# INTERNET LEGAL RESEARCH ON A BUDGET



SECOND EDITION

## FREE AND LOW-COST RESOURCES FOR LAWYERS

JUDY K. DAVIS AND CAROLE A. LEVITT

Cover design by Kelly Book/ABA Design



Printed in the United States of America.

24 23 22 21     5 4 3 2

**Library of Congress Cataloging-in-Publication Data**

Names: Levitt, Carole A., author. | Davis, Judy K., author. | American Bar Association. Law Practice Division, sponsoring body.
Title: Internet legal research on a budget : free and low-cost resources for lawyers / Judy K. Davis and Carole A. Levitt.
Description: Second edition. | Chicago, Illinois : American Bar Association, [2020] | Includes index. | Summary: "Our goal in writing the second edition of this book is to point lawyers to useful and reliable free (and low cost) Internet legal research resources and to explain how to use them effectively so they can become more satisfied using these resources"—Provided by publisher.
Identifiers: LCCN 2020023179 (print) | LCCN 2020023180 (ebook) | ISBN 9781641056069 (paperback) | ISBN 9781641056076 (epub)
Subjects: LCSH: Legal research—United States—Computer network resources. | Information storage and retrieval systems—Law—United States.
Classification: LCC KF242.A1 L479 2020 (print) | LCC KF242.A1 (ebook) | DDC 340.0285/4678—dc23
LC record available at https://lccn.loc.gov/2020023179
LC ebook record available at https://lccn.loc.gov/2020023180

# Dedication

## JUDY K. DAVIS

I would like to dedicate this book to Pavan. Thank you for your patience, support, and unwavering beliefs in my abilities.

## CAROLE A. LEVITT

I'd like to dedicate this book to my husband, Mark Rosch. I couldn't have asked for a better husband, best friend, and supportive work partner, all wrapped up into one person. If it wasn't for Mark, this book (and all the other books I've written) and our continuing legal education seminar company might never have come to fruition. When I first decided to switch careers (in 1999) to teach lawyers how to conduct Internet research on a budget, it was Mark who encouraged me to develop what became Internet For Lawyers (IFL). Mark then taught himself HTML to create IFL's website. Then, Mark taught me how to use PowerPoint so I could create slides for the seminars that I intended to present. He also edited all my articles and seminar materials. Eventually, Mark came on board full-time as my co-speaker and co-author.

Over the course of twenty years, we have co-authored six ABA Law Practice Division (ABA LPD) books and fourteen editions of our seminar book, *The Cybersleuth's Guide to the Internet*, and presented hundreds of CLE seminars all over the U.S. As online CLE got popular, it was Mark who developed IFL's webinar company (CLEwebinars.com). On December 27, 2019, after twenty years of working together at IFL, we will retire IFL. I'll focus on semi-retirement while Mark will focus on CLEwebinars.com. See you on the Web!

# Contents


*Dedication* ..... *iii*
*About the Authors* ..... *xi*
*Acknowledgments* ..... *xiii*
*Foreword* ..... *xv*
*Introduction* ..... *xvii*

**Part I General Research** **1**

**Chapter 1 Websites for General Legal Research** **3**

Articles ..... 3
Court Rules ..... 6
Dockets ..... 9
Expert Witnesses ..... 9
Forms: Court, Agency, and Transactional ..... 9
Jury Instructions ..... 12
Jury Verdicts and Expert Witnesses ..... 13
Samples of Case Documents and Oral Arguments ..... 14

**Chapter 2 Websites by Practice Area** **17**

Advertising Law ..... 17
Bankruptcy Law ..... 18
Class Action Lawsuits ..... 18
Copyright Law ..... 19
Corporate/Business Law ..... 19

Criminal Law ..... 20
Employment and Labor Law ..... 20
Family Law ..... 21
Foreign and International Law ..... 22
Immigration Law ..... 22
Insurance Law ..... 23
Intellectual Property—Copyright, Patents, and Trademarks ..... 24
Law and Medicine ..... 26
Legal Ethics and Professionalism ..... 27
Patent Law ..... 28
Real Estate and Property Law ..... 28
Securities Law ..... 29
Tax Law ..... 31
Trademark Law ..... 32

**Chapter 3 Apps for General Legal Research** 33

Case Law ..... 34
Code of Federal Regulations ..... 35
Congressional Record ..... 35
Court Rules ..... 35
Criminal Law ..... 36
Dictionaries (Legal) ..... 36
Legal Ethics and Professionalism ..... 37
State Statutes ..... 37
Taxation ..... 37
United States Code ..... 38
United States Constitution ..... 38

**Part II Legal Portals and Directories** 39

Assessing Legal Portals and Legal Directories ..... 40
The Top Legal Directories and Portals ..... 41

**Chapter 4 Free Commercial Portals and Directories** 43

Justia ..... 43
FindLaw ..... 48
HG.org (Formerly Hieros Gamos) ..... 50
Nolo Press ..... 51
Visalaw.com ..... 52

**Chapter 5 Government, Academic, and Association Portals and Directories** 53

Government Portals and Directories 53
Academic Portals and Directories 64
Cornell's Legal Information Institute 64
University of Southern California Gould School of Law 68
Legal Association Portals 69

**Part III Case Law Databases** 71

**Chapter 6 Free Commercial Online Case Law Databases** 73

Google Scholar 73
FindLaw 85
CourtListener Opinions 94
Casetext 101
The Public Library of Law (PLoL) 106
Justia 107

**Chapter 7 Free Governmental Online Case Law Databases** 109

govinfo United States Courts Opinions Collection 109
The Supreme Court of the United States 112
California Official Reports Public Access 116

**Chapter 8 An Introduction to Casemaker4** 123

Casemaker4 Content (Compilations) 124
Searching Casemaker4 124
- Reading and Navigating through a Case 128
- The Results List 131
- Save a Search 132
- Subsequent Treatment 133
- Limit Your Search to One or More Jurisdictions and Compilations 133
- Other Search Options: Recent Searches, Advanced Search, and Citation Search 137
- Citator Products (CasemakerPro) 140
- Searching Statutes 142
- Working with Documents 145
- Alerts 149

Personalize Your Search Experience at Casemaker4 151
Outside Vendors' Products 154

**Chapter 9 Fastcase 7: The Basics** 157

Introduction 157
Finding Resources on Fastcase 7 158
Case Law 163
Authority Check 166
Interactive Timeline 167
Bad Law Bot 169
Statutes 170
Authority Check for Statutes 172
Regulations 172
Secondary Resources 173
Treatises 174
Law Reviews 175
Working with Documents 176
The Fastcase Mobile Apps 179
Conclusion 183

**Chapter 10 Federal Statutory Research** 187

United States Constitution and the Declaration of Independence 187
United States Code (U.S.C.) 191
The OLRC United States Code 192
The Cornell LII U.S.C. Database 199
The govinfo United States Code Database 201

**Chapter 11 Federal Legislative and Congressional Materials** 205

Congress.gov 206
govinfo Legislative and Congressional Materials (Collections) 220
Additional Resources 224

**Chapter 12 Federal Executive and Administrative Law** 227

The Federal Register 227
The Code of Federal Regulations 229
The e-CFR 231
Searching the List of CFR Sections Affected (LSA) and the List of CFR Parts Affected 233
U.S. Regulation Tracker 236
govinfo and Presidential Materials 237
The White House 240
Federal Agencies 240

United States Government Manual .... 241
USA.gov .... 242
Finding Defunct Federal Agencies' and Commissions' Websites .... 243

**Chapter 13 State, Local, Territorial, and Tribal Law** **245**
USA.gov .... 245
LII's Law by Source: State .... 247
State and Local Government on the Net .... 250
Library of Congress .... 251
WashLaw Legal Research on the Web .... 252
Full-Text State Statutes and Legislation on the Internet .... 253
FindLaw .... 253
Open States .... 254
Legiscan .... 255
State Case Law Databases .... 256
State and Local Courts: Dockets .... 256
Tribal Government and Law .... 256
County and City Level .... 257
Local Codes at the County and City Level .... 258

**Chapter 14 Foreign, International, and Comparative Law Resources** **263**
The Law Library of Congress .... 264
The American Society of International Law .... 266
GlobaLex and Other NYU Law Resources .... 270
Hieros Gamos .... 273
Justia's Latin American Resources .... 276
Additional Resources for Foreign Law .... 278
Additional Resources for Subject-Specific International Law .... 279
Foreign Constitutions .... 280

**Part IV Additional Research Sources** **281**

**Chapter 15 Dockets and Case Documents** **283**
How Dockets and Case Documents Can Be Used for Legal and Investigative Research .... 284
Fees .... 284
Federal, State, and Local Court Docket Directory .... 285
Docket Websites .... 285
PACER .... 286

RECAP (PACER Spelled Backwards) Archive Free Federal Court Dockets and Case Documents Database ... 300
Justia Free Federal Dockets ... 308
U.S. Supreme Court Dockets and Case Documents (Oral Arguments—Audio Recordings and Transcripts, and Merit and Amicus Briefs) ... 311
State, Federal, and Local Complaints ... 317

**Chapter 16 Social Media** 319
Facebook ... 321
YouTube ... 324
Twitter Accounts ... 324
Instagram ... 326
LinkedIn ... 326
Pinterest ... 329
Snapchat ... 330
Social Media Profile Collection Vendors ... 331
Using Social Media to Research Lawyers or Legal Topics ... 333

**Chapter 17 Researching Legal Professionals** 335
Contact and Licensing Information ... 335
Lawyer Directories with Biographies ... 336
Judicial Directories ... 342
Articles by and about Judges or Attorneys ... 346
Using Legal Professional-Oriented Social Media to Research Legal Topics, Lawyers, or Judges ... 347

**Part V Cite Checking Your Research** 351

**Chapter 18 Cite Checking Cases** 353
Google Scholar ... 354
CourtListener ... 357
WorldLII's LawCite ... 359
Casetext ... 361
"Party Name as Keyword" Cite Checking ... 363

*Index* ... 367

# About the Authors

## JUDY K. DAVIS

Judy is a senior law librarian and adjunct assistant professor of law at the University of Southern California Gould School of Law. Prior to coming to USC, she worked at the University of San Diego Pardee Legal Research Center. Earlier, she practiced law before a wise person introduced her to the world of librarianship. She currently teaches legal research to USC law students, works in the law library's Reference department, and gives lectures and training sessions on legal research and related topics. When she isn't doing any of that, she can likely be found enjoying the great outdoors in beautiful Southern California.

## CAROLE A. LEVITT

Carole A. Levitt is the founder and President of Internet For Lawyers (www.netforlawyers.com) and Vice-President of CLEwebinars.com. She is a nationally recognized CLE seminar speaker and best-selling American Bar Association Law Practice Division (ABA LPD) author. She is an expert on Internet investigative and legal research; social media research; social media ethics; Google search and Google Cloud Apps; and technology for lawyers. Carole has been presenting CLE seminars full-time since 1999 throughout the United States.

Carole has co-authored six ABA LPD books with her husband/business partner, Mark Rosch, including: *The Lawyers Guide to Fact Finding on the Internet* (2nd edition in 2004 and the 3rd edition in 2006); *Find Info like a Pro*, Volume 1 (2010) and Volume 2 (2011); *Google for Lawyers: Essential Search Tips and Productivity Tools* (2010); and *Google Gmail and Calendar in One Hour for Lawyers* (2013). She has also co-authored fourteen editions of IFL Press's *The Cybersleuth's Guide to the Internet* with Mark Rosch, from 1999–2019 and hundreds of Internet research articles with Mark Rosch.

Previously, Carole was a California attorney, a law librarian in Chicago and Los Angeles, and a Legal Research and Writing Professor at Pepperdine University School of Law. She graduated with distinction from UIC John Marshall Law School where she was a member of the school's law review and worked full-time as a law librarian at the school. Carole has a Masters in Library Science and a B.A. in Political Science from the University of Illinois, Champaign-Urbana.

Carole is an active member of the ABA LPD, serving on its Publications Advisory Board since 2004 (to present) and on its Executive Council from 2006 to 2011. Carole is past Chair of the California State Bar's Law Practice Management & Technology (LPMT) Executive Committee and in 2013 she became the second recipient of LPMT's Lifetime Achievement Award. In 2012, Carole was inducted into the College of Law Practice Management, an honorary legal technology association, and in 2013 she received the "Fastcase Fifty" award, recognizing "50 of the smartest, most courageous innovators, techies, visionaries, and leaders in the law."

You can reach Carole at clevitt@netforlawyers.com.

# Acknowledgments


## JUDY K. DAVIS

I would like to thank the librarians and staff at the USC Gould Law Library for the support that allows me to continue working on projects like this. I could not have landed in a better profession or found better colleagues. Thanks also to Gould's IT staff who keep my computers and software running so that I can access and evaluate the many resources in this book. Finally, a huge thank you to my co-author, Carole Levitt, who took a chance on working with a new author almost seven years ago. I found a new colleague, and I found a new friend. I will miss writing with you, and I wish you the happy retirement you so deserve.

## CAROLE A. LEVITT

First, I would like to thank my co-author, Judy Davis, who agreed in 2013 to write the first edition of this book with me. It would have been a daunting task to write the first edition of this book on my own but, with Judy's help, this book was brought to fruition. Despite never having met in person, we were able to successfully collaborate on this book using the magic of e-mail and Google Hangouts. A few years later, I find myself thanking Judy again; this time for convincing me to write the 2nd edition of this book and especially for agreeing to take the lead on this book and writing a larger portion of it.

## JUDY K. DAVIS AND CAROLE LEVITT

We would like to thank:

- Brian Huddleston, Senior Reference Librarian at the Loyola University New Orleans College of Law Library, who guest wrote the chapter on Fastcase. Brian put in an inordinate amount of time to write that chapter . . . and then did it again when he had to revise the chapter when Fastcase launched an unexpected (to us) update. Brian also served as a peer reviewer for the entire book.
- Michael Spektor, Esq., our ABA LPD Liaison.
- Billie Jo Kaufman, Interim Law Library Director & Visiting Professor of Law Mercer University School of Law, our peer reviewer.
- Molly Montanaro, Program Manager, Lachina Creative, who project managed this book almost until the end. She was a joy to work with.
- Sarah Craig, Executive Editor, ABA Publishing, who came along to help us complete this project after Molly departed.

In addition, I (Carole) would like to express my appreciation to my University of Illinois library science legal research professors, Carol Boast and Nancy Johnson, for inspiring me to become a law librarian in 1976 and teaching me all about legal research (pre-Internet). I'm also grateful to my fellow law librarian, Cindy Chick, for introducing me (and many other law librarians) to the world of legal research on the Internet.

# Foreword

## ROBERT J. AMBROGI

*"Imagine instant access to virtually unlimited sources of legal information. Imagine receiving court decisions within hours of their release. Imagine consulting experts in any legal field, anywhere in the world, and having their answer within minutes. Imagine having statutes, bills and government documents at your fingertips. Imagine huge files of legal forms and pleadings at your disposal.*

*"Now imagine that this is all free and available to you right in your office, no matter how small or remote. No travel to distant libraries. No expensive search fees."*

It seems laughable now, but when I wrote those words in 1995, in an article introducing lawyers to the Internet, the legal research landscape I described was a pipe dream. Then, much of the Internet still consisted solely of text. Navigating it required knowledge of archaic and confusing commands and interfaces with names such as Gopher and Telnet.

Hyperlinked navigation of the Internet—what came to be called the World Wide Web—was invented in 1991 and only began to find broader use in 1993 with the development of the first two viable web browsers. Notably, one of those browsers, Cello, was developed specifically with lawyers in mind by the Legal Information Institute at Cornell Law School.

Back then, neither Westlaw nor LexisNexis were accessible through the Internet. Researchers could access them only through a dial-up terminal. Only a handful of courts had begun to publish their opinions on the Internet, and only newly released ones—there were no extensive archives to search. The vast majority of legal research was still done as it long had been, by trudging to the law library and poring over hard-copy books.

Fast forward almost three decades and that pipe dream is a reality, and then some. Every federal and state appellate opinion can be found online at no cost. Federal and state statutes are online, as are growing bodies of other primary legal materials, from federal regulations to municipal ordinances. Traditional law reviews now publish online while legal blogs are creating new forms of legal commentary and analysis. Search technology has become so sophisticated that we forget how difficult a search used to be. All of this is available to us wherever we are, in the office or on a mobile device sitting outside a courtroom.

This glut of legal research materials on the Internet is a good thing, of course. But it is also a mixed bag. Paid research services compete with free ones. Established publishers go against start-ups. So many resources are available that some of the most useful ones can be lost in the crowd. Even professional legal researchers have a hard time keeping score.

I will confess that I am a cheapskate. Way back when, when I started using the Internet, I was hoping to save a buck. I had just started my own practice. I did not want to pay the high cost of a Westlaw or LexisNexis subscription or invest in a library of hard-bound reporters. I went on the Internet to see what free resources I could find there.

All these years later, I am as budget-conscious as ever. *Internet Legal Research on a Budget* is written for any lawyer or legal researcher who is similarly budget-conscious—and I am willing to bet that most of us are. Carole Levitt and Judy Davis have scoped out the terrain. They have tested and evaluated a host of free and low-cost legal research sites and identified the best. Not only do they show you the sites, they provide detailed instructions on how to use them.

Much as I imagined twenty-five years ago, the Internet today offers legal professionals seemingly unlimited sources of legal information—much of it free. But that abundance can be daunting. Think of *Internet Legal Research on a Budget* as a roadmap to the best of what is out there. It will guide you to what you need, and save you a buck along the way.

ROBERT J. AMBROGI, PUBLISHER AND EDITOR-IN-CHIEF OF LEXBLOG.COM, ATTORNEY, EXECUTIVE DIRECTOR OF THE MASSACHUSETTS NEWSPAPER PUBLISHERS ASSOCIATION, AND AUTHOR OF "THE ESSENTIAL GUIDE TO THE BEST (AND WORST) LEGAL SITES ON THE WEB."
WWW.LAWSITESBLOG.COM
@BOBAMBROGI

# Introduction

## WHY A BOOK ABOUT FREE ONLINE LEGAL RESEARCH?

With cost-conscious clients scrutinizing legal bills, lawyers cannot afford to only depend on fee-based resources the way they used to, especially if there are reliable free resources available. Our goal in writing the second edition of this book is the same goal we had when we wrote the first edition: to point lawyers to useful and reliable free (and low cost) Internet legal research resources and to explain how to use them effectively so they can become more satisfied using these resources. In other words, our goal is to help you save time and money and avoid frustration in your legal research quest.

Reviewing the 103-page Online Research Report (completed by 622 lawyers) published as Volume 1 of 5 volumes by the American Bar Association Legal Technology Resource Center (*2019 Legal Technology Survey Report* at http://bit.ly/abaltrc2019survey), we learned that lawyers spend a good deal of their time on legal research and they mostly use free Internet services. For example, "Respondents admitted to the bar less than ten years and [who were] associates, on average, spend . . ." 25% of work time on legal research. Not falling far behind that percentage are respondents less than 40 years old (23%) and those between ages 40–49 years (21%). In that Report, we also learned that solos (who represented 30% of respondents to the Survey) reported spending 19% of their work time on legal research. Firms of 2–9 lawyers (who represented 30% of respondents to the Survey) reported spending 18% of their work time on legal research. Firms of 10–49 lawyers (who represented 15% of respondents to the Survey) reported spending 15% of their work time on legal research, while firms of 100 or more (who represented 18% of respondents to the Survey) reported spending 15% of their work time on legal research.

In that Report, we also learned that 90% of lawyers who responded to the survey stated that they use free Internet services (65% regularly and 25% occasionally). The large amount of time both newer admittees and older lawyers spend on legal research and that 90% of that research focuses on free Internet services confirms the usefulness of a book on free Internet legal research.

We have tested and evaluated each site, described and explained how to actually use the site, often step-by-step, and have included numerous screenshots to better illustrate the steps. If you didn't receive Internet legal research training in law school or at your firm, of if the Internet did not even exist then, this book is for you.

This book focuses primarily on "pure" Internet legal research (cases, statutes, dockets, ordinances, legal blogs, etc.). We know that a lawyer's research can sometimes also involve investigative and background research. For those who want to learn about that, please read *The Cybersleuth's Guide to the Internet*, 14th edition revised (2019), by Carole Levitt and Mark E. Rosch (https://www.netforlawyers.com/products).

## THE AUTHORS OF THIS BOOK ARE UNIQUELY QUALIFIED TO WRITE THIS BOOK

The authors of this book share a common background that uniquely qualifies them to write this book: We have both had careers as lawyers as well as law librarians. Carole worked as a law librarian at corporate legal departments, law schools, and law firms in Chicago and Los Angeles. Judy currently works as a senior law librarian at the University of Southern California (USC) Gould School of Law and previously at the University of San Diego Pardee Legal Research Center. We have also both taught Legal Research at law schools (Judy currently teaches at the USC Gould School of Law and Carole taught at Pepperdine University School of Law and at the West Los Angeles College's Paralegal School). In 1999, Carole founded Internet For Lawyers (IFL) to teach Internet research CLE seminars to lawyers and paralegals throughout the United States. By the time you read this book, she will have retired from IFL, but continues as the Vice-President of IFL's webinar division founded in 2015 (CLEwebinars.com).

Because of this background, we understand how lawyers think when it comes to legal research, so we decided to put our heads together to write a current book on Internet legal research, discussing government, academic, and commercial (free and pay) websites as well as apps, blogs, Twitter feeds, and crowdsourced sites.

## WHAT'S NEW IN THE SECOND EDITION?

In the second edition of the book, we updated information about resources discussed in the first edition, deleted resources no longer available, and added new resources. We have taken all new screen shots of every site. Also, we've expanded the chapters on Casemaker and Fastcase because lawyers in every state can now access one or both of these for free through membership to a state, local, or specialty bar association (or other legal entities, such as the Los Angeles Law Library). We don't go into great detail about Artificial Intelligence (AI) products because this book is about free (or low-cost) online resources and AI resources are neither free nor low-cost. Also, AI resources are primarily limited to case law and this book goes well beyond case law research.

## IS FREE ALWAYS BEST?

We know, as it is with most anything, that price is a major consideration when deciding between alternative research resources—and we all agree that all other things being equal, free is better. With that said, we do make note of pay databases when they have more useful features than the free sites. Sometimes it makes sense to pay for data—especially if the pay databases have something the free ones are lacking (content or functionality), or when using the pay databases can simply save you time, and thus money.

## HOW THIS BOOK IS ORGANIZED

This book is primarily organized by type of material. For example, there are chapters about websites for statutes, cases, dockets, and so on. One chapter is organized by practice area, from advertising law to trademarks. That law chapter includes both websites and blogs. We also included a chapter about general legal research (such as where to find free law review articles, forms, court rules, etc.) websites and apps.

We only show you the best sites. We begin each chapter with the most useful or comprehensive site for a specific topic. We then discuss a few alternative sites. We include tips about the most useful aspect of each site (content and functionality) and let you know if there are any hidden functions.

## CONVENTIONS USED IN THIS BOOK

Throughout the book we will use boldfaced type to indicate exact text that appears on a web page (links, buttons, dropdown menus, etc.), and italics to indicate the exact text of search terms/keywords used in sample searches we conducted to evaluate the sites we discuss. Website URLs, descriptions, and screenshots are accurate and up to date as of October 2019.

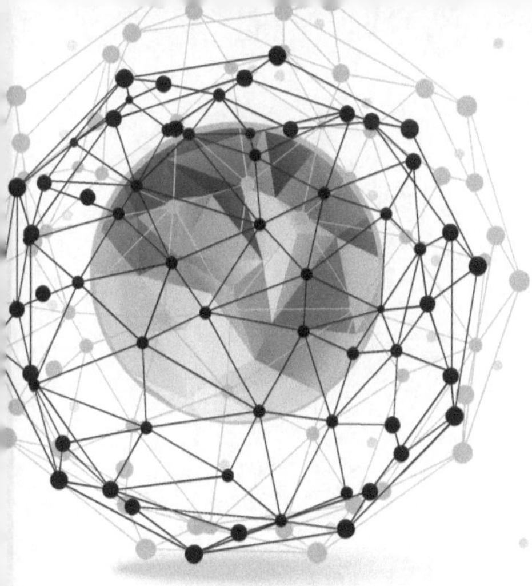

# Part I

## GENERAL RESEARCH

Part I will focus on free and low-cost general legal research sites, blawgs (law blogs), and apps. We will begin in Chapter 1 by discussing websites that provide general resources such as articles, forms, and case document samples. Chapter 2 will address subject-specific websites. Chapter 3 focuses on legal research apps for your phone or other devices.

# Chapter 1

## WEBSITES FOR GENERAL LEGAL RESEARCH

Attorneys usually associate legal research with searching for primary law, such as court opinions, statutes, and regulations. But sometimes it is faster and easier to begin your research using secondary legal sources, such as articles or sample pleadings and briefs. These secondary resources explain and analyze primary law and direct you to the primary law relevant to your project. We will begin this book by discussing secondary legal sources. We will also discuss websites that contain helpful resources, such as court rules, jury verdicts, and expert witness directories.

## ARTICLES

### Journals and Magazines (General)

- Before using any pay sites, visit your public library's website to see if it provides library card holders with free remote access to pay databases that include articles from journals, magazines, and newspapers. See also information about free (and pay) articles via Google Scholar in Chapter 6. Your local public law library may also provide access to pay legal databases, although you may need to be physically present in the library to use them.
- **IngentaConnect** (http://www.ingentaconnect.com) allows visitors to search (by keyword, title, author, etc.) the full text of articles from 13,000

professional and academic publications. The article abstract results can be viewed for free, but to read the full text of most articles, visitors must pay via credit card; prices vary, but tend to be expensive. The site offers a handy **Access Key** with colored symbols so the researcher can scan the list of results and quickly see which articles are available free of charge.

- In addition, sometimes you can find a free article simply by searching for the title as a phrase with a general search engine such as Google or Bing.

## Articles (Legal)

- **Social Science Research Network (SSRN)** (https://ssrn.com) is an enormous repository of working and accepted scholarly papers in law, business, the social sciences, and other areas. The site provides over 500,000 free full-text articles for download, along with many additional abstracts. The homepage has a simple search box where you can enter keywords to search the title, author, abstract, and full text of articles. An **Advanced Search** page (http://bit.ly/SSRNAdvanced) allows you to keyword search the Title Only, the Title, Abstract & Keywords, or the Title, Abstract, Keywords & Full Text. A separate box lets you simultaneously keyword search the Author(s), and a drop-down menu lets you choose a Date range. You can also filter by the various SSRN Networks, such as Law, Finance, Criminal Justice, and more. A **Browse by Network and Subject Area** tab at the top of the Advanced Search page lets you drill down through the many subject categories on SSRN. (The third tab on the Advanced Search page, Browse by JEL Code, allows you to browse by the *Journal of Economic Literature* (JEL) classification system.)
- **Law Commons** (http://network.bepress.com/law), part of the Digital Commons network, allows you to browse, search, and read free, full-text articles and other scholarly legal publications from over 350 universities and colleges around the globe. The simple search feature searches all terms you enter in the full text as well as in any field, such as author, title, etc. Besides keyword searching, researchers can pre- and post-filter searches by refinements, such as law sub-discipline, institution, publication, publication year, and publication type. Coverage dates vary by publication and institution.
- **Law Review Commons** (http://lawreviewcommons.com/) is a subset of Law Commons and describes itself as "the largest collection of free and open

law review scholarship." Launched in 2013, it contains both current and archived materials from over 150 law reviews dating as far back as 100 years.

In addition to the browsing and searching functions available for Law Commons, Law Review Commons also offers **Advanced Search** features (http://bit.ly/LRCadvanced). Users can keyword search all, one, or multiple fields, which include Abstract, Subject, Author, Institution, Title, Document Type, Publication, and "All Fields." A date range filter is available, as is the option to sort results by relevance or publication date. Users can format search results as a list of links or as a downloadable Bibliography Export text file. (See Figure 1.1) The **Help with Search** page (http://bit.ly/LRChelp) provides additional search tips, such as using special characters for wildcard searching and "fuzzy matches" (e.g., colour vs. color).

After creating a free account, you can save your Law Review Commons searches. You can also sign up to receive the Law Review Commons RSS feed, and for "bealerts," weekly email updates on new content that fits your search criteria.

**Figure 1.1** Law Review Commons Advanced Search page. Screenshot from Law Review Commons used with permission.

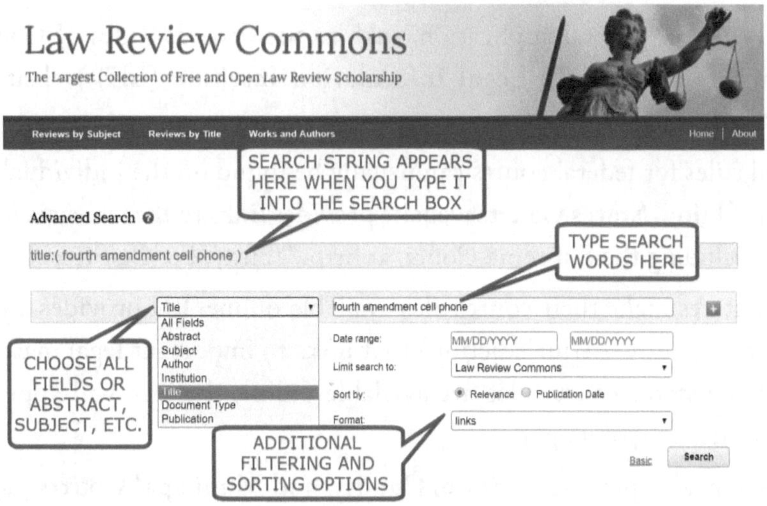


- The **ABA Legal Technology Resource Center** (http://bit.ly/ABAfreeFT) provides a Google-powered search engine to keyword search over 400 law reviews and law journals with some amount of free, full-text online. The database contains mostly U.S., but some foreign and international journals, some academic papers, and publications such as Congressional Research

Service reports. Coverage dates and availability of full-text articles vary from publication to publication. If you scroll down the page, you will also find a list of links to journals with free full-text content that are not part of this searchable database but that can be searched or browsed individually at each journal's site.

- **Lexology** (https://www.lexology.com) publishes over 450 articles every day from over 800 leading U.S. and foreign law firms and service providers. The articles cover 50 practice areas and vary from analyzing important case decisions and legislative topics, to offering practical guidance, such as checklists for creating contracts (e.g., a physician's employment contract). Their free searchable archive contains 650,000+ articles. If you want to receive an RSS feed in your morning inbox on topics of your choice, you can sign up for free. This site can be useful to determine trends in legal practice or to keep up-to-date on your practice area. You can also search the archives to obtain a quick overview of an area of law if you need to prepare for a last-minute meeting.

## COURT RULES

Federal rules of general application, such as the Federal Rules of Civil Procedure, are available at **Cornell's Legal Information Institute** (LII) website at https://www.law.cornell.edu/rules.

Local rules for federal courts can usually be found on the individual court's website. The **United States Courts** website provides links to the websites of U.S. federal courts, including the Supreme Court, at http://bit.ly/FedCtsSites.

Most states make their court rules available online. **LII** provides a page for each state (http://bit.ly/LIIJurisdiction) that links to important legal materials for that state. If the state's court rules are available online, the link will appear under the **Judiciary** heading of its page.

**USA.gov** also provides a **State, County, and Municipal Courts** page that links to websites and other online resources (https://www.usa.gov/state-courts). Under the **State Courts** heading on this page is a link to the National Center for State Courts (NCSC) website, where you can find links to judicial branch resources for each state (http://bit.ly/NCSCStates). See Figure 1.2.

**Figure 1.2** NCSC State Courts page.

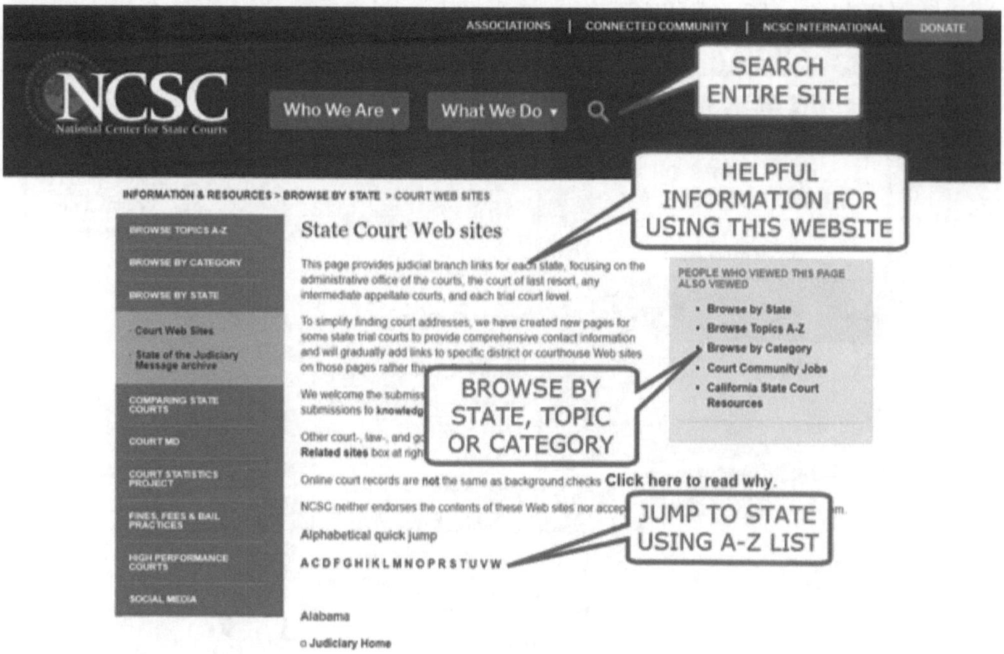


Under the **County Courts** heading of the State, County, and Municipal Courts page, you will find a link to a county information website run by NACo, the National Association of Counties (ce.naco.org). The NACo site provides interactive maps where you can find county profiles as well as search for and compare indicators like federal funding and demographics. To find general information, click the county of your choice on the interactive map of all U.S. counties. (You can also search for counties by name, topic, zip code, etc. in the search box at the upper right corner of the page; see Figure 1.3.) A pop-up screen will appear with that county's information, such as the County Seat, Total Square Miles, and Government Type, along with its website address. To find information on a specific topic (e.g., housing affordability, demographic, transportation, infrastructure, and more), click one of the two tabs at the top of the home page—**Maps** or **Profiles**. Then choose a category from the dropdown menu that appears. From there, you will see various sub-categories to choose from. Once you choose a sub-category, a different interactive map of all the counties, often color-coded, will appear (see Figure 1.3). You can then select a county to see additional information, or double click multiple counties to compare them. (Scroll down the page to see the comparison.)

**Figure 1.3** NACo County Explorer interactive map with county information. County Explorer is the property of the National Association of Counties (NACo). Image used with permission.

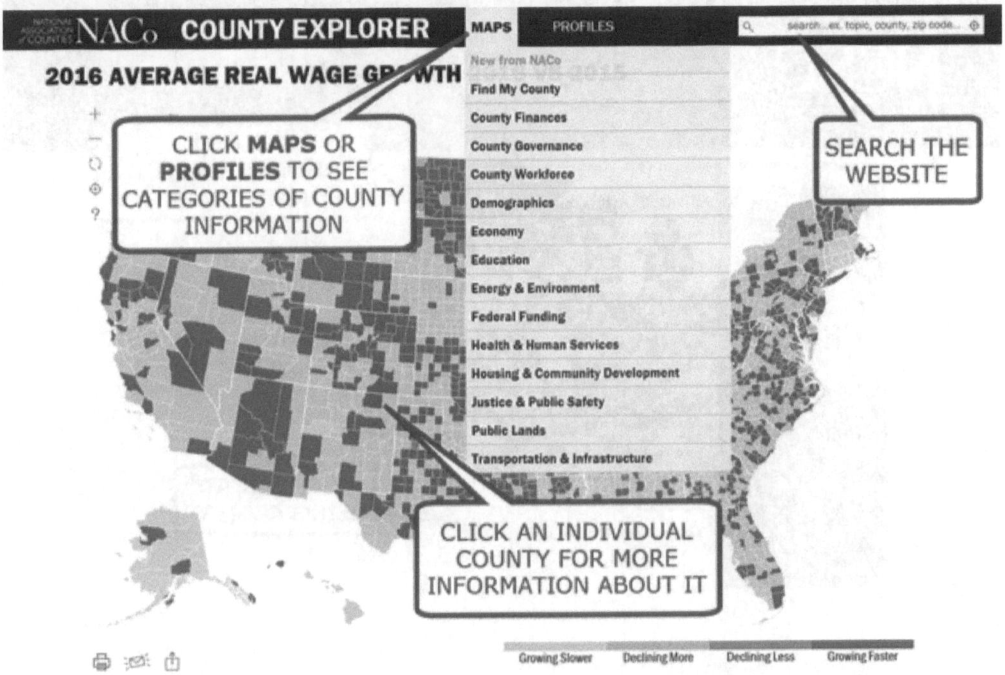


Finally, the **Municipal Courts** heading on USA.gov's State, County, and Municipal Courts page (https://www.usa.gov/state-courts) provides two links that may be helpful if you are trying to locate rules or other information for a municipal court. The first of the two links goes to the NCSC web page described previously (http://bit.ly/NCSCStates). You can use some of the resources linked from this page to find municipal court information. For example, if you click the **Administrative Office of Courts** link under the **Alabama** heading, you will be taken to Alabama's Administrative Office of Courts site (alacourt.gov). You can then choose the **Municipal Courts** link from the topics displayed at the top of the page.

Sometimes it can be more challenging to find the information you need from the NCSC page. If you were looking for Arizona municipal courts, for example, you could click the **Administrative Office of the Courts** link under the **Arizona** heading. Once you reach Arizona's Administrative Office of the Courts website, you will not find a link to municipal courts, however, so you must look for this information. If you hover over the **AZ Courts** heading on the menu at the top of the page, a drop-down menu appears. One link in the drop-down menu is **City Courts** (see Figure 1.4). If you click that link, you will go to a page that explains that a municipal court may also be called a city court or magistrate court—at least in Arizona. From there, you can continue your research.

**Figure 1.4** Click **City Courts** to find information about Arizona municipal courts.

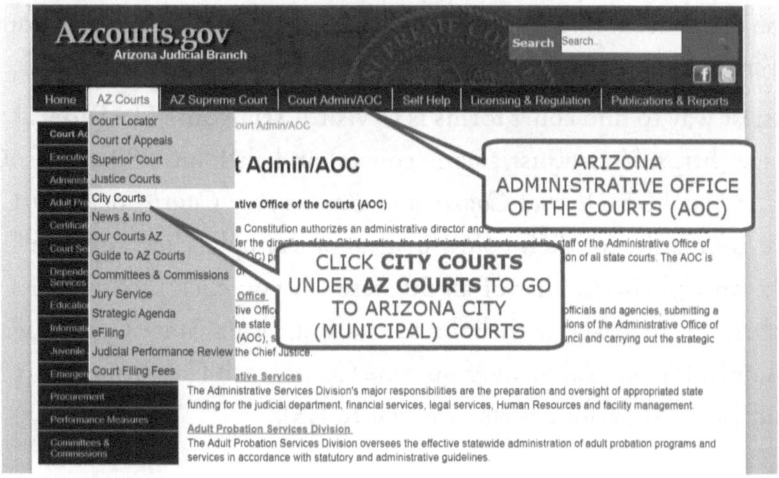


The second link under the **Municipal Courts** heading takes you to the NACo County Explorer page described above. Use the interactive map as described above to locate municipal court information, if it is available. For example, click the county you want on the map, and then look under the **County Contact** heading. From the county website, you can often navigate your way to the court websites.

## DOCKETS

For Docket information, see the section on Samples of Case Documents and Oral Arguments in this chapter, and see Chapter 15 for an in-depth discussion of docket websites.

## EXPERT WITNESSES

See Jury Verdicts and Expert Witnesses, later in this chapter.

## FORMS: COURT, AGENCY, AND TRANSACTIONAL

Numerous federal, state, local, and tribal government agency and court forms can be found at **USA.gov**. Federal agency forms are listed alphabetically by agency name (https://www.usa.gov/forms). For example, to locate passport forms published by the Department of State, click "S" (for State) and scan the list of all federal agencies beginning with the letter "S" until you find the State Department (DOS) link. To locate state, local, and tribal government forms, enter the keyword *form* and a description of the form into the search box at the top of the USA.gov home page—e.g., *new york state tax forms.*

The easiest way to find court forms is to visit **Justia.com's US Federal and State Courts** page (https://www.justia.com/courts) and click on *US Supreme Court, US Courts of Appeals, US District Courts and Bankruptcy Courts,* or *State Courts* and search that court's site for their court forms. For example, clicking State Courts will take you to an alphabetical list of all 50 states. If you click the link for California, you will then go to a page with links to the California State Court's website and individual links for the California Supreme Court, each California court of appeal, and the individual superior courts (see Figure 1.5).

**Figure 1.5** Justia provides links to many court websites where you can search for forms and other materials. Screenshot from Justia used with permission.

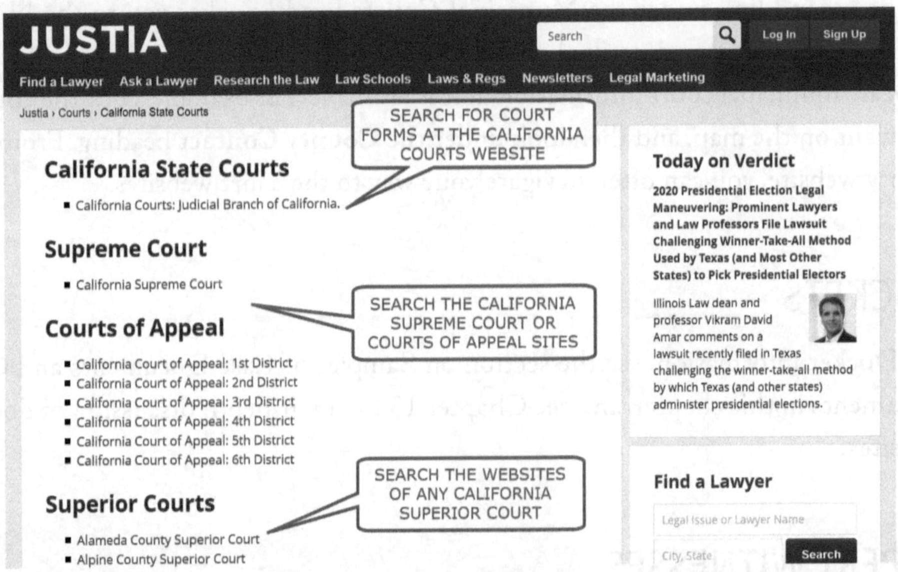


At the IRS's **Forms, Instructions, & Publications** web page http://bit.ly/IRSForms, you can keyword search current tax forms, instructions, and publications, using multiple keywords, including years or form numbers. To search older ones as far back as 1864, choose the **Prior Year** link in the left sidebar. There is no documentation explaining how the keyword search function works, and we found the search results to be confusing at times. For instance, our search for *3468 investment credit* brought back that particular form and its instructions but also brought back 216 other results, which did not necessarily contain our keywords, causing us to wonder if the default Boolean connector is *or* when *and* would be more logical.

Conducting the same search but placing *"investment credit"* in quotation marks, however, brought our results down to 4, and this time, every result contained the keyword *3468*, as well as the phrase *"investment credit."*

You can also find accessible forms and instructions (for those using assistive technology such as screen reading software) by choosing **Accessible** from the left sidebar menu. If you select this option, you will be taken to a page with a list of links to accessible IRS products, as well as additional links to helpful information such as videos in American Sign Language and information about free tax preparation for qualifying taxpayers. You can also find accessible forms and instructions by first searching current or prior years, and then using the dropdown menu that appears above the search results to choose **Accessible.** You can also use the dropdown menu to filter for **Current** year, **Prior** years, or **All** results (see Figure 1.6).

**Figure 1.6** IRS forms search results.

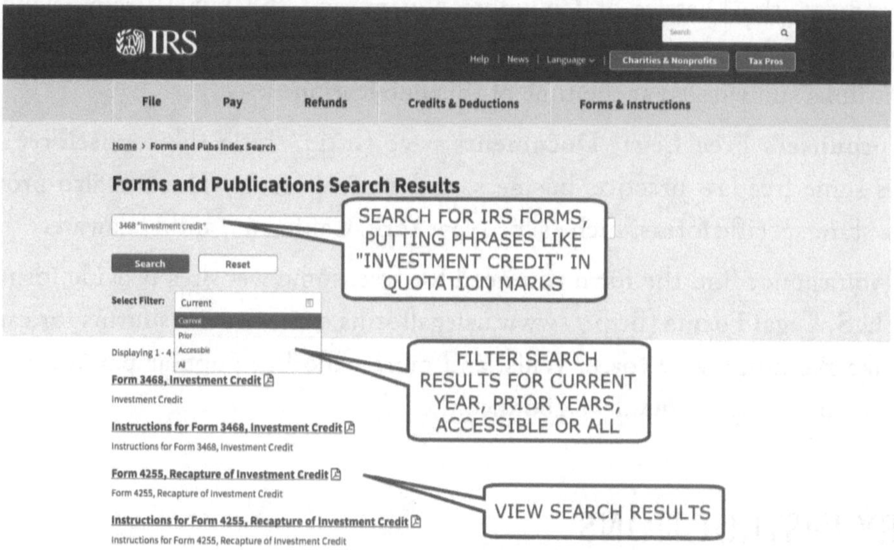


The **IRS Tax Map** page (https://taxmap.irs.gov) provides several options if you prefer to browse instead of search. An A-Z Topic Index and three specialized indexes are available, and users may browse five "Tax Products": Forms, Publications, Tax Topics, Worksheets, and FAQs. Archives for the IRS Tax Map are available back to 2012.

Many forms on the IRS site can be filled in online and saved to your hard drive. For those forms that are not fillable, you can save them to your hard drive and use Adobe Acrobat's "Fill & Sign" feature to complete them, even without purchasing the full version of Adobe Acrobat.

For links to state tax forms, see the **Federation of Tax Administrators'** site (http://bit.ly/FTAForms). The site provides links to tax forms from all 50 states, Washington, D.C., Puerto Rico, New York City, and Philadelphia.

For access to over 2,000 generic and state-specific business and personal forms, from quitclaim deeds to employment agreements and wills and name change forms, see **Publiclegalforms.com**, a product of the **Internet Legal Research Group** (ILRG) site (http://www.ilrg.com/forms). You can browse by topic or enter a keyword into the search box on the home page and then select a state from the drop-down menu. You can view a free preview of the form, but it won't be usable because it has a watermark. If you want to use the form, you will have to pay to download their "Professional MS Word and PDF formatting" version (at $9.99 per form), which is editable and reusable. ILRG also provides a page with links to official corporate and business entity forms that are maintained by each state government, the District of Columbia, Guam, and the U.S. Virgin Islands, at https://www.ilrg.com/corp. Although the page was last updated in 2016, almost all of the links still worked at the time of this publication.

**Upcounsel's Free Legal Documents** page (http://bit.ly/UpcounselFree) also offers some free law practice, business, and general forms. The site also provides some state-specific forms, such as for New York, California, and Delaware.

If you cannot find the form you need for free, some websites provide forms for sale. **U.S. Legal Forms** (http://www.uslegalforms.com) provides forms for categories like Bankruptcy, Divorce, Wills, and more. Another popular pay form site is **LegalZoom** (http://www.legalzoom.com).

## JURY INSTRUCTIONS

The **National Center for State Courts** provides a list of states that publish jury instructions online at http://bit.ly/NCSCJury. (A few of the links no longer work, however.)

Also, in 2015, Jan Bissett and Margi Heinen published an article in the *Michigan Bar Journal*, "**Accurately Instructed in the Law: Finding State Jury Instructions**" (http://bit.ly/Bissett2015). This article followed up on an earlier (now outdated) article they wrote on a similar topic. The 2015 article contains a chart showing which states have jury instructions available in the major pay and low-cost databases of Bloomberg Law, Casemaker, Fastcase, Lexis Advance, and Westlaw Next. In addition, however, many states on the chart have a corresponding footnote that provides a link to the state's free online version of their jury instructions.

If the state you need is not listed in either of the above sources, or if the links no longer work, you can try searching for the court's website to see if they may have posted jury instructions. Not all states make jury instructions freely available online; for example, several states put them on their state bar website, available to state bar members only. Many federal circuits also provide pattern jury instructions on the court website; check the individual court's website.

## JURY VERDICTS AND EXPERT WITNESSES

Researching verdicts and settlements of cases similar to your case might help you assess a case's worth and also help you identify experts.

**MoreLaw.com** (http://www.morelaw.com/verdicts) provides a free jury verdicts and settlements database. To locate experts who have testified in cases similar to one that you are handling, search by keywords describing your case and limit the search to the **Plaintiff(s) Experts** or **Defendant(s) Experts** field. To research verdicts/settlements, search by keywords describing your case and limit the search to the **Case Description** or **Verdict** field. You can further limit any of your searches by state. The site also provides an **Expert Witnesses** directory, accessed via the sidebar on the right side of the page (see Figure 1.7).

**Figure 1.7** MoreLaw.com helps you find jury verdicts, settlements, and expert witnesses. Screenshot from MoreLaw.com used with permission.

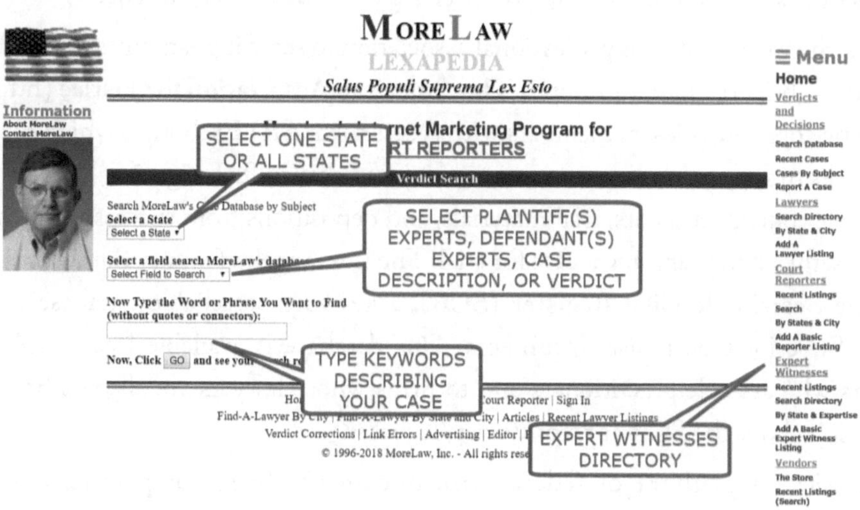


**Jurispro.com** (http://www.jurispro.com) allows you to search for an expert witness by name or by expertise to get background information about the expert. Most experts' profiles include the expert's photo, C.V., a list of published articles (and sometimes the full text of one or more articles), references (including phone numbers), and a link to their website. Some have even placed an audio or video file in their profile so you can listen to their voice or watch them in action to decide if you want to contact them.

The founder of Jurispro, along with three other authors, also maintain a report entitled *Finding and Researching Experts and Their Testimony* (4th Edition, 2018) (http://www.expertwitnesswhitepaper.com). This document provides detailed instructions on finding expert witnesses and contains a plethora of expert witness links.

If you need to verify an expert's credentials, the **National Student Clearinghouse** (http://bit.ly/NSCverify) may be useful. For a fee, this service offers to verify such credentials as degree, school certificate, or professional certificate, as well as current enrollment and dates of attendance.

## SAMPLES OF CASE DOCUMENTS AND ORAL ARGUMENTS

Instead of drafting case documents and pleadings (such as complaints, answers, briefs, or summary judgment motions) from scratch, consider searching for samples to speed these tasks along. Samples can also serve as research guides to the leading cases and statutes on the topic. Some courts, government agencies, professional associations, and law firms offer access to these types of case documents (some free and some for a fee) which, in turn, you can use as samples. You can even retrieve samples of oral arguments to help you prepare for your oral argument.

Check the website of your professional association to see if it posts any sample pleadings or has a brief bank. For example, **The American Association for Justice** (https://www.justice.org) provides its members with access to its **AAJ Exchange**, which consists of resources to support the representation of injured clients. Its **Litigation Packets** contain sample court documents, trial materials, and depositions from successful cases and may be useful when preparing a case for trial. The Los Angeles County Bar Association offers the **Searchable Civil Register (SCR)**, a keyword-searchable database of Los Angeles Superior Court case documents. This database is available free to LACBA members who are sole practitioners and to firms whose lawyers are all members. See information about the SCR at http://bit.ly/lacbascr.

To retrieve a plethora of federal case documents (e.g., complaints, answers, motions, and sometimes briefs) from federal district, bankruptcy, and appellate court cases, use **PACER** (https://www.pacer.gov) or **RECAP** (https://www.courtlistener.com/recap). See Chapter 15, Dockets and Case Documents, for more information on using **PACER** and **RECAP**.

Some state and local courts also provide access to case documents. For instance, the **Los Angeles Superior Court** (http://bit.ly/LACourtOnline) offers access to PDF images of case documents, searchable by case number or part name, for a fee (see Figure 1.8).

**Figure 1.8** Some courts, such as the Los Angeles Superior Court, offer access to PDF images of case documents.

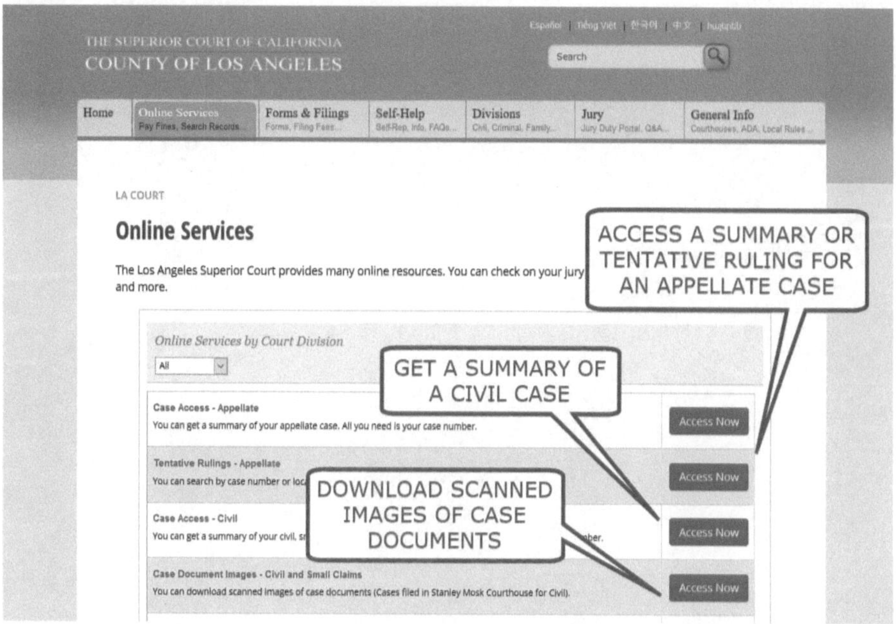


At the **Supreme Court of the United States** site (https://www.supremecourt.gov/docket/docket.aspx), you can retrieve Supreme Court merit and amicus briefs for free. See Chapter 15, Dockets and Case Documents, to learn how to search the site and find out dates of coverage.

There are several sites where you can retrieve Supreme Court and Federal Appellate Court audio files. The three sites for Supreme Court audio recordings are: **Supreme Court of the United States** (http://bit.ly/sctoralargaudio), **Oyez** (http://www.oyez.org/cases), and **CourtListener** (https://www.courtlistener.com/audio). The one site for audio recordings of oral arguments from the Federal Courts of Appeals, First through the Ninth Circuits, the D.C. Circuit, and the Federal Circuit is **CourtListener** (https://www.courtlistener.com/audio). The one site for Supreme Court transcripts is: **Supreme Court of the United States** (http://bit.ly/sctoralargtran). See Chapter 15, Dockets and Case Documents, to learn how to search the sites and find out their dates of coverage.

# Chapter 2

## WEBSITES BY PRACTICE AREA

This chapter will focus on traditional Internet resources that are practice area-specific. A practice area-specific legal site focuses on one area of law (such as advertising law) and either provides content at its site or links to other sites that focus on that practice area. Because there are so many areas of practice, we will discuss only a few practice areas. If your topic is not listed here, you can try searching one of the general legal research websites discussed in Chapter 1, or one of the portals and directories discussed in Chapters 4 and 5.

## ADVERTISING LAW

The law firm of Reed Smith originally created an advertising and marketing law website, which was updated bi-weekly, but it has now morphed into a blog—**AdLaw By Request** (http://www.adlawbyrequest.com)—and is updated more frequently. The blog's keyword search engine is located at the top of the right-hand sidebar. If you scroll down, you will also see a heading on the right side, labeled **Topics**. From there you can select a topic, such as **Children's Advertising, In the Courts, Intellectual Property, Product Placement,** etc., to focus on a specific area of advertising law. The firm also has several other blogs on various legal topics (http://bit.ly/ReedSmithBlogs).

For other advertising law blogs, see the list at **Justia's BlawgSearch** (http://bit.ly/JustiaAdLawBlogs).

## BANKRUPTCY LAW

The Administrative Office of the **U.S. Courts** provides information on **Bankruptcy Basics** (http://bit.ly/USCtsBK). As the name implies, the site gives general and introductory information about bankruptcy laws, but it also provides links to several useful sources such as a glossary, bankruptcy forms, and a schedule of fees associated with filing for bankruptcy. Individual bankruptcy court websites may also provide helpful information. The **U.S. Courts** website also provides a list of all bankruptcy courts and other federal court websites (http://bit.ly/FedCtsSites).

For information about Bankruptcy Courts and opinions, see Chapters 6 and 7 on Free Case Law, and for information about Bankruptcy dockets, see Chapter 15 on Dockets and Case Documents.

For Bankruptcy law blogs, see the list at **Justia's BlawgSearch** (http://bit.ly/JustiaBKBlogs).

## CLASS ACTION LAWSUITS

Timothy E. Eble, a contributing author to a leading treatise on class actions (*Newberg on Class Actions*), is the site owner of **Class Action Litigation Information** (http://www.classactionlitigation.com). The site contains the full text of the *Federal Class Action Practice Manual—Internet Edition* (1999), by Timothy E. Eble. Although the site has not been updated since 2015, it still contains useful links to class action articles, legislation, and more.

Despite focusing mostly on their own firm's class action cases, the sites of two big players in this arena, **Robbins Geller Rudman & Dowd LLP** (http://www.rgrdlaw.com) and **Milberg** (http://www.milberg.com), each provide useful research information about their cases. At the Robbins' site, you can click on **Cases** to get details about settled and pending cases, including complaints and settlement agreements.

**Classified: The Class Action Blog** (http://classifiedclassaction.com) is written by attorneys at the law firm of Carlton Fields. You can search the blog or browse by topics such as **Construction, Health Care,** and **Privacy & Technology**. For more class action blogs, see the list at **Justia's BlawgSearch** (http://bit.ly/JustiaClassActionBlogs).

## COPYRIGHT LAW

See Intellectual Property—Copyright, Patents and Trademarks, later in this chapter.

## CORPORATE/BUSINESS LAW

Since many corporations are incorporated in Delaware, attorneys researching corporate law may find it useful to visit the **Delaware State Court** site (http://courts.delaware.gov). As the site explains, "The Delaware Court of Chancery is widely recognized as the nation's preeminent forum for the determination of disputes involving the internal affairs of the thousands upon thousands of Delaware corporations and other business entities through which a vast amount of the world's commercial affairs is conducted. Its unique competence in and exposure to issues of business law are unmatched" (see https://courts.delaware.gov/chancery).

- The **Court of Chancery** home page (https://courts.delaware.gov/chancery), contains several useful links; the left side of the page provides information such as **Jurisdiction**, with detailed information about the Court's jurisdiction; **Chancery Opinions and Orders**, for decisions by the Court; and **Rules & Amendments** for information about Court procedures. The right side of the page also provides **Guidelines** for those litigating in the Court of Chancery and **Operating Procedures** for the Court, among other helpful information.
- The **Opinions and Orders** database (accessed by the **Opinions** tab at the top of each page) is keyword searchable with coverage back to 1983. There are no instructions on how to search, and our test searches were inconclusive. For example, sometimes a phrase search (enclosing two words in parentheses) worked and sometimes it didn't. Sometimes searches for certain keywords would return documents that did not contain the words. To browse, select one or more of the drop-down menu categories, such as **Court of Chancery** and **Decision Date**; to sort results, click any of the column headings, such as **Parties/Caption, Date, Court,** etc. (For a better keyword search experience of Delaware court opinions and orders, use other free or member-benefit case law databases such as Google Scholar, Casemaker, or Fastcase, which are discussed in Chapters 6, 8, and 9, respectively.)

- Under the **eServices** dropdown menu at the top of each page, you can link to the various electronic filing services used by the Delaware courts. Fees and procedures vary by service.

**The M&A Profs** blog (http://lawprofessors.typepad.com/mergers) is written by two law professors and a practicing attorney. You can read their posts, which focus on mergers and acquisitions, or search by keyword. For more blogs about various areas of business and corporate law, see **Justia's BlawgSearch** (http://bit.ly/JustiaBusinessBlogs). Blog titles range from the **Harvard Law School Forum on Corporate Governance and Financial Regulation** to **Indian Company Law**.

## CRIMINAL LAW

The **National Association of Criminal Defense Lawyers'** (NACDL) site (http://www.criminaljustice.org) has information about criminal law, but mostly from the defense viewpoint. Some information is available free to nonmembers (e.g., links to **News of Interest** and abstracts from select publications by other organizations that are relevant to the criminal justice field) while other information is available only to members, such as the **Brief & Motion Bank** and *The Champion*, NADCL's journal.

For prosecutors and researchers interested in the prosecutorial point of view, see the **National District Attorneys Association's (NDAA)** site (http://www.ndaa.org). While most of the site is for members only, there are some free publications listed at http://bit.ly/NDAAPubsVideos. For example, you can read current and past issues of *Between the Lines*, the National Traffic Law Center's newsletter (http://bit.ly/NDAALines), or download a PDF of the guide, *Cross-Examination for Prosecutors*.

For blogs about various areas of criminal law, see the list at **Justia's BlawgSearch** (http://bit.ly/JustiaCrimLawBlogs). Areas range from Chicago DUI law to prisoners' rights.

## EMPLOYMENT AND LABOR LAW

The **Employment Law Information Network** (**ELIN**) website (http://www.elinfonet.com) includes articles, sample personnel policies and forms, summaries of federal and state employment cases, and an attorney directory. The site is aimed at management-side employment lawyers, in-house employment lawyers, and human resource staff. The content is supplied by affiliates of ELIN, which include several law firms, one corporate affiliate, the University of Pennsylvania's Wharton School of Business, and Cornell University's School of Industrial & Labor Relations (http://bit.ly/ELINAffilates).

**HG.org's Employment Law** page (http://www.hg.org/employ.html) links to articles, organizations, lawyers, websites, laws, and government agencies (e.g., the U.S. Department of Labor and the labor departments in all fifty states and the District of Columbia) dealing with employment/labor law for both the employer and the employee. In addition, HG includes international and foreign labor law links.

Another website that provides extensive black-letter employment law is **Workplace Fairness** (https://www.workplacefairness.org). To research specific areas of government and administrative employment law, several government websites are available. Check the U.S. **Equal Employment Opportunity Commission** at eeoc.gov, the **Office of Personnel Management** (opm.gov) and the **U.S. Merit System Protection Board** (mspb.gov).

If you are looking for a specific union or list of unions, **Cornell University Library** provides a guide that lists **Labor Union Directories** at http://bit.ly/CornellUnionDirectories. **FindLaw's List of Labor Unions** page (http://bit.ly/FindLawUnions) may also be useful. To find local union websites, first click the parent union name. The AFL-CIO website (http://bit.ly/AFLCIOUnions) lists links to all 56 of its **Affiliated Unions, State Federations and Labor Councils**, and more.

For blogs about various areas of employment and labor law, see the list at **Justia's BlawgSearch** (http://bit.ly/JustiaEmploymentBlogs). Popular blog titles range from **New York Public Personnel Law** to **Whistleblower Protection Blog**.

## FAMILY LAW

**DivorceNet** (http://www.divorcenet.com), a site created by Nolo (publisher of do-it-yourself legal guides), includes a family law blog, articles, and referrals to attorneys and experts. The site also provides some state-by-state family law links, such as **Best Interests of the Child State-by-State** (http://bit.ly/DNBestInterests) and **Divorce and Property Laws by State** (http://bit.ly/DNWhoGetsWhat).

Also useful is **Cornell's Divorce Law Overview** (http://bit.ly/LIIDivorce). If you scroll down to the **Menu of Sources** heading, you will find links to uniform laws and recent federal cases about divorce and related family law issues. For links to all fifty states' divorce laws, visit http://bit.ly/LIIFamilyState.

**Illinoisdivorce.com** (http://illinoisdivorce.com) has several articles on its **Legal Advice** page (http://bit.ly/IDArticles) covering various areas of divorce law in Illinois, from Annulment to Same-Sex Marriage and Divorce, to Enforcing Child Support Orders. This site is an example of e-lawyering. Everything is handled online. For $499 they will handle an uncontested divorce (from filing the papers to representing clients in court), and for $149 they will fill out paperwork and coach clients to file their own papers and represent themselves.

If issues of sexual orientation and gender come into play in a family law matter you are handling, you may want to check the **Williams Institute** (http://williamsinstitute.law.ucla.edu), a sexual orientation and gender research think tank. You can keyword search various reports or choose a topic from the menu bar at the top of the page. The American Society for Reproductive Medicine's **ReproductiveFacts** site (http://www.reproductivefacts.org) may be a useful site if you encounter a divorce involving the custody of frozen embryos or cross-border reproductive care, for example.

## FOREIGN AND INTERNATIONAL LAW

See Chapter 14.

## IMMIGRATION LAW

The federal government regulates immigration law. It's not surprising then, that some of the most helpful (and free) websites are from the federal government. The **U.S. Department of Homeland Security** (https://www.dhs.gov) oversees several agencies that regulate immigration, including **U.S. Citizenship and Immigration Services** (https://www.uscis.gov), **U.S. Customs and Border Protection** (https://www.cbp.gov), and **U.S. Immigration and Customs Enforcement** (https://www.ice.gov). Check these websites and their tools (USCIS), research libraries (ICE), fact sheets, and links to primary law for immigration law information.

The **American Immigration Council** (https://www.americanimmigrationcouncil.org) is a nonprofit immigration advocacy group that provides a wealth of information on its site. The **Topics** tab on the home page provides links to categories like **Immigration 101, Immigration Benefits and Relief, Due Process and the Courts**, and much more. A magnifying glass icon in the upper right corner of the page reveals a search box that allows you to keyword search the site.

The **ImmigrationProf Blog** (http://lawprofessors.typepad.com/immigration) is written by four immigration law professors. You can browse or search the blog, as well as subscribe for email updates. For more blogs on immigration law, try searching **Justia's BlawgSearch** (http://bit.ly/JustiaImmigrationBlogs).

See Chapter 4, Legal Portals and Directories, to learn about Siskind Susser's **VISALAW.com** immigration website (http://www.visalaw.com).

## INSURANCE LAW

The **National Association of Insurance Commissioners (NAIC)** has a website that, although geared primarily toward association members, provides some useful information for researchers (https://naic.org). The site's **Library** page (http://bit.ly/NAICLibrary) links to several helpful resources, including **My State's Insurance Department Contact Information**, a map of U.S. states and territories that provides the name and contact information for the head of each state's insurance department. Clicking a state's name takes you to the insurance department website for that state. The Library page also provides links to additional resources, such as an extensive **Glossary of Insurance Terms**, and the **NAIC Publications, Manuals, Guides and Reports** page, which you can search and browse by topic. Although some publications are for sale, many, such as white papers and statistical reports, are free.

Although **Insure.com** is a commercial site that provides instant quotes from insurers and insurance brokerage, it also provides useful articles about various lines of insurance at http://www.insure.com. Click the **Life Insurance, Auto Insurance, Health Insurance, Home Insurance,** and **Insurance Calculators & Tools** tabs to find information. The site also provides links to every state insurance department (http://www.insure.com/states-insurance).

For blogs about various areas of insurance law, see the list at **Justia's BlawgSearch** (http://bit.ly/JustiaInsuranceBlogs). The blog topics range from reinsurance to coverage and many also focus on the insurance law of a specific state.

## INTELLECTUAL PROPERTY—COPYRIGHT, PATENTS, AND TRADEMARKS

The **U.S. Copyright Office** (http://www.copyright.gov), a department of the Library of Congress, provides online access to forms, regulations, and laws relating to copyright; it also posts a primer about copyright.

- The U.S. Copyright Office website also has a user-friendly searchable database of over 20 million copyright records dating back to 1978 (http://cocatalog.loc.gov). The catalog includes registrations and pre-registrations for books, music, films, sound recordings, maps, software, photographs, art, multimedia, periodicals, magazines, journals, newspapers, and so on. Also included are records for assignments, transfers, and miscellaneous documents relating to copyright ownership.
- To search the database, click the **Search the Catalog** link. This link leads to the **Basic Search** page, where you can search by **Title, Name, Keyword, Registration Number, Document Number**, or **Command Keyword** (Boolean, phrase, and wildcard searching). Sample searches are available for each of the five categories above; click the linked category name near the top of the page to see samples for that category. For more detailed searching, click the **Other Search Options** tab.
- To access pre-1977 records, researchers have three options. First, they can go to the Copyright Office in Washington, D.C. and use the physical card catalog. Second, they can use the online **Catalogs of Copyright Entries** (CCEs) (http://bit.ly/CopyrightCCE), an ongoing project to digitize the records of copyright ownership back to 1891. The CCEs contain registration records only; no information about transfer, assignment, or other documents recorded in the Copyright Office is included. (For more information, researchers have to contact the Copyright Office directly.) Third, a researcher can hire the Copyright Office to search the records. Start by completing the online Search Estimate form (http://bit.ly/COSearchEstimate) to request a search. Fees start at $200 per hour.

While the **Copyright & Fair Use** site (http://fairuse.stanford.edu) appears on the Stanford University website, several entities actually sponsor it—the Stanford Libraries, Justia, NOLO, LibraryLaw.com, and Onecle. Tabs under the site's **What's New** heading (scroll down the page to see it) link to copyright-related **Opinions, Dockets, Legislation, Regulations, Articles, Blogs**, and **Our Blog**—Stanford's own **Fairly Used** blog (http://fairuse.stanford.edu/blog).

For other copyright law blogs, see the list at Justia's **BlawgSearch** (http://bit.ly/JustiaCopyrightBlogs).

Visit the **U.S. Patent and Trademark Office** (USPTO) site (https://www.uspto.gov) to search patent and trademark text and image databases for the U.S. and some other countries. (The USPTO does not handle copyrights—only patents and trademarks. See the paragraphs above for copyright research.)

- The USPTO offers a database of patents back to 1790 at http://bit.ly/USPTOPatents. The **Quick Search** feature allows you to search full-text, using keywords with Boolean connectors and fields. You can also conduct a **Patent Number Search** and an **Advanced Search**. The Advanced Search uses command line syntax to search with keywords and phrases and to include fields (e.g., inventor's name). A **Help** page (http://bit.ly/USPTOHelp) explains how to do this.
- Users can search patents full text for 1976 to the present. For 1790 to 1975, you can only search by Issue Date, Patent Number, and Current Classification. The database also includes full-page images (http://bit.ly/USPTOImages), but they can be searched only by number.
- Patent applications are searchable back to March 2001 using **Quick Search**, **Publication Number Search**, and **Advanced Search** (http://bit.ly/USPTOApplications). The search features work like the ones described above for searching patents.
- The USPTO also disseminates public patent and trademark bulk data products. They can be prepackaged or user-customized. See the **Bulk Data Products** page (http://bit.ly/USPTOBulkData) for information and resources for downloading bulk data.
- In 2017, USPTO decommissioned its Global Patent Search Network (GPSN) that allowed full-text searching of Chinese patent-related documents. Many alternative search platforms are available, however. Sites that USPTO recommends include the **State Intellectual Property Office of the People's Republic of China** (http://english.sipo.gov.cn). Access to machine translation of Chinese patents is available on that site. Another useful site is the **World Intellectual Property Organization** (WIPO), which provides PATENTSCOPE Search Service. PATENTSCOPE allows full-text searching of international Patent Cooperation Treaty (PCT) applications on the day of publication and also provides a list of international patent databases (http://www.wipo.int/patentscope/en). The **USPTO** site also links to other useful international and foreign countries' IP offices (http://bit.ly/USPTOOther).

**Google Patents** (https://patents.google.com) uses Google's familiar search interface to provide access to over 87 million patent publications from 17 patent offices worldwide, dating back to 1790. Google Patents' **Advanced Search** page (https://patents.google.com/advanced) allows for keyword and phrase searches similar to those on the Google Advanced Search page. Additionally, you can search for information in specific areas of a patent document, such as Patent number, Title, Inventor, Assignee, and more.

For trademark research, use TESS, the **Trademark Electronic Search System** (http://tmsearch.uspto.gov), to search over 4 million pending, registered, and dead federal trademarks at the USPTO site. There are three search options: (1) the **Basic Word Mark Search (New User)** allows you to search word marks; (2) **Word and/or Design Mark Search (Structured)** allows you to search word and/or design marks after you look up Design Codes in the **Design Search Code Manual** (http://bit.ly/USPTODesignCodes); and (3) **Word and/or Design Mark Search (Free Form)** allows you to search word and/or design mark searches with Boolean operators and multiple search fields.

For patent and other IP resources, see the **American Intellectual Property Law Association**'s (AIPLA) website (http://www.aipla.org). The AIPLA is an association of 17,000 attorneys who work with national and international intellectual property issues. Portions of its site are member-only, but some information is available to the public. Use the search box on the right side of the home page to search the site. Results may include books, article abstracts (full text for members only), and AIPLA's advocacy materials—statements, briefs, and testimony submitted to Congress, executive agencies, federal courts, and international organizations and governments. You can also browse the advocacy materials by selecting the **IP Policy & Advocacy** tab from the home page.

For blogs about various areas of IP, see the list at **Justia's BlawgSearch** (http://bit.ly/JustiaIPBlogs). The blog titles range from **Likelihood of Confusion** to **Hollywood, Esq.**

## LAW AND MEDICINE

The **American Medical Association** (AMA) site (http://www.ama-assn.org) is a good starting point to find information about nearly every one of the 814,000 licensed physicians in the United States. Unfortunately, their **DoctorFinder** feature has become even more difficult to find since the last edition of this book. Go to https://apps.ama-assn.org/doctorfinder and enter the words or numbers you see in the Captcha image. Then click the image labeled **for Patients.** Next, click the **DoctorFinder** link, read the disclaimer, and click **Accept.** You can search by **Last Name** or by **Specialty**; a State or ZIP Code is required for either search. Adding a First Name or City is optional. You can select the option for a sound-like name search if you are unsure of the spelling. AMA members and non-members are displayed separately, and the results return basic background and contact information.

You won't find discipline information at the AMA database, but you might find some if you visit the **Administrators in Medicine DocFinder** site (http://docfinder.docboard.org). This site simultaneously searches 16 states' physician license databases and two osteopathic license databases. Discipline information is sometimes included. The site also provides links to the other states' licensing boards, where you might find discipline information.

To conduct medical-related research, begin with the **National Library of Medicine (NLM)** at (https://www.nlm.nih.gov). From the home page, you can choose a popular database from among the links in the left sidebar to search. Probably the most useful individual NLM database to lawyers who are researching medical issues is **PubMed** (http://bit.ly/NLMPubMed), which provides over 27 million citations from MEDLINE, life science journals, and online books. Some citations link to free full-text content from PubMed Central or publishers' websites. Use the search box at the top of the home page to keyword search for medical articles. The NLM also provides a search page specifically for **PubMed Central**, a free full-text archive (https://www.ncbi.nlm.nih.gov/pmc); PubMedCentral contains 4.5 million free articles.

For blogs about various areas of Medical Malpractice and Personal Injury Law, see the list at **Justia's BlawgSearch** (http://bit.ly/JustiaMedMalBlogs). The blog titles can range from very narrow topics such as **Pharmacy Error Injury Lawyer Blog** to the more general, like **Nursing Law Blog**.

## LEGAL ETHICS AND PROFESSIONALISM

The **ABA Center for Professional Responsibility (CPR)** site (http://bit.ly/ABA_CPR) describes itself as "provid[ing] national leadership in developing and interpreting standards and scholarly resources in legal and judicial ethics, professional regulation, professionalism and client protection." CPR posts the Model Rules of Professional Conduct (with comments), its Table of Contents, and its subject index for free (http://bit.ly/ABAModelRules).

- Recent Formal Ethics Opinions are available for free (http://bit.ly/ABAEthicsOpinions) to ABA members only for one year from the opinion's date of release while CPR members have full-text access to all opinions since 1983. The opinions are organized by date of issue and by subject. Archived opinions can be purchased online for $7.50 each.
- The CPR site also links to **State Ethics Rules** and an **Alphabetical List of States Adopting Model Rules** among other state ethics related topics (http://bit.ly/StateEthicsLinks). Most states publish their ethics opinions for free, usually on the state's bar association website. If you don't find them there, try the court's website. If you have a free member subscription to **Fastcase** (Chapter 9) or **Casemaker** (Chapter 8), check to see if they offer ethics opinions for your state.
- **ETHICSearch** (http://bit.ly/ETHICSearch) is a service offered on the ABA site to any ABA member, although nonmembers can also subscribe to ETHICSearch annually. The service provides free initial consultations to ethics inquiries. From the left-hand column of the page you can link to **Ethics Tips Archives, Eye on Ethics Articles,** and more free resources.

**Legal Profession Blog** (http://bit.ly/LProfessionBlog) is part of the Law Professor Blogs Network. Edited by four professors, it covers various legal areas but focuses primarily on ethics, professional responsibility, and the practice of law. This and other ethics blogs can be found on **Justia's BlawgSearch** (http://bit.ly/JustiaEthicsBlogs).

## PATENT LAW

See Intellectual Property—Copyright, Patents, and Trademarks, earlier in this chapter.

## REAL ESTATE AND PROPERTY LAW

**Justia** provides an overview of real estate law and links to additional resources on its **Real Estate Law** page at (https://www.justia.com/real-estate).

For "quick and dirty" price estimates of over 110 million U.S. homes, including homes for sale, homes for rent, and homes not currently on the market, see **Zillow.com** (www.zillow.com).

For blogs about various areas of Real Estate and Property Law, see the list at **Justia's BlawgSearch** (http://bit.ly/JustiaRealEstateBlogs). The blog titles vary from **inversecondemnation.com** to **Florida HOA Lawyer Blog**.

## SECURITIES LAW

The **U.S. Securities and Exchange Commission's (SEC)** site (http://www.sec.gov) has reams of SEC documents online that can be accessed either by entering keywords/phrases into the SEC documents search box on the upper right-hand side of the home page or by selecting one of the tabs listed on the top of the home page (**Divisions, Enforcement, Regulation, Education, Filings, News**). Each tab offers a drop-down menu with more selections. For instance, from the **Enforcement** tab's drop-down menu you can select **Litigation Releases, Administrative Proceedings**, and so on.

- From the **Filings** tab's drop-down menu, you can access free "real time" SEC company filings using **EDGAR** (Electronic Data Gathering, Analysis, and Retrieval), the SEC's online public database that contains documents submitted by companies and other entities that are required to file forms with the SEC. EDGAR offers full-text searching of filings from the last four years (http://bit.ly/EDGARFullText). (Soon EDGAR will let you search the past ten years of filings.)
- If you click the **Advanced Search Page** link to the right of the search box, you can narrow down your keyword search by Company Name, Central Index Key (CIK, the unique identifying number the SEC assigns to each company), or Standard Industrial Classification (SIC) number, the U.S. government's numerical classification system that describes a company's line of business.
- For earlier years' filings, you can search by Company Name at http://bit.ly/EDGARCompany and also by, file number, state, country, or SIC number, if you click the **More Options** link. For more ways to search EDGAR, visit the Search Tools page at http://bit.ly/EDGARSearchTools.

**SEC Info** (http://www.secinfo.com) offers free, full-text searching of U.S. Securities and Exchange Commission filings. The following search options are available: **Name, Industry, Business, SIC** (Standard Industrial Classification) **Code, Topic, CIK** (Central Index Key), **Accession Number, File Number, Date,**

and **ZIP Code**. Additionally, although not listed as one of the available criteria next to the Search box, you can also search by NAICS (North American Industrial Classification System numbers—the government's newer numerical classification system that describes a company's business, adopted to replace the SIC Codes). While you can search the site and also receive a list of results without registering, free registration is required to view full-text filings and to receive new filing e-mail notifications.

**Rank and Filed** (rankandfiled.com) describes itself as "SEC filings for humans." This resource collects data from EDGAR, indexes it, and provides it in a form that allows researchers to study, compare, and investigate companies. Type the name of a company, broker-dealer, or other entity into the search box at the top of the home page and choose from a list of results in the drop-down menu that appears.

If you need filings from years earlier than 1994, you can order the document(s) from the **SEC** (http://bit.ly/SECInfo). If you need to keyword search older filings, you will need to subscribe to a pay database such as **Intelligize** (https://www.intelligize.com) or Securities Mosaic (http://bit.ly/SecuritiesMosaic), both owned by LexisNexis.

To obtain dockets for over 4,000 class action securities fraud matters filed since 1995, with the full text of over 47,000 complaints, briefs, and orders, see **Stanford Law School Securities Class Action Clearinghouse** (SCAC), a site created in cooperation with **Cornerstone Research** (http://securities.stanford.edu). The SCAC also contains opinions, articles, settlement news, reports, and charts about securities litigation. You can keyword-search the entire collection by using the search box on the top right-hand side of the homepage. The tabs across the top of the page also lead to many useful resources:

- **Filings Database:**
  - Browse filings in reverse chronological order or
  - Type a Filing Name or Company into the search box on the right-hand side or
  - View charts, statistics, and lists relating to **Heat Maps & Related Filings, Top Ten, Key Stats, Filings by Year,** or **Filings by Circuit** by clicking any one of their tabs
- **Resources:** Leads to sub-tabs for **News & Blogs Excerpts, Academic Articles, Related Sites,** or **Conferences & Seminars.** You can also use the search box to keyword-search News & Blogs Excerpts.

- **Litigation Activity Indices:** Displays a sidebar on the left side with links to indices such as the **Median Lag Time,** which shows the number of days between the end of class periods and the filing dates starting from 1997.
- **Clearinghouse Resources:** Read research reports about filings and settlements dating from 1996.

Check out your broker's background at the **Financial Industry Regulatory Authority (FINRA)** site's free **BrokerCheck** database (http://brokercheck.finra.org). Note: FINRA was formerly known as the National Association of Securities Dealers (NASD). You will be able to find BrokerCheck Reports for brokers currently registered with FINRA, registered with FINRA within the past 10 years, or whose registration terminated over 10 years ago. Report summaries provide overviews of brokers, their credentials, listings of current registrations or licenses, industry exams passed, and registration and employment history.

FINRA also provides two other databases: **FINRA Disciplinary Actions Online** (http://disciplinaryactions.finra.org) and **FINRA Arbitration Awards Online** (http://finraawardsonline.finra.org).

For blogs about various areas of Securities Law, see the list at **Justia's Blawg-Search** (http://bit.ly/JustiaSecuritiesBlogs). The blog titles range from **The Race to the Bottom,** with postings from professionals, law faculty, and law students about corporate and securities law, to **Stock Broker Fraud Blog** to **Hedge Fund Law Blog.**

## TAX LAW

The **IRS** site (http://www.irs.gov) provides tax forms and publications online for free. The **U.S. Tax Court** website provides many of its decisions in a searchable database. Its **TC and Memorandum Decisions** (September 25, 1995–present), its **TC Opinions** (January 11, 2010–present), and its **Summary Decisions** (January 10, 2001–present) are available at http://bit.ly/TaxCtOpinions. You can search by one or more of the following criteria: **Text Search** (keywords), **Date Search, Case Name Keyword, Judge,** and **Opinion Type** (choose **All Types, Memorandum, Summary,** or **TC Opinion**). Dockets are also online for cases filed on or after May 1, 1986 and can be searched by **Docket Number, Individual Party Name** (a state and year can be entered to narrow the search), or **Corporate Name Keyword** (http://bit.ly/TaxCtDockets). Some case documents, such as a stipulated agreement, may also be online.

For blogs about various areas of Tax Law, see the list at **Justia's BlawgSearch** (http://bit.ly/JustiaTaxBlogs). The blog titles include **Taxable Talk, State and Local Tax Talk,** and **Tax Policy Blog.**

The **Federation of Tax Administrators** (https://www.taxadmin.org) was organized in 1937 and provides services to U.S. states, including research and information exchange, training, and interstate coordination. Its website may be useful for researching state tax law issues. Among other resources, the site provides a **State Tax Agencies** page that lists each state tax agency's website (http://bit.ly/taxadmin-state). **State Tax Agency Research Links** (http://bit.ly/taxadmin-research) lists economic and tax policy research websites, ordered by state. The site also provides a page of links to **Other Tax Policy and Administration Websites** (http://bit.ly/taxadmin-other) that may help researchers.

## TRADEMARK LAW

See Intellectual Property—Copyright, Patents, and Trademarks, earlier in this chapter.

# Chapter 3

## APPS FOR GENERAL LEGAL RESEARCH

App is short for *software application*. Apps are designed to run on smartphones, tablet computers, and other mobile devices. They are usually obtained from the Apple App Store (for iOS mobile devices—iPads or iPhones), Google Play (for Android mobile devices—phones and tablets), or the Windows Phone Store. Sometimes there are also apps for Blackberry devices. For each app listed below, we will indicate if it is available for iOS and/or Android devices. It's always a good idea to go online and check to see if the iOS apps we mention are now available for the Android and vice versa.

To search for and download apps, locate the "App Store" icon on your device. To find a specific app, you usually have to know its exact name, so they can sometimes be challenging to locate. Both Google Play and Apple's App Store will allow you to keyword search the apps database for apps for a specific purpose—legal dictionaries, for example. You can then filter your results by categories such as price and user ratings.

If you want to receive updates and reviews of new legal apps, you can subscribe to Brett Burney's free **Apps in Law** newsletter. The website (appsinlaw.com) also features a searchable database of reviews, as well as podcasts and links to the site's Twitter and YouTube feeds.

To help you get started with some useful apps, we have listed a sampling in this chapter by topic or practice area. Most are free or low-cost. Many provide at least some content for free, but to access additional content may require one or more in-app purchases.

## CASE LAW

- **Fastcase** (iOS and Android): This app is free even to non-subscribers, but they will need to register with Fastcase to use the app. The app does not offer the full content or functionality of the computer version. It only allows you to search cases and statutes by keyword or citation and limit the search by jurisdiction and date. The Authority feature is also available on the app. If you have a subscription to Fastcase, you can also sync between your computer and mobile devices. For example, if you mark a case as a **Favorite** when researching from your computer, your favorites will automatically be synced to your iPhone, iPad, and/or Android Fastcase App. If you **Save** a document when you are researching from the Fastcase App, that document will be synced to your computer and all your other mobile devices. You can print the document when you later log into your Fastcase account on your computer by clicking **My Library** and then clicking **Go to Recent Documents**.

  See Chapter 9 to learn about using Fastcase on your computer.
- **Oyez** (iOS): This app is free for iOS devices and contains briefs of over 850 Supreme Court cases, as well as voting information for the cases and audio recordings of oral arguments. Cases range from the current term to as far back as 1789. Provided by Justia, the app provides all the information on the Oyez website.
- **PushLegal's Statutes and Case Law Library** (iOS): Search annotated case law (linking to Google Scholar), statutes (California, Delaware, Florida, Illinois, New York, and Texas), and court rules. The app is free to download and it comes with the Federal Rules of Evidence for free. Other materials are available by subscription for $1.99 a month for each "book." For instance, the California Evidence Code is considered a separate book from the California Probate Code so each one would cost $1.99 a month. Although we were able to sign up and use the iOS version, the Android version was problematic, so we are not sure whether this app is being updated for Android.
- **Casemaker** (iOS, Android): The app is free to download, but you must subscribe to Casemaker in order to use it. Casemaker subscribers can obtain a reference code by logging into Casemaker online and then entering the code into the app on their mobile device. Law students can obtain a free CasemakerX account, which will also allow them to use the app. See Chapter 8 on Casemaker to learn what's available and how to search on your computer.

## CODE OF FEDERAL REGULATIONS

- **GovRegs** (Android): This free app allows you to search or browse the Code of Federal Regulations, the U.S. Code, and the U.S. Constitution. Unlike many free apps, GovRegs tells you how current (by CFR and USC title) its materials are. Also, relative to other free apps, the materials are quite current; for example, no title of the CFR was more than six months old at the time of this writing.
- See also **LawStack** (iOS), discussed in the Court Rules section of this chapter.

## CONGRESSIONAL RECORD

- **Congressional Record (CR)** (iOS): The Library of Congress offers the CR for free from 1995–present. Using your iPad or iPhone, you can keyword search the CR, copy text, save text as a PDF, and e-mail it. The app also tracks Congress's current activity.

## COURT RULES

- **Rulebook** (iOS): Mobile access to federal and state court rules using full-text searching. You can highlight text, add notes, copy, print, and/or bookmark text. The app is free and so are the Federal Rules of Evidence, the U.S. Constitution and a few other documents, but it will cost anywhere from $3.99 to $4.99 to purchase other court rules, or up to $39.99 to purchase *The Bluebook*, for example. This app is powered by Casemaker.
- **LawStack** (iOS): This free app includes the U.S. Constitution and Federal Rules for free. You can also add additional state and federal rules; some are free and some require purchase. Tekk Innovations, which provides LawStack, sells several apps in the LawStack series with specialized content ranging from Title 11 Bankruptcy ("11 USC Bankruptcy") to the Florida Rules of Civil Procedure, to individual titles of the Code of Federal Regulations. Annual subscription fees range from $4.99 to $29.99.
- **US Constitution & Federal Laws** (Android): This free app comes with the Rules of the Supreme Court of the United States, the Federal Rules of

Appellate Procedure, Civil Procedure, Criminal Procedure, Evidence, and Bankruptcy, and the U.S. Constitution. You can browse or keyword search each category.

## CRIMINAL LAW

- The Association of Federal Defense Attorneys (**AFDA**) has migrated its entire website to a free app (iOS and Android). The app provides several free features and some paid features. Free features include a collection of blogs on federal criminal law topics, discussion forums for each federal district, and an archive of AFDA's recorded webinars from 2012–2016. You need to set up a free account to use the free features.

## DICTIONARIES (LEGAL)

- One free legal dictionary that is available for both Android and iOS is provided by Farlex, Inc. The Android version is called **Legal Dictionary by Farlex**, and the iOS is **Legal Dictionary—Law Definitions and Thesaurus.** Both versions provide over 58,000 legal terms as well as more than 42,000 audio pronunciations.
- **Law Dictionary & Guide** (iOS, Android) by TheLaw.com. This free app for both iOS and Android contains over 14,000 offline legal definitions and over 28,000 online. Users can search, browse, and bookmark entries.
- **Nolo's English Law Dictionary** (iOS) This free app contains almost 4,000 legal definitions, in plain English.
- **Black's Law Dictionary** (10th ed.) by Thomson Reuters (iOS): $54.99. The latest edition of the Black's app contains over 50,000 terms. It's not free, but we included it here because it is such a classic resource. Unfortunately, although the dictionary is easy to use and search, the app itself appears to lack some basic functionality such as page numbers for citations, support for recent editions of the iPhone, and more. This app is no longer available for Android devices.
- **Wolfram Lawyer's Professional Assistant** (iOS) is not just a dictionary, but we have included it in this category because it does contain a small legal

dictionary. For $4.99, Wolfram Alpha, a computational knowledge company, provides an app that includes not only the dictionary but also statutes of limitations for each U.S. state, visa information, crime statistics, and such tools as demographic data, international calculators, currency converters, real estate calculators, and more. Professional Assistant can also perform calendar computations, as well as calculate fees, settlements, and interest-rates.

## LEGAL ETHICS AND PROFESSIONALISM

- **Model Rules of Professional Conduct** (iOS): This app, introduced by the ABA Center for Professional Responsibility, costs $24.99. We thought it was worth mentioning here, however, since every state except California has adopted the format used by the Model Rules. You must first download the Ready Reference Apps' free Rulebook app (http://bit.ly/RulebookApp) and then make an in-app purchase of the Model Rules.

## STATE STATUTES

- See **LawStack** noted earlier in the Court Rules section in this chapter.
- See **Fastcase, PushLegal,** and **Casemaker** noted earlier in the Case Law section in this chapter.

## TAXATION

- **TouchTax Code and Regs** (Android and iOS): For $5.99 for Android or $3.99 for the iOS version, this app provides offline access on your mobile device to all 7,700+ sections of the latest edition of the Internal Revenue Code of 1986, as amended, as well as the Treasury Regulations in Title 26 of the CFR, the Internal Revenue Bulletins since 2003, Circular 230, Revenue Procedures, Revenue Rulings, and Notices and Announcements since 2003. The app page states that this app is updated regularly; Internal Revenue Bulletins, Revenue Procedures, Revenue Rulings, and Notices and Announcements are updated approximately weekly and appear automatically on your device.

## UNITED STATES CODE

- **United States Code All Titles Free** (Android): contains the entire U.S. Code. You can search title headings or, within a specific title, search sub-title headings or sections. You can "favorite" an item for faster access later. The app is free but contains ads.
- **US Code, Titles 1 to 54 Codes** (iOS): For an annual subscription of $9.99 this app provides all 54 titles of the U.S. Code without the need for internet access. See also **LawStack** in the Court Rules section earlier in this chapter.
- See also **Fastcase, PushLegal,** and **Casemaker,** noted in the Case Law section earlier in this chapter.

## UNITED STATES CONSTITUTION

- **U.S. Constitution Annotated** (iOS): Also provided by the Library of Congress, this free app is a treatise written by the attorneys of the Congressional Research Service. It delivers the full text of "Constitution of the United States of America: Analysis and Interpretation," with a clause-by-clause discussion of the entire Constitution. It discusses U.S. Supreme Courts cases and other documents that interpret the Constitution and lists laws struck down by the Supreme Court. You can navigate via a table of contents, table of cases, and an index, or you can search by keyword. As with the Congressional Record app, you can share documents via email; or save them to your preferred PDF reader.
- See also **Rulebook, LawStack,** and **US Federal Law,** all in the Court Rules section of this chapter.

# Part II

## LEGAL PORTALS AND DIRECTORIES

Legal directories attempt to categorize websites by areas of law, jurisdiction, or both, and then provide links to those legal content websites. Legal portals, while also providing directories, go a step further and provide "added value," such as a full-text, keyword-searchable database of court cases or subject-specific articles about an area of law. Portals are more than a directory of links to other legal content sites because they include substantive legal content right on their sites. Even with this added value, most portals are still free (or partially free) because advertisers (and other alliances) support the cost of running the site.

Portals and directories differ greatly from a search engine. Search engines return their results via automated software programs that do not rely on human intervention. In contrast, legal portals and directories employ people to create their product. These people (usually law librarians or lawyers) have the subject expertise to be able to categorize the sites (just as a librarian would catalog a book by subject) and to judge whether a site is reliable before adding it to the portal or directory. This ensures that you can easily pinpoint relevant and reliable sites.

Free legal portals and directories are usually sponsored by one of five types of groups, all of which have their own reasons for sponsorship: (1) commercial entities, which support the free portion of their site through advertising or by selling related paid products or services (such as FindLaw or Justia, which both advertise their lawyer website businesses on their free portals); (2) law firms, which are using their sites to attract clients; (3) governmental entities, which are using their sites to make government documents and services more accessible to the public; (4) academic institutions, which are using their sites for scholarly reasons; and (5) associations, which are using their sites to offer value to their members (and sometimes to educate the general public).

## ASSESSING LEGAL PORTALS AND LEGAL DIRECTORIES

If you want to use a portal or directory we have not mentioned in this book, you should assess its quality before relying upon it. A high-quality, useful legal portal or directory should do the following: (1) include a subject (or practice area) directory and preferably also include a jurisdictional directory; (2) include an internal search engine so you can search the site with keywords; (3) be user-friendly (intuitive); (4) link directly to many relevant sites; (5) in the case of a portal, include added value (and make it easy to access this added value); and (6) be reliable—by which we mean it's credible, up to date, and objective. An example of a legal portal that meets these qualifications is **Justia** (http://www.justia.com) (see Figure II.1).

**Figure II.1** Example of a legal portal. Screenshot from Justia used with permission.

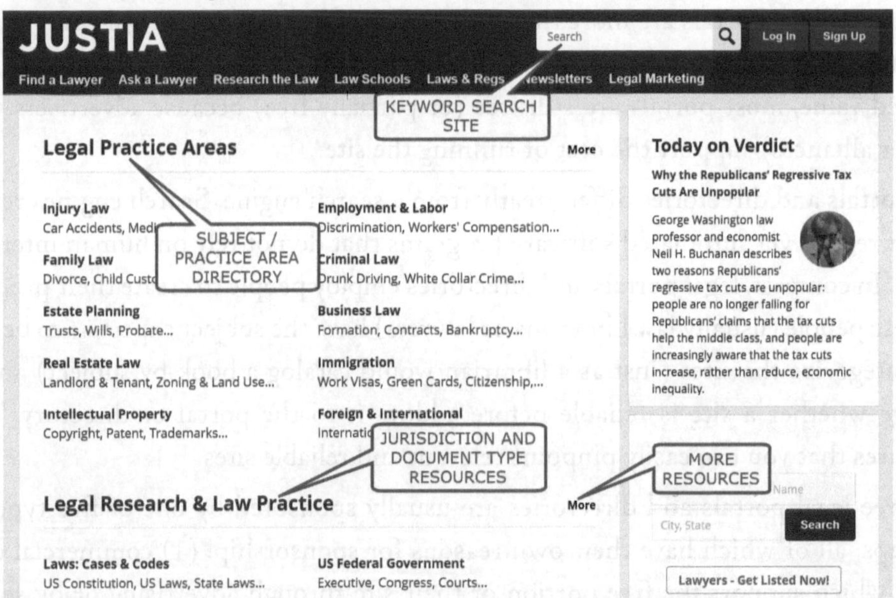


As you review the Justia home page, it's easy to see that it meets most of our "high-quality" tests by (1) having practice area, jurisdictional, and document type directories; (2) offering a keyword search box; (3) being user-friendly (intuitive) by providing an easy-to-read and easy-to-navigate home page; (4) linking directly to many relevant sites that appear once you start clicking on the practice areas or jurisdiction links; and (5) offering added value. Some examples of added value (on the home page but not shown in the figure) are Justia's **Supreme Court Center**, a database of all U.S. Supreme Court decisions since the 1790s, links to **Recall Warnings**, and the **Stanford Copyright and Fair Use Center**. Also not shown in the figure, note that about halfway down the home page is a section on Latin American legal research resources, as well as a link to Justia's Federal Dockets database at the bottom of the page.

Justia also meets the final criteria of the quality test—our three-pronged reliability test. Scroll down to the bottom of the home page to locate the **Company** link. Clicking this link and then selecting the **About Justia** link helps you decide that. For the first prong of our reliability test, credibility, Tim Stanley is listed as the leader of the Justia team. Tim is well-known in the Internet legal research field and is the former CEO and co-founder of FindLaw.

For the second prong of our reliability test, objectivity, "Justia works with educational, public interest and other socially focused organizations to bring legal and consumer information to the online community" (http://bit.ly/JustiaAbout). For the third prong of our reliability test (being up-to-date), Justia adds cases and dockets to its database on a daily basis.

## THE TOP LEGAL DIRECTORIES AND PORTALS

Some of the top legal directories and portals are FindLaw, Justia.com, Nolo.com, Law.com, HG.org, USA.gov, Cornell Law School's Legal Information Institute (LII), the American Bar Association, and VISALAW, each of which will be discussed in the following two chapters. We'll divide them into the following categories: Free Commercial, Governmental, Academic, and Legal Association. Chapter 4 will discuss Free Commercial portals. Chapter 5 will discuss Governmental, Academic, and Legal Association portals.

# Chapter 4

# FREE COMMERCIAL PORTALS AND DIRECTORIES

## JUSTIA

**Justia** (http://www.justia.com) is a free legal portal that offers a directory to help researchers find legal research websites and also offers free added-value databases. Justia does not require registration.

Figure 4.1 shows the following features:

- A Google-powered search box to full-text search Justia with keywords and phrases (and Boolean connectors). (Justia's **Legal Web** search engine, which locates legal-specific information on the web and is also powered by Google, is described later in this chapter.) Note: many sites' internal search engines are powered by Google, but only some indicate that fact. If they are powered by Google, you will be able to construct more precise searches using Google's Boolean, Proximity, and Phrase search features. Later in this chapter we'll provide details about these features.
- **Legal Practice Areas** is one of two directories located below the search box. Those who prefer to browse rather than keyword search can browse by legal topic (e.g., **Immigration**).

**Figure 4.1** Justia home page features. Screenshot from Justia used with permission.

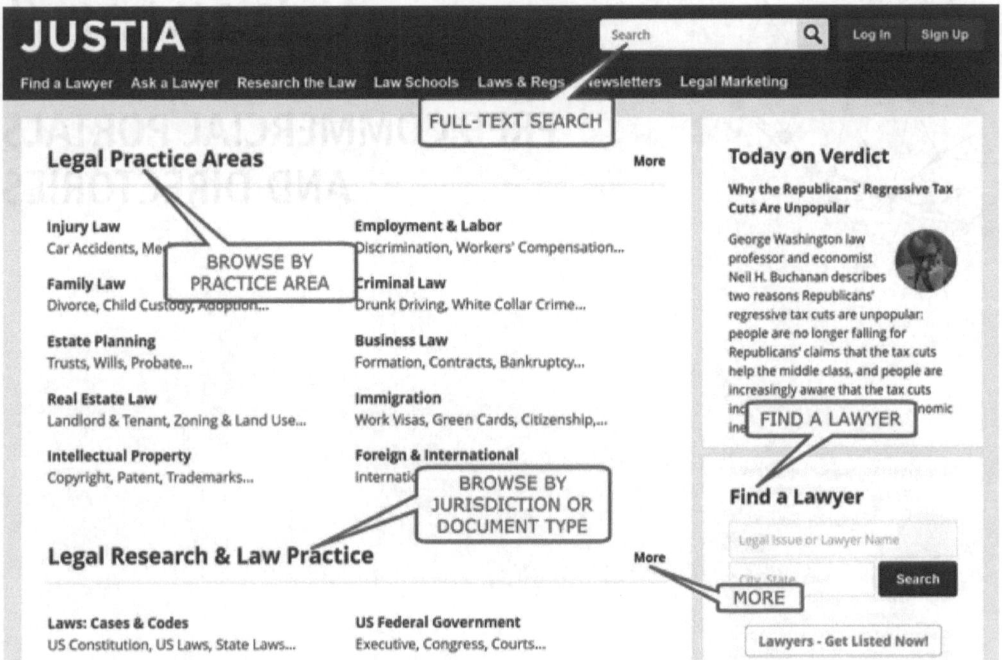


- The second directory, **Legal Research & Law Practice**, can be browsed by jurisdiction (e.g., **U.S. Federal Government, U.S. States,** etc.) or by document type (e.g., **U.S. Constitution, Texas Supreme Court Decisions, Legal Forms,** etc.).
- The **Find a Lawyer** directory, **Ask a Lawyer,** and more tabs.

Figure 4.2 shows these other features that you can see after scrolling down the Justia.com home page:

- Additional added-value Justia resources are found by clicking the **More** tabs on the home page—to the right of the major headings on the main part of the page, and also under the abbreviated lists in the categories at the bottom of the page, under **Justia Legal Resources.**
- **Justia Legal Resources** include additional research aids such as subject-specific lawyer directories, business resources, and a federal docket database.

## Justia's Google-Powered Internal Search Engine

Because so many sites include an internal Google-powered search engine, let's review Google search syntax.

**Figure 4.2** Justia Legal Resources at the bottom of the home page. Screenshot from Justia used with permission.

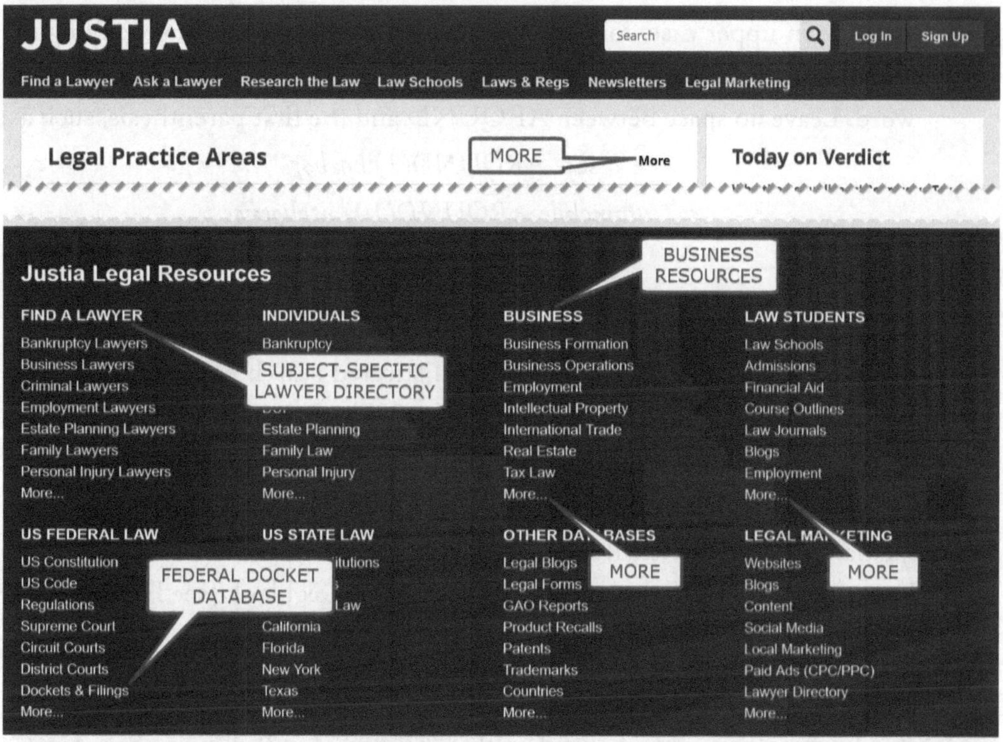


- Google, like all search engines, uses Boolean connectors, so you can instruct the search engine how to connect your keywords and phrases. The default Boolean connector is AND. Leaving a space between words automatically connects your keywords/phrases with the AND Boolean connector so there is no need to type the word AND.
- Google also offers phrase searching if you surround your phrase(s) with quotation marks.
- Google offers the Boolean connector OR but requires you to place it in upper case:

  *nevada OR arizona.*

- If you are excluding a word, you would place a minus sign before the word without any space. Google does not recognize the Boolean connector NOT:

  *"homeland security" nevada -arizona.*

- Google is the only major search engine that offers a proximity connector, although it is not documented on their site. This connector—

AROUND—allows you to instruct the search engine how closely you want a word or phrase to occur in relation to the next word or phrase. AROUND must be in upper case, followed by a number in parentheses specifying the maximum number of words that can occur between the first and second word. Leave no space between AROUND and the first parenthesis, such as:

*safe AROUND(1) harbor*

*automobile AROUND(10) negligence*

## Justia's Legal Web Search

One of Justia's most notable features is a sophisticated search engine, **Legal Web,** which locates legal-specific information on the Web. It is powered by Google's search engine technology.

To actually run a Legal Web search at Justia, enter no keywords into the search box at Justia.com. Instead, click the **magnifying glass** button at the right of the search box on the home page, while leaving the search box blank (see Figure 4.3).

Figure 4.3 How to find Justia's Legal Web search. Screenshot from Justia used with permission.

Then a **Legal Web** tab will appear over the search box (see Figure 4.4). After selecting **Legal Web,** enter your search into the search box and click the **Search Legal Web Resources** option.

Below your search results (see Figure 4.5), a group of suggestions is displayed to help you refine the initial results list—although they are less than helpful because they seem to be the same for every search. Also, depending on your browser, the search results page may display paid Google Ads above the suggested refinements.

**Figure 4.4** Choose Legal Web before entering your search terms. Screenshot from Justia used with permission.

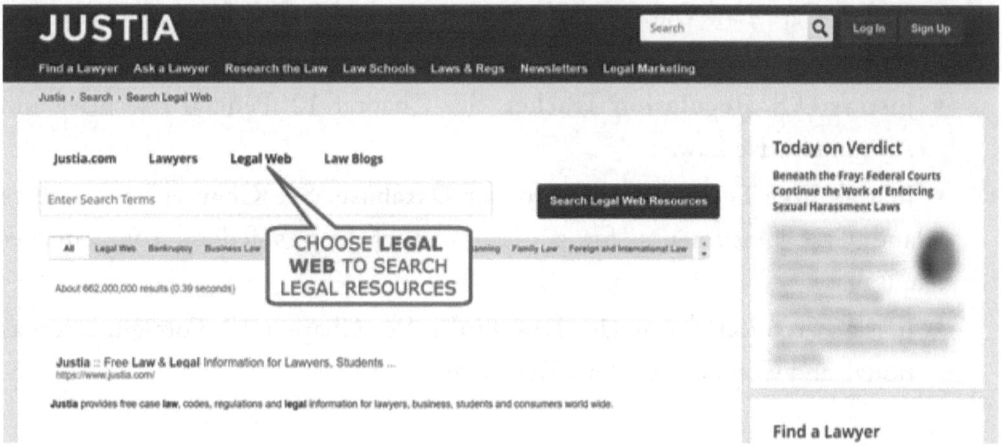


**Figure 4.5** Justia Legal Web search results. Screenshot from Justia used with permission.

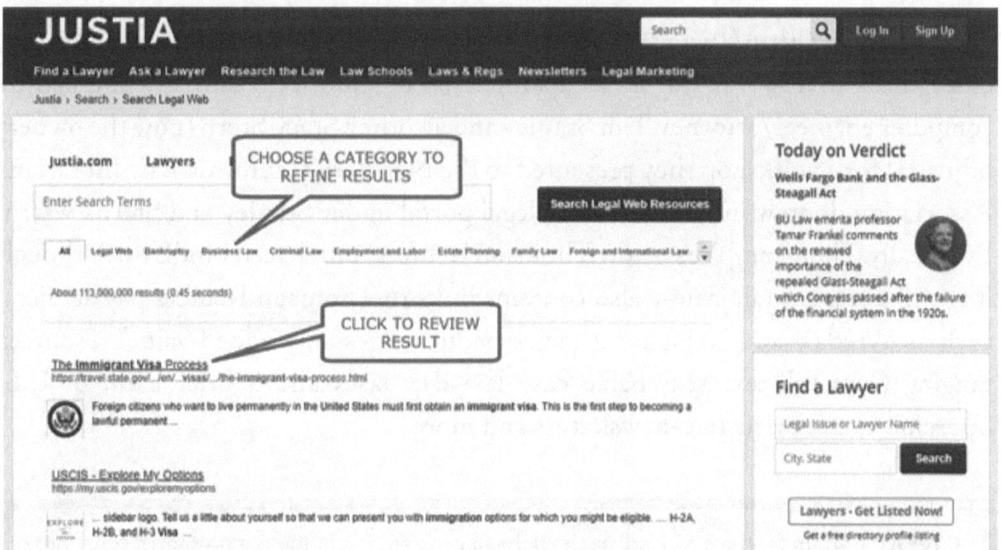


## Justia's Free Court Opinion Newsletters

Justia offers free daily court opinion summary newsletters for all federal appellate and all state supreme courts, as well as weekly practice area newsletters. They can be received by e-mail or news feeds (http://bit.ly/JustiaSummaries).

The following specific features of Justia will be discussed in the chapters indicated:

- **Justia's Free Online Case Law Databases.** See Chapter 6, Free Commercial Online Case Law Databases, for a discussion of Justia's free online case law database.
- **Justia's U.S. Regulation Tracker.** See Chapter 12, Federal Executive and Administrative Law.
- **Justia's Free Federal Court Docket Database.** See Chapter 15, Dockets and Case Documents, for a discussion of Justia's federal court docket database.
- **Justia's Free Latin America Law Links.** See Chapter 14, Foreign, International, and Comparative Law Resources.

## FINDLAW

The **FindLaw** (http://www.findlaw.com) portal is one of the oldest legal portals, dating back to 1995. It started as a simple list of Internet resources compiled by computer engineer/attorney Tim Stanley and attorney Stacy Stern (now the owners of Justia) for a workshop they presented to the Northern California Law Librarians Association. It grew into a full-blown legal portal under Stanley and Stern's watch. Eventually, Thomson/West (now Thomson Reuters) purchased FindLaw. Although it is still a free portal, it now also contains links to Thomson Reuters pay services, such as Westlaw and KeyCite. It includes directories and "added-value" resources ranging from full-text searchable case law databases and a brief bank of U.S. Supreme Court briefs to e-newsletters and more.

**CAVEAT:** Certain features of FindLaw have been problematic in the past—search functions that did not work properly, databases that were not kept up to date, and so forth. We pointed out the problems to FindLaw while writing the previous edition of this book and were assured that they were working on a fix. Since then, many issues have been fixed, and other features that were not working properly have been fixed or removed. Although some issues remain, we are keeping FindLaw in this book because we find it useful, and it works most of the time.

FindLaw focuses on two audiences—the legal professional and the consumer—and is divided into those two categories. If you use the direct URL http://www.findlaw.com, you will find yourself on the consumer side of the site. Probably the most useful data on the consumer side for both consumers and legal professionals is FindLaw's Find a Lawyer directory.

To reach the site created for legal professionals, click the link at the top of the home page labeled **For Legal Professionals** (see Figure 4.6) or use this URL: http://lp.findlaw.com.

**Figure 4.6** FindLaw is still a free portal, but it also links to Thomson Reuters pay services. Originally appeared on FindLaw.com. Used with permission.

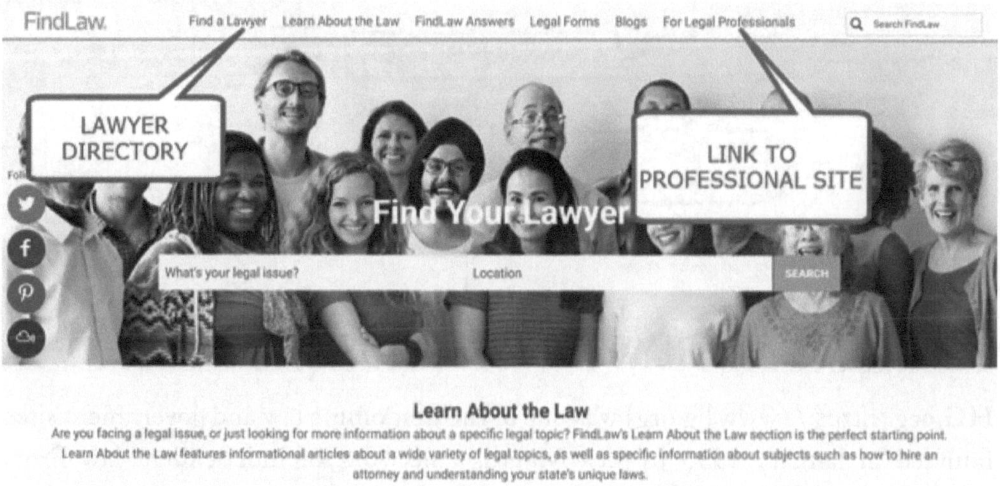


The FindLaw Legal Professionals site's home page (see Figure 4.7) has a lot going on. Much of its information can be accessed by clicking the tabs located in one of the two rows of tabs running horizontally beneath the FindLaw logo, such as **Cases & Codes** on the top row (left side) or **Forms** on the second row (left side). The **Forms** tab takes you to free sample business contracts and free forms (and also pay forms). Beneath the **Browse Research Materials** section, notice the links to browse **by Research Type, by Jurisdiction,** and **by Practice Area.** The **Cases & Codes** section contains links to state, local, and federal resources (constitutions, statutes, cases, ordinances, and more).

**Figure 4.7** FindLaw's site for Legal Professionals. Originally appeared on FindLaw.com. Used with permission.

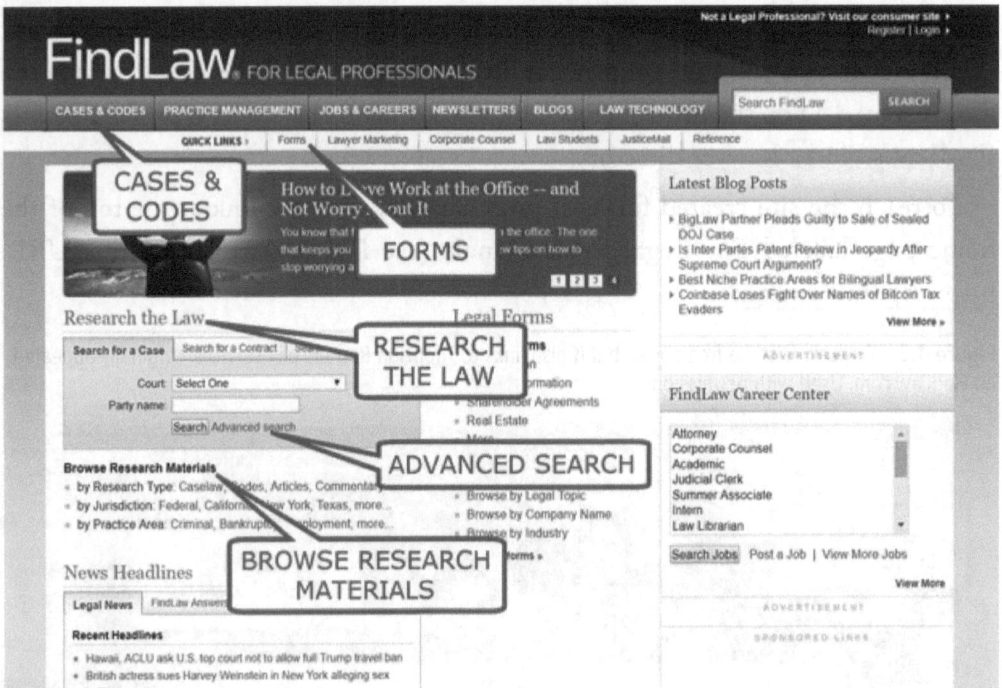


## HG.ORG (FORMERLY HIEROS GAMOS)

**HG.org** (https://www.hg.org) was one of the first online law and government sites, founded in January 1995 by Lex Mundi, a network of independent law firms. HG.org is a bit of a mix between Law.com, FindLaw, and Justia.

HG.org provides an expert witness directory (free) and an employment search. Like FindLaw and Justia, HG provides a lawyer directory and a directory of law-related websites arranged by subject and jurisdictional categories. On the home page, scroll down to the **Learn About the Law** section, which contains an abbreviated list of some of the subjects HG covers. Click the **260 law guides** link to go to HG's Law Center, which has over seventy "core areas of law" and 260 "sub areas of practice." HG explains that, "The Center provides information on U.S. (Federal and State), European and International Laws. An abundance of information dealing with the specific area of law is also integrated into each page, including: Publications, Articles, Organizations, Resources, Attorneys and Law Firms" (https://www.hg.org/practiceareas.html). When we chose Bankruptcy, HG displayed a summary of bankruptcy law, links to websites (primarily U.S.) explaining bankruptcy, the U.S. Bankruptcy Code, the U.S. Bankruptcy Courts, organizations related to bankruptcy, bankruptcy lawyers, and articles about bankruptcy.

HG has a Google-powered search box on the top right-hand side of the home page to keyword search the site (see Figure 4.8). Searching the two words *Dubai escrow* returned several results, with one of the top ones being an article titled "Buying Property in Dubai." The search engine also appears to recognize other Google connectors such as AROUND(#), described earlier in this chapter. We especially like HG for its foreign and international links; see Chapter 14 for additional discussion of this.

**Figure 4.8** HG.org homepage. Screenshot from HG.org used with permission.

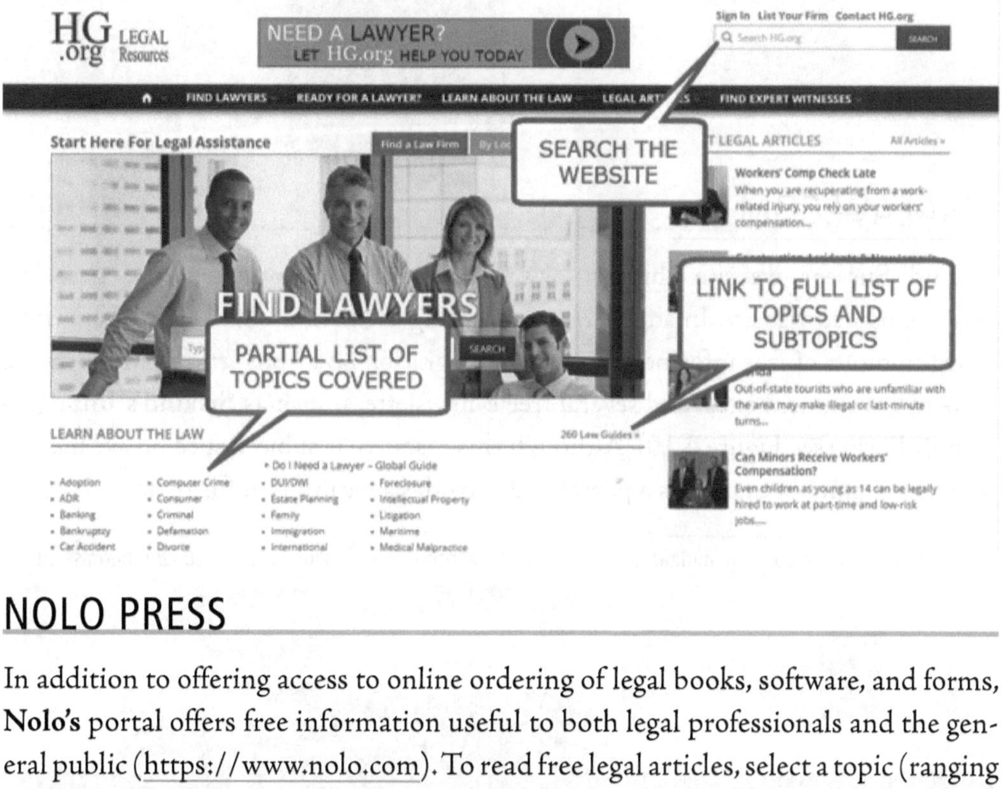


## NOLO PRESS

In addition to offering access to online ordering of legal books, software, and forms, **Nolo's** portal offers free information useful to both legal professionals and the general public (https://www.nolo.com). To read free legal articles, select a topic (ranging from **Auto Accidents** to **Workers Compensation**) listed under the **Legal Articles** tab at the top of the home page (see Figure 4.9).

Also at Nolo, you will find the following free resources by using these direct URLs or by scrolling down to the bottom of the home page and clicking on their links:

- **Lawyer Directory**: http://www.nolo.com/lawyers
- **Law Dictionary**: http://www.nolo.com/dictionary
- **Legal Research** (basic instructions for finding legal resources): https://www.nolo.com/legal-research
- **Law Blog**: http://blog.nolo.com

Figure 4.9 Nolo legal articles. Screenshot from Nolo used with permission.

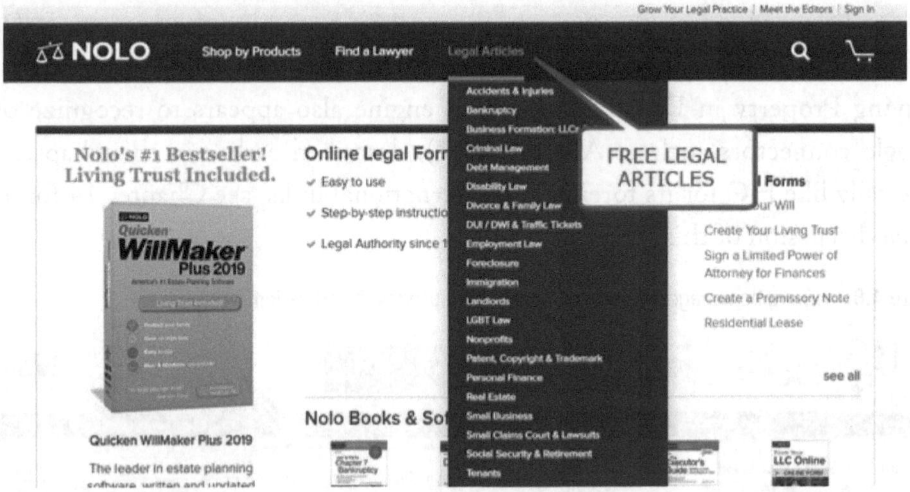


## VISALAW.COM

Siskind Susser's website (http://www.visalaw.com) was probably the first law firm-sponsored website. In addition to promoting the firm itself, the site offers enormous amounts of free information about immigration law, from articles and forms to links to government sites, and several free e-newsletters, such as **Siskind's Immigration Bulletin** (see Figure 4.10). Although this resource is subject-specific, we include it in this chapter because it is a portal and provides a wealth of information.

Figure 4.10 Visalaw.com, an immigration law portal. Screenshot from Siskind Susser used with permission.

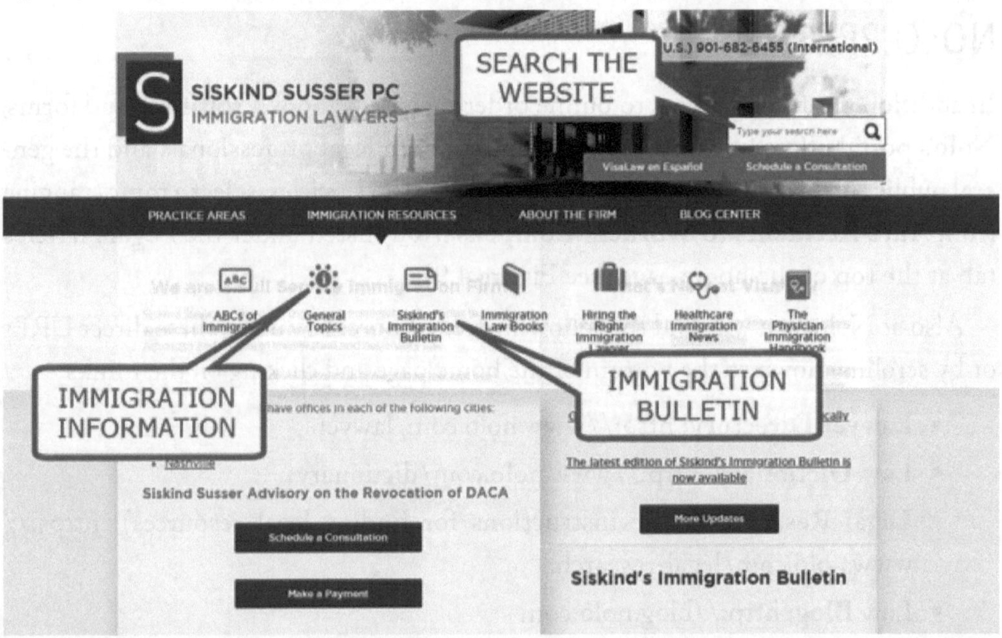

# Chapter 5

# GOVERNMENT, ACADEMIC, AND ASSOCIATION PORTALS AND DIRECTORIES

This chapter continues the previous chapter's discussion of legal portals and directories but will focus on Government, Academic, and Legal Association portals. For an overview of the characteristics of legal portals and directories, as well as a detailed discussion on assessing their quality, see the introduction to Part II.

## GOVERNMENT PORTALS AND DIRECTORIES

### USA.gov

**USA.gov** (https://www.usa.gov) is the federal government's primary information portal, with many resources that can be useful for legal research. USA.gov searches millions of web pages from all levels of the United States government: federal, state, local, tribal, the District of Columbia, and the U.S. territories (see Figure 5.1). Although results occasionally bring back court opinions, this is not the right site to search for them. Instead, see Chapter 6 for the databases of Justia and FindLaw, and also Chapters 8 (Casemaker), and 9 (Fastcase), where free case law research is discussed.

**Figure 5.1** USA.gov home page.

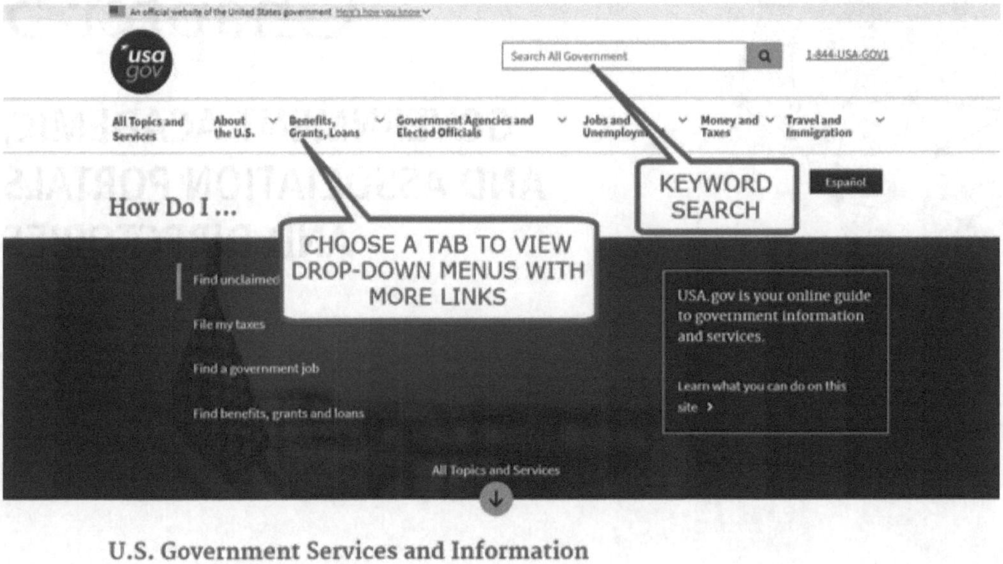


In addition to offering keyword searching, USA.gov offers the ability to browse by a government service, topic, agency, or government contact. To browse instead of keyword search, select one of the seven tabs listed below the search box on USA .gov's home page: **Government Agencies and Elected Officials; Benefits, Grants, Loans; Housing; Jobs and Unemployment; Money and Consumer Issues; Travel and Immigration**; and **More Topics and Services.** Once you select one of these tabs, a drop-down menu with more links will appear.

Under the heading **How Do I. . .** are links to additional resources, such as government forms, passport renewals, and job searches. USA.gov also serves as a forum in which to conduct business online with government agencies. For instance, if you click the **Find government forms** link under **How Do I. . .**, you will find an A–Z list of government forms, by agency. You can do everything from applying for a Social Security card to completing U.S. Customs forms, and more.

USA.gov's internal search engine (the search box on USA.gov's home page) is powered by Bing. You can use the search box to search government documents by keyword or phrase. Unfortunately, USA.gov provides no search tips about how to construct a search and use Boolean connectors and this information is difficult to find at Bing, as well.

USA.gov has removed the advanced search page from its website, much to our disappointment. However, you can still perform advanced search functions using the Bing-powered search engine on USA.gov, if you know how. We will therefore provide a brief Bing/USA.gov tutorial.

**Figure 5.2** Bing advanced search options.

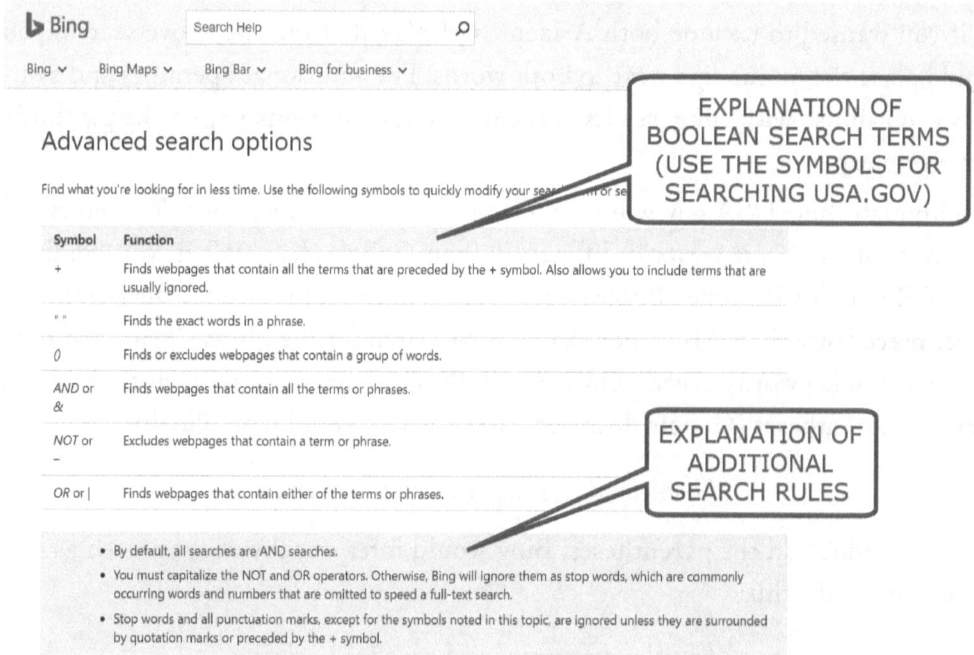


Like Google, Bing/USA.gov allows the use of Boolean connectors to link keywords and phrases. Create phrases by surrounding your phrase with quotation marks. Bing/USA.gov's default Boolean connector is *AND*. Leaving a space between words automatically connects your keywords/phrases with the *AND* Boolean connector so there is no need to type the word *AND*. In our test searches, the USA.gov search function did not recognize the *AND*, *OR*, or *NOT* connectors, although it did recognize the corresponding symbols—&, | (vertical bar, which is found above the Enter key on most computers; it shares the same key as the backward slash) and – (minus sign); see Figure 5.2.

The regular Bing search site appears to recognize both the words and the symbols for connectors, although strangely, the results of our test searches at Bing.com were slightly different when we tried the same searches with the words versus the symbols. So, some differences exist between USA.gov's Bing search and the standard Bing search, and you may have to experiment to get your searches to work the way you want.

If you are excluding a word at Bing/USA.gov, you would place a minus sign (–) before the word with no space, to mean *NOT*, just as you would at Google. To search USA.gov for the phrase *"homeland security"* and the keywords *nevada NOT arizona*, for example, we recommend constructing your search like this example (since the USA.gov version of Bing search does not recognize the connector word *NOT*):

*"homeland security" nevada -arizona*

If you wanted to exclude both Arizona and Nevada from the above search, you would place the minus sign next to both words. For additional operators and symbols you can use with Bing, see its **Advanced search options** page at http://bit.ly/BingBoolean.

Although Bing/USA.gov will recognize the Boolean connector *OR* when typed as a vertical bar (|), it treats it differently than Google does. When you combine your *OR* search with other Boolean connectors in the same search, Bing gives *OR* lower precedence than *AND*. For example, to search for the phrase *"homeland security"* and the keywords *nevada OR arizona*, Bing requires you to enclose your *OR* terms in parentheses (Google does not). Your search would look like this:

*"homeland security" (nevada | arizona)*

If you didn't add the parentheses, Bing would interpret the above search as if it were written like this:

*("homeland security" and nevada) | arizona*

If you are only searching the keywords *nevada OR arizona*, your Bing/USA.gov search would need no parentheses and would look like this:

*nevada | arizona*

For more information about Bing's order of operators, see the **Operator Precedence** page at http://bit.ly/BingPrecedence.

In addition to removing its advanced search page, USA.gov has also removed many of the search filters that used to exist. You can still filter your searches by a few categories, however. After you run a search, you can switch from searching All Government (the default) to searching only the USA.gov website by clicking the **Search USA.gov Only** link above the search box on the results page. You can also limit your results to images or videos by clicking the corresponding links that appear above the search box. If you limit your search results to videos, you can then sort them by **Most recent** or **Best match**, and you can filter them by date.

## govinfo

In early 2016, the **U.S. Government Publishing Office (GPO)** released the Beta version of a new website at https://www.govinfo.gov, and in early 2018, govinfo left the beta phase. In late 2018, this site replaced the **FDsys.gov** site, which has been retired.

Cleaner and more intuitive than FDsys, we like what we have seen so far from govinfo. Like FDsys, govinfo provides free online access to official publications from all three branches of the Federal Government. The site arranges its database into Collections, which include **Budget of the United States Government, Code of Federal Regulations, Congressional Bills, Congressional Record, Federal Register, Statutes at Large, United States Code**, and **United States Court Opinions**, among others.

All content formerly available on FDsys is available through govinfo. You can get any pdf, xml, text or other content file that was available on FDsys. Also, all Browse and Content Details pages that were on FDsys have equivalent pages on govinfo (https://www.govinfo.gov/help/faqs).

The website and all the Collections use the same search protocols (keyword/phrase/citation searching and Boolean and proximity connectors). Results can also be displayed and sorted in the same way throughout the Collections, so we will use this section to explain how to search govinfo in general.

You can use the search box on the govinfo home page (under the **Search** tab) to search the entire site. This is govinfo's Basic Search. If you are looking for a particular document or type of document but do not have the citation (something from the Congressional Record or U.S. Code, for example), you will probably want to use the **Advanced** search tab, as it allows you to tailor your search more easily than with a Basic Search. If you know the citation for the document you want, you can use the **Citation** tab to enter the citation. Finally, you can also use the **Browse** feature, via the link near the upper left corner of the home page, or the tiles below the search box, to browse all the Collections alphabetically with the **A-Z** list, or by **Category, Date, Committee,** or **Author.** We will explain each of these search options below.

Whether you are performing a Basic or Advanced Search, you can create simple or complex queries. We will highlight some of the search queries available at govinfo, but for more detailed information and examples, see the **Search Operators** page (http://bit.ly/govinfoSearchOperators).

When researching at govinfo, you can use the Boolean connector *AND* or leave a space between words because *AND* is the default connector. Boolean connectors are case insensitive at govinfo (while Boolean connectors such as *OR* and *NOT* must be in uppercase at Google, for example). The govinfo search function recognizes *NOT* as well as the minus sign (-) to exclude a term from the search results. Finally, govinfo allows for additional types of complex queries (most of which are not found at Google), such as:

- Proximity connectors *adj, before/#, near/#*:
    - *adj* specifies that one word is adjacent to another.
    - *before/#* ( e.g., *handgun before/3 protection*) specifies that the first word is within whatever number of words that you select of the second word and that the first word must precede the second word. Thus, *handgun* must appear one, two, or three words before *protection*.
    - *near/#* (e.g., *handgun near/10 protection*) specifies that the first word is within whatever number of words that you select of the second word and in any order. (See Chapter 4, pages 45–46 to learn about Google's proximity connector.)
- Wildcards, which are indicated by:
    - the question mark symbol (?) to replace only one character before, within, or after a search term.
    - the asterisk symbol (*) to replace one or more characters before, within, or after a search term.
        - Typing *int*state* into the search box indicates a search for any word that begins with *int*, is followed by at least one character, and then ends with *state*. The search results might include the words *interstate, intrastate, intestate*, or all three words.
        - Typing *amend** into the search box indicates a search for the word amend and any word that begins with *amend*, such as *amendment, amending*, or *amends*.
- Parentheses, which should be used when creating complex searches such as those where you use multiple proximity connectors and/or multiple Field operators (discussed below). The following is an example:

    *(congressional OR executive) AND hearing AND (member:sanders)*

Figure 5.3 shows a Basic Search with a simple query. We have entered two keywords (*negligence entrustment*) separated with a space into the Basic Search box. This will search all the govinfo Collections together for both words.

govinfo also allows you to construct a complex query on the simple search page by using field operators. Field operators allow you to restrict your keywords to specific metadata fields (parts of a document), such as:

**Figure 5.3** A basic search on govinfo.

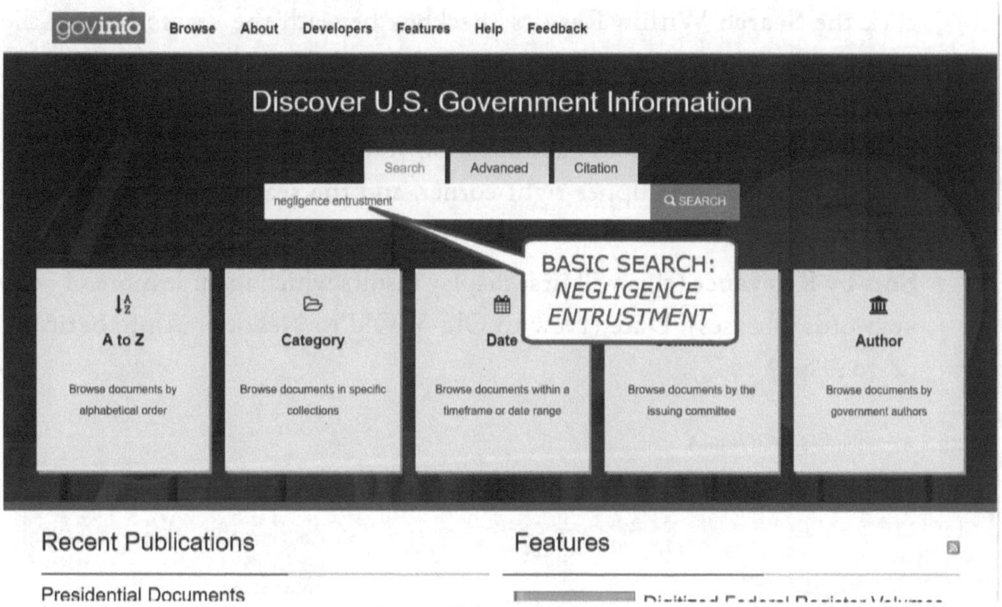


- Congress Member: To search by this field, enter your search this way: *member:sanders*
- President: To search by this field, enter your search this way: *president:kennedy*
- You can search using multiple Fields, such as *title:homeland* and *member:collins*

Commonly used field operators that apply to all or most of the Collections can be found at http://bit.ly/govinfoField. Descriptions of each Collection's unique field operators are also available; go to the **Help with a Specific Collection** page (http://bit.ly/govinfoCollectionHelp), click the link for the Collection you want from the alphabetized list of Collections, and then scroll down to the **Metadata Fields and Values** heading for that Collection's page.

Once you run your search, you can filter or sort the results. Figure 5.4 shows how your search results are displayed, and how you can do the following:

- **Refine Your Search** by filtering results with the categories in the left-side column. Although in the illustration, only **Collection** and **Date** are expanded to show all filtering options just for those two categories, you could click the minus sign (–) beside **Government Author** or **Organization** to expand those categories, too.

- After you have run a search, if you would like to search within those results, click the **Search Within Results** checkbox beneath the search box on the results page. This allows you to enter one or more keywords and re-run your search within your original search results to narrow down your search further. If the search box does not appear on your results page, click the orange **Search** button in the upper right corner, and the search box and tabs will appear.
- **Sort by Relevance** (this will first display results which include more of your keywords/phrases), **Date** (New to Old or Old to New), or **Alphabetically** (Z to A or A to Z).

**Figure 5.4** govinfo search results.

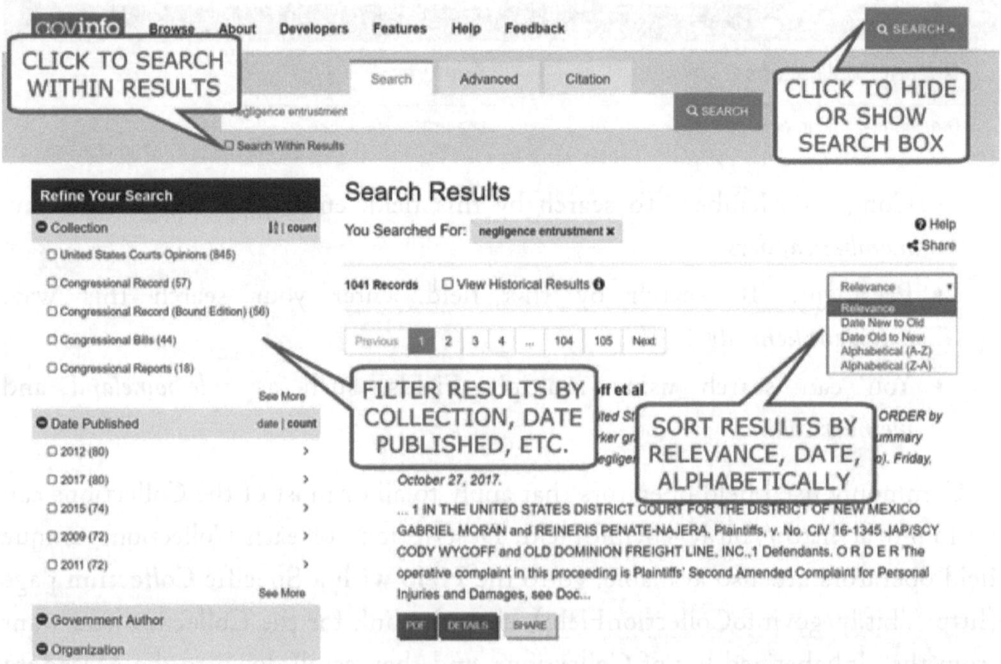


The **Advanced Search** page (https://www.govinfo.gov/#advanced) is illustrated in Figure 5.5. The page is essentially a form.

- Starting on the left side of the page, you can choose a date or range of dates in the **Date Range** column on the left, or you can leave the default choice of All Dates.
- In the center column, **Refine by Collection**, you can choose one or more Collections to search.

**Figure 5.5** govinfo Advanced Search page.

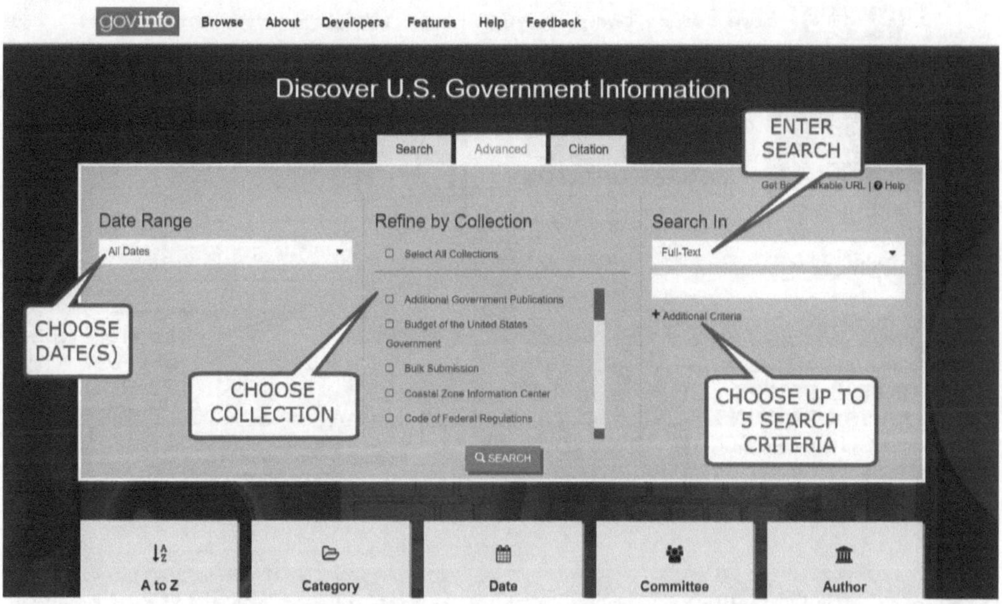


- After you choose to search one or more Collections, you will need to select your search criteria from the **Search In** column on the right side of the page. Note that **Full-Text** is the default criteria for all Collections. Once you choose a Collection, a different menu with other search criteria appropriate for that Collection will be displayed in a pop-up list when you click the down arrow to the right of the **Full-Text** criteria box.
  - For example, if you choose the United States Code, its search criteria would include a search by **Title, U.S. Code Amendments,** or **U.S. Code Future Amendments** among others, while the Collection of **United States Court Opinions** would include much different search criteria options, such as **Party Name** or **Court Name,** among others. (See Figure 5.6.)
  - If you choose more than one Collection, the Search In column provides only those criteria that are common to all the Collections you have selected; for example, Court Type is a criterion available only in the **United States Courts Opinions** Collection, so if you search the **Statutes at Large** Collection at the same time as the **United States Courts Opinions** Collection, the **Court Type** criterion disappears from the Search In menu because there is no Court Type criterion for Statutes at Large.

**Figure 5.6** govinfo search criteria correspond to the Collection(s) chosen.

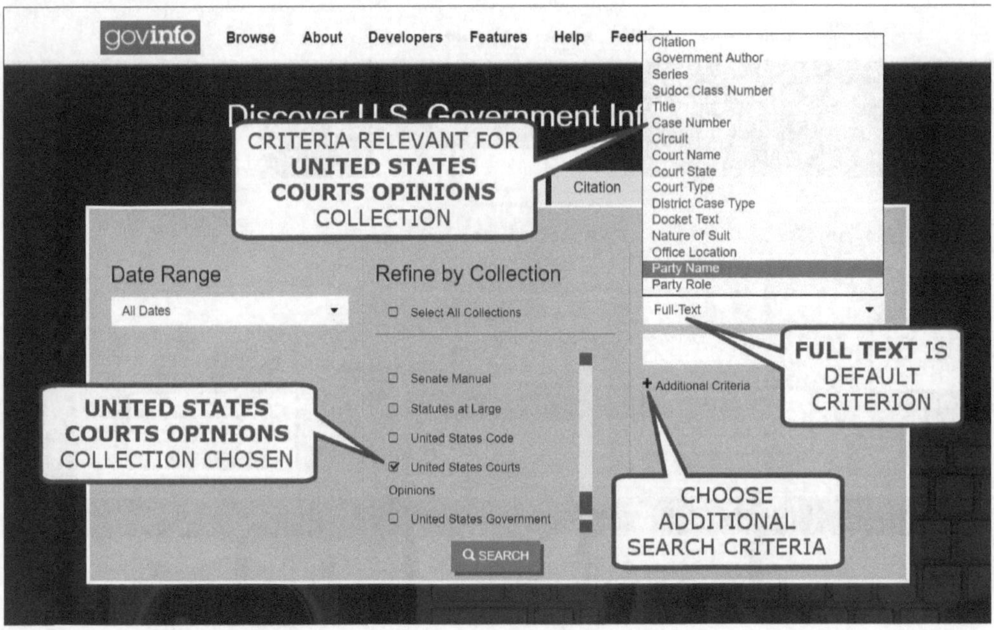


Because of the differences in searching each Collection and because of the different topics on which the Collections focus, we will discuss them individually in later chapters and then refer you back here for a refresher on general govinfo search protocol strategies.

If you have the citation for the document you want, you can choose the **Citation** tab on the govinfo home page (to the right of the Search and Advanced tabs). From the **Citation** page, you must first choose a Collection from the drop-down menu above the orange Search button. For example, in the Figure 5.7, we chose the **Code of Federal Regulations** (CFR) Collection.

After choosing the **Code of Federal Regulations** Collection, the search menu that is appropriate for a CFR citation is displayed. Type the elements of the citation into the boxes to run your search. If you leave a box blank that is required (such as Part for the CFR), you will receive a message telling you that it is required. If you have pop-up blockers enabled when you run a citation search, a message will appear near the top of the screen that says, "Click here if content does not open. This could happen because of a pop-up blocker."

To browse specific govinfo Collections, click the **Browse** link near the upper left corner of govinfo, and then choose from the five browsing options in the drop-down menu: **A–Z, Category, Date, Committee,** or **Author.** You can also choose one of the five tiles below the search box; they contain the same categories as the drop-down menu (see Figure 5.8).

**Figure 5.7** Searching govinfo with a citation.

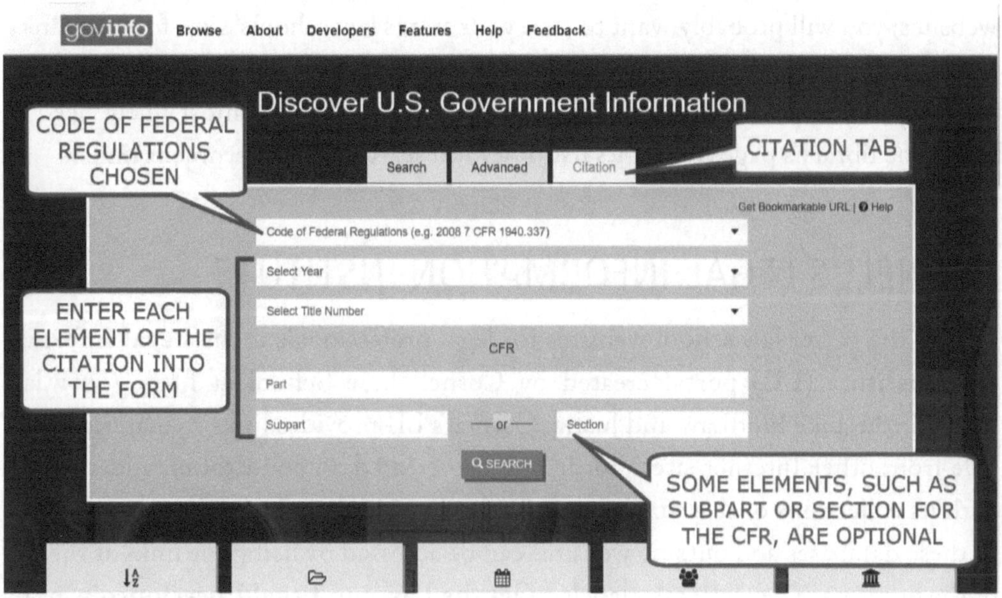


**Figure 5.8** Browsing govinfo.

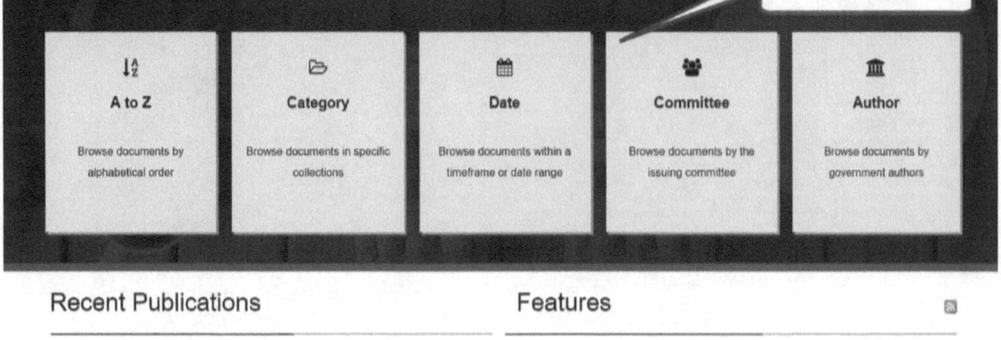

## ACADEMIC PORTALS AND DIRECTORIES

There are many excellent academic portals and directories for Internet legal and government research, with most created by law school librarians. Academic portals are useful for linking to their own state and local legal research and government websites; you will probably want to visit your state's law schools' sites for local links. For a list of all law school websites, see **FindLaw** (http://bit.ly/FindLawLawSchools). Once you link to the relevant law school, you will most likely need to locate the library's page to find its list of legal research and government links.

## CORNELL'S LEGAL INFORMATION INSTITUTE

One of the better law school websites for legal professionals is the **Legal Information Institute** (LII) portal created by Cornell Law School at http://www.law.cornell.edu. Like FindLaw and Justia, Cornell's LII provides links to material available from other Internet sites, but it has also created a good deal of "added value" with its collections of searchable legal databases hosted on LII's own servers. Many of these databases and outside websites can be accessed by using the links at the top of the home page beneath tabs labeled **Get the Law** and **Legal Encyclopedia,** or by conducting a keyword search from the home page's search box (see Figure 5.9).

**Figure 5.9** Legal Information Institute (LII) home page. Screenshot from the Legal Information Institute at Cornell Law School used with permission.

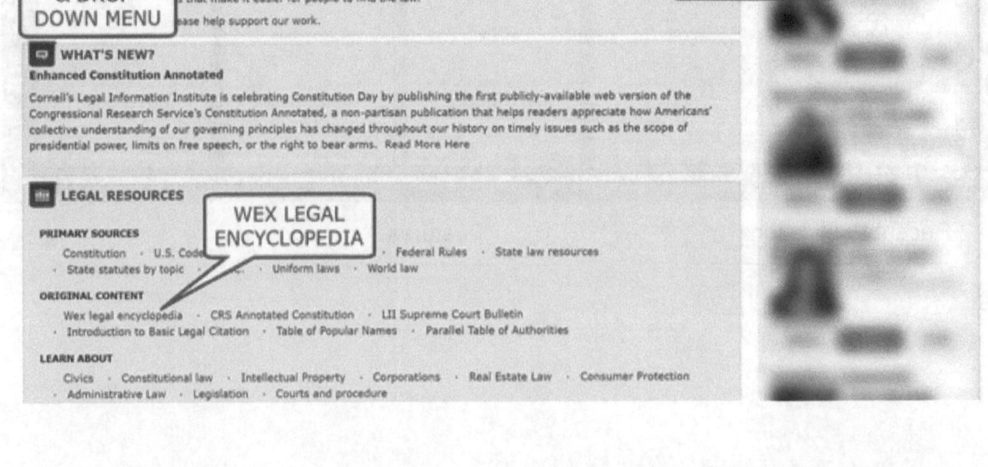

If you hover your mouse over the **Get the Law** heading at the top of the home page, a drop-down menu appears with links to several topics, some with submenus containing additional topics (see Figure 5.9). The links are:

- Constitution
- Supreme Court
- U.S. Code
- CFR
- Federal Rules
- U.C.C.
- Law by Jurisdiction

If you click the links, you will go to a page with an outline or table of contents, with additional links you can browse. The one exception is the **U.S. Code** page, which provides a citation form at the top of the page so that you can look up a statute by its citation.

If you want to keyword search the topics and subtopics under **Get the Law**, you must first conduct a keyword search from the home page's search box (see Figure 5.9). Then use the filters that appear on the right side of the search results page to see only results from a specific database. We entered the search terms *warrantless search* into the search box (see Figure 5.10). On the search results page, we then had the option of filtering by **content type** (CFR, Supreme Court, U.S. Code, etc.).

**Figure 5.10** LII search results and filters. Screenshot from the Legal Information Institute at Cornell Law School used with permission.

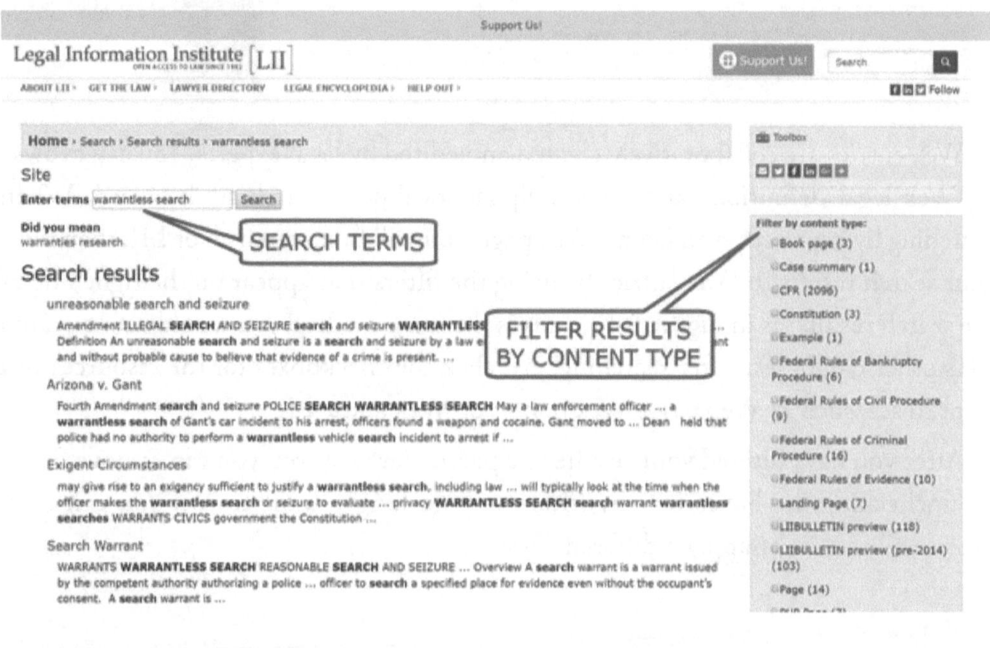

The **Legal Encyclopedia** heading at the top of the home page functions similarly to Get the Law. Hover over it, and a drop-down menu appears that lists several topics such as Business Law, Constitutional Law, Criminal Law, and others. You can click the **More** link at the bottom of the drop-down menu to go to a page with the full list of topics. To go to the main page of **Wex** (http://www.law.cornell.edu/wex), a free legal dictionary and encyclopedia sponsored and hosted by the **LII**, scroll down the home page to the **Legal Resources** heading and click **Wex Legal Encyclopedia**, under **Original Content** subheading (see Figure 5.9). This page, shown in Figure 5.11, provides a menu near the top of the page where you can browse **All Pages** of Wex, browse **Articles**, see Wex articles in **Español**, and **Search** the site.

Figure 5.11 LII's Wex: Free Legal Dictionary and Encyclopedia. Screenshot from the Legal Information Institute at Cornell Law School used with permission.

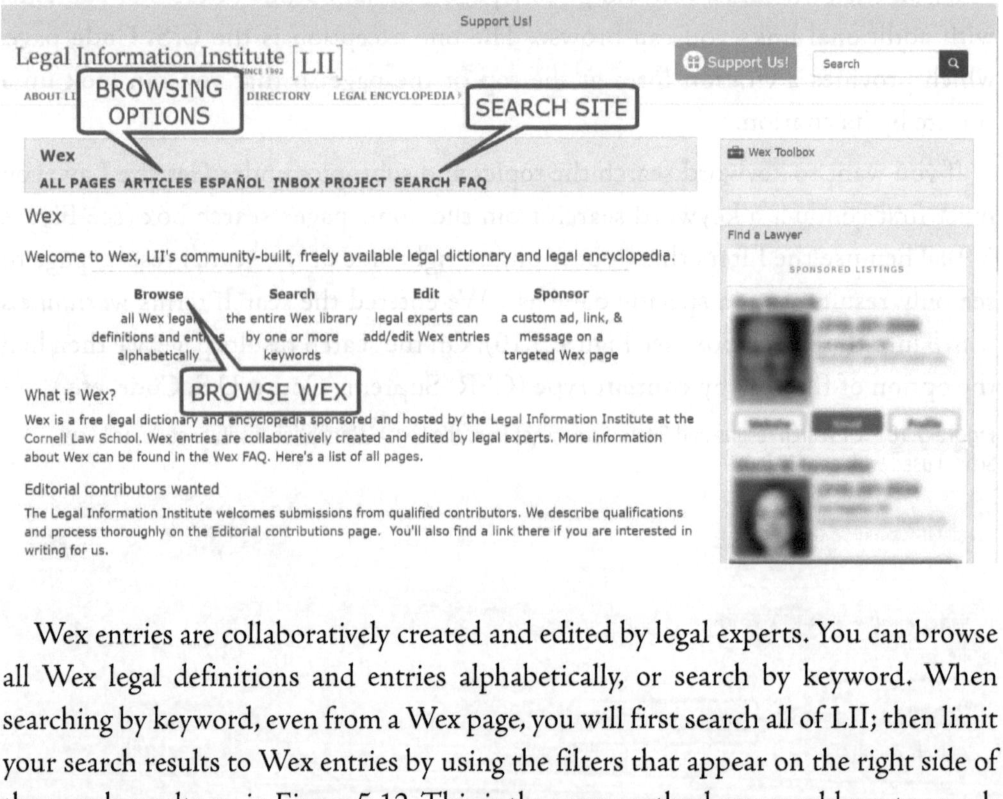


Wex entries are collaboratively created and edited by legal experts. You can browse all Wex legal definitions and entries alphabetically, or search by keyword. When searching by keyword, even from a Wex page, you will first search all of LII; then limit your search results to Wex entries by using the filters that appear on the right side of the search results, as in Figure 5.12. This is the same method you would use to search LII's other databases. After searching, just click the checkboxes for the resources you want to see, such as **Wex page, Wex paper,** or **Wex statute list**.

After you have filtered your results to a particular resource, you can remove filters by unchecking the boxes for any filters you no longer want to see. You can then browse all results or apply a different filter.

**Figure 5.12** Filter results to Wex on LII. Screenshot from the Legal Information Institute at Cornell Law School used with permission.

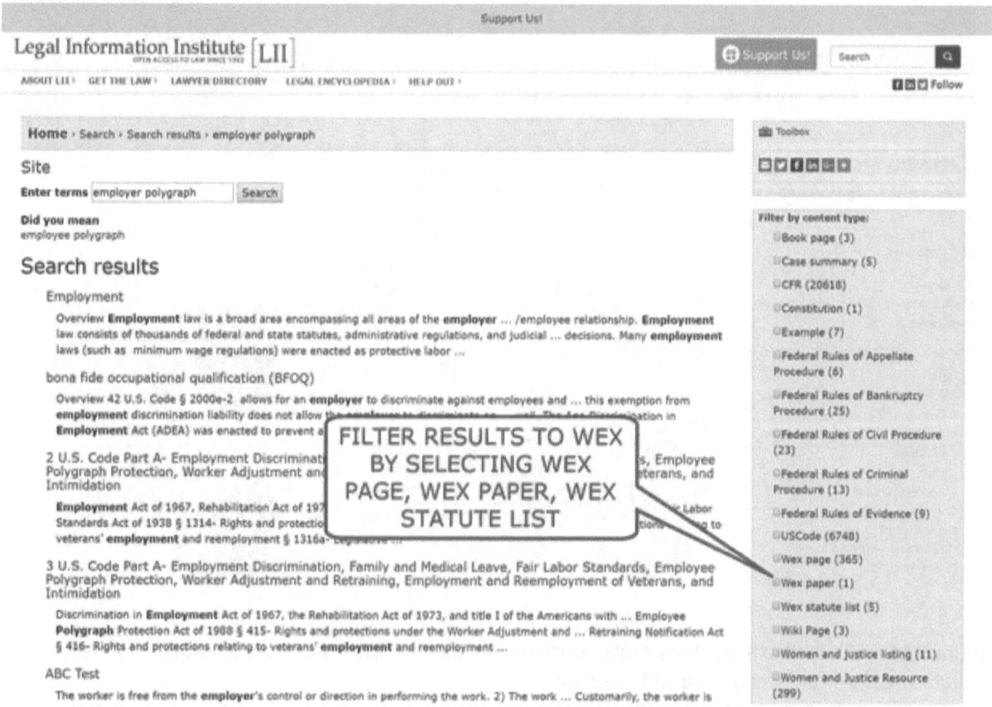


In previous versions of LII's search function, you could continue searching within the filter you had just set (Wex pages, for example). That feature appears to have been removed, however, so if you want to search within Wex pages (or another filter) again, you must search the entire site and then filter your results each time.

Another highlight of LII is its **State Statutes by Topic** database (http://bit.ly/LIIStateStatutes), which links to all fifty states' statutes on topics ranging from **Agriculture** to **Water Code** (see Figure 5.13). Not every state's statutory scheme is organized in a topical breakdown similar to this database. Some topics will display a state's name with a link to the home page of that state's statutory database. A link to a list of all state statutes on the web is also available on this page.

One other LII feature of note is the **Toolbox**, a box that appears near the upper right corner of some pages. Although the box is often empty, it does contain helpful information in some instances. Content appears in the Toolbox when you select any topic from **Get the Law**, except Law by Jurisdiction. For example, when we selected the **U.S. Code**, a U.S. Code Toolbox appeared, containing links to such resources as **Law about. . .Articles from Wex**, a **Table of Popular Names**, a **Parallel Table of Authorities**, and a **How current is this?** link (see Figure 5.14).

**Figure 5.13** LII's Topical Index of State Statutes. Screenshot from the Legal Information Institute at Cornell Law School used with permission.

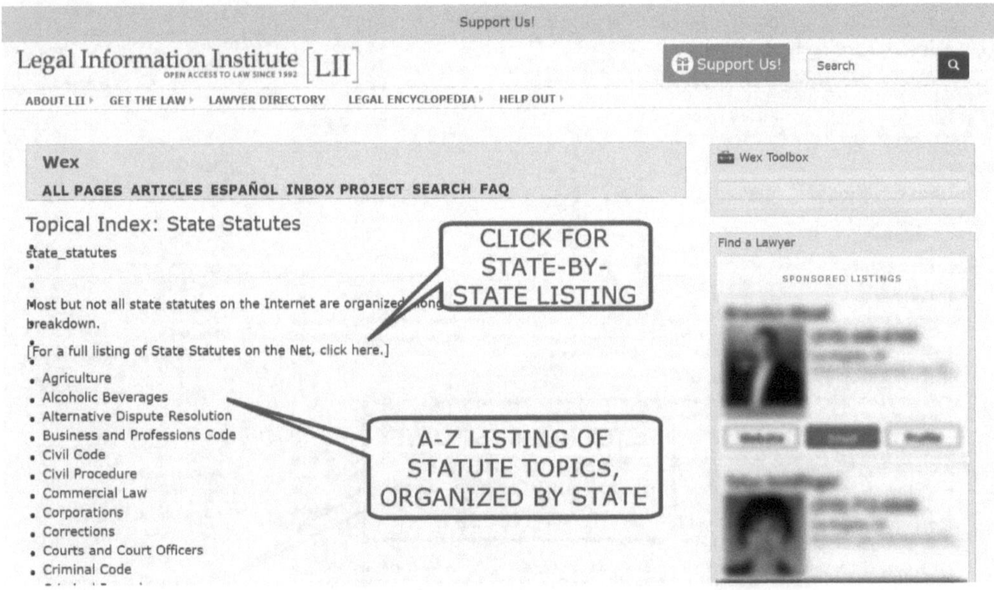


**Figure 5.14** LII's Toolbox sometimes contains helpful information. Screenshot from the Legal Information Institute at Cornell Law School used with permission.

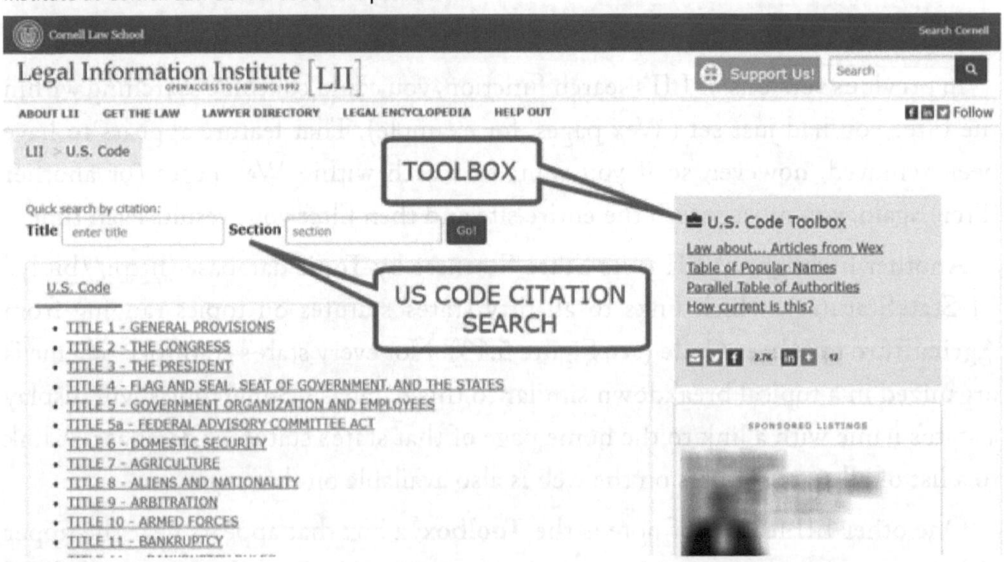


## UNIVERSITY OF SOUTHERN CALIFORNIA GOULD SCHOOL OF LAW

The University of Southern California (USC) Gould School of Law's **Asa V. Call Law Library** (http://bit.ly/USCFree) provides a guide with links to Free Legal Web

Resources such as **General Research Links, Federal Research Links, California Research Links,** and **Foreign & International Research Links** (see Figure 5.15).

**Figure 5.15** USC Gould School of Law provides a guide for free legal web resources.

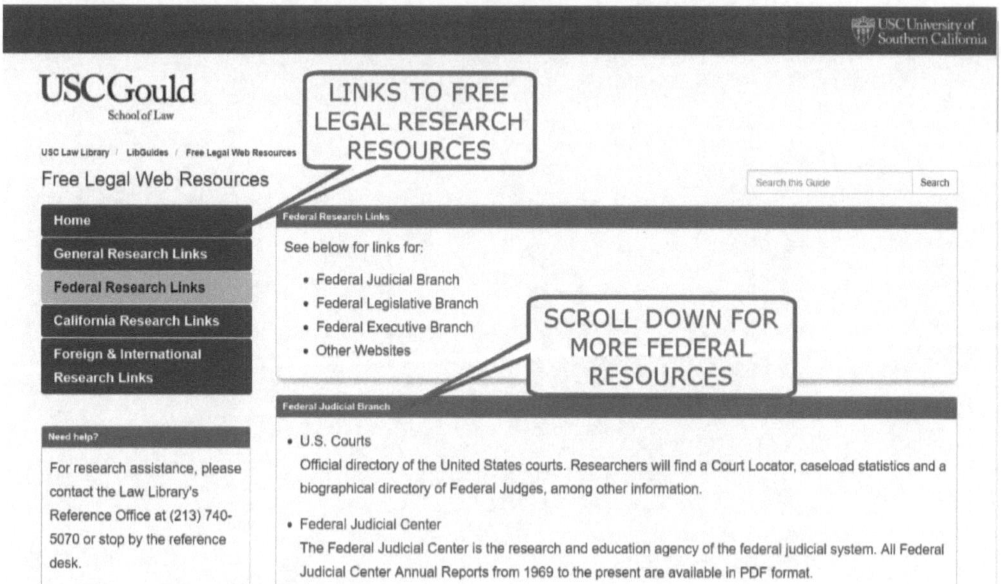


# LEGAL ASSOCIATION PORTALS

Many legal associations have created websites that not only provide information about the association, but also provide links to law-related websites that relate to the association's area of focus and that may interest their members. Many have also added original content such as online seminars and discussion groups. Even when association sites are restricted to members only, they often make some information available to the public.

## American Bar Association

The ABA website provides a **State and Local Bar Association Resources** page, with an interactive map containing links to free state and local resources (http://bit.ly/ABAStateLocal). Just click the state that you want (or the District of Columbia) from a map of the United States, and you can see a list of links to freely available legal resources for that jurisdiction.

For additional state and local resources, check your state or local bar associations for links and other resources they provide. To find nearby bar associations, see the **ABA's State & Local Bar Associations** directory at http://bit.ly/ABASLDirectory.

# Part III

## CASE LAW DATABASES

In Part III, we will discuss several free case law databases. Most free case law databases are limited in some way; they may have limited dates of coverage, provide cases only from certain courts, provide a browse function but no search function, or lack other features that paid databases provide. Probably no databases (even including paid ones) are 100 percent reliable, so researchers must always cite-check their cases. However, even the cite-checking databases are not 100 percent infallible.

Chapter 6 will focus on free commercial websites that provide online case law databases, including those found in the legal portals discussed in Chapter 4 (e.g., Justia and FindLaw). We will also discuss free commercial "stand-alone" case law databases such as the Public Library of Law (PLoL), Google Scholar, and Casetext. Chapter 7 will focus on free government websites that provide free case law.

Casemaker and Fastcase, which are case law databases free to many lawyers as a bar association "member benefit," will be discussed in Part IV's Chapters 8 and 9. (If you have free access to them, we would recommend using Casemaker or Fastcase over all other free databases. They offer more search functions and provide access to more than just case law—for example, statutes, regulations, etc.)

# Chapter 6

## FREE COMMERCIAL ONLINE CASE LAW DATABASES

This chapter describes free commercial websites that provide online case law databases. We will explain how to find case law on legal portals such as Justia and FindLaw, as well as on "stand-alone" case law databases such as Google Scholar, CourtListener, Casetext, and the Public Library of Law (PLoL). We will begin our discussion with Google Scholar, not because it's the best database or the most reliable, but because: (1) it offers more court and date coverage than the other free databases we will discuss in this chapter, and (2) it also finds articles (some free and some pay) and not just case law.

## GOOGLE SCHOLAR

In 2009, Google launched a free case law database and legal articles index (Legal Opinions and Journals), accessed via Scholar. In this chapter, we will only focus on the case law portion of Google Scholar. Use the URL: https://scholar.google.com because it cannot be reached from the Google.com homepage. We recommend you bookmark it if you use if often.

The cases come from a variety of sources, such as Cornell LII, Justia, Public .Resource.org, and official court sites. Scholar contains opinions from the following:

- All U.S. state appellate and state supreme courts back to 1950
- U.S. federal district, appellate, tax, and bankruptcy courts back to 1923
- Court of Claims from 1929 to 1982 (when the court was abolished)
- Court of Customs and Patent Appeals from 1929 to 1982 (when the court was abolished)
- Customs Court from 1949 to 1980 (when it was replaced by the Court of International Trade)
- Court of International Trade from 1980 (when it replaced the Customs Court) to the present
- Board of Tax Appeals from 1924 (when it was established) to 1942 (when it became the Tax Court)
- Tax Court from 1943 (when it replaced the Board of Tax Appeals) to the present
- U.S. Supreme Court back to 1791

Google states that it does not guarantee its coverage to be complete or accurate. The Customs Court and Tax Court, for example, do not appear to be complete for all years, especially for older years. It would be a good idea to double-check your research in another database if possible, especially for older cases. If a particular case is not available online for free in full-text format, Google Scholar search results will include only a citation.

## Searching Google Scholar

There are three ways to search case law using Google Scholar. To use any of the three methods, first select the **Case law** radio button under the search box. Three pre-filtering options will then appear—a **Federal Courts** radio button, a radio button for the state you are in (or the jurisdiction you have saved in a previous search), and a **Select courts. . .** link (see Figure 6.1; for copyright reasons, Google screenshots that appear in this book do not contain callout boxes or other superimposed graphics).

After you have selected **Case law**, you can search in one of three ways: (1) enter your search terms directly into the search box, which will search all jurisdictions; (2) enter your search terms into the **Advanced search** feature, which we will explain below; or (3) pre-filter your search by selecting certain courts to search, such as Federal courts or Texas courts, or by using the **Select courts** link, as in Figure 6.1. If you use the first or second methods (and enter your search terms now), you may

**Figure 6.1** Select case law and choose courts on Google Scholar. Google and the Google logo are registered trademarks of Google LLC, used with permission.

still want to filter the results by court or other criteria afterward. We will discuss how to do this below.

If you click **Select courts** (see Figure 6.1, second row of radio buttons below the search box), a screen containing all the courts Google Scholar covers will appear. You can then use the checkboxes to choose any combination of courts to search (see Figure 6.2).

**Figure 6.2** Google Scholar's Select courts feature. Google and the Google logo are registered trademarks of Google LLC, used with permission.

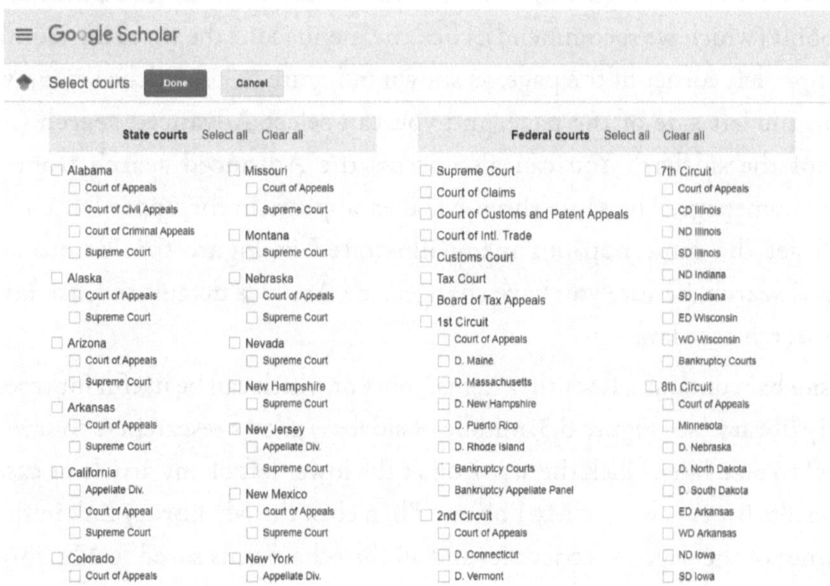

For example, to search all federal court opinions, you would click the **Select all** link just to the right of the **Federal courts** heading. This will select all federal courts, including the U.S. Supreme Court, all federal appellate courts and district courts (1st through 11th and D.C. Circuits), the Federal Circuit, the Tax Courts and Board of Tax Appeals, Bankruptcy Courts, and so on. Or, you could search one federal court or multiple federal courts. You could also mix and match federal and state courts.

To search all state court opinions, you would click the **Select all** link beside the **State courts** heading. To search only the state courts of Missouri, click the **Clear all** link beside the **State courts** heading (as well as the one beside **Federal courts**, if you had selected any) and then check the box next to Missouri. If you only want the Missouri Supreme Court but not the Missouri Court of Appeals, simply click the **Court of Appeals** box to uncheck it. (This will also uncheck the main Missouri box, as well.) When you have made your court selections, click **Done** (near the upper left corner) to close the courts screen.

When you click the **Select courts** link to use the check boxes to select jurisdictions before entering a search (Figure 6.2), clicking **Done** takes you to a screen with a single Google Scholar search box and the instructions **Please enter a query in the search box above** (see Figure 6.3). If you wish to use the **Advanced search** feature at this point (which we recommend), click the menu icon (the three horizontal bars) in the upper left corner of the page, as shown in Figure 6.3. A sidebar menu will pop out from the left side of the page, and you can select **Advanced search** (near the bottom of the sidebar). You can also access the **Advanced search** from Google Scholar's homepage. The same three-bar icon appears in the upper left corner, and you will get the same pop-out menu illustrated in Figure 6.3. Before selecting **Advanced search,** be sure you have changed the **Articles** default to **Case law** if you want to search case law.

The sidebar contains a few other items, some of which can be useful for researching cases. **My library** (see Figure 6.3, middle of sidebar) allows researchers to save articles (or cases) to read later. Click the star icon at the lower left of any article or case in the search results list to save it to **My library.** Then click the **My library** link in the upper right corner of the page to retrieve it (and all the other items saved to **My library;** see Figure 6.4). The **My library** feature requires you to create a free Google account. The **Alerts** link (under **My library** in Figure 6.3) allows you to save a search and have Google email you when new articles meeting your search criteria are added to the database. You can create an alert for case law by running a search for cases and then

**Figure 6.3** Google Scholar's Advanced search link for case law. Google and the Google logo are registered trademarks of Google LLC, used with permission.

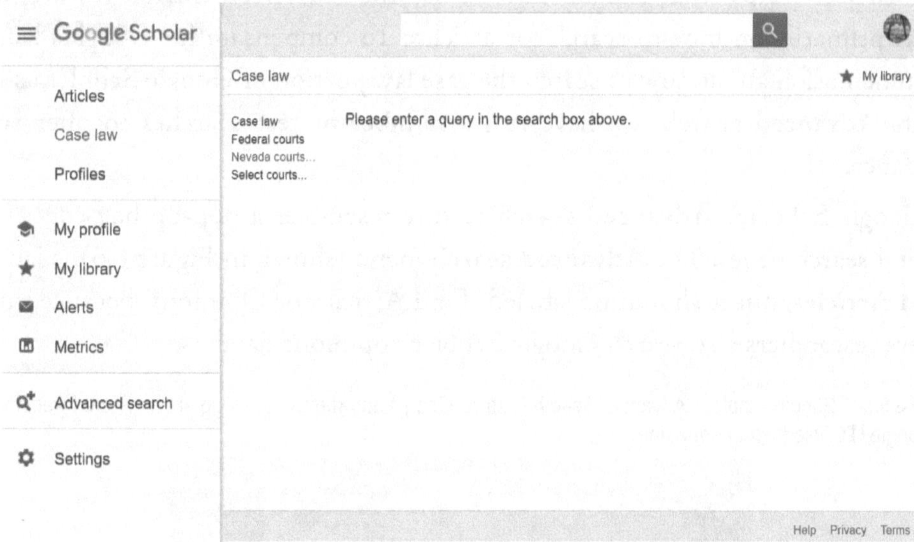


clicking **Create alert** at the bottom of the left sidebar on the results list page (see Figure 6.4). We will discuss this feature in greater detail later in this chapter. The links for **Profiles, My profile,** and **Metrics** relate to articles and not case law.

**Figure 6.4** Creating alerts and saving cases to My library in Google Scholar. Google and the Google logo are registered trademarks of Google LLC, used with permission.

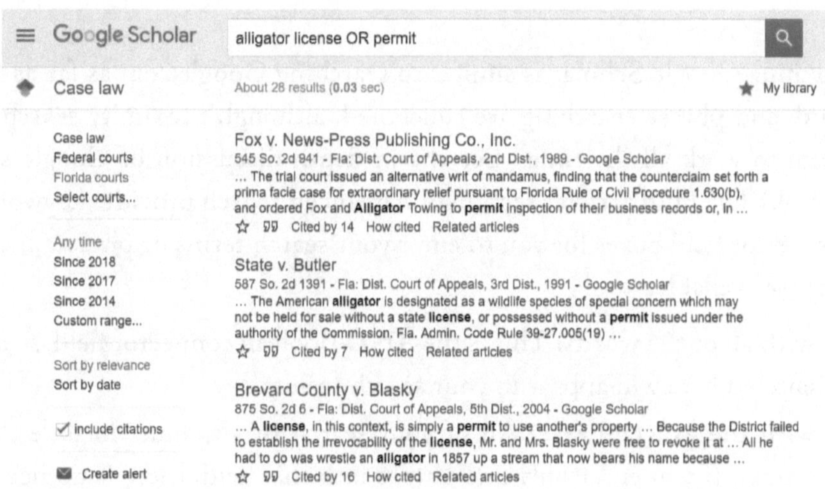

Although Google Scholar provides some specific search tips (http://bit.ly/ScholarSearchTips) that explain how to use the **Advanced Search** feature, they focus primarily on how to search for articles. To compensate for Google's lack of documentation about how to search the case law portion of Google Scholar as well as its **Advanced search**, we have run a number of test searches to offer some guidance.

Google Scholar's **Advanced search** feature resembles a pop-up box containing several search boxes. The **Advanced search** menu (shown in Figure 6.5) is labeled **Find Articles**, but it should be labeled "Find Articles or Opinions" because this is where researchers also search Google Scholar's opinions database.

**Figure 6.5** Google Scholar's Advanced Search Feature. Google and the Google logo are registered trademarks of Google LLC, used with permission.

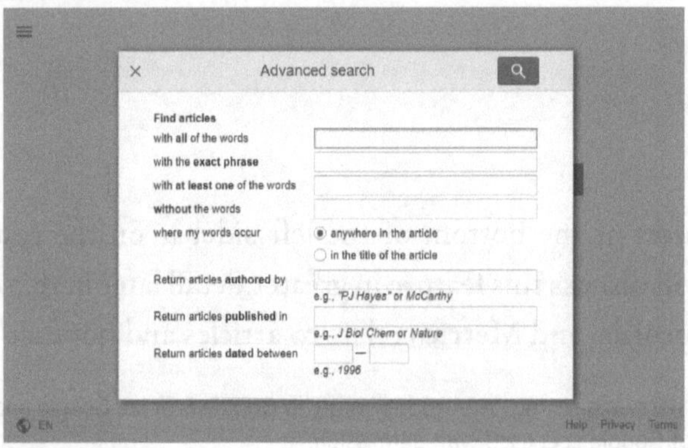


Searching Google Scholar is similar to searching Google.com as far as Boolean, keyword, and phrase searching are concerned, although proximity searching does not seem to work all the time. (See the in-depth discussion of Google syntax in Chapter 4.) The **Find articles** section of **Advanced search** provides keyword/Boolean connector field boxes for you to enter your search terms or phrases into. These options are available:

- **with all of the words:** This is the **AND** Boolean connector field, so all words entered here will appear in your search results.
- **with the exact phrase:** All of your search results must include this exact phrase. If you enter only one phrase into this field, there is no need to surround the phrase with quotation marks. If you enter more than one phrase, however, each will require quotation marks.

- **with at least one of the words:** This is the *OR* Boolean connector field, so at least one of the words entered will be included in the search results.
- **without the words:** This is the *NOT* Boolean connector field, so all documents containing the words or phrases entered into this field will be excluded from the search results.

In addition, these fields allow you to create searches unique to opinions. For example, to force a search by citation, enter the citation, in Bluebook style, into the **with the exact phrase** search box. You will notice that the results for this search include not only your case but also cases that have cited to it, similar to using a citator (such as Shepard's or KeyCite, for example). We will discuss using Google Scholar as a citator later in Chapter 18 Cite-Checking Cases.

You can use the **where my words occur** option to select either **anywhere in the article** (think of it as "anywhere in the *case*") to run a full-text search, or **in the title of the article** (think of it as "in the *party names* of the *case*") to search for the case name.

You can also search for a case name using a slightly more precise method. First, limit the results to a specific court (e.g., the California Supreme Court) if you know which court decided the case. Next, enter the name of the case (e.g., *Tarasoff v. Regents of the University of California*) into the **with the exact phrase** search box, using *v.* and not *versus* or *vs.* Finally, from the **where my words occur** section, select **in the title of the article.** (N.B. This search actually brought back no full-text cases until we removed "the" from the search phrase, even though *Tarasoff v. Regents of the University of California* is the correct name of the case, and the case is in Google's database. Removing "the" returned one result—the *Tarasoff v. Regents of the University of California* case; see Figure 6.6.) The full-text case in Google's database omits the "the" in the case name. This is one example of why you should double check your work whenever possible, especially when using a free resource.

If you wanted to research how courts have cited to *Tarasoff*, you would first select the courts you want to search from the **Select courts** page. Then enter the party names as a phrase (e.g., *Tarasoff v. Regents*) into the **with the exact phrase** search box under **Find articles.** From the **where my words occur** drop-down menu, select **anywhere in the article.** This will bring back cases that include the phrase "Tarasoff v. Regents" anywhere in the opinion and not just in the case title (unlike the previous search). This should return a list of cases that have cited to your case. This technique is useful for the party name cite checking technique, which we will discuss below.

**Figure 6.6** Using Google Scholar to search for a case name. Google and the Google logo are registered trademarks of Google LLC, used with permission.

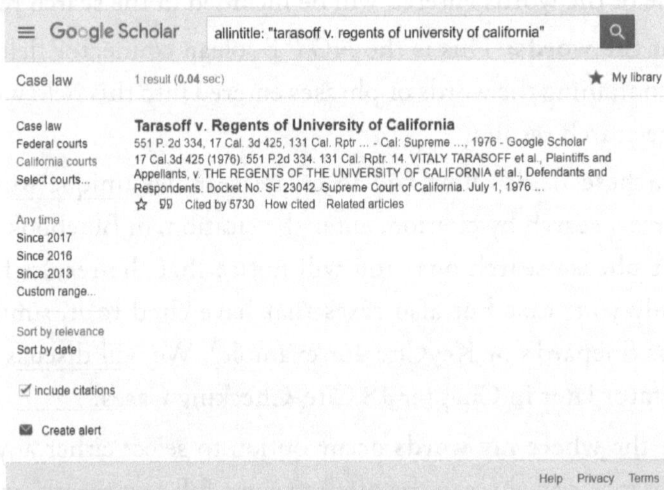


The remainder of the **Advanced search** box provides search fields for **Author**, **Publication**, and **Date**. You can think of the **Author** field as the equivalent of **Judge** because you can enter a judge's name here when researching opinions. Test searches indicate that this field does not necessarily return opinions (or concurrences or dissents) authored by the judge searched, however. Any case in which the judge's name appears (e.g., if he or she heard the case but did not author the opinion) can appear in the search results.

You can try to force a search to return a judge as author. If you want only cases in which a specified U.S. Supreme Court Justice delivered the opinion, for example, you would first select that court and then add the justice's name and the word "delivered" into the search box labeled **Find articles with all of the words.** For other jurisdictions—Arizona, for example—if you wanted opinions written by Eckerstrom, you would first select Arizona and then enter *opinion Eckerstrom* into the exact phrase box. (Check several cases to see if the court you are searching uses a standardized format to indicate the judge who authored the opinion.) This approach is very hit-or-miss, however. It's possible that search results could include cases in which someone else delivered the opinion but the specified judge was mentioned regarding his or her delivery of another opinion cited to in the case you are viewing.

Or it could miss relevant opinions altogether if the spacing or punctuation of your search phrase differs slightly from some opinions, or if the judge co-authored an opinion and his or her name is not the next word after *opinion*.

You may also use the **Advanced search** box to search for cases published in a particular reporter by using the **Return articles published in** field. Test searches indicate that when you restrict your search to case law, the **Return articles published in** field allows you to search for the abbreviation of the case reporters—e.g., *A.2d, P.3d, NY 2d,* and so on. (Searches in the **Return articles published in** field for words such as *reports* or *supreme court* retrieve no results; only the reporter's abbreviation will work.) For example, if you were searching for *Smith v. Jones* and only knew that the case was published in the Atlantic Reporter, you could enter *Smith v. Jones* into the **with the exact phrase** box and still narrow your search significantly by entering *A.2d* (or *A.3d,* etc.) in the **Return articles published in** field.

The **Collections** and **Legal opinions and journals** sections that were available on Google's "old venerable" advanced search page allowed you to search law journals and cases together. Although those were removed when the old page was retired in 2012, researchers can still approximate this function with Google Scholar's post-search filters. We will explain how below.

## Search Results in Google Scholar

Always remember to select the **Case law** radio button on the main Google Scholar page when beginning your research. Doing so will help ensure that your search results are within the legal field, although this feature is not infallible. (Unfortunately for researchers in other disciplines, law is currently the only subject—or "collection"—for which Google even attempts to pre-filter search results.)

Once you have selected which courts to search and entered your search terms, you will receive a list of results. Because you selected the **Case law** option when you began searching, however, Google Scholar will provide search result filtering options specific to legal document searches. You can use these to refine your research even more. The filtering options appear in a sidebar on the left side of the search results page. (See Figure 6.7.)

**Figure 6.7** Google Scholar case law search results and filters. Google and the Google logo are registered trademarks of Google LLC, used with permission.

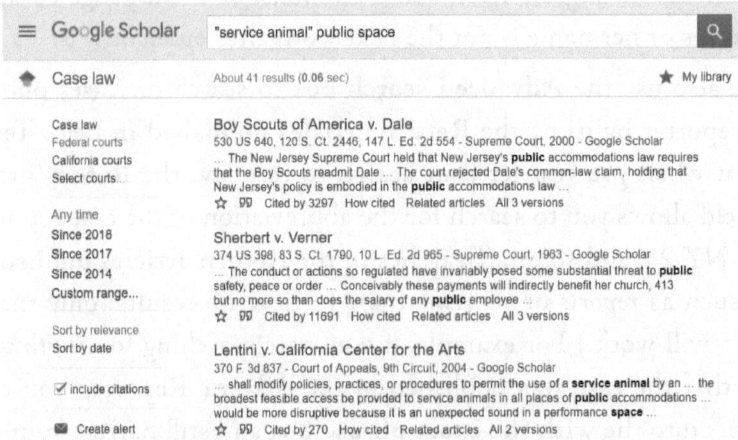


We will discuss the filters from top to bottom as they appear on the search results page. Google has moved the links that allow you to switch between articles and case law in your results. To find the links, you now click the three-bar menu icon in the upper left corner of the screen, shown in Figures 6.3 and 6.8. Then, the left sidebar menu will pop out from the left, and you can choose **Articles** or **Case law** at the top of the sidebar (see Figure 6.8). Clicking these links will refresh your results list to show the relevant type of documents. (To return to your original search results without refreshing them, simply click in the search results part of the screen, and the sidebar will disappear.)

Although you may have already selected the jurisdictions you wished to search before you reached this page, you can now adjust them while retaining your search terms. If you click **Select courts** near the upper left corner of the search results page (see Figure 6.7), you will go to the same jurisdiction menu that appeared if you chose **Select courts** from the original Google Scholar search page. You can now use this menu to see your search results in different courts.

The next two groups of filters are for date. You may want to find more recent cases (or journal articles), so the filters allow you to select **Any time**, various dates in recent years, or your own custom date range. If you click the **Custom range** link, two boxes will appear beneath the link. You enter the four-digit beginning and ending years of the dates you wish to include in your search results and then click the Search button that appears below the two boxes. The next filtering option allows you to sort your search results by date (instead of relevance), with the newest items appearing first.

**Figure 6.8** Use the menu icon to switch search results between Articles and Case law. Google and the Google logo are registered trademarks of Google LLC, used with permission.

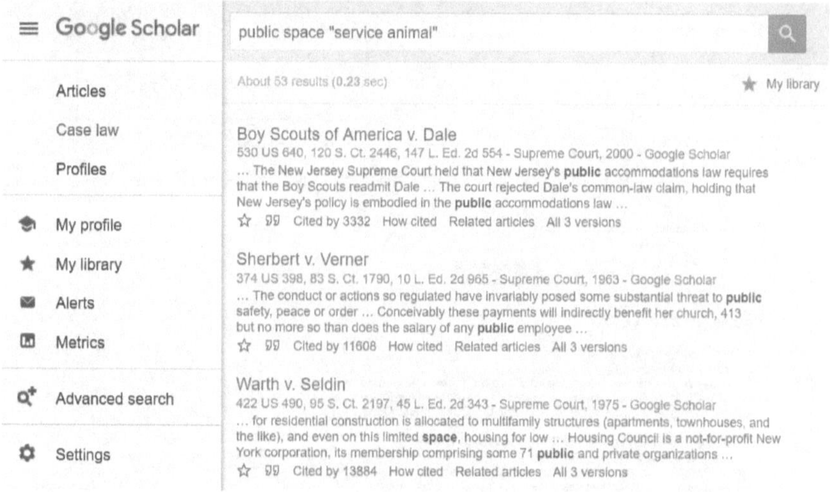


The next link in the list of filtering options is a checkbox to **include citations.** As mentioned earlier, Google will search cases that include your search terms but to which it (and you) may not have full-text access. If you only want to see search results that include the full text of cases, you can uncheck the box next to **include citations.** If you have other sources for viewing case law, however, it might be a good idea to leave this option checked, in case there are citations to relevant cases that you can access elsewhere.

The final item in the list is not a filtering option, but it is a useful feature that Google has added. **Create alert** allows researchers to receive regular e-mail alerts about cases on any chosen topic emanating from any chosen court. You can also set up alerts using a citation or keywords, such as a party, judge, or attorney name. The alert defaults to your current search, but you can revise the alert by typing in other keywords/phrases and selecting up to ten or up to twenty results at a time (see Figure 6.9). If you want to revise the jurisdiction or change from courts to articles (or vice versa), however, you will have to go back and revise your search first. You do not need to have a Google account to set up an alert, although if you don't, Google may require you to click a verification link in order to begin receiving alerts.

**Figure 6.9** Setting up a Google Scholar Alert for your search terms. Google and the Google logo are registered trademarks of Google LLC, used with permission.

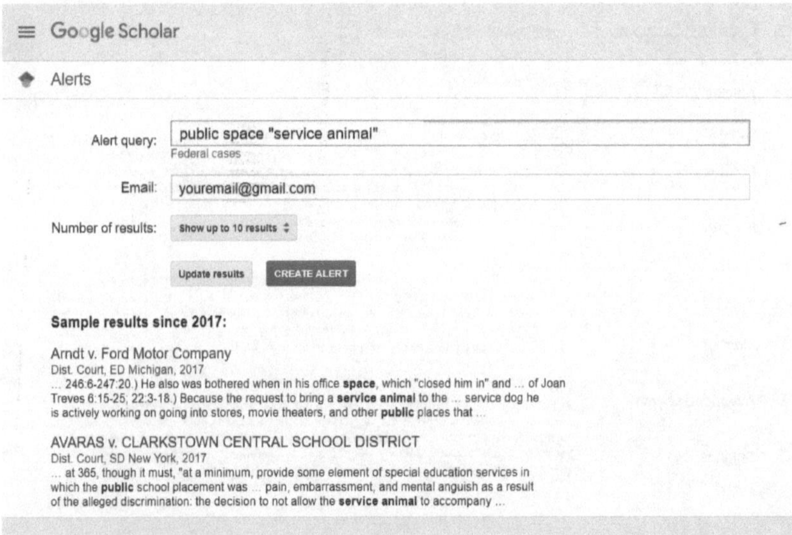


## Viewing Cases in Google Scholar

Once you have executed a search and refined your results, you will begin reviewing the cases you have found. Figure 6.10 shows an example of what you will see when you click a search result link to view a full-text opinion with Google Scholar.

Keywords are no longer highlighted as they were in the past, but you can use your computer's Control/Command + F (for a PC/for a Mac) to search for them. Page numbers (in gray) in the left-hand margin and throughout the text of the opinion correspond to the pages in the printed reporter (usually the official reporter), as shown in the Federal Supplement opinion in Figure 6.10. The upper left corner of the screen contains three links—**Read** and **How cited** (under the case name), and a **back arrow** (to the left of the case name). The **Read** link is inactive on this screen because you are already reading the case. Clicking **How cited** will show other cases that cited this case and can help you conduct a rudimentary citation check of your case. (See Chapter 18 for details about Google's citation features.) To return to the list of search results, click the **back arrow**.

Google provides this disclaimer about using its case law database: "Legal opinions in Google Scholar are provided for informational purposes only and should not be relied on as a substitute for legal advice from a licensed lawyer. Google does not warrant that the information is complete or accurate." (See http://bit.ly/ScholarDisclaimer.) Disclaimers like this can even be found at official courts' websites

**Figure 6.10** Viewing the text of an opinion in Google Scholar. Google and the Google logo are registered trademarks of Google LLC, used with permission.

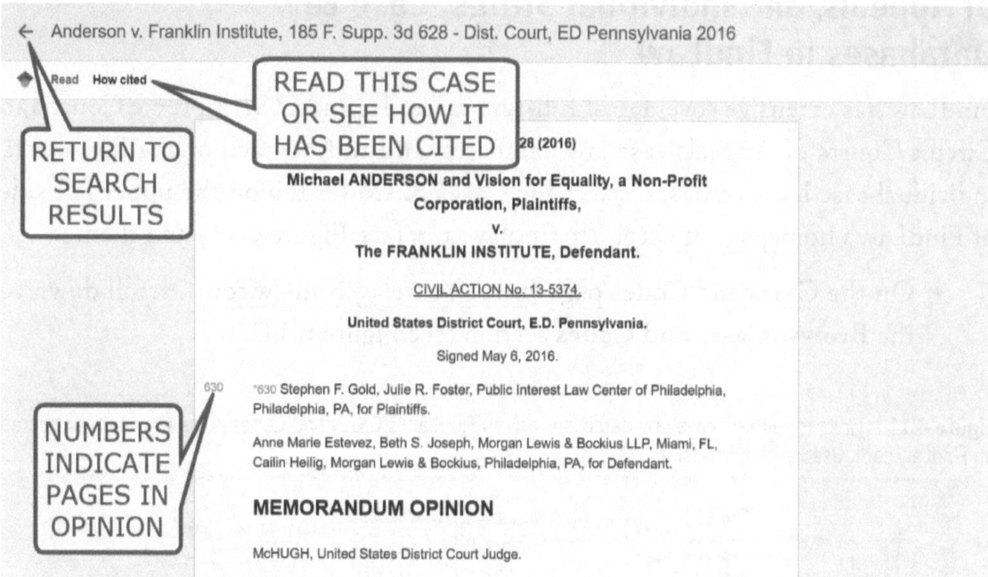


where they are providing a database of their own legal opinions. As with any case law research, it's imperative that you determine that you are using cases that have not been overruled or reversed. You can do this by using the citation features at Google Scholar (see Chapter 18, which also discusses other free citator-like resources), or by conducting a citation check using either (1) a pay resource such as KeyCite, Shepard's, or BCite; or (2) a member-benefit resource such as Fastcase (Chapter 9) or Casemaker (Chapter 8). In addition, you should always run a keyword search by party name when using any free or low-cost database, to double check its citations feature.

## FINDLAW

In Chapter 4, we noted that **FindLaw** is classified as a portal because it has added something of value at its site: free case law databases. In the previous edition of this book, we noted that we found many problems with FindLaw's databases. We alerted FindLaw about the problems and were informed they were fixing them. Since then, we have seen some positive changes to the website. Although not all the issues have been fixed in the ways we would like, many features have been improved. When its databases work, FindLaw's are the next best for case law after Google Scholar. We will point out any continuing issues with FindLaw databases in the sections below.

## Finding U.S. Supreme Court, Federal Circuit Courts of Appeals, and Individual States' Case Law Databases in FindLaw

FindLaw has extensive coverage of full-text cases. To find U.S. Supreme Court and Circuit Courts of Appeals case law databases, and to find each of the fifty states' individual case law databases, select the **Cases & Codes** tab on the upper left side of FindLaw's homepage at http://lp.findlaw.com (see Figure 6.11) and then:

- On the Cases and Codes page (http://caselaw.findlaw.com), scroll down to the **Browse Cases and Codes** section (see Figure 6.11).

**Figure 6.11** Links to full-text case law databases are on FindLaw's Cases and Codes page. Originally appeared on FindLaw.com. Used with permission.

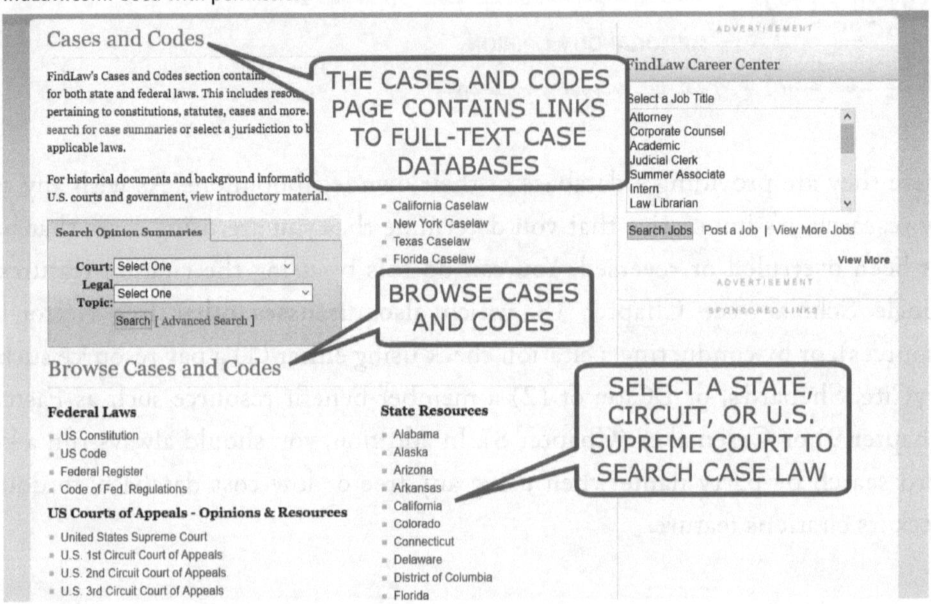


- Select the jurisdiction you want from the lists of links—U.S. Supreme Court, one of the Circuit Courts of Appeals, or one of the states and territories listed beneath **State Resources.**
- If you selected a link for the Supreme Court or a Circuit Court, you will go directly to a search page similar to the one in Figure 6.13.
- Links for **State Resources** go to individual pages for each state. (These pages provide links to FindLaw's searchable case law databases for each state, as

well as other links to state case law, the state's official court site, and additional resources. Sometimes the State Resources pages also link to non-official sites that may offer additional searchable case law databases.) From the State Resources page, you can select the link for the court you want—such as court of appeals or state supreme court—under the **State Court Opinions** heading (see Figure 6.12).

- After selecting a federal or state court from FindLaw's **Cases and Codes** page at http://caselaw.findlaw.com (or from a **State Resources** page, if you are researching state law), you will be taken to a page with case law database search menus.

**Figure 6.12** From a state law page on FindLaw you can select a court to search full-text opinions. Originally appeared on FindLaw.com. Used with permission.

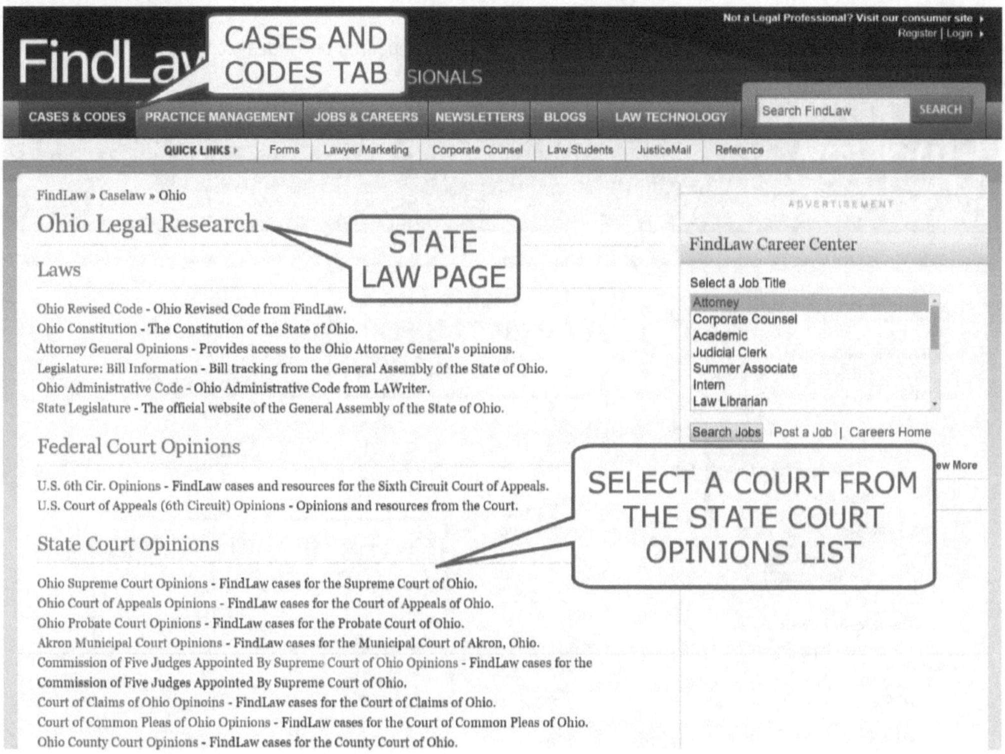

## Searching Case Law Databases in FindLaw

FindLaw no longer has a search help page to assist users with its full-text search feature, but the following search tips will work for all the databases we have just discussed—U.S. Supreme Court, U.S. Courts of Appeals, and all the state court case databases provided by FindLaw.

- On the case law page, select the **Free Text Search** tab at the top of the blue search box (see Figure 6.13).
- The Boolean operators *AND* and *OR* and the proximity operator *NEAR* (which in theory places words on the same page, although our test searches have indicated they can be farther apart) can be used to connect keywords and phrases. Note that the above operators must be in all capital letters; otherwise the search engine will treat them as regular search terms.

**Figure 6.13** FindLaw's full-text case law search box. Originally appeared on FindLaw.com. Used with permission.

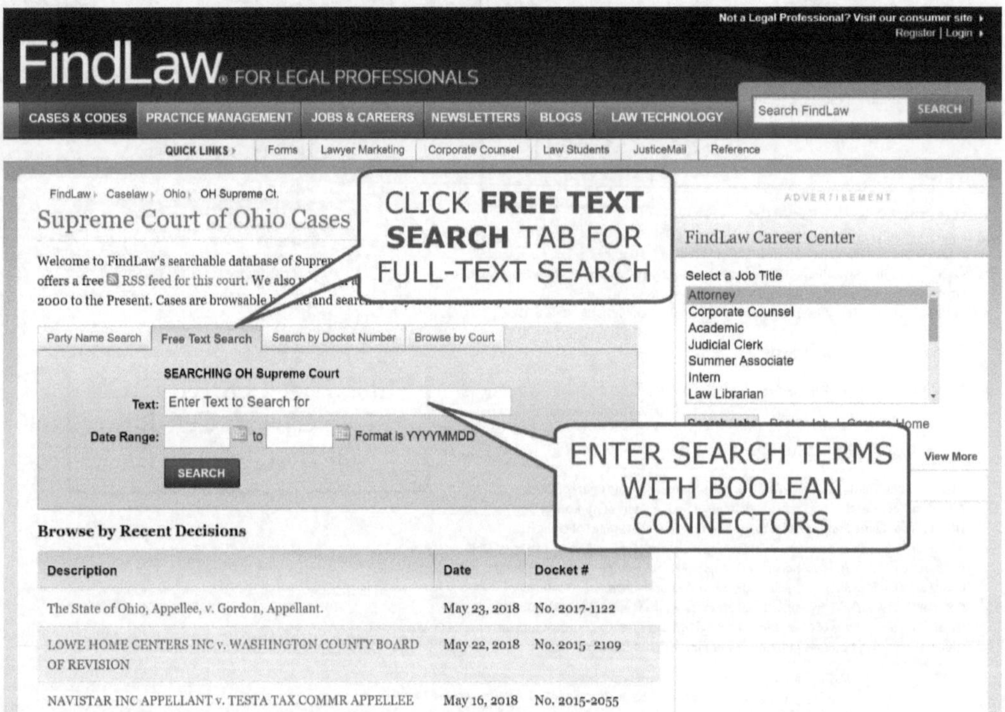


- The operator *AND NOT*, which should exclude specified search terms, does not work. FindLaw appears to treat the words *AND NOT* like any other search terms.
- To search for an exact phrase, enclose it in quotation marks.

- Finally, note that the default search tab for FindLaw's full-text case databases is **Party Name Search.** Every time you enter a full-text search, you have to select the **Free Text Search** tab, or you will be searching in the Party name field—even if you have just run a full-text search and are on the search results page (Figure 6.13). We had to redo several searches after realizing we received no results because we had accidentally searched by Party name instead of full text.

If you want to search by **Party Name**, enter one or more words from one or both of the names of the parties in the case. You can connect the names with *v.*, but we do not recommend connecting them with *and* because *and* does not always work. For example, to retrieve the U.S. Supreme Court case of *Brown v. Board of Education*, you could type *brown* or *brown board* or *brown v. board* but not *brown and board.* (Many, if not most, of FindLaw's case law databases actually do work when you attempt to connect party names with *and*. Our test searches indicate that at least the United States Supreme Court database does not work with *and*, however. Because not all of FindLaw's databases work when you connect party names with *and*, we therefore recommend including *v.* in the search, as in *brown v. board*; this seems to work more consistently.)

You can also search for cases by **Docket Number**, and for U.S. Supreme Court cases, you can search by **Citation**, as well. All the case law search tabs will allow you to also restrict your search by **Date Range**.

FindLaw only searches one court at a time. If you need to search multiple courts (for free), see the discussions elsewhere in this chapter of Google Scholar or Casetext, both of which can search all or multiple courts together, or see the "member-benefit" Casemaker and Fastcase chapters (Chapters 8 and 9). Also, see the discussion later in this chapter about Justia's Supreme Court Center, which offers additional resources for researching the U.S. Supreme Court.

In addition to searching, you can also browse cases in a few ways. Below the search box (on each jurisdiction's court page) is the heading, **Browse by Recent Decisions** (see Figure 6.14). To browse all of one jurisdiction's court decisions that are in FindLaw's database, scroll farther down the page to the **Browse opinions by calendar year** heading. The **Browse by Court** tab on the far right of the blue search box (shown in Figure 6.14) also links to case law, but only for selected jurisdictions. If you click **Browse by Court**, links will appear to the U.S. Supreme Court, all Circuit Courts, supreme courts of the states of California, Colorado, Delaware, Florida, Illinois, Minnesota, New Jersey, Ohio, Texas, and the New York Court of Appeals. When you browse cases, opinions are displayed in reverse chronological

**Figure 6.14** Features of FindLaw state case law database. Originally appeared on FindLaw.com. Used with permission.

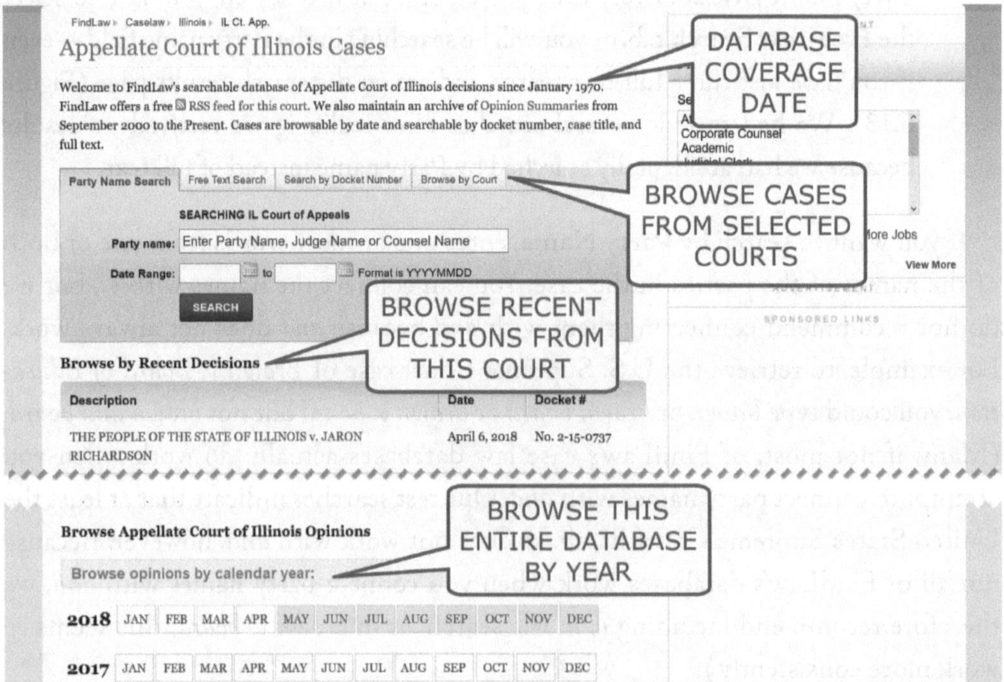


order, except for U.S. Supreme Court opinions, which are listed (for the most part) in alphabetical order by the first party's name.

FindLaw's coverage varies by court. Supreme Court cases go back to 1760. U.S. Courts of Appeals Cases coverage varies by circuit, with most going back to 1995. The First Circuit goes back to 1984, however. State court coverage varies, although many go back to 1997. You can find the coverage of a state court database near the top of the state court search page (see Figure 6.14).

## FindLaw's Opinion Summaries Archive

In addition to its extensive databases of full-text cases, FindLaw also has an **Opinion Summaries Archive** (http://caselaw.findlaw.com/summary) that includes case summaries written by FindLaw staff. For an illustration of the Opinion Summaries Archive page, see Figure 6.17.

The opinion summaries are uploaded to the Archive soon after the cases are released. After reading a summary, you can click a **Read** link on the page to read the full text of a case. The Opinion Summaries Archive covers opinions dating back to 2000 from the U.S. Supreme Court, all thirteen U.S. Circuit Courts of Appeals, and six states: the supreme and appellate courts of California and Illinois, the supreme courts of Delaware, Florida, and New York, and the supreme and criminal appeals courts of Texas. Each court must be searched individually. (To search farther back in time and to search all states' cases, see the earlier section of this chapter, Finding U.S. Supreme Court, Federal Circuit Courts of Appeals, and Individual States' Case Law Databases in FindLaw.)

**Figure 6.15** FindLaw homepage. Originally appeared on FindLaw.com. Used with permission.

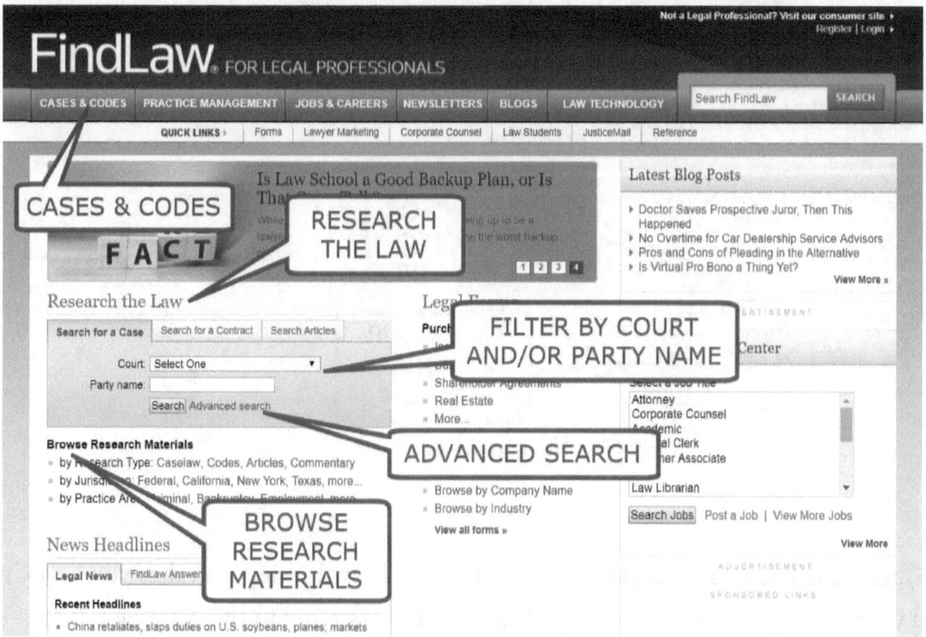


In addition to using the direct URL link (http://caselaw.findlaw.com/summary), you can also access the **Opinions Summaries Archive** from two places on the FindLaw website: from the **Research the Law** search box in the middle of FindLaw's homepage (http://lp.findlaw.com) and from the **Cases & Codes** tab on the top left side of the homepage (see Figure 6.15). The access points are slightly different, so we will describe them both.

The **Research the Law** search box has three tabs; in addition to the **Search for a Case** tab, it also has tabs labeled **Search for a Contract** and **Search Articles** (Figure 6.15). Under the **Search for a Case** tab, you can type in a Party name and search, or you can type in a Party name and also choose a Court from a drop-down list. If you click the Search button without either selecting a Court or typing in a Party name, however, you will get zero search results. (You could also get zero results if your case is not in the summaries archive.) An Advanced search link to the right of the Search button takes you to the **Opinion Summaries Archive** page (http://caselaw.findlaw.com/summary).

**Figure 6.16** FindLaw's Cases and Codes search (basic). Originally appeared on FindLaw.com. Used with permission.

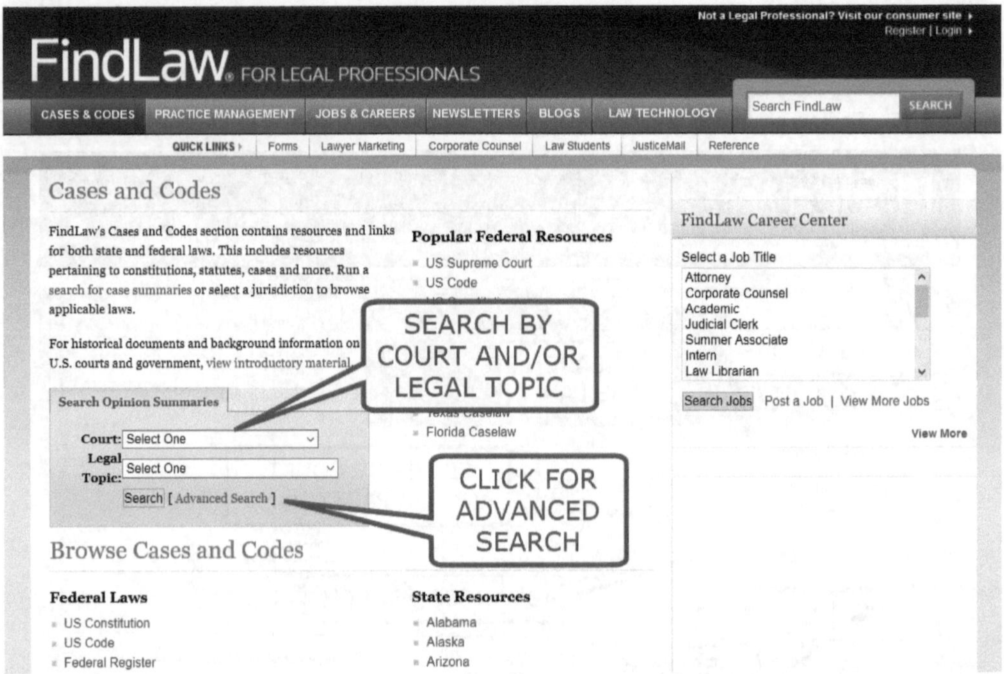


Clicking the **Cases & Codes** tab from the FindLaw homepage takes you to a **Cases and Codes** basic search menu page (Figure 6.16). The menu has a single tab that says **Search Opinion Summaries.** The Cases and Codes menu offers the same Court drop-down menu as the Research the Law search box. Instead of a Party name search box, however, the Cases & Codes page provides a drop-down menu listing several Legal Topics (see Figure 6.16). From this menu, you can also click an **Advanced Search** link. This **Advanced Search** link takes you to the same **Opinion Summaries Archive** page at http://caselaw.findlaw.com/summary as the **Advanced search** link from the **Research the Law** box on the FindLaw homepage (see Figure 6.15). Thus, you see the same Advanced search menu with the same search fields (Court, Legal Topic, Industry, Docket Number, Party Name, Date, and Date Range; see Figure 6.17).

The default view of the **Advanced search** menu, described above, is under a tab titled **Opinion Summary Search** (see Figure 6.17). The menu also has a second tab called **Full Text Search.** This option might be better titled "Keyword Search of Summaries" because it does not search the full text of opinions but rather, it keyword searches the same opinion summaries as the Opinion Summary Search tab (see Figure 6.17). Our test searches indicated that the Full Text Search function operates

**Figure 6.17** FindLaw Opinion Summaries Archive Advanced Search. Originally appeared on FindLaw.com. Used with permission.

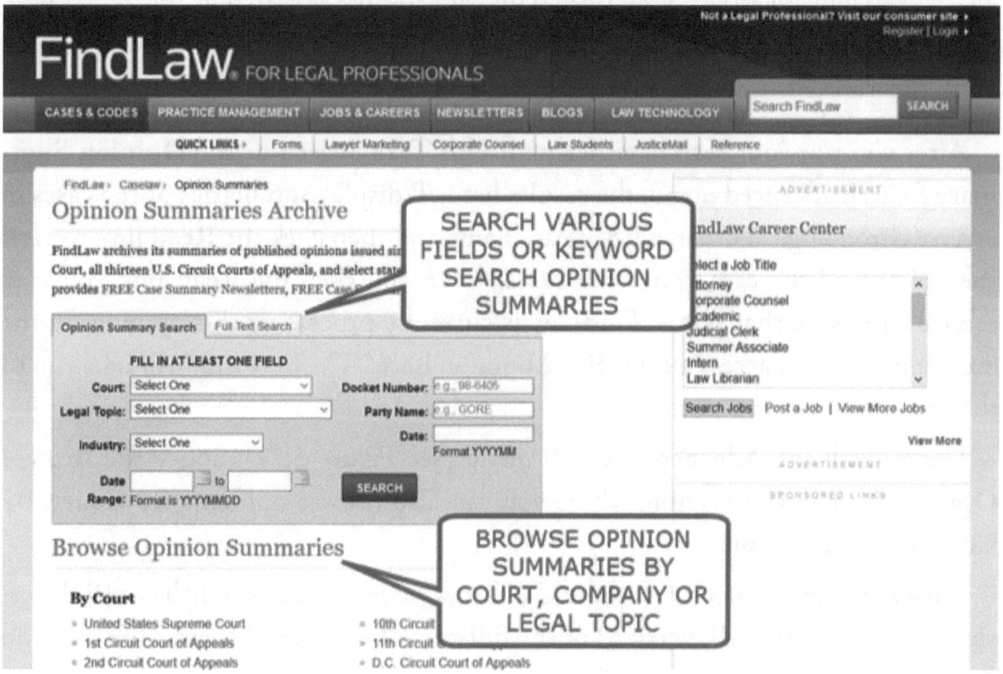


independently of the Opinion Summary Search (advanced search) function. In other words, you cannot use the Opinion Summary Search menu to filter to a specific court, date, etc. and then refine your results by keyword using the Full Text Search tab. You also cannot do the reverse—i.e. perform a keyword search and then restrict the results to a particular court, legal topic, or other field offered in the Opinion Summary Search menu. The two search functions used to work together to allow more refined searching, but they no longer do; thus, the Advanced search feature is not as useful as it used to be.

Our test searches indicated that the **Full Text Search** feature for the Opinion Summaries Archive does not work like a natural language search or a Google search. In other words, you must either use Boolean connectors between search terms or limit your keyword search to one word or phrase; otherwise, the search will not work. We were able to get the following search techniques to work:

- The Boolean connectors **AND, OR,** and **NOT** worked in our test searches. Capitalizing the connectors is not necessary.
- We were unable to get any proximity connectors (*NEAR, AROUND, /#,* etc.) to function, and we received zero search results when we tried them.
- When we searched for more than one keyword without a Boolean connector between them, the search engine treated the words as a phrase. Placing

quotation marks around phrases did not make a difference; for example, searching for *service dog* returned the same results as searching for *"service dog."*

- We were able to connect phrases with other search terms using Boolean connectors. For example, searching for *service dog and ADA* will return results.

After you run your search, either with **Full Text Search** or the **Opinion Summary Search** advanced menu, the results list will display summaries of the cases in reverse chronological order. Click a case name and then click the **Read** link to view the full text of the case. For some cases, when you click the **Read** link you may receive a message that states "FindLaw is currently processing this opinion. In the meantime, you can access a copy of the opinion **here**." The **here** link will take you to the slip opinion of the case.

Underneath the **Advanced Search** menu (see Figure 6.17), notice the **Browse Opinion Summaries** section, where you can also browse opinions **By Court, By Company**, or **By Topic**.

**California Differences:** For some California cases, FindLaw only has a PDF version (and not an HTML version) of the full-text of the case. If these PDF cases do not open in your browser, you will be prompted to download or save.

## COURTLISTENER OPINIONS

CourtListener (https://www.courtlistener.com) is a free legal research website provided by the Free Law Project. Its database, which has extensive coverage of legal opinions from federal and state courts, was created over the course of many years and from many sources. CourtListener explains its coverage this way: "We do not currently claim to have complete coverage of judicial opinions, but we believe that we will one day soon" (http://bit.ly/CourtListenerCoverage). The database includes the complete United States Reports (back to 1759), the second series of the Federal Reporter, volumes 1–491 of the third series of the Federal Reporter, and many state court opinions. Since 2010, CourtListener began to gather opinions directly from court websites via their Juriscraper tool. Currently, CourtListener scrapes opinions from hundreds of court websites daily and can also provide instant, daily, weekly, or monthly alerts from these courts (http://bit.ly/CourtListenerJurisdictions). CourtListener is planning an audit to ensure every opinion from both WestLaw and LexisNexis is available at CourtListener. As of December 2018, CourtListener offered access to 4,177,084 opinions (https://www.courtlistener.com/coverage).

On the **Advanced Opinion Search** page (https://www.courtlistener.com/opinion), below the logo and to the right of the **Opinions** link, are links to other CourtListener databases, which we discuss in Chapter 15, Dockets and Case Documents (**RECAP Archive** and **Oral Arguments**).

Courtlistener's **Advanced Opinion Search** page (https://www.courtlistener.com/opinion) lets you search specific parts of opinions, like the **Case Name** and the **Judge** for a particular case, a technique often called field searching. You can also combine field searching with keyword searching, and you can specify a range of dates in your search. You can also search by citation or docket number. See Figure 6.18, as we explain in the next few pages how to search.

**Figure 6.18** CourtListener's Advanced Opinion Search page. Screenshot from CourtListener used with permission.

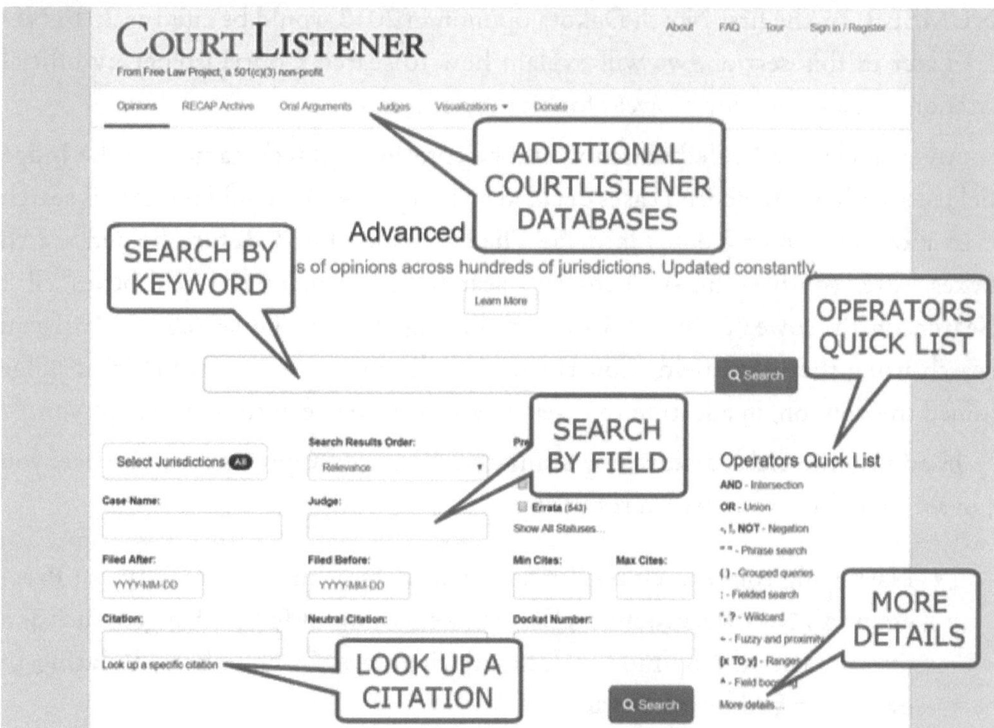


To keyword search, enter one or more keywords (or phrases) into the top search box and click Search on the right-hand side of the search box. You can create a more sophisticated keyword/phrase search by using one or multiple advanced query techniques displayed in the **Operators Quick List** found on the right side of the search menu. To learn how to use these operators (often called "connectors" at other websites and search engines), wildcards, fielded queries, and other search techniques, click the **More details** beneath the Operators Quick List. You can also learn about the **Operators Quick List** by reading the How to Search RECAP section in Chapter 15 (see Figure 15.15).

If you want to refine your keyword search, you can add more information into one (or more) of the various fielded search boxes located below the large keyword/phrase search box. As noted earlier, you can, in the alternative, leave off keywords and conduct a fielded-only search. The fielded search boxes let you search by: **Jurisdictions** (one, multiple, or all), **Case Name, Filed After:YYYY-MM-DD, Filed Before:YYYY-MM-DD, Judge, Docket Number, Citation,** and **Neutral Citation.** (Neutral citations are citations that some courts affix to their work as they publish opinions on their websites, instead of waiting for an official citation to be assigned for print reporters. Neutral citations use the format: YEAR JURISDICTION NUMBER; so, the first North Dakota opinion in 2013 would be cited as 2013 ND 1.) Later in this section, we will explain how to search CourtListener by official citation and also provide a caveat for citation searching.

An example of a fielded search would be entering a judge's name into the **Judge** fielded search box to do find cases decided by that judge. You could refine this search even more by entering dates into the **Filed After** or **Filed Before** fielded search boxes. After you have finished entering search criteria using the field boxes, click **Search** on the lower right-hand side of the page to run the search. (NB: If you search using the Judge field, CourtListener will return cases in which that judge joined the opinion, in addition to cases in which she or he authored the opinion.)

In addition to fielded searching using the Advanced Opinion Search page, you can sort and filter your search results by:

- Narrowing your search results to one or more of these opinion types: **Precedential, Non-Precedential, Errata** (something added or changed, such as a dissent, after the opinion is decided), **Separate, In-chambers, Relating-to orders,** or **Unknown Status.**
- Clicking **Search Results Order**, near the middle of the **Advanced Opinion Search** page, to change the order in which the results are displayed. The default order is Relevance, but you can change it to Newest First, Oldest First, Most Cited First, or Least Cited First.

We keyword searched *abortion*, which returned 23,021 opinions, sorted by Relevance (the default). The first case in the results list was the seminal abortion case, *Roe v. Wade* (see Figure 6.19). CourtListener's relevance engine determines relevance in part by a case's **CiteGeist** score, which factors in not only the number of citations a case has, but also how important the citing cases are.

**Figure 6.19** Search results on CourtListener. Screenshot from CourtListener used with permission.

Once you retrieve a results list, notice the left column (see Figure 6.19), where you can refine your results with many of the same options listed above for searching. If you scroll down this page, you can also set up an Alert (not shown) for this search.

Click a case title from the results list to read the opinion—e.g., *Roe v. Wade,* shown in Figure 6.20. At the top of the left-hand column of the case page, you can see how many cases cited *Roe v. Wade* with the **Cited By (3081)** heading. Farther down the left column, the **Authorities (97)** heading indicates how many cases *Roe v. Wade* relied on, and below that, **Visualizations** provides links to various visual resources, such as charts and graphs, about *Roe v. Wade.*

**Visualizations** may be helpful to researchers in several ways. The graphs can illustrate which cases have been highly cited; they can also provide quick access to cases that may discuss similar areas of law. To explain Visualizations, we chose the link for **Very Large Abortion Network: Roe (1973) to Whole Woman's Health . . .** from the **Visualizations** feature. When you click the link, the first thing you will see is a chart (called a citation network), titled **Very Large Abortion Network: Roe (1973) to Whole Woman's Health (2016)** (see Figure 6.21). This chart shows the

**Figure 6.20** A case page on CourtListener. Screenshot from CourtListener used with permission.

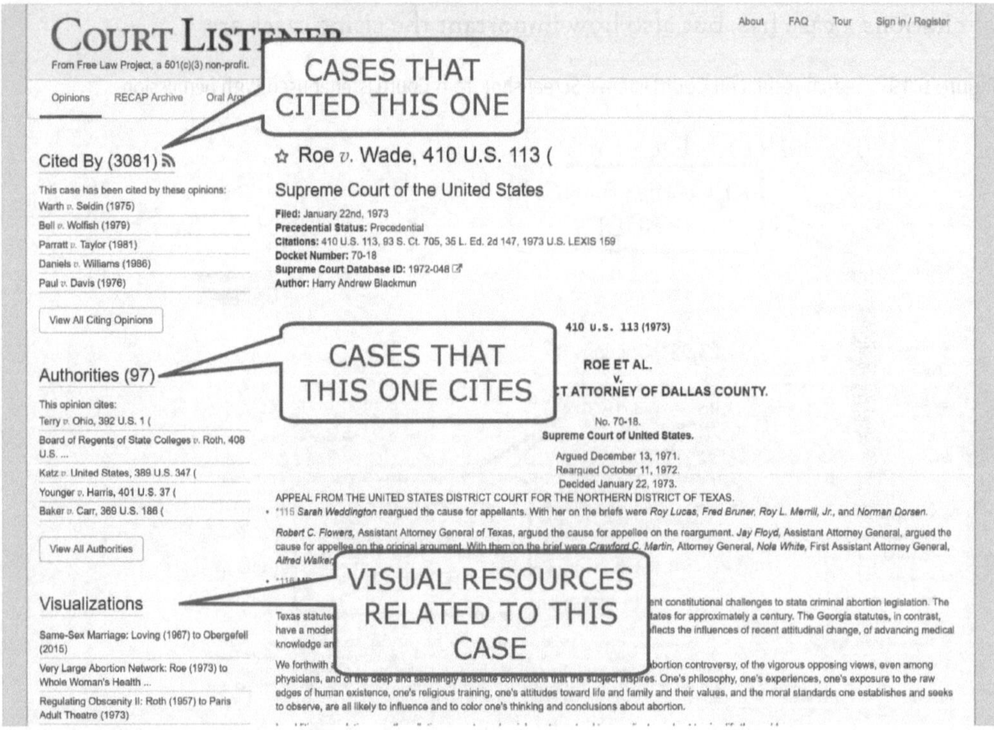


citation relationship between *Roe* and *Whole Woman's Health*. You will notice a large purple circle placed beside both of these cases. The purple circles indicate that *Roe* and *Whole Woman's Health* are separated by one degree (i.e., *Whole Woman's Health* directly cites *Roe*). A red circle beside a case indicates two degrees of separation between *Roe* and *Whole Woman's Health*—e.g., *Whole Woman's Health* cites *Harris* (which has a red circle), and *Harris* cites *Roe*. A green circle indicates three degrees of separation between *Roe* and *Whole Woman's Health*. (CourtListener does not provide analysis for more than three degrees of separation.)

If you scroll down the page (Figure 6.21), you can use drop-down menus to reorganize the chart, based on three types of criteria: **Chart Type, Timeline Spacing,** and **Degrees of Separation.** Below the three drop-down menus are the following tabs (shown in Figure 6.21):

- **Description:** This tab provides any description or notes about this citation network from its creator. (If the creator did not write a description, there will be a notation under the tab indicating that.)
- **Cases:** This tab lists all cases in this citation network, along with information about the cases. Case information includes a link to each case's Supreme Court Database (**SCDB**) entry on the Washington University Law website

**Figure 6.21** A citation network chart on CourtListener visualizes citation relationships between cases. Screenshot from CourtListener used with permission.

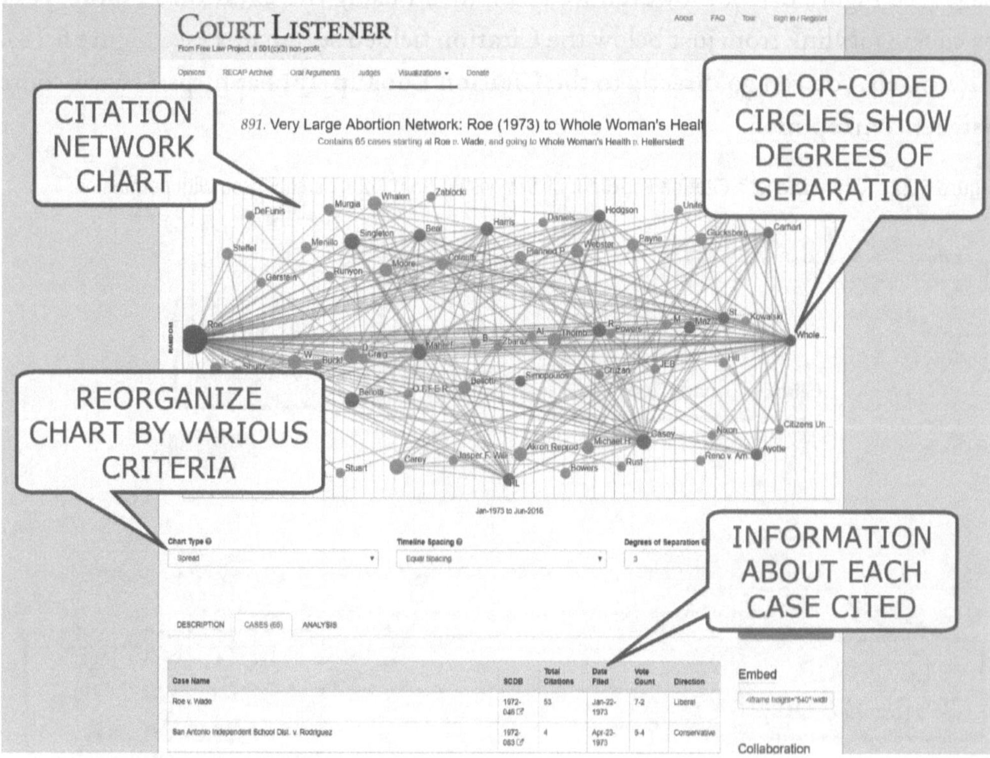


(http://scdb.wustl.edu), its **Date Filed, Total Citations** within this citation network, **Vote Count, Direction** (Liberal or Conservative), and a link to the full text of the case on CourtListener.

- **Analysis:** This tab takes you to a **Degree of Dissent** graph. As explained by CourtListener, "We use Degree of Dissent (DoD) in our visualizations of Supreme Court networks to indicate the average level of disagreement in the cases shown. For example, in a network that shows two cases, each with unanimous 9-0 votes, there would be no dissent, and so the score would be 0. By contrast, if a network had only two cases, each with 5-4 decisions, the DoD would be 1.0, indicating a highly dissenting network. Mathematically, the DoD for a given case is calculated by multiplying the number of dissents by 0.25. This means that a 9-0 case will have the same DoD as a 8-0 case (0.0) and a 6-3 will have the same DoD as 5-3 case" (https://www.courtlistener.com/faq/#dod).

Earlier, we said we'd discuss how to find an opinion on CourtListener by citation and also provide a caveat about citation searching, so let's look at that now. You can find an opinion by citation on CourtListener in two main ways. You can enter a citation into the **Citation** fielded search box on the **Advanced Opinion Search** page (see Figure 6.18). However, we recommend using the **Citation Lookup Tool** by clicking its link from just below the **Citation** fielded search box (see Figure 6.18). Alternately, you can go directly to the **Citation Lookup Tool** at https://www.courtlistener.com/opinion.

**Figure 6.22** CourtListener's Citation Lookup Tool. Screenshot from CourtListener used with permission.

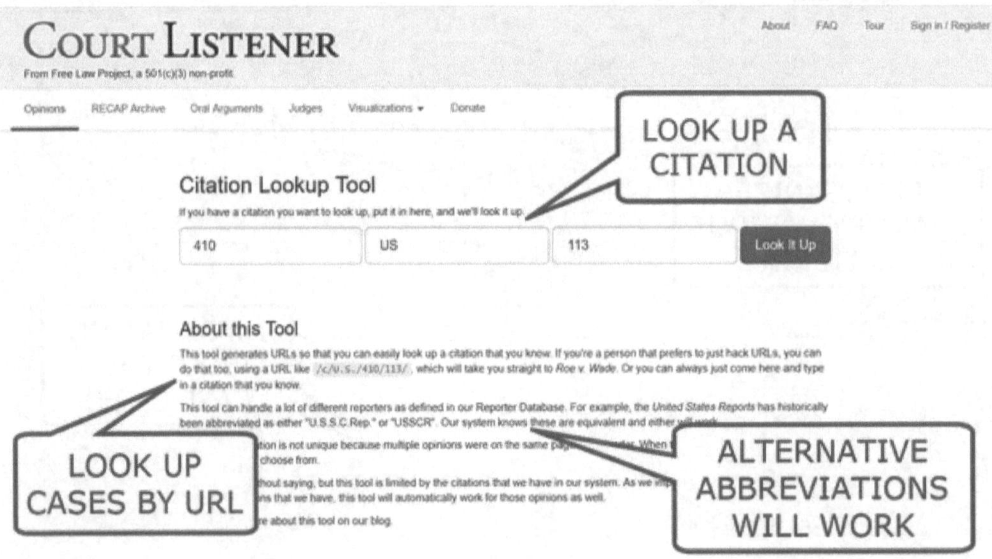


The caveat is that although each option allows you to enter official or unofficial citations, such as: *558 U.S. 310* or *130 S. Ct. 876* or *175 L. Ed. 2d 753* or *2010 U.S. LEXIS 766*, only the **Citation Lookup Tool** allows you to search by alternative reporter names and abbreviations. That's why we recommend using it instead of the **Citation** fielded search box on the **Advanced Opinion Search** page. For example, to search the U.S. Reports at the **Citation Lookup Tool** page, you can use any of these abbreviations: *US, U.S., U.S.S.C.Rep*, or *USSCR*. Thus, when we searched for *410 US 113* with the **Citation Lookup Tool** (see Figure 6.22), the search worked. But it did not work when we entered the same search into the **Citation** fielded search box on the **Advanced Opinion Search** page; only *410 U.S. 113* (with periods after U and S) worked.

Those who are more technologically inclined can also retrieve a case from CourtListener's site by entering a citation in URL format directly into the browser bar. There's no need to even be on CourtListener's site. To retrieve a case this way, type the URL in this format:

*https://www.courtlistener.com/c/**REPORTER/VOLUME/PAGE.***

So, if you wanted to read *Citizen's United v. Federal Elections Commission,* 558 U.S. 310, enter this into your browser bar:

*https://www.courtlistener.com/c/**U.S.S.C.Rep./558/310***

(For more details about the **Citation Lookup Tool**, see http://bit.ly/CourtListenerCitation.)

## CASETEXT

Casetext (https://casetext.com) is a relative newcomer to the online legal research community. Created by two lawyers who believed the legal publishing market was overpriced, Casetext provides free access to most federal primary law (federal cases, statutes, and regulations), as well as many state resources. In addition, Casetext is known for fostering a community of attorneys who add analyses to Casetext's primary law resources. Although you can search Casetext for free, you must set up a free account to see the full text of your results (see Figure 6.23). Casetext has a paid feature called CARA (Case Analysis Research Assistant), an AI (artificial intelligence)-assisted resource that can find cases related to a brief or other legal document but that are not cited in it. We will focus on Casetext's free features, however.

Casetext has extensive coverage of most U.S. case law. All U.S. Supreme Court opinions are available, along with federal Circuit and District Court opinions from 1925–present. In addition, unpublished District Court opinions from 2000–present and several other federal courts are available. State supreme court and appellate court opinions are available back to at least 1950, and earlier for some jurisdictions. Many state trial court opinions are available, as well. Casetext also provides federal statutes and regulations, and statutes for the states of California, Delaware, Florida, New Jersey, and New York.

To create a free Casetext account, click the **Sign In** link in the upper right corner of the homepage (see callout #1 in Figure 6.23). A pop-up will appear, where you can sign in to an existing account or create a new free account with the **Sign up** link (see callout #2 in Figure 6.23). (The **Free Trial** link next to the Sign In link lets you sign up for a 14-day trial of Casetext's paid features.)

**Figure 6.23** Casetext homepage with pop-up box where you can sign in or create a free account. Screenshot from Casetext used with permission.

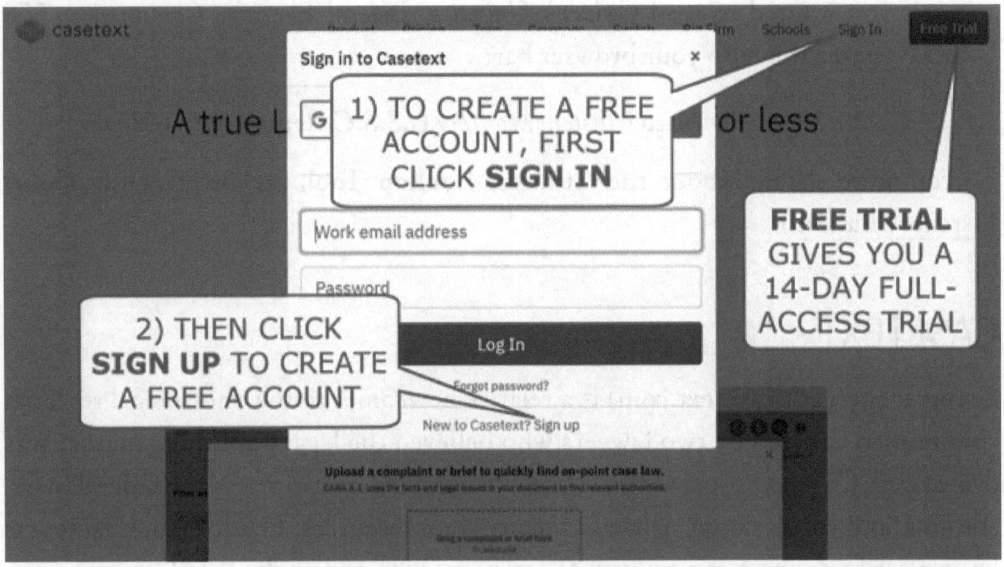


**Figure 6.24** Casetext homepage with Search Techniques menu. Screenshot from Casetext used with permission.

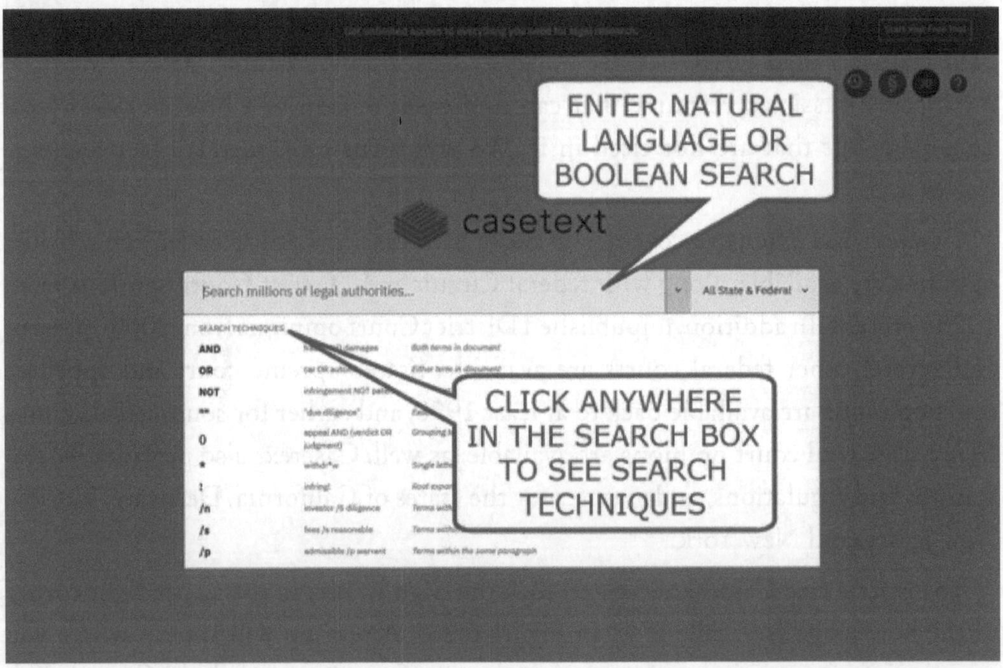


Once you have created your free account, sign in and go to the homepage (https://casetext.com). On the homepage, clicking anywhere in the search box causes a drop-down menu to appear below the search box (see Figure 6.24). The menu indicates the keyword search features that are available. Casetext's search features include:

- Boolean AND, OR, and NOT.
- Proximity connectors /n (n=number of words between terms); /s to find terms in the same sentence; and /p to find terms in the same paragraph.
- Quotation marks to retrieve an exact match for phrases.
- Parentheses to group search terms and their connectors.
- Wildcards—the asterisk (*) substitutes for one letter of a word, and the exclamation point (!) substitutes for one or more letters at the end of a word.

**Figure 6.25** Casetext search results. Screenshot from Casetext used with permission.

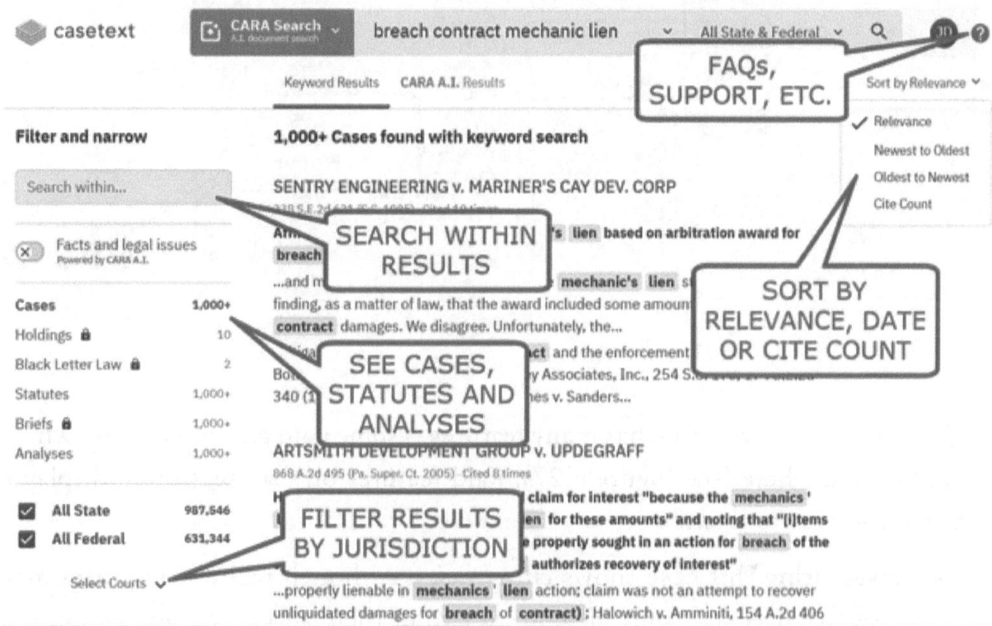


After typing your search terms, click the **Keyword Search** button, which appears after you begin typing, to run your search. (The CARA Search button only works if you have a free trial or have paid for full access.) After you enter your search terms (our example used *breach contract mechanic lien*), you will get a results list of all relevant cases (see Figure 6.25). Casetext has a robust jurisdiction filter that allows you to choose from any, multiple, or all of the courts that it covers. To filter search results by jurisdiction, click the **Select Courts** link in the left column of the page, as shown in Figure 6.25. You will then see a menu of all jurisdictions (see Figure 6.26). Click each jurisdiction you want to include in your search results, and then click **Apply Jurisdictions** to see the filtered results. You can also pre-filter by jurisdiction by clicking the (default) **All State & Federal** link to the right of the search box (see Figure 6.24). You will then be taken to the same menu of jurisdictions (see Figure 6.26). After selecting the courts you want, click **Apply Jurisdictions** to return to the homepage.

**Figure 6.26** Casetext jurisdiction filter. Screenshot from Casetext used with permission.

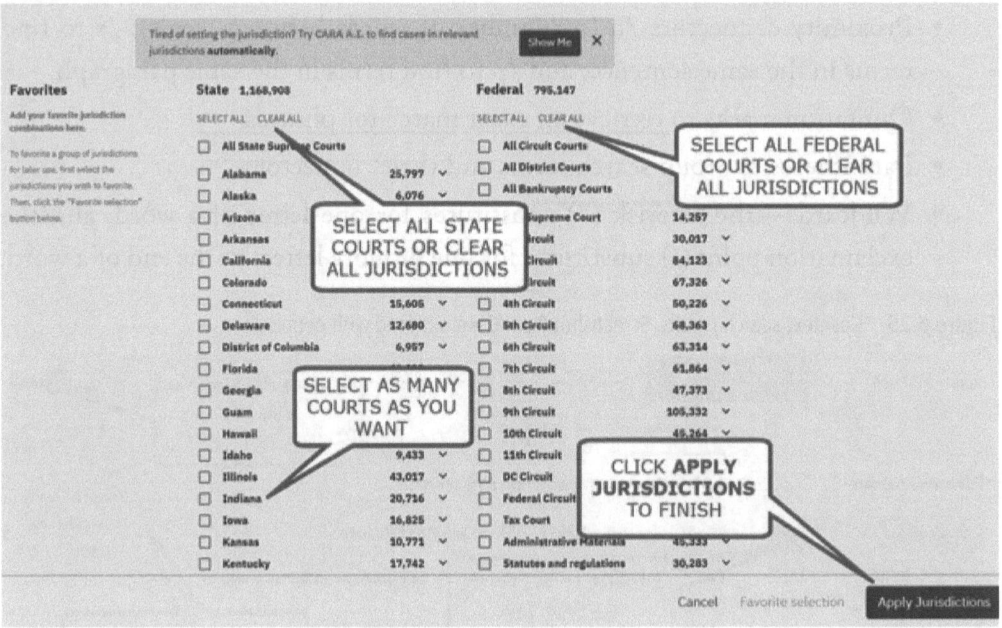


Casetext's case view screen has many features—some paid and some free—which we will describe here (see Figure 6.27). Paid features on Casetext often display a padlock icon next to them.

- **Cases citing this case** shows citing cases. Although many citing cases may exist, free users can only view up to two of them (if two citing cases exist). Viewing all citing cases or using the citator feature requires a paid subscription. This limitation makes Casetext less useful to free users because a case that you cannot see could potentially reverse or overrule your case.
- **Summaries** appear below the case title. Summaries are passages from newer cases that cite and summarize the case you are reading. Although many Summaries may be available to paid subscribers, free users (who have created a free account) can view one Summary and click a link to the citing (summarizing) case.
- **Attorney Analyses** are case annotations written by law firms and attorneys. If any Analyses for your case exist, they will appear above the case name, next to the **Read** link.

Figure 6.27 Casetext case view page. Screenshot from Casetext used with permission.

- **Hyperlinked citations** within opinions (not shown in Figure 6.27) appear in blue text and let you jump directly to other primary law (including federal statutes) in Casetext's database.

As noted earlier, several resources on the case page (shown in Figure 6.27) are only available to paid subscribers. Examples of paid resources include the downloading, printing, and citator features. In the top center of the screen, above the case name, are links for Citing Briefs and Citing Cases. Small padlock icons indicate that these are paid features. If you click any paid-feature links, you will usually receive a pop-up asking if you want to pay for full access. (Our tests indicated that the padlock icon and pop-up may not be used consistently throughout the site, however. If you repeatedly click a link that appears to be free, but nothing happens, it may be a paid feature that is not labeled as such.) If a more recent case has summarized the case you are reading, you can view a case summary written by a judge, below the case title. Although non-subscribers can read that one summary for free, if any more are available, you need a paid subscription to access them.

## THE PUBLIC LIBRARY OF LAW (PLOL)

**PLoL** (http://www.plol.org) is a free, full-text keyword-searchable database of cases provided by Fastcase (see Chapter 9 on Fastcase), but PLoL only includes a limited number of courts and a limited range of dates. To search more courts and date ranges, PLoL includes a link to the paid content found at the Fastcase database. Before paying for Fastcase, see Chapter 9 to learn if your state provides Fastcase as a free "member benefit" and also see Chapter 3's discussion of the free Fastcase mobile app. PLoL requires registration (including a telephone number) to view the full text of cases from these courts:

- All fifty states' (and Guam's) appellate and supreme court cases from 1997 to present
- All U.S. Supreme Court cases from 1754 to present
- All federal Circuit Courts of Appeals cases from 1950 to present (except for the 11th Circuit, which provides cases from 1981 to present, and the Federal Circuit, which provides cases from 1982 to present)

The PLoL case law database does not include federal district cases, federal bankruptcy cases, or any non-case-law legal materials. Sometimes, a notation appears at the top of the search results that indicates the number of additional results available to Fastcase subscribers.

To search case law, select the **Case Law** tab at the top of the page, and enter a citation, docket number, party name, or keywords and phrases into the search box. This will search all jurisdictions for which PLoL has cases. Choose the **Advanced Options** link (just under the main search box) to limit your search by a date range (month/year), a specific state's case law, a specific federal circuit, or the U.S. Supreme Court. (You can leave the court search boxes blank to search all courts included in the PLoL database.) PLoL only allows researchers to select one jurisdiction or all jurisdictions. Searches can include Boolean connectors (*AND, OR, NOT*), phrase searching, wildcard characters (the asterisk to search words beginning with the same stem, as in *employ**), and proximity connectors (*w/#* to indicate a word within a certain number of words of another word).

Although there are tabs to the right of the **Case Law** tab (**Statutes, Regulations, Court Rules, Constitutions,** and **Legal Forms**), they only link to the official government websites where you can search those materials. When we checked these links, we found that many of them are out of date or do not work.

# JUSTIA

## U.S. Supreme Court Online Case Law Database

Justia's U.S. Supreme Court Center database can be reached either by clicking the **Supreme Court Center** link found near the bottom of Justia's homepage (https://www.justia.com) or by using this URL: https://supreme.justia.com. The database coverage reaches back to Volume 1 of the U.S. Reports (1791).

**Figure 6.28** Justia's U.S. Supreme Court Center allows you to browse opinions by year. Screenshot from Justia used with permission.

To full-text search, enter keywords or phrases into the search box at the top right-hand side of the page (see Figure 6.28) and connect them with Boolean connectors. Justia's search protocols are the same as Google's. Even though it's not apparent, you can also enter a citation (e.g., *1 U.S. 1*) or a party name into the full-text search box. You can also browse by **Year** (see Figure 6.28). Justia had traditionally allowed users to search by court, via a drop-down menu next to the search box. That feature has been removed, however, so you now must search the entire site and then browse all results to locate the cases you want.

Justia also offers free subscriptions to case opinion summary newsletters for the U.S. Supreme Court and other U.S. appellate and state courts. You will need to create a free Justia account and subscribe (http://law.justia.com/subscriptions) to select the free newsletters you wish to receive. You can also follow Justia on several social media sites.

For databases that offer additional free U.S. Supreme Court resources, such as audio files of both the oral arguments and opinion announcements, see **Oyez** (https://www.oyez.org). Also see Chapter 15, Dockets and Case Documents, for additional discussion on U.S. Supreme Court resources, including oral argument transcripts.

## Justia Federal and State Courts' Online Case Law Database

You can browse federal and state court cases on Justia at https://law.justia.com/cases. Here you first select the court you want, then the year, and then browse the cases in reverse chronological order. Dates of coverage vary by court.

Justia also provides links to the official sites of all federal and state courts at https://www.justia.com/courts. After choosing a federal or state court, you will be taken to the official website for that court. Most of the court sites will have a link to opinions on the homepage, either in a side bar, or in a row of tabs near the top of the screen. Each court's site is different, however, so to search or browse opinions you may have to search for the link.

As with any case law research, be sure to cite check your cases before filing a brief. (See Chapter 18, Cite-Checking Cases, for information on free cite checking sites.)

# Chapter 7

## FREE GOVERNMENTAL ONLINE CASE LAW DATABASES

This chapter will focus on two governmental websites that provide free online case law databases. We will also discuss a stand-alone, free case-law database for California cases found at the California Court's official site but supplied by LexisNexis. Free non-government-affiliated online case law databases are discussed in Chapter 6. Other online case law databases, such as those that are available for free as a member benefit through certain bar associations, will be discussed in Chapters 8 and 9.

All of the free, governmental case law databases have some sort of limitation, such as limited ranges of dates, limited court coverage, no search option (just browsing), or limited documentation. Although governmental databases have high reliability, we recommend using member-benefit databases (Casemaker, Fastcase, or others) because they usually offer more sophisticated searching. Regardless of which database you use, probably none of them is 100 percent reliable, so it is imperative that researchers cite check their cases (see Chapter 18, Cite-Checking Cases).

## GOVINFO UNITED STATES COURTS OPINIONS COLLECTION

As we discussed in Chapter 5, the Government Publishing Office (GPO) retired FDsys at the end of 2018 and replaced it with a new source for federal government documents, called **govinfo** (https://www.govinfo.gov). All documents that were available on FDsys are available on govinfo, including the U.S. Courts Opinions collection.

Originally, court opinions were not included in FDsys, but in a project that began in 2011, several courts' opinions from the U.S. appellate, district, and bankruptcy courts (going back to April 2004) have been added. This project, operated jointly by the U.S. Government Printing Office (GPO) and the Administrative Office of the United States Courts (AOUSC), is meant "to provide public access to opinions from selected United States appellate, district, and bankruptcy courts" (http://bit.ly/AboutUSCtsOpinions). The project now includes over 130 courts (appellate courts, district courts, bankruptcy courts, and the United States Court of International Trade).

**CAVEAT:** Although the GPO continues to expand the U.S. Courts Opinions collection, at the time of this book's publication, the collection still lacks many courts and years of coverage. We therefore recommend that you check the coverage of this collection before using it; if it still has significant gaps, we suggest you choose one of the case law databases described in Chapters 6, 8, or 9. The collection currently includes these courts:

UNITED STATES COURTS OF APPEALS:

- First through Eleventh, D.C., and Federal Circuits.

UNITED STATES DISTRICT COURTS:

- Over fifty district and territorial courts, including federal district courts from thirty-eight states and the District of Columbia, and territorial courts from Guam, Puerto Rico, and the U.S. Virgin Islands.

BANKRUPTCY COURTS:

- Over sixty courts from thirty-five states and the District of Columbia.

NATIONAL COURT:

- The United States Court of International Trade.

Court opinions are searched in the same way any other govinfo Collection is searched, except that some of the search fields are unique to court opinions, such as the party name and docket search fields. Figure 7.1 shows an **Advanced Search** (https://www.govinfo.gov/#advanced) in the United States Courts Opinions Collection.

**Figure 7.1** Searching U.S. Courts Opinions with govinfo's Advanced Search page.

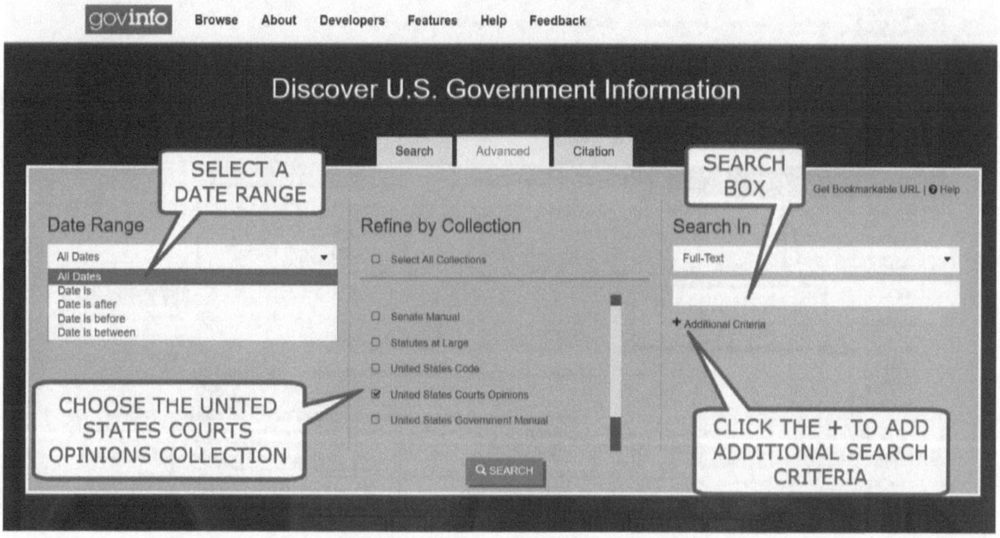


To search U.S. Courts Opinions, first select a **Date Range** in the left column or leave the default setting (All Dates). Next, in the center column, titled **Refine by Collection**, choose the collection(s) to search—in this instance the United States Courts Opinions. Finally, in the right-hand column, **Search In**, choose which criteria to search. The default criterion is Full-Text. You can use the drop-down menu to select a different criterion, or add additional search criteria by using the plus (+) link under the search box. An example of search results is shown in Figure 7.2.

The results can be:

- Sorted by **Relevance, Date** (New to Old or Old to New), or **Alphabetically** (Z to A or A to Z).
- Re-sorted (see the left-side column) by **Collection, Date Published, Government Author, Organization, Person, Court Type** (District or Appellate), **Court Name, Circuit,** or **State.**
- Narrowed by clicking the **Search Within Results** checkbox under the search box and then entering one or more keywords into the search box to re-run the new keywords within the original search results.

For each result, you can click links to view a **PDF** of the opinion or see the **Details,** which consist of a two-tabbed page. The first tab is titled **Summary** and summarizes the case with information such as the SuDoc (Superintendent of Documents) Class Number, Court Type, Court Name, Circuit, Office Location, Case Type, and more. The second tab is called **Document in Context.** Although some of our tests returned

**Figure 7.2** U.S. Courts Opinions search results.

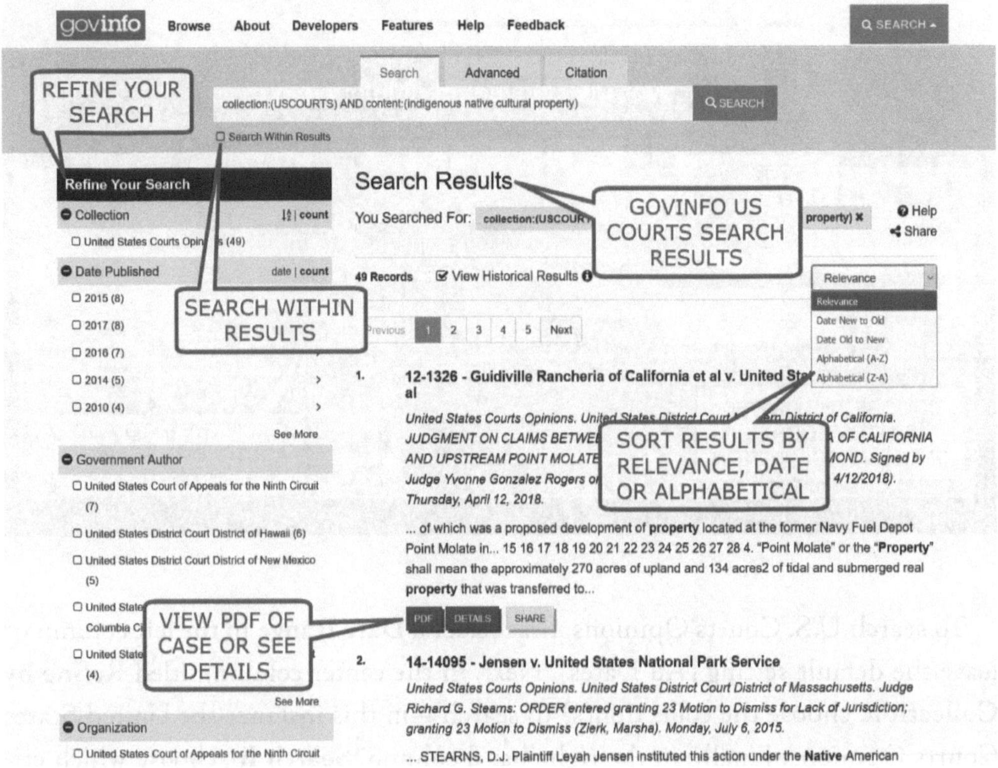


errors for this tab, when it works, it provides all other orders and opinions related to the case (the same information provided on the **More Information** page of the old FDsys system). Each result also has a third link titled **Share**, which you can use to share information via social media and other methods. (Note that you may have to disable anti-tracking software installed on your browser to get the **Share** link to work.)

## THE SUPREME COURT OF THE UNITED STATES

The **Supreme Court of the United States** provides a website (http://www.supremecourt.gov) that may be helpful for some legal researchers. Although this site may not always be the best choice for finding Supreme Court opinions, we will briefly describe it here because it provides useful resources and information (and because govinfo does not provide a searchable database of Supreme Court opinions). See Chapters 6, 8, and 9 for other free websites that have better search options and date coverage for Supreme Court opinions. Opinions are typically available on the site within five minutes of being released from the Bench. Older opinions date back only to the 1991 Term, however, so this site may be more useful for researching recent Supreme Court opinions than older ones.

The Supreme Court website's homepage has a full-text keyword search box in the upper right corner. This search box searches the entire website, including court opinions (which are in PDF format). To search only court opinions, use the **Advanced Search** feature. First click the **Advanced Search** link to the right of the search box (see Figure 7.3), and then select the checkbox next to **Opinions** near the bottom of the Advanced Search page. (The Advanced Search page also allows you choose from any or all of several other categories, such as Court Orders, Rules of the Court, and Argument Transcripts, among others.)

**Figure 7.3** The United States Supreme Court homepage.

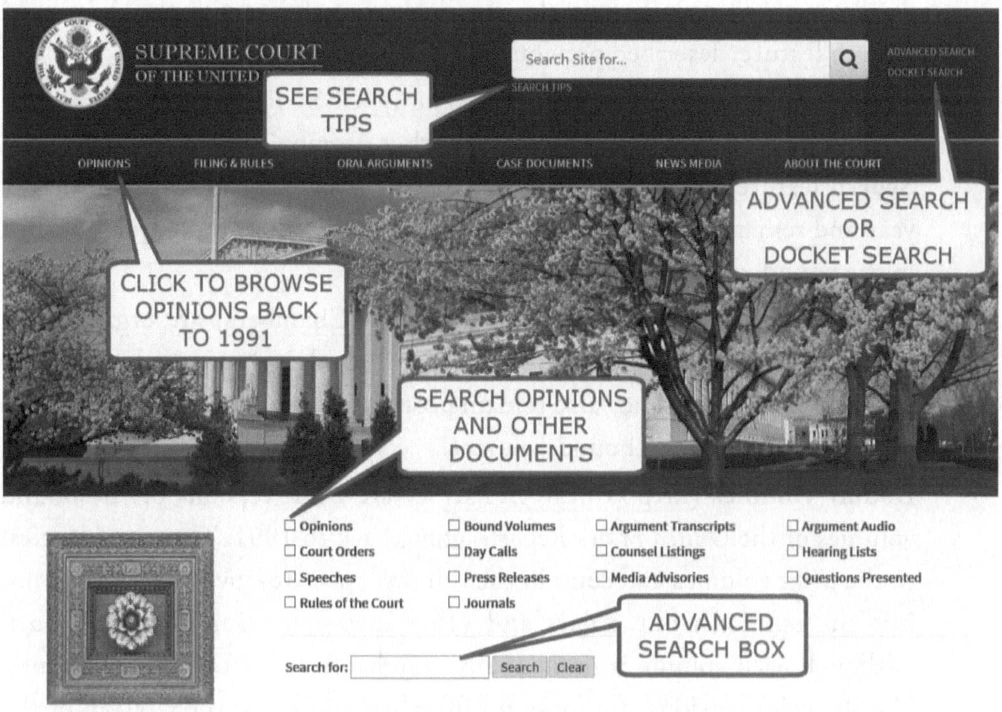


A **Search Tips** link below the main search box takes you to a page (http://bit.ly/USSCTips) that explains the site's search function. The search function recognizes the Boolean operators *AND, OR, NEAR* (within fifty words), and *NOT* (to exclude a term). You can put exact phrases in quotation marks, and you can use parentheses to create more sophisticated searches. For example, searching for *(supreme NEAR court) AND (miranda NEAR warning)* would require *supreme* to appear near *court* and *miranda* to appear near *warning,* but it would not require that all four words appear near each other. An asterisk (*) acts as a wildcard for letters at the end of a word; so searching *justi** would search for *justice, justify, justification,* etc. Searches are not case-sensitive, even when words are put inside quotation marks. (Remember that your search terms can also include the name of a party, an attorney, or a judge.)

On the **Opinions** page (http://bit.ly/USSCOpinions), a menu in the left column provides links to several opinion-related pages for the U.S. Supreme Court:

- **Opinions of the Court** (http://bit.ly/USSCSlip) allows you to browse PDF versions of Supreme Court slip opinions. These opinions are organized in reverse chronological order by year. Slip opinions remain posted on the site until the opinions for the entire term are published in bound volumes of the *United States Reports*—usually about five or six years. (You can also keyword search all opinions on the site, including these, with the **Advanced Search** feature, described previously in this section.)
- **Opinions Relating to Orders** (http://bit.ly/USSCRelatingOrders) can be browsed (and keyword searched with other opinions, using the **Advanced Search** feature). They are also organized in reverse chronological order by year and remain posted until the opinions for the entire term are published in the bound volumes.
- **In-Chambers Opinions** (http://bit.ly/USSCChambers) are organized in reverse chronological order and can be browsed and searched like other opinions on the site. They also remain posted until the entire term's opinions have been published in bound volumes.
- **Bound Volumes** (http://bit.ly/2HjxfNe) are PDF versions of the bound volumes of the *United States Reports,* going back to 1991. They are identical to the print volumes and contain the full text cover-to-cover—including not just the opinions, but orders and other materials issued by the Court. Although each volume is individually searchable as a PDF, these volumes, like the print versions, are more useful when you know the citation of the case you want. The Bound Volumes are included when you conduct an **Opinions** keyword search using the site's **Advanced Search** feature.
- **Internet Sources Cited in Opinions** (http://bit.ly/USSCCitedURLs) provides links to online sources (such as reports, press releases, web pages, etc.) cited in U.S. Supreme Court opinions going back to 2005. The sources are arranged in reverse chronological order by year.
- **Media Resources** (http://bit.ly/USSCMedia) provides links to media files (video or audio files from a lower court record, for example) to which U.S.

Supreme Court opinions cite. Links to these files, which go back to 2006, are in reverse chronological order.

- **Case Citation Finder** (http://bit.ly/USSCCasefinder) allows you to enter terms into a search box to find the citation for any signed, *per curiam*, or in-chambers Supreme Court opinion that is published or will be published soon in the *United States Reports*. This resource goes back farther in time than the rest of the site, but it only searches the citation information (including party names), not the full text of the opinion. Likewise, its search results only include citation information. Once you have the full citation, however, you can use it to look up the full text of the case, either on this site (if the case is from 1991 to the present), or from one of the other sources discussed in this book, such as Google Scholar (Chapter 6) or Cornell's LII (Chapter 5). To use the Case Citation Finder, enter any information you know from the citation, such as a party name. The default connector for Case Citation Finder is the Boolean *OR*. You can use *AND* as a Boolean connector (by typing it in) and enclose phrases in quotation marks to make your query more specific. A drop-down menu allows you to sort your results by **Volume number**, or alphabetically by **Petitioner**, or **Respondent** (see Figure 7.4).

**Figure 7.4** U.S. Supreme Court's Case Citation Search Results.

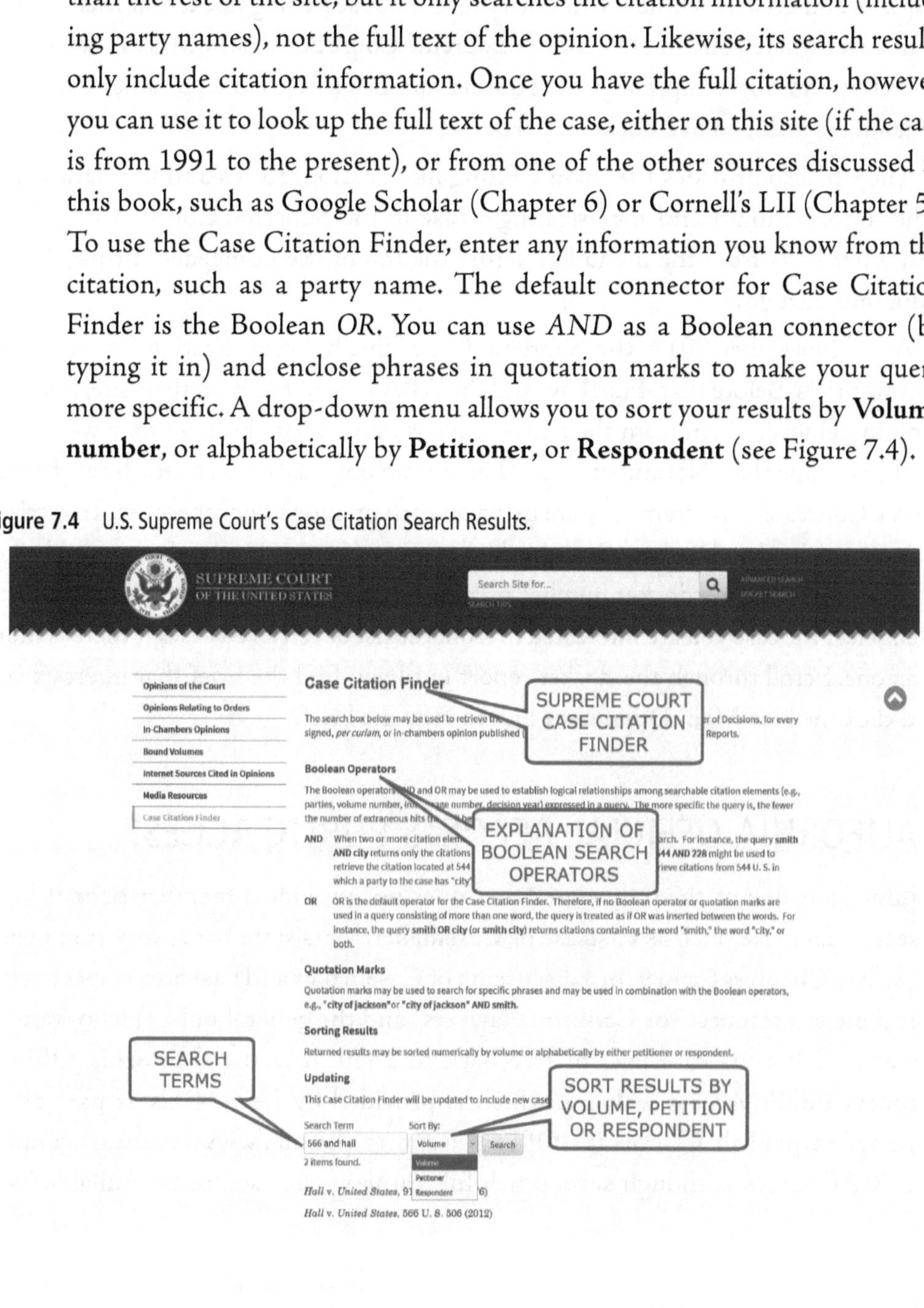

## Additional Resources on the U.S. Supreme Court Website

The Supreme Court website provides additional resources that may be useful to some researchers. A **Docket Search** link appears below the Advanced Search link beside the main search box. This docket database (http://bit.ly/USSCDocket) contains complete information regarding the status of cases filed since the beginning of the 2001 Term. (See "U.S. Supreme Court Dockets and Case Documents" in Chapter 15, Dockets and Case Documents, to learn more about searching dockets at this site and to discover where you can obtain older Supreme Court dockets.) Users can search the docket by entering a Supreme Court docket number, a case name, or other keywords or numbers included in a docket report.

The site also provides **Electronic Filing** information, **Rules and Guidance**, and other information useful for litigating a case in the Supreme Court. Access these and other links from the menu bar across the top of the homepage (https://www.supremecourt.gov).

As of November 2017, the Supreme Court finally began hosting its merit and amicus briefs. Before that, **FindLaw** and the **ABA** hosted them on their site, but they recently removed them from their sites. This is unfortunate because they went back further in time than November 2017. There is no obvious access to the briefs hosted on the Court's site. Instead, they are listed on each opinion's docket report. To retrieve a brief, visit the **Docket Search** page (https://www.supremecourt.gov/docket/docket.aspx), enter a docket number or a case name into the docket search box, and then select the case you are interested in from the list of retrieved cases if there is more than one. Scroll through the docket report until you find the brief that interests you and click the blue **Main Document** link to view the brief.

# CALIFORNIA OFFICIAL REPORTS PUBLIC ACCESS

California is one of the only states that does not provide a member-benefit legal research database, such as Fastcase or Casemaker, to its state bar association members. (See Chapters 8 and 9 for a discussion of Casemaker and Fastcase, respectively.) But there is a resource for California lawyers (and the general public) who want to research California case law for free back to 1850. It is the **California Official Reports Public Access website**, which is provided by LexisNexis as part of its contract to publish California's Official Reports (http://www.lexisnexis.com/clients/CACourts). Although several helpful features that used to be available have been removed (including the option to search unpublished opinions), the site is still a good resource because of its sophisticated search functions and depth of coverage. At the time of this book's publication, California appears to be the only state with a case law database of this nature provided by LexisNexis. Check your state court's official site to find out if another vendor provides a similar free database for your state.

You do not need to be a member of the California State Bar to use the site, but you must agree to the terms and conditions of use by checking a box and clicking the **Begin Searching Opinions** link. This link goes to the search page (see Figure 7.5) where users can search **CA Supreme Court Cases from 1850** and **California Court of Appeals Cases** together or separately. Two radio buttons appear below the search box. The default selection is **Search all sources on this page.** If you select the other one—**Select sources to search**—you can select **CA Supreme Court Cases from 1850** or **California Court of Appeals Cases,** or both. Begin by typing your research issue into the search box using keywords, phrases, lists, Boolean search terms, or a "natural language" sentence—e.g., *Where can I find cases about "negligence per se" and also products or goods?*

**Figure 7.5** California Courts search page.

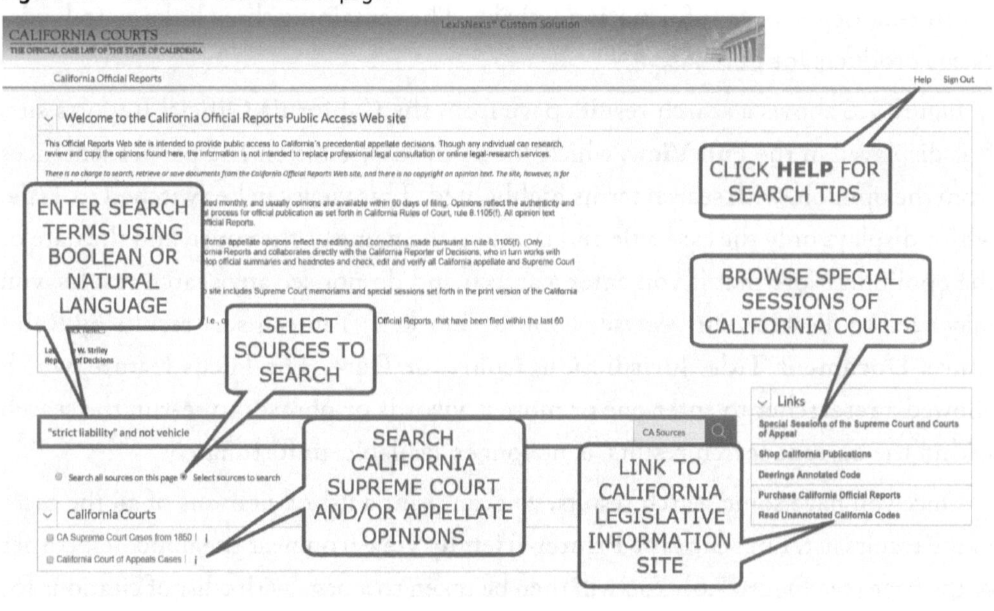


LexisNexis provides a search **Help** link in the upper right corner of the search page (see Figure 7.5). Although the Help link leads to some useful tips for searching

LexisNexis databases, we will give an overview here because this site provides for more complex Boolean searching than most free sites.

The Boolean searching on this website functions similarly to Terms and Connectors searching on the pay LexisNexis databases. The basic connectors *and*, *or*, and *and not* are available, as are several proximity connectors, such as *w/n* (within *n* words of the next word or phrase), *w/s* (within the same sentence as), *w/p* (within the same paragraph as), and *w/seg* (within the same segment as). *And not* can also be combined with the proximity connectors for even more advanced searching. In addition, several search commands, such as *atleast*, *allcaps*, *caps*, *nocaps*, *plural*, and *singular* are available to researchers, as are the wildcard symbols (*!* for multiple characters and * for a single character). The Boolean and proximity connectors and the search commands are case insensitive. Note that it is always a good idea to put phrases in quotation marks to ensure the search engine recognizes the words as a phrase. Figure 7.5 shows an example of a Boolean search.

Besides the search feature, the search page of the California Courts site also provides a list of **Links** in the lower right-hand corner (see Figure 7.5). The first link in the list allows you to browse documents from **Special Sessions of the Supreme Court and Courts of Appeal** for California. The bottom link goes to the official **California Legislative Information** website. The remaining three links go to LexisNexis products for purchase.

Figure 7.6 shows a search results page from the California Official Reports site. It is displayed in the **Full View**, which shows the case citation and partial sentences from the opinion, with search terms highlighted. This view can be switched to **Title**, which displays only the case title and citation, the name of the court, and the date of the opinion. (Note that if you enter a search and do not see any search results, you may need to disable your browser's pop-up blocker.) You can sort results by **Relevance**, **Document Title**, **Jurisdiction**, **Court**, or **Date**. The Focus feature, which allowed a researcher to enter one or more keywords or phrases to re-run the search within the current search results, is no longer available, unfortunately.

Once you have some search results, you can print a list of citations of all the cases in the results list. First click the **Printer-friendly view** icon near the upper left corner of the page (see Figure 7.6). You will then be taken to a page with a list of citations for your search results. Click the blue **Print** link in the upper right corner of the page, or use your browser's print function (CTRL or Command + P) to print the list.

The results page also has some features that do not appear to work. Each search result has a checkbox beside it, but checking the boxes doesn't accomplish anything.

If you check a box, a blue dropdown menu with the number of checked boxes appears above the upper left corner of the search results. When you click the menu, however, you receive a popup box with a list of the cases you selected and the words "In Plan -None-" next to each case.

**Figure 7.6** California Courts search results.

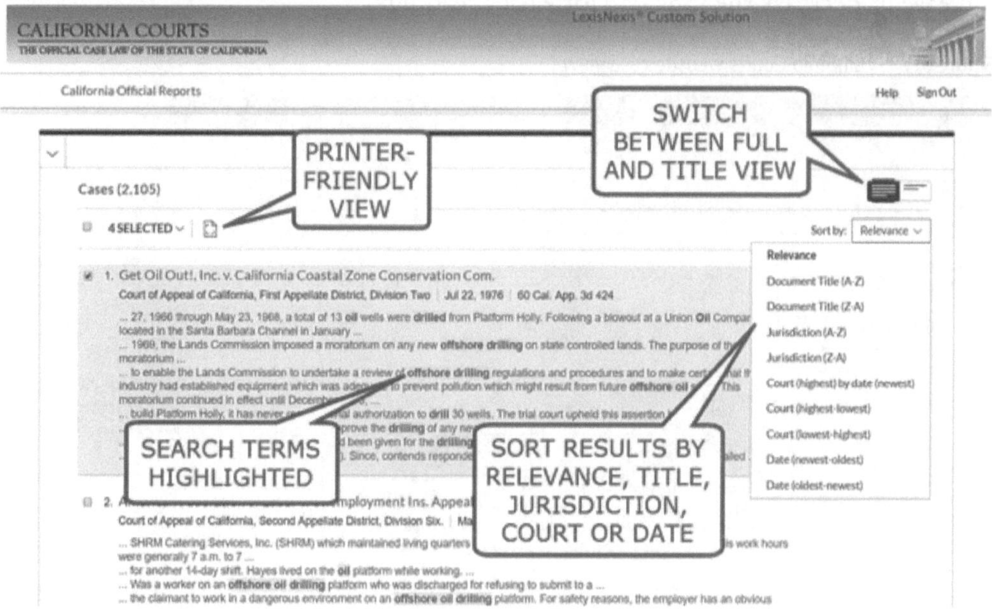


One of the most useful features of this or any free legal research site had been the color-coded Shepard's "treatment" flags that indicate how other cases have treated your case (e.g., positive, negative, etc., treatment). LexisNexis has removed that feature from this site, unfortunately. When you view a list of search results in the printer-friendly view, you may see a red symbol with a stylized "S" in it (see Figure 7.7). This indicates that a Shepard's report is available for the case. The icon itself does not link to anything, however, so if you want to see the Shepard's report, you will need a paid subscription to LexisNexis. (See Chapter 18 to learn how to cite check for free.)

When viewing an individual case, there are a few features to be aware of. First, underneath the case title is a **Copy Citation** link (see Figure 7.7). Clicking this link will allow you to copy and export the case's citation in the correct format for any of the fifty states, the ALWD Guide to Legal Citation (similar to Bluebook) or the "Standard" format (which also closely aligns with Bluebook format).

As with the official print reporters, cases viewed on this site contain the official headnotes (but not the LexisNexis headnotes). Like the search results list, individual cases are available in a printer-friendly format. Finally, the case view page has a **reading mode**; if you click the square icon with four arrows near the upper right corner of the page (see Figure 7.7), the view changes to a screen that allows you to increase or decrease the font size for easier reading.

**Figure 7.7** California Courts website case view.

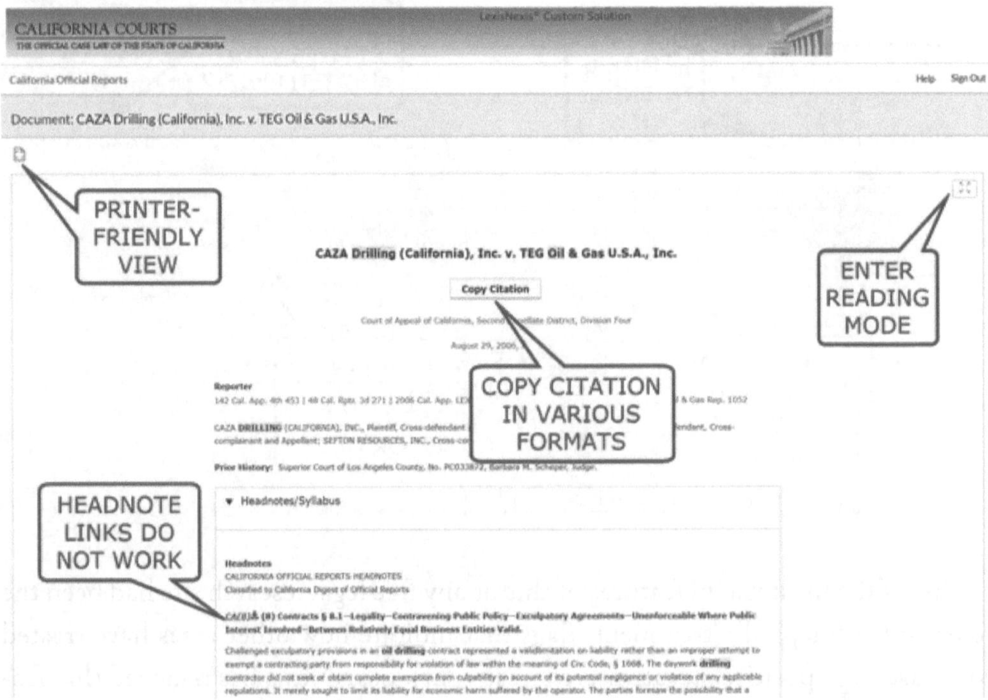


LexisNexis has removed many customizable printing features previously available for this website. You can still print the full text of a case, however. On the case view page, choose the **Printer-friendly** view by clicking the icon at the top left corner of the page (see Figure 7.7). It is identical to the standard view, except that a **Print** link that appears in the upper right corner of the page. The Print link does the same thing as using your browser's print function (CTRL or Command + P). To print anything else from this website, simply use your browser's print function.

**Important Note:** According to the California Courts website, the LexisNexis California database is updated monthly, and opinions are usually available within 60 days of filing. For those who prefer using LexisNexis's California database, it's important to use another free (or pay) database to update your research to ensure you do not miss any new cases. To cut down on retrieving cases already retrieved from the LexisNexis search, the Public Library of Law (http://www.plol.org) and CourtListener (https://www.courtlistener.com) are the better choices of the free databases (see Chapter 6), because they allow for a combined keyword and month/year/date range search. (Google Scholar's keyword search only offers a date range search by year.)

# Chapter 8

## AN INTRODUCTION TO CASEMAKER4

Casemaker4 is an online legal research system that many lawyers can access for free through their bar association memberships. If your bar does not offer Casemaker4 (or if you are a member of the public), you can subscribe to Casemaker4 for $60.00 monthly or $600.00 annually (http://bit.ly/cm4pubsubscribe). To add on its Citator products, the cost rises to $95.00 monthly or $950.00 annually (http://bit.ly/cm4subscribe).

**Casemaker** updated its entire platform and launched **Casemaker4** on June 5, 2019. The update includes a new interface (the "look and feel"), new features (e.g., **Alerts**), re-named features (e.g., **Data Types** are now called **Compilations**), improvements to some features (e.g., **Advanced Search** and **Search Within**), and new content (e.g., **Tribal** courts). We will explain how to use **Casemaker4** in this chapter. For those of you who used the earlier version of **Casemaker** and want to learn detailed information about the differences between **Casemaker** and **Casemaker4**, see Casemakers' "Overview of Casemaker 4 Enhancements" (http://bit.ly/cm4improve).

As of June 2019, a consortium of twenty-one state bars and seven city and county bar associations subscribe to Casemaker4. The State bars include Alabama, Alaska, Colorado, Connecticut, Idaho, Indiana, Kansas, Kentucky, Maine, Michigan, Nebraska, New Hampshire, North Dakota, Ohio, Pennsylvania, Rhode Island, Texas, Utah, Vermont, Washington, and Wyoming. City and county bars include five from New York (Erie County, Monroe County, New York City Bar, Oneida County, and Schenectady County); one from Massachusetts (Hampden County); and one from California (Santa Clara County). To see a current list, visit http://bit.ly/cm4members.

If your bar association is part of the consortium, visit your bar's website to access Casemaker4. The Casemaker4 link will either be on the homepage (e.g., the Alaska State Bar has placed it on the upper right-hand side of its homepage) or it might be hidden (e.g., the Alabama State Bar first has you click the *Membership* tab, then you click *Member Benefits*, and finally, you click *Casemaker*). Instead of clicking around the site, you can simply enter *Casemaker4* into the Bar's search box on its homepage. All subscribers have access to the mobile Casemaker4 App (see Chapter 3).

All law students have free access to Casemaker4 (http://www.casemakerx.com/).

## CASEMAKER4 CONTENT (COMPILATIONS)

Note that Casemaker4 calls content "**Compilations**." Casemaker4 includes a variety of current and archival state, District of Columbia, and federal legal primary and secondary content, and tribal court cases (see Figure 8.13). Also, Casemaker4 offers two citator products (free to consortium members) and several third-party products that require extra fees, which we'll detail in this chapter.

All Casemaker4 consortium members have access to all **Federal** and **Tribal** materials, but not necessarily to all state and District of Columbia compilations. If a state (or the District of Columbia) has added extra compilations (e.g., municipal codes) beyond Casemaker4's "core" compilations (state cases, statutes/codes, session laws, constitutions, court rules, and regulations), it varies from state to state whether you can search that state's additional compilations.

## SEARCHING CASEMAKER4

Casemaker4 offers many ways to search, and they all begin from the homepage. The first way to search is the "default" **All States, All Compilations** search, where you search all state compilations simultaneously (Figure 8.1). You can easily switch to other search types by clicking one of the tabs (e.g., **Federal**) in the left column (or by changing your **Start Page**, which we'll explain later).

**Figure 8.1** Casemaker's Homepage. Screenshot from Casemaker used with permission.

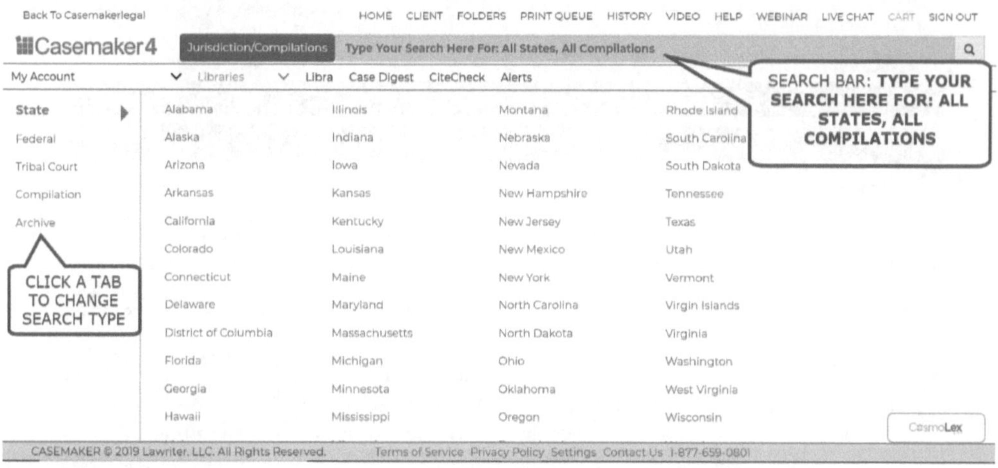


## Keyword Searching and Search Tips

If you are unfamiliar about how to construct a keyword search in **Casemaker4**, a **Search Tips** tab appears in a drop-down menu as soon as you place your cursor into the search bar (see Figure 8.2). Two other tabs, **Recent Searches** and **Advanced Search**, also appear, which we'll explain later.

**Figure 8.2** Select Search Tips Tab From Drop-Down Menu. Screenshot from Casemaker used with permission.

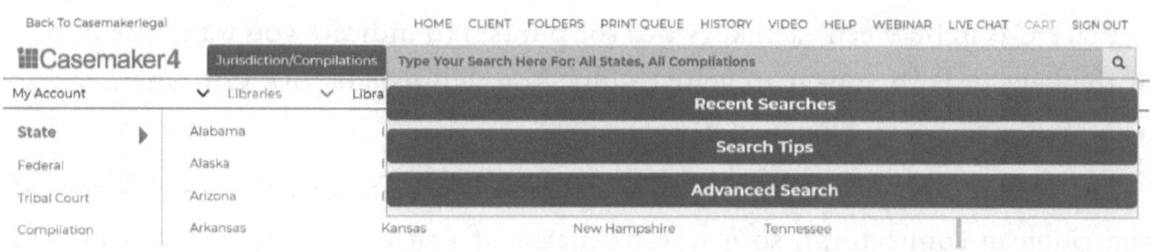


After you click **Search Tips** a **Search Types, Examples,** and **Results chart** is displayed (see Figure 8.3). The **Search Tips** work the same for most any of **Casemaker4**'s compilations.

The first three **Search Types** (**AND, OR, NOT**) should look familiar to you because they are the same Boolean connectors you use to connect your keywords at most pay legal research systems. For the **AND** search type, you don't actually type **AND** in between each keyword (or phrase) because it is the default every time you

**Figure 8.3** Search Tips Chart. Screenshot from Casemaker used with permission.

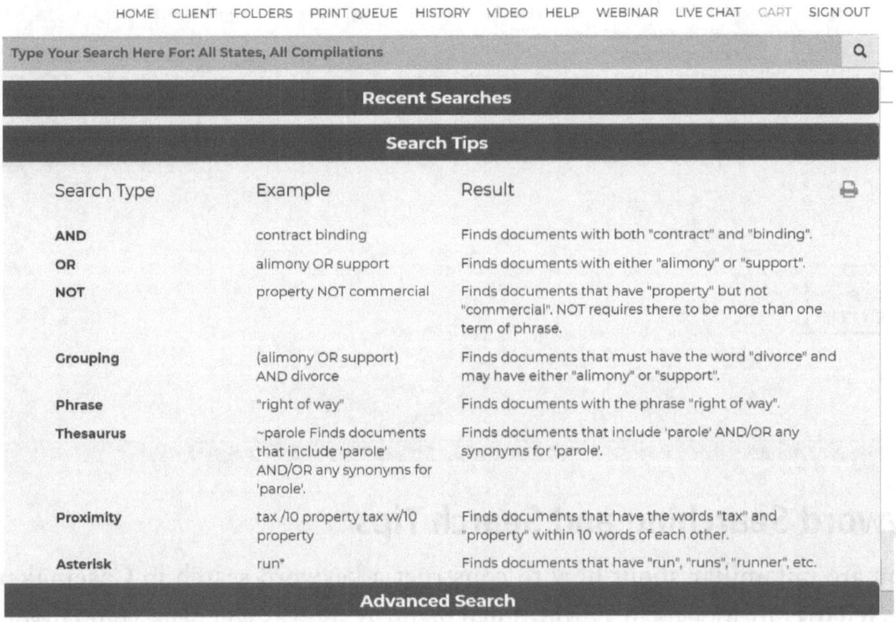


| Search Type | Example | Result |
|---|---|---|
| **AND** | contract binding | Finds documents with both "contract" and "binding". |
| **OR** | alimony OR support | Finds documents with either "alimony" or "support". |
| **NOT** | property NOT commercial | Finds documents that have "property" but not "commercial". NOT requires there to be more than one term of phrase. |
| **Grouping** | (alimony OR support) AND divorce | Finds documents that must have the word "divorce" and may have either "alimony" or "support". |
| **Phrase** | "right of way" | Finds documents with the phrase "right of way". |
| **Thesaurus** | ~parole Finds documents that include 'parole' AND/OR any synonyms for 'parole'. | Finds documents that include 'parole' AND/OR any synonyms for 'parole'. |
| **Proximity** | tax /10 property tax w/10 property | Finds documents that have the words "tax" and "property" within 10 words of each other. |
| **Asterisk** | run* | Finds documents that have "run", "runs", "runner", etc. |

leave a space between a keyword or phrase; an **AND** search indicates you want all the keywords or phrases to appear in your results.

Place **OR** in between each keyword (or phrase) to indicate you want one or both of the keywords to appear in your results. You will usually use **OR** when you are using synonyms (*e.g., alimony OR support*).

Let's create a Keyword Search. (Casemaker4 is case-insensitive [as to keywords and Boolean connectors], so it doesn't matter if you use upper or lower case for them.) We'll connect our keywords with many of the Boolean connectors listed in the **Search Tips** and a few of the other **Search Types** listed there (**Grouping, Phrase, Thesaurus, Proximity**, and **Asterisk**) and enter our search into the search box on Casemaker4's homepage. Even though this is a very broad search, because it defaults to all states and all compilations, you can narrow your search to specific jurisdictions or compilations once you retrieve your results list.

You have a client who wants to bring a personal injury lawsuit after he fell on a snow-covered sidewalk, so let's enter this keyword search into the homepage's search bar:

*~sidewalk snow* (fall* or fell)*

After reading several cases about bank robbers wearing ski masks who fell on a snow-covered sidewalk during their escape, you decide to change your search to exclude ski masks in hopes of finding cases relevant only to personal injury. Your new search (see Figure 8.4) is:

*~sidewalk snow* (fall* or fell) NOT "ski mask*"*

**Figure 8.4** Keyword Search. Screenshot from Casemaker used with permission.

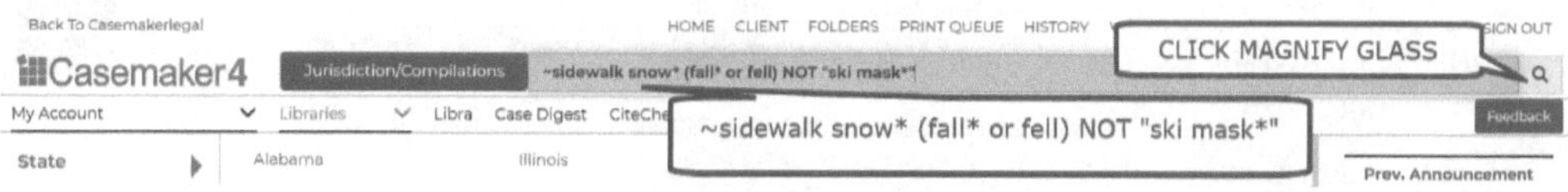


The following explains this keyword search:

- *~sidewalk:* This is a **Thesaurus** search, which is indicated by placing a tilde ~ before the keyword, without a space; this will bring back synonyms such as: *side-walk, walkway, path,* etc. The space between *~sidewalk* and *snow** makes this an **AND** search because a space between words (or a phrase or a grouping of words), serves as the Boolean connector **AND.**
- *snow**: This is an **Asterisk** search, indicated by the * placed after the keyword *snow,* without a space. Results will include any keyword that begins with *snow* because the * extends *snow* to *snowing, snowed, snow-covered,* etc. The space between *snow** and the next grouping of words within the parentheses makes this an **AND** search as explained in the above *~sidewalk* bullet point.
- *(fall* OR fell)*: The parentheses indicate that this is a **Grouping** search. Results will include *fall* or *fell* or both words. This is also an **Asterisk** search because the * extends the word *fall* to any keyword that begins with *fall* (e.g., *falling, fallen,* etc.).
- *NOT "SKI mask*"*: This is a **NOT**, a **Phrase**, and an **Asterisk** search. The Boolean connector **NOT** serves to exclude what follows, which, in this case is the **Phrase**, *"ski mask*"* as indicated by the quotation marks around the two words. The **Asterisk** after *mask* will retrieve any keyword that begins with *mask* (e.g., *masked, masks,* etc.).

Click the magnifying glass icon to submit this search (see Figure 8.4).

## Selecting a Case from the Search Results

Figure 8.5 shows the search results page from our **All States, All Compilations** search. Casemaker4 divides its search results page into two frames, left and right (see Figure 8.5). Later we will explain the left frame and various features in both frames, but for now, we'll focus on the right frame (the search results list) to select a case to read. Simply click its citation (see Figure 8.5) and its full text will appear (see Figure 8.6).

**Figure 8.5** Search Results List. Screenshot from Casemaker used with permission.

## Reading and Navigating through a Case

Figure 8.6 displays the full text of the case you selected. Official, parallel, and pin-point citations are color coded. Citations to other cases within the case you are reading are boldfaced in dark blue. These are hyperlinks, so you can click to read them without having to conduct a new search. As you begin reading a document, you can quickly scroll through the document for your search terms because they are boldfaced in black.

**Figure 8.6** Read Full Text Case. Screenshot from Casemaker used with permission.

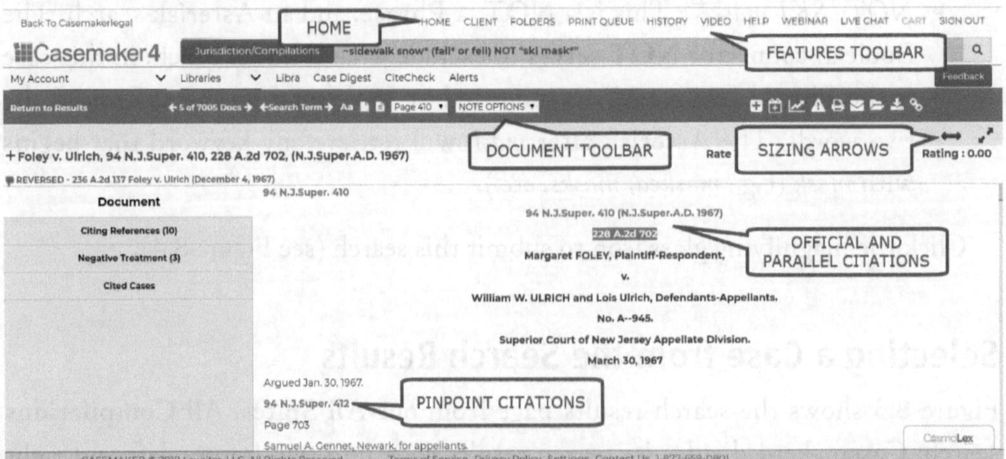

If you want to read a document without the left frame taking up space, click the horizontal sizing arrows on the far right in the right frame, just below the Document Toolbar. This will hide the left frame. The toolbars and the search box will still be displayed. Click the horizontal sizing arrows again to re-display the left frame. If you want to also eliminate the toolbars and the search box, click the diagonal arrows (this is the **Full screen mode**). To exit the **Full screen mode**, click the ESC (Escape) key on your keyboard.

If you want to start over with a new search (instead of, or after, reading the case you clicked on), click the **Home** link in the Features Toolbar on the top (it's on almost every page).

The Document Toolbar has many useful features that you will use, whether you are reading a case, statute, etc. There are tools to help you return to your results list, navigate within a document, and also between documents (see Figure 8.7). We will focus on the left side of the Document Toolbar here (ending with **Note Options**). After we discuss how to search Statutes, we'll explain the right side of the Document Toolbar (see Figure 8.20 and the following text).

**Figure 8.7** Document Toolbar (Left Side). Screenshot from Casemaker used with permission.

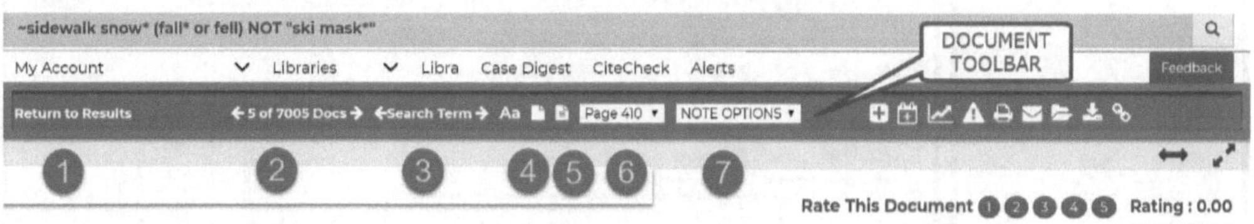


1. To go back to the full results list, click **Return to Results.**
2. To go to the next or previous document, click the left or right **Doc** arrows.
3. You can jump from search term to search term by clicking the right or left arrow on either side of the **Search Term** tab. Your search terms will now be highlighted in yellow.
4. To read only those paragraphs that include your search terms, click the **Paragraph with hits** icon (but with so many paragraphs missing, you might find it difficult to read this way).
5. Click the Page icon to return to reading the full document in page order.
6. You can enter a page number into the **Page** selection bar to jump to that page to read. If you are reading a statute, the selection bar is used to enter a subsection number to jump to that subsection (see Figure 8.17).
7. Another option on the Document Toolbar is **Note Options.** Click this to add a note to yourself about the document.

## Return to Results

After you are done reading a case, you can return to your results to read other document types, narrow your results, and more, by using different features in the left and right frames of the results page, as we'll now describe.

## Left Frame: The Compilations List

The left frame is the **Compilations** list (see Figure 8.8), which shows the total number of documents (**Total Docs**) retrieved and the number of documents retrieved for each **Compilation.** When you search **All Compilations** as we did, **Case Law** is always shown as the first compilation (in both frames). You can control what you see in the right frame (the results list) by selecting it from the left frame. For example, to change the **Case Law** results list to **Statutes**, select it from the left frame and the right frame will change to a list of **Statute** results.

**Figure 8.8** Left Frame: Compilations List: Narrowing Results. Screenshot from Casemaker used with permission.

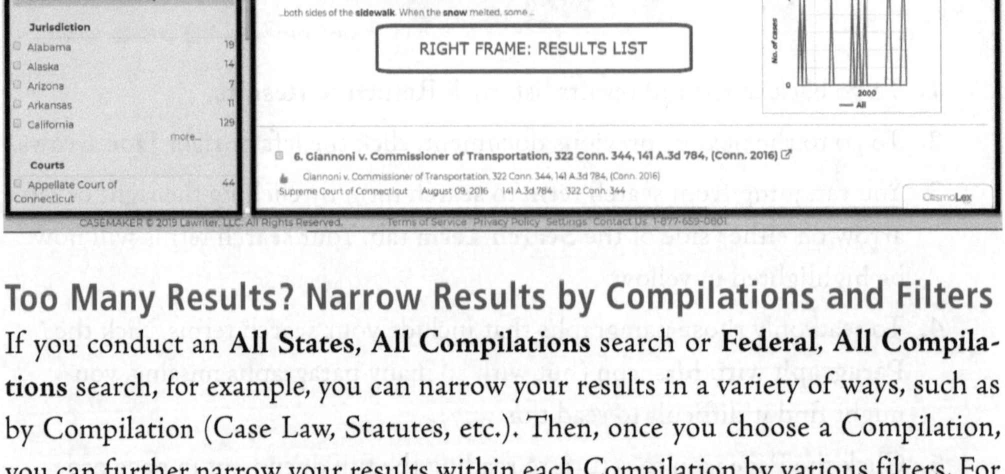


## Too Many Results? Narrow Results by Compilations and Filters

If you conduct an **All States, All Compilations** search or **Federal, All Compilations** search, for example, you can narrow your results in a variety of ways, such as by Compilation (Case Law, Statutes, etc.). Then, once you choose a Compilation, you can further narrow your results within each Compilation by various filters. For Case Law the filters would be: **Jurisdictions, Courts, Date Range,** or **Case Type (Published or Unpublished).** (See Figure 8.5.) So, if you wanted to filter to Alaska cases from 2011–2020, you would check **Alaska** from the **Jurisdictions** filter and 2011–2020 from the **Date Range** filter. To reveal the full list under each filter, click **more.** If you click to another **Compilation,** such as **Statutes,** the filters change to **Jurisdictions** and **Chapters/Titles.**

## Too Many Results? Narrow by Using "Search Within Results"

Another way to narrow your search results is to click the **Search Within Results** Bar (Figure 8.8) in the left frame. A new frame slides in from the left (Figure 8.9) with options to add a new keyword or phrase into the **Search Within Results** box, or narrow by **Cite, Docket Number, Case Name, Judge,** or **Attorney.** To return to the original left frame results, click the X on the top right of the **Search Within Results** menu (Figure 8.9).

**Figure 8.9** Search Within Results. Screenshot from Casemaker used with permission.

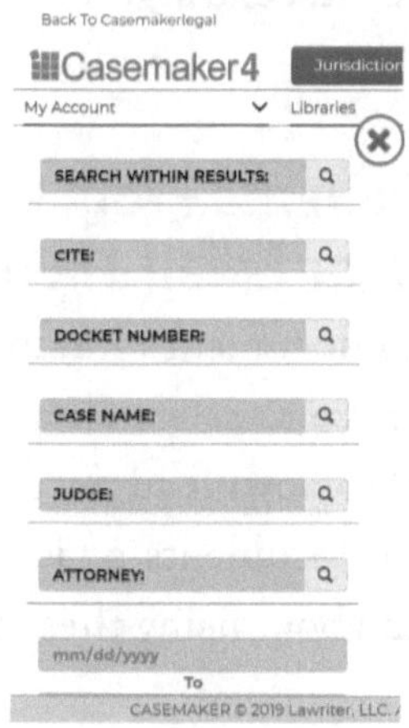


## Right Frame: The Results List

As noted earlier, the right frame is the results list. Before you decide to click a case to read, this is where you can re-sort the results list, navigate through the results if there are multiple pages, and get a preview about each case, and learn about subsequent treatment of each case.

**Figure 8.10** Right Frame: The Results List. Screenshot from Casemaker used with permission.

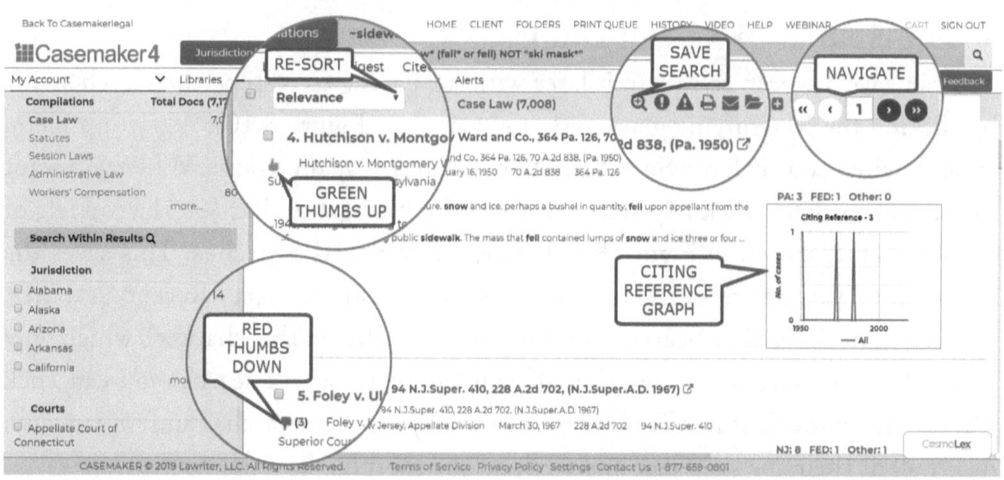

## Re-sort the Results List

Casemaker4's results always default to **Relevance** order. Click the down-arrow to the right of **Relevance** to re-sort (see Figure 8.10). For Case Law, a drop-down menu appears with these re-sorting options: **State Ascending, State Descending, Case Date Ascending, Case Date Descending, Citing References Ascending, Citing References Descending,** and **Court Level.** The re-sorting choices vary depending on the **Compilation** you have chosen. For example, if you choose **Statutes,** you won't see **Case Date Ascending,** but will instead see **CodeSec Ascending.**

## Save One or Multiple Documents From a Results List to a Folder, or Download Them, or Email Them (or Their Citations)

Check the boxes to the left of each document's number in the results list (or click the check box to the left of **Relevance** to select all documents) to: (1) save one or more documents to a Folder, or (2) to download documents (or just their citations) to your hard drive, or (3) to email documents or just their citations. (See Figure 8.20 and the text following to learn about using these tools.)

## Navigate Through the Results List

Use the two left arrows on the far right of the Document Toolbar to go back to the first page of results and the two right arrows to go to the last page of results (see Figure 8.10). Use the one left arrow to go back to the previous page of results and the one right arrow to go to the next page of results.

If you want to read a document in a new tab, click the diagonal arrow inside a box (to the right of the case title).

## Save a Search to Re-run Later

You can save a search to re-run it later without having to re-type the search string by clicking the Magnifying glass with a + icon (see Figure 8.10). A pop-up menu appears when you click the **Save Search** icon. Click it again to save. When you want to return to it later, click **My Account** from the Navigation bar (on the top left of the left frame, shown in Figure 8.10). Then click **Saved Searches.** This saves the search until you delete it, in contrast to **Recent Searches** (see "Recent Searches" subsection in the "Other Search Options" section earlier in this chapter), which only keeps the most recent five searches. If you forgot to save a search, you can click **History** from the Features Toolbar to review all your past searches and: re-run any; delete all of them; or keep just one week or one month.

## Get a Preview About Each Case and Learn About Subsequent Treatment

As you review the **Case Law** results list in the right frame, you can quickly learn a few important things about each case before you even click to read it. For example, the green thumbs-up symbol indicates there is no subsequent negative treatment of your case and the red thumbs-down indicates there *is* subsequent negative treatment of your case by one or more subsequent cases (see Figure 8.10). All cases will show one or the other of these symbols. The *Foley* case shows a red thumbs-down. You now know, even before reading this case, that it might have been reversed (or questioned, etc.). You'll have to review the subsequent case(s) that treated *Foley* negatively.

The **Citing Reference** graph (see Figure 8.10), placed to the far right of each case result, might help you decide how important a case is because it shows how often your case has been cited and by which court, and also how long ago your case has been cited. For example, the graph in the *Hutchison* case (see Figure 8.10) shows **Citing Reference – 3** and that three are from Pennsylvania state courts and one from a Federal court (this now says **Citing Reference – 4**; there was a temporary error that Casemaker4 fixed after we pointed out that 3 plus 1 equals 4!). The *Hutchison* case was first cited to by a subsequent case in 1950 and last cited in 2000. If you click the graph, it will pop-out in a larger format to read more easily. Once you are viewing a case in full-text mode, you must click the **Citing Reference** icon (see Figure 8.20, number 3) in the Document Toolbar to view the **Citing Reference** graph.

# Limit Your Search to One or More Jurisdictions and Compilations

If you don't want to start with the default search (**All States, All Compilations**) as we did in our first search, there are ways to limit your search to a specific jurisdiction(s) and compilation(s). We'll start with jurisdiction.

## Limit Jurisdiction to Federal

To limit your search to the federal jurisdiction, select the **Federal** tab from the left frame of home page. This will then display all thirty-two federal compilations available in Casemaker4 (see Figure 8.11). Click **View Currency** to see a list of the currency and the scope of each compilation. For example, the Bankruptcy Reporter is updated daily and begins with 1 B.R. (1979). You can search all federal compilations together by entering your search into the search bar at the top (**All Compilations, All Federal**) or you can search one federal compilation individually by clicking it. To search multiple compilations (and jurisdictions) by mixing and matching, you would click the **Jurisdiction/Compilations** tab (see Figure 8.13).

Figure 8.11 Federal Jurisdiction Compilations. Screenshot from Casemaker used with permission.

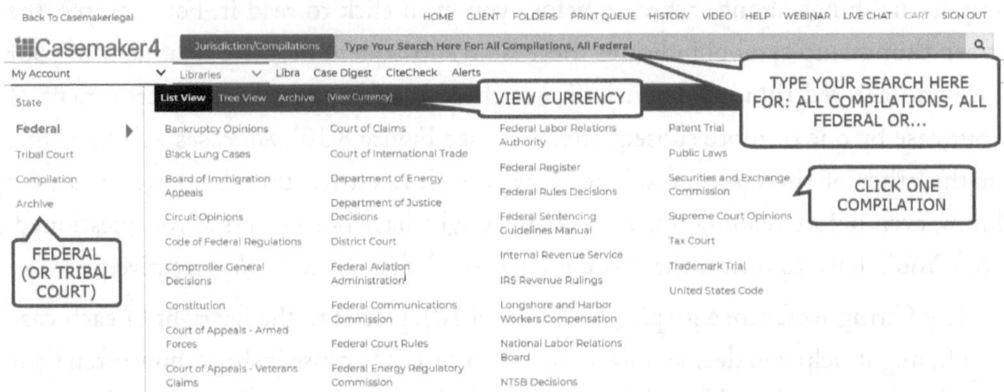


## Limit Jurisdiction to Tribal

To limit your search to the Tribal jurisdiction, select the **Tribal Court** tab in the left frame of the home page (Figure 8.11). This will display all 62 tribes (not shown here), which you can search together or individually. There are 525 recognized tribes, so Casemaker4 has a way to go until the Library is complete (they assure us it's a growing collection).

## Limit Jurisdiction to One State

To limit your search to one state, click that state's link displayed on the homepage (see Figure 8.1). Since lawyers are often searching their own state, let's take a closer look at one state's compilations, using Alaska as our example. After you select Alaska, you are shown its available compilations and the scope and currency of each compilation (see Figure 8.12). In our Alaska example, Alaska's **Case Law** compilation is shown as **Current: Updated Daily** and its **Scope** is shown as going back to **348 P.2d (1950)**.

To search all of Alaska's (or another state's) compilations together, enter your keywords into the top Search Bar. In this example the Search Bar displays **Type Your Search Here For: Alaska, All Compilations.** To search one of Alaska's compilations, click it and then enter your keywords into the same Search Bar at the top. The Search Bar will display the compilation you chose to search.

**Figure 8.12** State Compilation Example: Alaska. Screenshot from Casemaker used with permission.

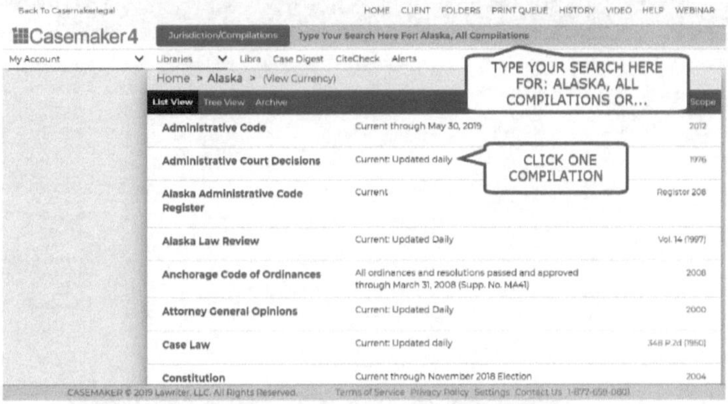


## Mix and Match Jurisdictions and Compilations

You can also search by mixing and matching jurisdictions and compilations by clicking the **Jurisdiction/Compilations** tab to the right of the Casemaker4 logo. It is displayed on almost every page (Figure 8.12). A **Jurisdiction/Compilations** menu will appear (Figure 8.13). Before you start checking off your selections, click the **Clear All Checks** tab at the top of the menu. Then you can check off one, multiple, or all jurisdictions from the state or federal columns (or both). You can also save time by checking off **All States, All Federal, All Tribal,** if you want to search an entire group of jurisdictions. These groups can also be mixed and matched. Likewise, you can check off one, multiple, or all compilations from the last column or check off the entire group of compilations by checking **All Compilations.**

The **Related Federal** and **Related States** column headings only apply to Case Law results, so only check these off if you have chosen **Case Law** or **All Compilations.** Checking off **California** and **Related Federal** would retrieve cases from all California state courts, all California Federal District Courts, and the 9th Circuit Court of Appeals, but only California cases (not the other states that comprise the 9th Circuit). An important point to note is that you cannot check off **Related Federal** and **All Federal** simultaneously, because they cancel each other out.

The **Related States** column heading is new and only works if you have checked off **Circuit Opinions** below **All Federal.** This allows you to search one, all, or

**Figure 8.13** Jurisdiction/Compilations Menu. Screenshot from Casemaker used with permission.

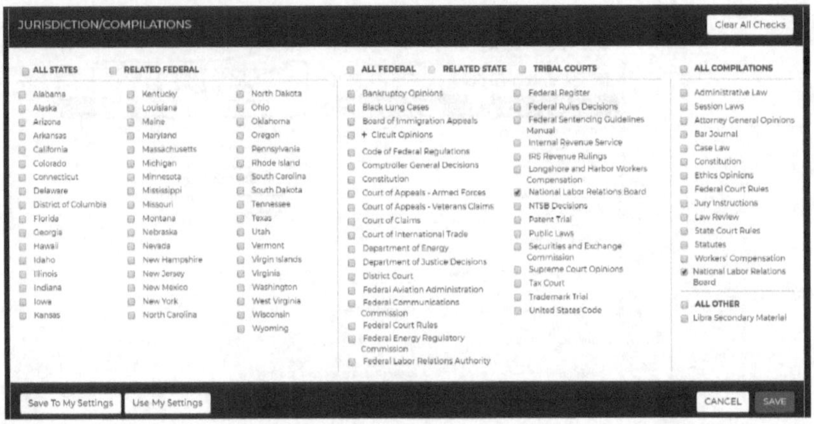


multiple federal circuit courts' opinions and also opinions from the states within the particular federal circuit courts you selected. For example, if you chose **Circuit Opinions**, then 9th Circuit, and **Related States**, you would retrieve federal opinions from the 9th Circuit and state opinions from all states in that circuit (California, Oregon, etc.).

After you are done selecting your **Jurisdictions** and **Compilations**, scroll down and click **SAVE** (see Figure 8.13 on the bottom far right-side) to use these new settings now. These new settings will stick until you either click **Home** or **Sign Out** (both on the Features Bar; see Figure 8.11), at which point the settings reverts to your original **Saved Settings** (or Casemaker's default settings if you never changed them). If you want these new settings to become your permanent settings, click **Save To My Settings**.

If you want to use your **Jurisdictions** and **Compilations** settings, instead of selecting new ones, click **Use My Settings**. Click **CANCEL** to return to your previous search results page and its settings.

## Limit Your Search to One or More Compilations or to Archives

To limit your search to one of the roughly twenty **Compilations** (such as **Administrative Codes, Attorney General Opinions, Bar Journals, Case Law, Constitutions, Ethics Opinions**), but across all jurisdictions, click the **Compilation** tab from the left frame of the homepage (see Figure 8.11).

You can also limit your search to historical versions of federal and state **Administrative Codes, Constitutions, Court Rules** (**Federal** or **State**), **Session Laws, Practice Book**, and **Statutes** by clicking the **Archives** tab from that same left frame of the homepage (see Figure 8.11). If you are already viewing a specific section of a current Compilation (or an archived Compilation), select **Archive** from the left pane. You will then see a list of all available archived Compilations (arranged by year) for just that section, which you can choose to view.

## Other Search Options: Recent Searches, Advanced Search, and Citation Search

There are hidden search options that are not revealed until you place your cursor into the search bar (from almost any page, not just the homepage), at which point a drop-down menu with three choices appears (Figure 8.2). We've already explained one of three options (**Search Tips**), so now we'll explain the **Recent Searches** and **Advanced Search** options.

### Recent Searches

If you click **Recent Searches** (see Figure 8.14), your most recent five searches would appear (not shown in Figure 8.14) and you could then select one. (As discussed earlier, to re-run past searches beyond just the recent five, click **History** from the Features Toolbar or click **My Account** from the Navigation Bar and then **Saved Searches**.)

### Advanced Search

If you click **Advanced Search** from the drop-down menu (Figure 8.14), another drop-down menu appears, the **Advanced Search** menu (Figure 8.14), which allows you to combine a **Search Term** search with one or more Fields, such as **Case Citation, Code Citation, Attorney, Judge, Short/Long Party** (or you can leave the **Search Term** search box empty and just use the Field boxes).

Using Fields, in addition to search terms, is useful when you only know bits and pieces about a case because you can enter what you know into the **Advanced Search's Search Term** box and Field boxes to create a more targeted search than a **Search Term**-only search. For example, let's say you need to gather background information about attorney Lloyd Levitt of Chattanooga, who you are opposing at trial (or considering hiring). In particular, you want to learn about what types of cases he handles (in any jurisdiction) and what the outcomes were. To eliminate any false hits where parties, judges, or witnesses are also named *Lloyd Levitt*, use the **Advanced Search** to enter *Lloyd Levitt* into the **Attorney** field box, enter *Chattanooga* into the

**Figure 8.14** Advanced Search. Screenshot from Casemaker used with permission.

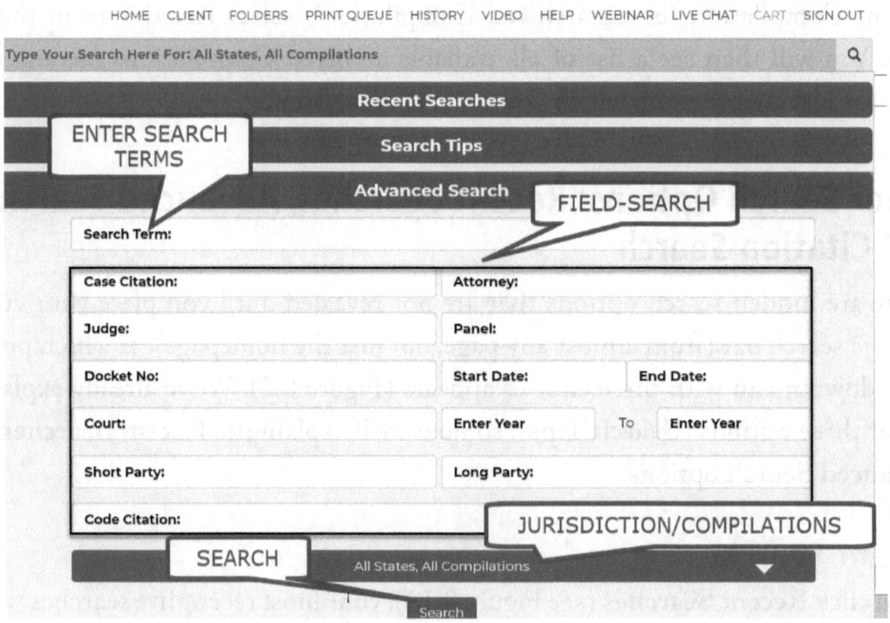


**Search Term** search box, and click **Search.** This retrieves twelve documents where *Lloyd Levitt* is the attorney of record.

You can use more than one field box at a time (with or without search terms as noted earlier). For example, enter Lloyd Levitt into the **Attorney** field box and *Susano* into the **Judge** field box to learn if Lloyd Levitt ever appeared before Judge *Susano*. You will retrieve one result.

If you want to retrieve a particular statute, such as *Conn. Gen. Stat. 8-2,* enter it (in Bluebook format) into the **Advanced Search** menu's **Code Citation** field box. Capitalization matters in this search; entering *conn. gen. stat. 8-2* retrieved no documents. If you had typed this citation into the default **Search Term** search box on the homepage, you would have needed to remember to enclose it in quotation marks and even then, you would retrieve every mention of that statute in any compilation (e.g., Case Law, Statutes, etc.).

Field searching by party name can be useful to learn how litigious someone is or to learn who typically represents them. You can enter a party name into one of these Field boxes:

- **Long Party:** Enter both party names into this field box (e.g., **Vincent v. Voight**). Some citations use "v" between the party names while others use "vs" or "versus." Casemaker4 only recognizes the "**v.**"
- **Short Party:** Enter just one party's name into this field box.

When you want to create a combined **Search Term** and Field **Advanced Search,** there are a few caveats: Although you *can* connect your search terms with the same search operators shown in the Search Tips chart (see Figure 8.3), that is not the case when entering text into Field boxes. You cannot use operators in the **Case** or **Code Citation, Docket No., Start Date/End Date,** or **Enter Year To Enter Year** Field boxes. With the **Attorney, Judge, Long Party,** or **Short Party** Field boxes, it also does not appear that you can use operators, but this may change once Casemaker4 is out of beta.

The **Jurisdiction/Compilations** bar at the bottom of the Field menu is set to **All States, All Compilations** in Figure 8.14 because it is set to your last search. This can be re-set by clicking this bottom bar or by clicking the **Jurisdiction/Compilations** bar at the top of the page to the right of the Casemaker4 logo (not shown). In either case, the **Jurisdiction/Compilations** menu will pop-up for you to make selections (see Figure 8.13).

As you can see, entering information into Fields in the **Advanced Search** menu can help you eliminate a lot of false hits, home in on what you are looking for, and save time.

## Citation Search with "Type Ahead" Feature

If you want to view a document and you know its citation, whether it's a citation to a statute, regulation, or even a party name, start entering it into the search bar on the homepage, like this:

*777 f.supp*

Even before you complete typing the full citation, a drop-down menu appears with a list of possible matching documents. This is Casemaker4's new "Type Ahead" feature. If you don't see the document you want on the list, continue typing the rest of the citation. If you are retrieving too many false hits, enclose your full citation in quotation marks, or enter it into the **Case Citation** or **Code Citation** Field box on the **Advanced Search** menu that we just mentioned.

If you want to view a case and you know part of the case title, start entering it into the search bar on the homepage, like this:

*Cruz v. Bristol*

The "Type Ahead" feature would initiate a drop-down menu with a list of possible matching cases, from *Cruz v. Bristol* to *Cruz v. Bristol Meyers*, etc.

## Casemaker4's Citator Products (CasemakerPro)

**Casemaker4** offers two Citator products: **CaseCheck+** and **CiteCheck.** Together, they are referred to as **CasemakerPro.**

### CaseCheck+

**CaseCheck+** does NOT display information about positive treatment and does not include unpublished cases. Because many unpublished cases are included in Casemaker4's case law database, you will need to create your own citator-like search for those cases (as explained in the "'Party Name As Keyword' Cite-Checking" section of Chapter 18). Citators provided by **Bloomberg Law** (**BCite**), **Lexis** (**Shepard's**), and **Thomson Reuters Westlaw** (**KeyCite**) include positive treatment and also include both published and unpublished cases.

As you saw in Figure 8.6, after you click a case from the results page, the full text of the case appears in the right frame. The left frame displays **CaseCheck+** (although it is not labeled as such). Either a "red thumbs-down" symbol with the word **Reversed** is displayed or a "green thumbs-up" symbol is displayed. Note that "green thumbs-up" does not mean "affirmed" but simply means there is no negative history.

If you click the **Negative Treatment** tab from the left frame, the full text of the case disappears from the right frame and is replaced with a list of all subsequent cases that have negatively treated the original case (see Figure 8.15). There is also a text explanation (e.g., **Reversed, Questioned**, etc.) listed to the left of the case citation.

When you click the **Citing References** tab, you will see a list of every subsequent case that cited the original case (these are the same cases shown earlier in the **Citing Reference** graph in Figure 8.10). You would need to review each of these cases to see how they treated your case because there is no text explanation as there is when you click the **Negative Treatment** tab.

**Figure 8.15** CaseCheck+, Negative Treatment, and More. Screenshot from Casemaker used with permission.

You can click on any case listed in the **Citing Reference, Negative Treatment,** and **Cited Cases** tabs to review it. Casemaker4 used to take you to the page where your case was cited, but now just takes you to the first page of the case. To quickly find your case, simply use the Find Function on your keyboard (Control+F for a PC or Command+F for a Mac) and enter one of the party names from your case. If you want to return to your original search's results list, click the browser's back button.

The last tab, **Cited Cases,** displays a list of all the cases cited in the case you are reading. This might be the least useful feature of **CaseCheck+**. Click the **Document** tab in the left frame to return to the full text of the case.

No citator product is perfect. Casemaker4 and the other major legal research system vendors, except for Fastcase, use a combination of algorithms and human editors to find citing references. Fastcase only uses algorithms. In test searches by us (and others), each one has missed citing references.

## CiteCheck

**CasemakerPro** also offers another citator product, called **CiteCheck,** which is an automated cite checking software program used to extract the case citations from a brief, memo, or even just a document comprised of citations (click **CiteCheck** from the Navigation Toolbar shown in Figure 8.15). It then generates a report showing the subsequent negative treatment of each case. This is useful not only to cite check your own work, but also the opposition's. It is free to consortium members.

## Searching Statutes

Keyword searching Statutes (and other non-case law compilations, such as Session Laws, Administrative Codes, Registers, Constitutions, and Court Rules) is similar to Case Law searching, so we will conduct just one keyword search through Statutes.

Let's say you're a Texas personal injury attorney and you receive a call from a former client who tells you he has been charged with stealing gasoline. You will probably refer the case to a criminal law attorney, but you decide to conduct some research first to find statutes about this crime. To start a new search, remember you can click the **Home** link in the Features Toolbar (on the top of almost every page; see Figure 8.15 for instance). Then, click the **Jurisdiction/Compilations** bar to open its selection menu (see Figure 8.13) and check **Texas** from **All States** and check **Statutes** from **All Compilations.** (If you needed to search federal statutes, you would click **United States Code** from the **Jurisdiction/Compilations** bar or click the **Federal** tab on the homepage.) Now, enter your keywords *(burglary OR steal OR theft) (petroleum OR gas*)* into the Search bar labeled **Type Your Search Here For: Texas, Statutes** and click the magnifying glass.

This retrieves twenty-one results (see Figure 8.16). You will see a left frame and right frame, just as you did with case law (or multiple compilation) results. The left frame displays a **Search Within Results** tab, similar to case law, but the filters differ from case law; they are statute-specific: **Chapters/Titles.** You can check the box to the left of **Penal Code** to view only the five penal code results.

**Figure 8.16** Search Statutes. Screenshot from Casemaker used with permission.

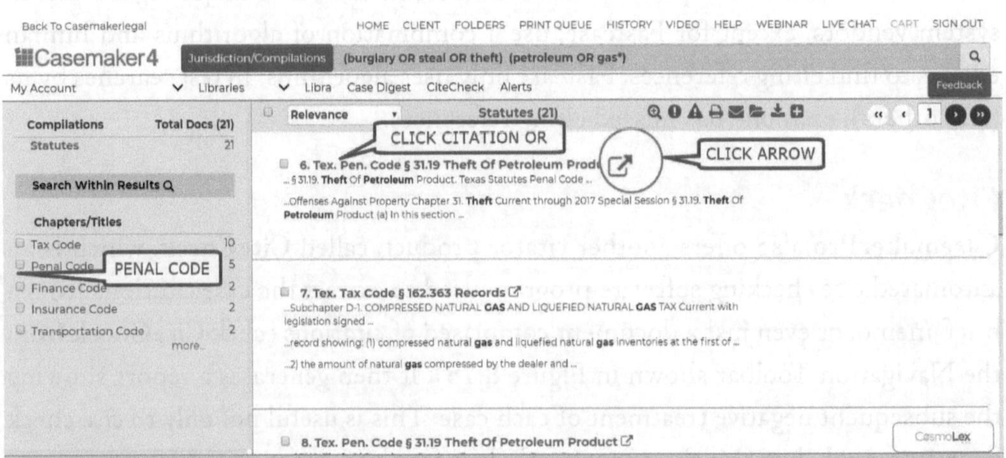

To read a specific section, either click the Section citation (Figure 8.16) to open it in the same tab or click the box icon that contains a diagonal arrow pointing up and to the right. The section will open in a new tab. In either case, it will look the same, as shown in Figure 8.17, with two frames appearing; the full text of the statute in the right frame and various tabs in the left frame.

Statutes (and other non-case law documents) have similar tools on their Document Toolbar (see Figure 8.17) as Case Law documents, such as adding notes, emailing a document, saving a document to a folder, creating alerts, and printing. For a detailed explanation of the Document Toolbar's left side, see Figure 8.7 and the bullet list that follows that figure. For a detailed explanation of the Document Toolbar's right side, see Figure 8.20 and the bullet list that follows that figure. However, there are some tools unique to the Statutes' Document Toolbar (see Figure 8.17), that allow you to:

- jump to any listed subsection if you click the drop-down arrow to the right of the sub-section selection bar that displays the section (a); or
- go back and forth to other sections of the Statutes, just like you would if you were browsing through a print version of the Statutes, by clicking the **Browse Documents** back and forth arrows.

**Figure 8.17** Full Text Statute. Screenshot from Casemaker used with permission.

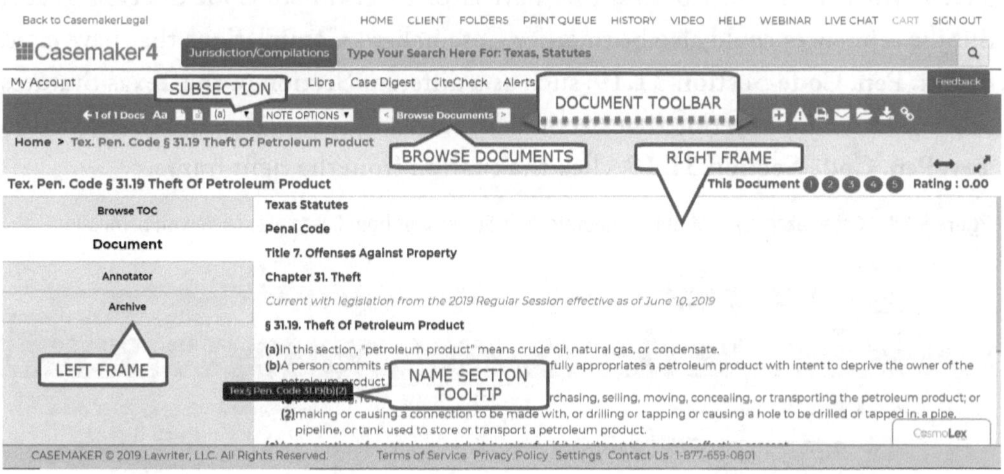


When you view the full text of a statute section in the right frame (Figure 8.17), you'll see some different features from when you viewed the full text of a case, such as:

- A currency date in red (above the section's text). This is always the most current edition of a state's (or United States') statutes. But, depending how often a state's legislature meets, this could be the prior year, or even two years prior. (For example, the Texas Legislature only meets every other year, so its most recent Statutes could be from two years ago.)
- A name section tooltip that pops up if you hover over any part of a section's citation, such as the (b)(2) beneath Section 31.19. The tooltip then displays the full citation: e.g., **Tex. Pen. Code Section 31.19(b)(2)**.
- The section's **History** (at the end of the text but not shown here).

As you look at a statute's full text, its left frame (Figure 8.17), shows some different tabs from those in a case law's left frame. For example, as you are reading **Tex. Pen. Code Section 31.19** (see Figure 8.17), if you click the **Browse TOC** (Table of Contents) tab in the left frame of Figure 8.17, this takes you to a Table of Contents of all other sections of that statute (e.g., to Sections 31.01 through 31.19). After you review the Table of Contents, you can then easily click to the next Section you want to read.

Another tab in the left frame is the **Annotator** tab (see Figures 8.17 and 8.18) It shows the number of other references to the Section you are reading. In Figure 8.18, we had already clicked **Annotator (61)** from the left frame, so this Figure now displays a new right frame with a list of those 61 references to **Tex. Pen. Code Section 31.19**, which are mostly to cases that have cited to **Tex. Pen. Code Section 31.19**. But the references could also be to other Casemaker4 Compilations that have cited to **Tex. Pen. Code Section 31.19**, such as a different Section of the Texas Statutes or a regulation interpreting that Section. To read any of the references that cited to **Tex. Pen. Code Section 31.19**, click the citation from the right frame.

**Figure 8.18** Casemaker: Texas Statutes Annotator Tab. Screenshot from Casemaker used with permission.

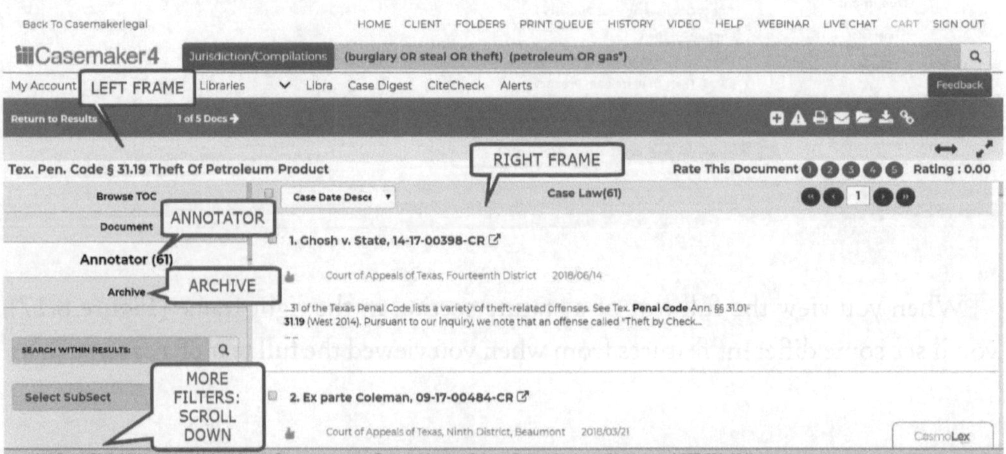

You can also use filters in the left frame (Figure 8.18) to narrow your **Annotator** results by:

- Keywords (Enter them into the **Search Within Results** filter box.); or
- Subsections (Click the **Select SubSect** drop-down arrow to select a Subsection from the list.); or
- Other filters, such as Compilations, Jurisdictions, etc. (not shown).

To return to the statute that you began with, click **Document** from the left frame.

If you click the **Archive** tab (Figure 8.18), a list of earlier versions of the section that you are reading appears in year order. If you want to read one of the earlier versions, click the year you are interested in.

## Browse through Statutes?

Instead of keyword searching, you can browse to a specific statute section, just like you browse through a print version of Statutes. Click a state from the homepage and then select **Statutes**. Click a Code (e.g., **Agriculture Code**) and then click the relevant Title, then Chapter, and then Section (or subsection) until you find what you want to read (see Figure 8.19). If you know the exact citation, enter it into the **Go to Section** box on the far right.

**Figure 8.19** Browse Statutes. Screenshot from Casemaker used with permission.

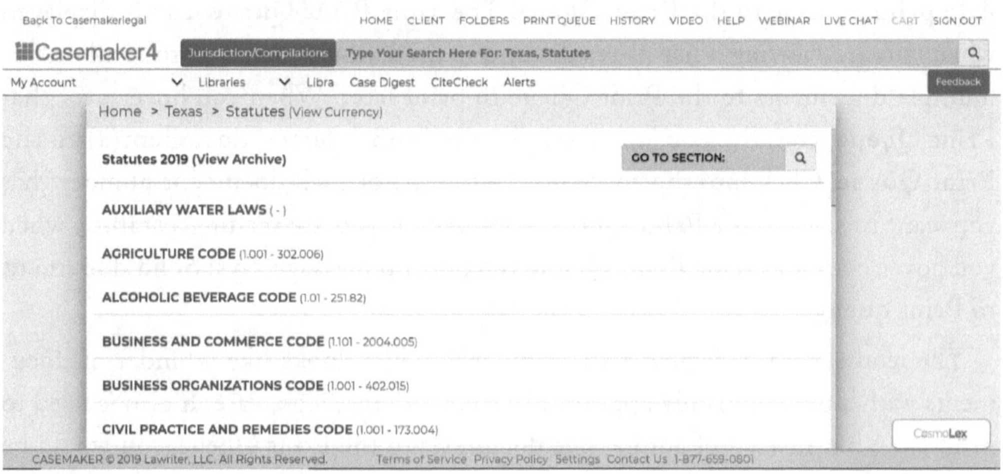


## Working with Documents

When we discussed the tools on the left half of the Document Toolbar earlier (see Figure 8.7), we noted that most of the tools on the Document Toolbar are the same no matter which document type you are working with (case law, statutes, regulations, etc.). Now we'll look at the tools on the right side of the Document Toolbar.

**Figure 8.20** Document Toolbar (Right Side). Screenshot from Casemaker used with permission.

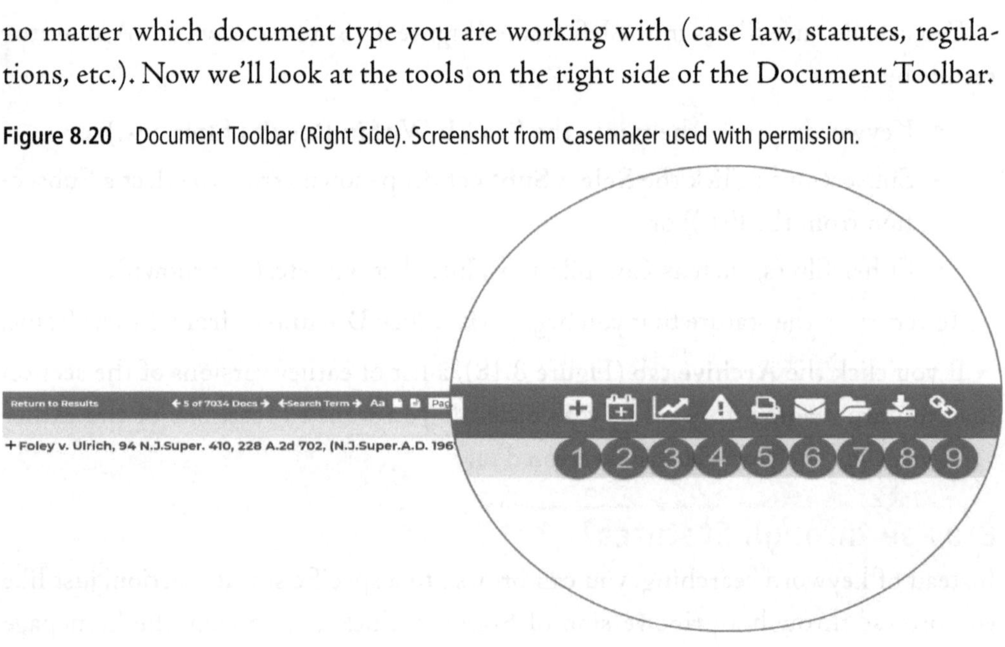


## Print Queue (Print Later)

The icon shown in Figure 8.20, number 1, which looks like a document with a plus sign, is the **Print Queue** icon and is used when you are reading one document and want to print it later. When you hover over that icon, the pop-up message says: **Add primary case to the Print Queue.** The same **Print Queue** icon is displayed when you are viewing a list of results and is used when you want to send one or multiple documents to the Print Queue to print later. When you hover over that **Print Queue** icon, the pop-up message says: **Send selected document(s) to the Print Queue.** Click into the check box to the left of each document number that you want to send to the **Print Queue.** However, if you are reading a statute, when you hover over that same **Print Queue** the pop-up message says: **Send document to Print queue.**

The icon shown in Figure 8.20, number 2, which looks like a binder of documents with a plus sign, only appears while you are reading a case. It also is used to print later, but instead of adding one document to the Print Queue, you would be adding the document you are reading and its related cases. When you hover over that icon the pop-up message says: **Add primary case and all related cases to the Print Queue.** Think twice before selecting this print later option because you could end up printing a lot of cases. (You can also print immediately, which we'll explain when we get to Figure 8.20, number 5.)

When you are ready to print documents that you sent to the Print Queue, click **Print Queue** from the Features Toolbar located at the top of almost all Casemaker4 pages (see Figure 8.19 or Figure 8.6). The **Quick Print Queue** page then appears. From there, you have many print choices, such as to: **Use default user setting when printing, Print All, Print Checked** (to print only cases you checked off), **Clear Checked Cases,** and **Check All Cases.** The three icons to the right of **Check All Cases** can be used to: **Remove checked documents from Quick Print Queue, Clear Print Queue,** or **Print History** (this was not working at the time we wrote this chapter).

Once you click **Print All** or **Print Checked,** a **Print** menu appears with most of the options you had when you printed immediately, but not the case-related and statute-related **Include** options (such as **Negative Treatment** cases or **Show Annotator,** respectively). However, you can now opt to just print a list of the citations instead of the full document by clicking the **List of items** radio button.

After you click the **Print Queue** from the Features Toolbar that we just noted (see Figure 8.19 or Figure 8.6), you have another print option, which is to use the search bar that appears at the top to **Enter up to 100 case citations to be added to the Quick Print Queue** (to print cases that are not part of your results, but to which you have citations). You can either type citations into the search bar or copy them (e.g., from a document on your computer or from a website) and paste them into the search bar. When you are done, click **Locate.**

## View Citing References Graph

The icon shown in Figure 8.20, number 3, which looks like a squiggly arrow, is displayed while you are reading a case. Click it to view the **Citing Reference** graph (this is the same graph that is placed to the far right of each case result; see Figure 8.10).

## Document Alerts

The icon shown in Figure 8.20, number 4, which looks like an exclamation point within a triangle, is the **Document Alert** tool. If you are reading a specific document, you can create a **Document Alert** by clicking it. We'll explain **Document Alerts** in more detail later (and also **Search Alerts**).

## Printing Immediately

While you are viewing a case or any document, you can print it immediately by clicking the Printer Icon on the Document Toolbar (see Figure 8.20, number 5). A **Print Documents** menu will pop up showing many print choices. You can choose the **Document Format** (**PDF** or **Word**), the **Page Layout** (**Single** or **Dual Column**), and whether you want search terms highlighted in your print job (**Term Highlighting**). You can also print more than just the one case that you are viewing by clicking any of these related case options: **Citing References, Cited Cases,** and **Negative Treatment** cases. Finally, you can attach one or both of these: a **Cover Page** or **Notes.**

The **Print Documents** menu for Statutes has a **Show Annotator** choice (instead of the **Negative Treatment** choice and other case law-related choices).

Some of the print choices can be pre-selected as your default by clicking **My Account** from the Navigation Bar located on the left side of the homepage (or almost any page) and then by clicking Settings and then the Email & Print Settings tab.

## Email One Document (or One Citation)

You can email a document by clicking the Envelope icon (see Figure 8.20, number 6), which inserts it into an email that is addressed to you (you can change the email address to someone else's). Enter a **Subject** line and a **Message** and click send.

## Save One Document to a Folder

You can save a document to a Folder on Casemaker4 by clicking the **Folder** icon (see Figure 8.20, number 7) and then entering a name for the Folder. Be sure to click **Save** and then **OK.**

To retrieve a document that you placed into a Folder, click **Folders** from the Features Toolbar (see Figure 8.19) and a **My Folders** screen will appear (not shown). If you saved a lot of documents and can't find the one you need, you can enter keywords describing it into the **Search Within Folders** search box in the left frame of **My Folders.** Or, you can sort your folders by **Title** or by **Date Added** (by clicking the arrow to the right of **Date Added** in the right frame). From **My Folders,** you can also create **New** Folders, **Re-name** Folders (click the arrow to the right of **Options**) or, send a Folder to the **Trash.**

## Download One Document (or One Citation) to Your Hard Drive

You can download one document to your hard drive by clicking the down-arrow icon pointing to a rectangle that is meant to like a hard drive (see Figure 8.20, number 8).

## Share a Link to a Document with a Non-Casemaker4 Subscriber

You can even create a shareable link to a document to email it to someone who is not a Casemaker4 subscriber *and* they will be able to read its full text. Do this by clicking the **Link** icon (see Figure 8.20, number 9). Then, a **Copy Shareable Link to the Clipboard** menu appears with a shareable link as shown Figure 8.21 (in this case it's https://links.casemakerlegal.com/docid/1076358?bookname=public_url&ci=95). Click the **Link** tab to the right of the link to copy it. Now paste it into an email (Control+v for a PC or Command+v for a Mac). If you instead click **Citation with Link**, this copies the full citation that you can paste into an email or document, but it will not be a shareable link.

**Figure 8.21** Copy Shareable Link to the Clipboard and Paste. Screenshot from Casemaker used with permission.

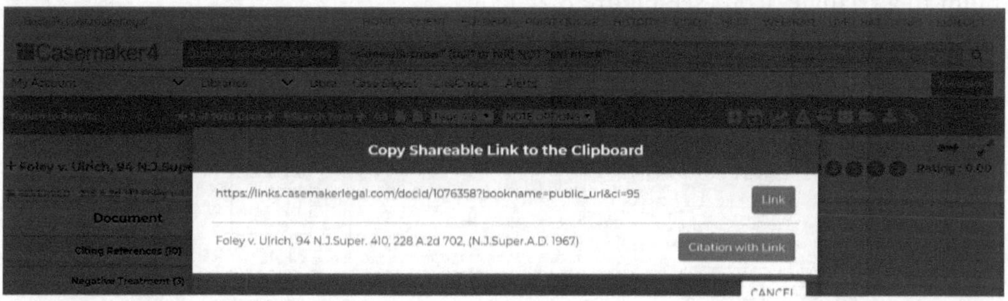


You can also copy and paste some or all of the text from a Casemaker4 document and email it or copy it into a Word document by simply highlighting any or all of the text and then right clicking it. A menu appears with three choices; click **Copy** and then paste the highlighted text into an email (or a document).

## Alerts

**Casemaker4** offers three types of alerts: **Search Alerts, Document Alerts,** and its **Case Digest.**

### Search Alerts and Document Alerts

If you want Casemaker4 to alert you whenever a new document matches a particular search query, such as: *~sidewalk snow* (fall* or fell)*, you would create a **Search Alert.** On the other hand, if you want Casemaker4 to alert you about the status of one or multiple documents, such as a specific statute or case, you would create a

**Document Alert.** We already explained how to create a **Document Alert** or add it to an existing alert while reading a single document (see Figure 8.20, number 4 and its discussion on clicking the "exclamation point in a triangle" icon), but there are two other ways to create **Document Alerts.**

**Document Alerts,** and also **Search Alerts,** can be created from scratch by clicking the **Alerts** link from the Navigation Toolbar (see Figure 8.22). Clicking this **Alerts** link also is where you can view and manage all your existing **Alerts.**

In addition, they can both be created while viewing a Results List.

To create a **Search Alert** that matches your search query click the "exclamation point in a circle" icon (see Figure 8.22).

To create a **Document Alert** (or add a document to an existing alert) from a Results List, first select one or more documents and then click the "exclamation point in a triangle" icon (see Figure 8.22).

**Figure 8.22** Alerts and Case Digest. Screenshot from Casemaker used with permission.

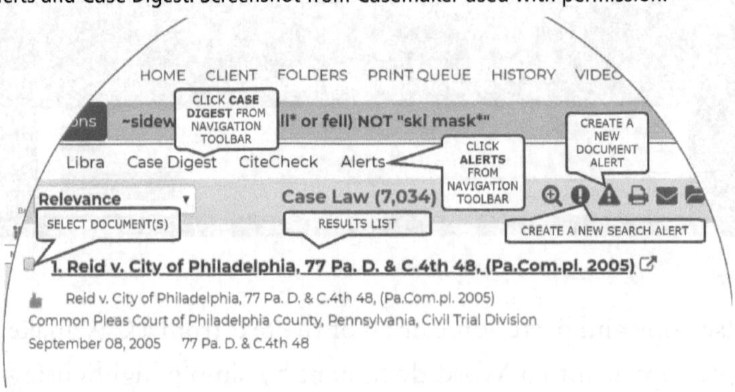


After you click **Search Alert,** a menu pops up for you to: add your email address; enter an **Alert Name** and **Alert Description;** and choose the **Frequency** for receiving alerts (by clicking into either the **Daily** or **Weekly** radio button).

After you click **Document Alerts,** the menu will include the above options, but will also include a **Selected Tracking Option.** If the **Document Alert** is for a **Statute,** the **Selected Tracking Option** offers to alert you to: **Changes** (e.g., if the statute gets amended or repealed), or **Annotations** (if the statute is cited to in a case), or both. The **Selected Tracking Option** for a case offers to alert you to one or more of these: **Citing References** (if your case is cited to by another case), **Negative Treatment** (if your case is reversed, overruled, questioned, etc., by another case), or **New Citation** (if a case is assigned a parallel citation or assigned a citation if it only had had a docket number).

Click **Save** when you are done making all your choices so Casemaker4 can send you an email **Alert** if there is a match.

### Case Digest Alerts

**Casemaker4** summarizes state appellate and federal circuit decisions within twenty-four hours of when they are decided to create its **Case Digest.** (Note: Casemaker4 adds new cases to its database as soon as they are released by the courts; it's only **Case Digest** that has a twenty-four-hour delay.) Click the **Case Digest** tab on the Navigation Toolbar (see Figure 8.22) to set up **Case Digest Alerts** and receive emails. (You can also use this tab to just read the **Case Digest** at the Casemaker4 website.) If you set up a **Case Digest Alert,** you will receive a free daily email alert of all summarized cases or you can customize **Case Digest Alerts** by choosing one or more of these filters: practice areas (there are fifty-seven), courts, or judges. You will then receive **Case Digest Alerts** via email that meet your filters only. Or you can enter a search query into the **Keyword** search box to receive **Case Digest Alerts** via email when a case includes the keywords from your search query.

# PERSONALIZE YOUR SEARCH EXPERIENCE AT CASEMAKER4

## My Account/Settings

To personalize your search experience, go to **My Accounts** in the Navigation Bar (on the home page or on most any page) and click **Settings.** A menu then pops up (Figure 8.23) with four **Settings** tabs to change Casemaker4's default settings to your own. These defaults will apply to all your searches until you return to **Settings** to change them or until you make *ad hoc* changes while you are searching.

### Settings and General Settings Menu

After you click **Settings,** the **General Settings** menu is the default page (see Figure 8.23). From there, you can set defaults for a variety of items such as:

- **History Records Per Page:** Choose 20, 50, or 100 (you will see that number of your search histories when you click **History** from the homepage).

**Figure 8.23** Settings Menu. Screenshot from Casemaker used with permission.

- **My Start Page:** Choose from **All States** or click down-arrow for more choices: **One State** (then **Select State** from list), **Federal, Tribal Court, Compilations,** or **Archive.**

Remember to click **Save** to save your settings or click **Reset** to start over.

## Search Settings Menu

After you click the **Search Settings** tab (see Figure 8.23), you can set defaults for a variety of items such as:

- **Home Page Search Settings:** Click the **Jurisdiction/Compilations** tab to pop out the Jurisdiction (and Compilations) menu and make choices as shown in Figure 8.13, Jurisdiction/Compilations Menu.
- **Default Sort for Case Law:** Click the drop-down arrow to the right of **Relevance** to select a sort by default other than **Relevance** (such as **Court Level, State Ascending, State Descending, Case Date Ascending, Case Date Descending,** etc.).

Click **Save** to save your settings or click **Reset** to start over.

## Email and Print Settings Menu

After you click the **Email and Print Settings** tab (see Figure 8.23), notice that your email address appears in the **E-mail** box as the default as (see Figure 8.24), but you can change it to a different email address (e.g., a client's, a co-counsel's, etc.).

**Figure 8.24** Email and Print Settings Menu. Screenshot from Casemaker used with permission.

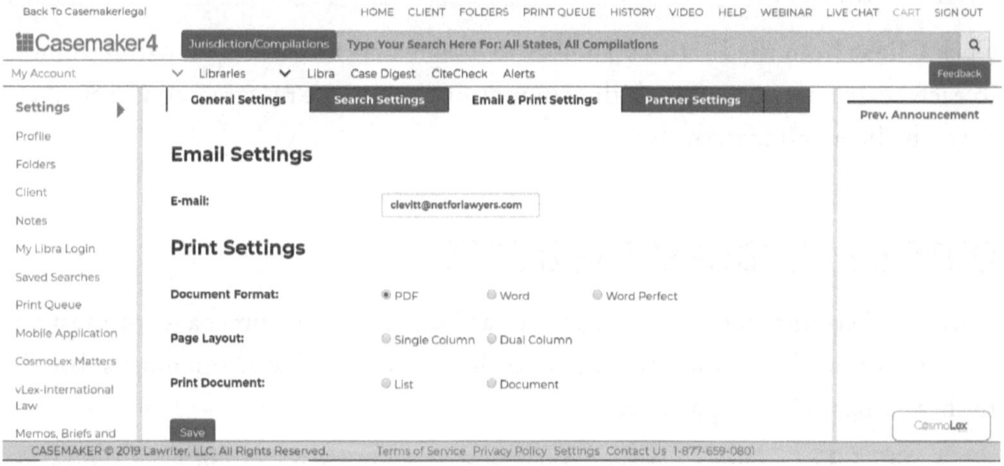


On the **Print Settings** section of this menu, choose from these selections:

- **Document Format: PDF, Word, Word Perfect**
- **Page Layout: Single Column** or **Dual Column**
- **Print Document: List** (just of citations) or **Document** (full-text)

Remember to click **Save** when you are done. (For more details on printing, see pages 176–177.)

## Partner Settings Menu

After you click the **Partner Settings** tab (see Figure 8.23), If you subscribe to Cosmolex (a cloud-based, law practice management software program) via Casemaker4, Select **Yes** or **No** to display it or not. Remember to click **Save** when you are done.

# GETTING MORE HELP (SEE THE FEATURES TOOLBAR)

If you need more help, you can find it on the Features Toolbar (which appears on every Casemaker4 page, not just the homepage). Clicking **Help** brings you to the user guide and the archive of weekly tips. You can register for free live webinars by clicking **Webinar**. You can click **Video** to watch tutorials on various topics, such as how to create folders or how to use CaseCheck+. And finally, you can instant message with customer support (note, if an operator is not available, you will receive an email answer later) by clicking **Live Chat**.

## TIME KEEPING

Click **Client** from the Features Toolbar to assign a client name and matter number to each search session to track the amount of time spent researching Casemaker4 for each client and matter.

## OUTSIDE VENDORS' PRODUCTS

Click **My Account** from the Navigation Bar located on the homepage (or most any page) to see the drop-down menu to outside vendors' products. You must subscribe to these separately and pay a fee.

- **My Libra** offers treatises, practice guides, and continuing legal education materials, published by state bars, the ABA, and others. After you click Libra, click By Publisher or By Practice Area (from the left pane) to view the list of available materials. Libra results are integrated into all search results, but a subscription is required to view the full text. Cosmolex is a cloud-based, law practice management software provider, integrated with Casemaker4 to allow users to track and bill Casemaker4 research time. Among other benefits, Casemaker4 users receive a lifetime discount with Cosmolex.
- **vLex—International Law** offers foreign case law and legislation from 100+ countries and editorial content with daily analysis from 1,000+ collaborating publishers (accessible in real time on a smart-search platform leveraged by machine learning). More Canadian materials will be added. The content is in both English and the native language. vLex results will appear in your search results, but you will need to subscribe to view the full text. A free trial is available.
- **Memos, Briefs, and Discovery** is a freelance legal research company.
- **US Legal Forms** offers over 65,000 legal forms available for download at a 10% discount.

## CONCLUSION

This chapter was meant to give you as in-depth an overview as we could without writing an entire book on Casemaker4. Although we did not show you how to search every document type, you should be armed with enough knowledge to search all document types. And, because the chapter was written during Casemaker4's Alpha and Beta modes, some features and tools may look different or be located in different places, but as we mentioned in the Getting More Help section of this chapter, Casemaker4 offers its customers a variety of ways to get the help you might need.

# Chapter 9

## FASTCASE 7

THE BASICS

**By Brian Huddleston***

## INTRODUCTION

Fastcase is a legal research service that provides primary legal resources for most U.S. jurisdictions, as well as an increasingly useful amount of secondary resources. Members of over forty state, local, and specialty bar associations have access to Fastcase included as part of their bar membership. The list of bar associations that provide Fastcase for its users is available at http://www.fastcase.com/bar-associations. If you're not a member of one of the bar associations that provides access to Fastcase, subscriptions are reasonably priced and start at $65 a month, depending on the plan you select. If you pre-pay for a full year, it is even less. For more information about Fastcase's subscription options, see http://www.fastcase.com/pricing-plans. You can also sign up for a free 24-hour trial of Fastcase through that page.

In 2017, Fastcase released a totally new version of its legal research service and called it Fastcase 7. The new version includes a complete redesign and significantly improves the way users access and search its resources. Fastcase also introduced several new tools that are available only on Fastcase 7. In 2019, Fastcase made more revisions and continually tweaks its service, which means, what we describe here, could look slightly different when you log into Fastcase.

* Brian Huddleston is the Senior Reference Librarian at the Loyola University New Orleans College of Law Library. He has an M.L.I.S. from the University of Washington and a J.D. from the University of Alabama.

Most bar associations that provide their members with access to Fastcase have enabled the **toggle switch** on the site that allows users to switch between the default "Fastcase Classic" (also referred to as Fastcase 6) and Fastcase 7 (see Figure 9.1).

**Figure 9.1** Toggle Switches to change between Fastcase Classic and Fastcase 7. Screenshot from Fastcase used with permission.

## FINDING RESOURCES ON FASTCASE 7

One big change that Fastcase 7 made is the way you find specific legal resources. You can, of course, search everything on Fastcase 7 at the same time, but if you are looking only for regulations from Massachusetts, or statutes from Florida, or cases from California, it can be inefficient to search everything and then sort through the results to find what you need. Luckily, Fastcase 7 organizes each type of legal resource from specific jurisdictions into separate Libraries. This makes it easy to find the Library for the type of resource you need and only search within that Library. Here's how that works.

Figure 9.2 shows the home page for Fastcase 7. (Note that depending on your computer and screen resolution, the "Jurisdiction & Sources" button in Figure 9.2 might just say "Sources" and the Main Search Box might look slightly different; Fastcase 7 dynamically scales the layout of its main page to fit lower screen resolutions.) If you want to search everything on Fastcase 7, just start typing in the Main Search Box on this page. (Even though searching everything is a very broad search, after your results are displayed, you can narrow you search results by the types of documents you find and their jurisdiction.) But if you want to select only a specific type of resource to search, click the **Jurisdiction & Sources** button to bring up the Filter Sources drop-down menu shown in Figure 9.3.

**Figure 9.2** Fastcase 7 Main Page with Main Search Box and Jurisdiction & Sources Button. Screenshot from Fastcase used with permission.

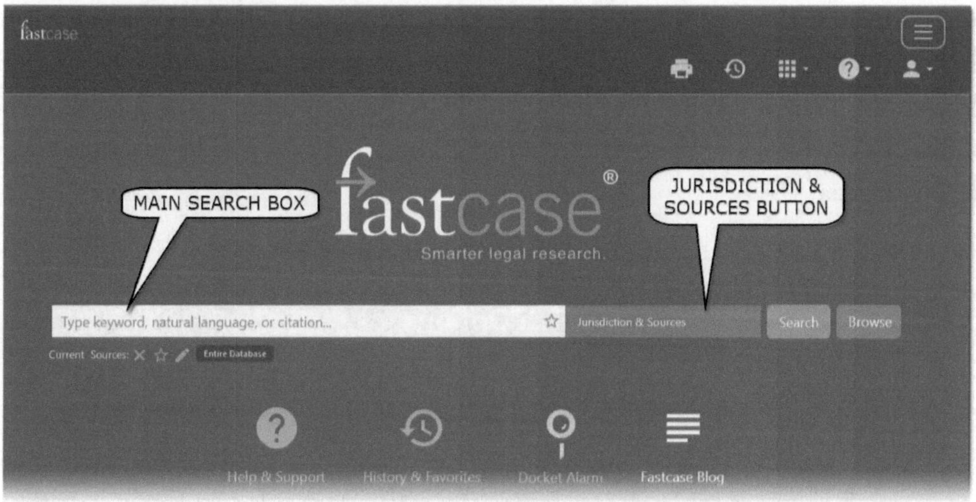


**Figure 9.3** Fastcase 7 Filter Sources drop-down menu and Filter Bar. Screenshot from Fastcase used with permission.

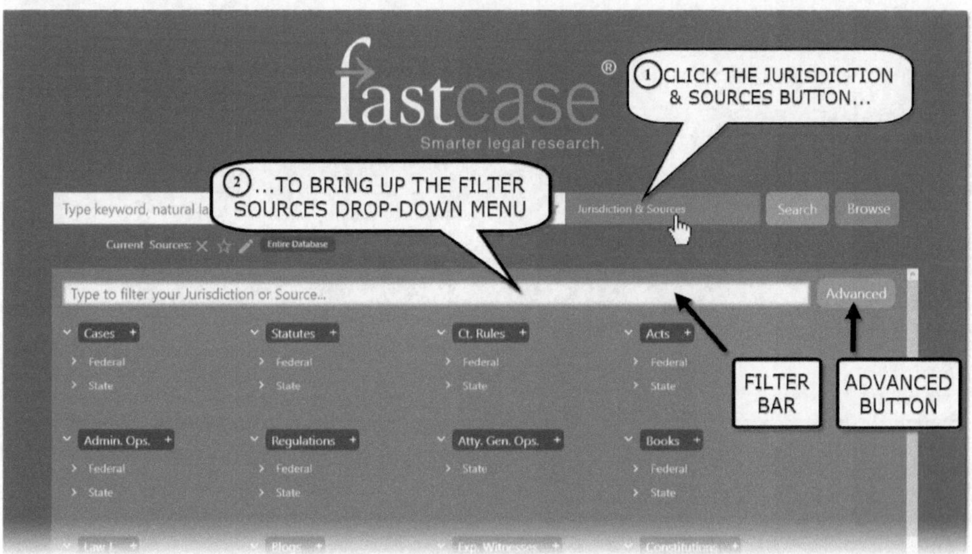


From the Filter Sources drop-down menu, you can click one or more sources to add to your list of **Current Sources** to search. For some of the sources, you can also filter to **State** or **Federal.** Or, you can type the name of a jurisdiction (e.g., California) into the Filter Bar to change the drop-down menu to display that jurisdiction's sources. To add a displayed jurisdiction or source to your search query, click on the jurisdiction or source name, and it will be added to your **Current Sources** list.

To the right of the Filter Bar is the **Advanced** button; click this button to access the Search Options page, shown in Figure 9.4. There are four tabs on this page: **Jurisdiction & Sources, Guided Search, Saved Scopes,** and **Advanced.** Each of these links displays various search options or tools; the Jurisdictions & Sources drop-down menu is displayed by default. A **Date Range** option is also offered at the bottom of the Jurisdictions & Sources page. The other tabs will be discussed later in this chapter.

**Figure 9.4** Fastcase 7 Search Options. Screenshot from Fastcase used with permission.

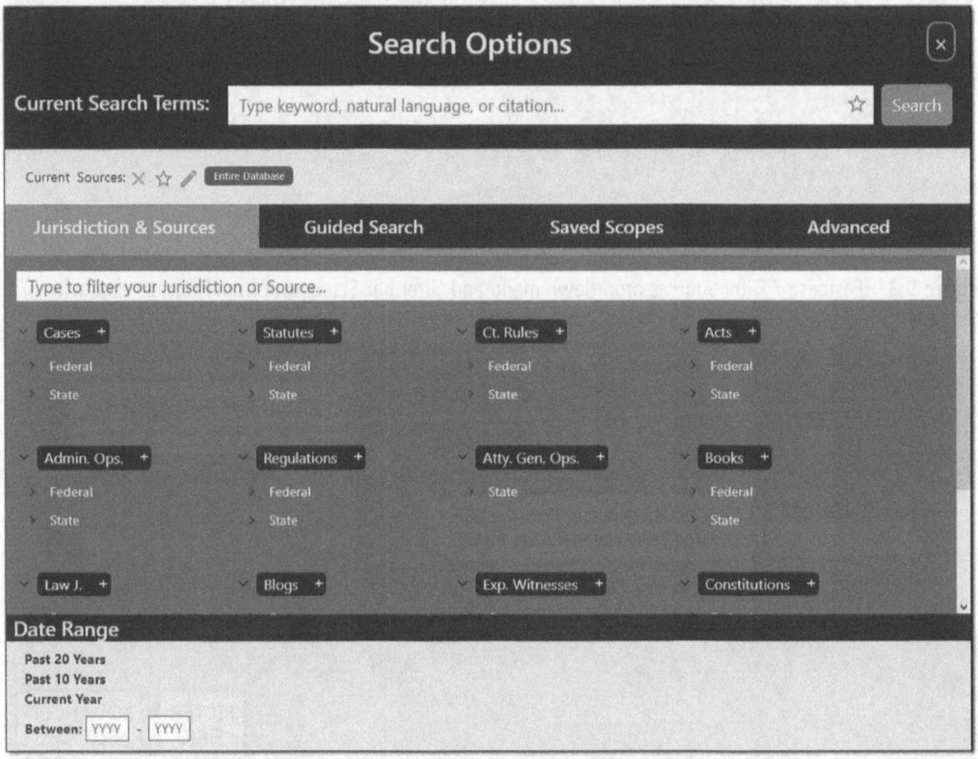

## Searching on Fastcase 7

If you have the citation to a case or other document, just type it into either the search box on the main Fastcase page (Figure 9.5), or the search box on the **Search Options** page (Figure 9.6). Note that Fastcase does not have a separate search box to search by citation (or judge or attorney) like other legal research services, such as Casemaker (see Chapter 8).

One new feature of Fastcase 7 is Type-Ahead Search. When you start typing any search, Type-Ahead Search provides suggested terms and documents. If you are searching by case name, Type-Ahead Search does a good job of displaying the most-likely matches to the case you are looking for. For example, if you don't remember the citation for *Miranda v. Arizona*, just start typing the case name, and Type-Ahead Search gives you a list of possible matches (shown in Figure 9.5), including the full citation to this landmark case. Similarly, if you search by citation to a case, statute, or other document, Type-Ahead Search auto-completes your citation, with the most likely choices at the top of the dynamic list that it generates. If you are searching for keywords (also called Search terms), Type-Ahead Search gives you suggested terms that start with your keyword.

**Figure 9.5** Fastcase 7 Type-Ahead Search. Screenshot from Fastcase used with permission.

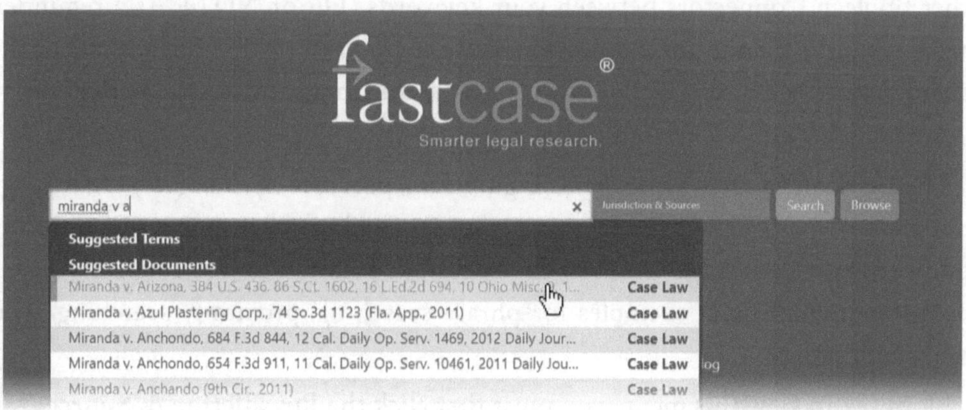


If you do not have a citation and need to search for a relevant case or other document, Fastcase 7 (like Fastcase 6) lets you use either a Keyword Search (also known as a Boolean or terms and connectors search) or a Natural Language Search.

However, as of this writing, Fastcase 7 has not fully implemented its plan to detect whether you are typing a Keyword or a Natural Language Search, so it is running all searches as a Keyword Search. Perhaps by the time you are reading this, Fastcase will have addressed this issue.

## Natural Language Searching

A Natural Language Search, as the name suggests, lets you search by typing a plain English query, such as: *is a landlord liable for injuries caused by a tenant's dog*. Even on Classic Fastcase, where Natural Language Searching works fine, you often get thousands of results, many of which may not be useful to your research. To find more useful, accurate search results, a Keyword Search is usually the better option.

## Keyword Searching

You can enter one or more keywords (or phrases) into the **Current Search Terms** Bar on the homepage (Figure 9.5). By default, your keywords will be connected with the *AND* Boolean Connector (Connectors are also called Operators). Your results will then include all your keywords. You also have the option of adding two other Boolean Connectors between your keywords (*OR* or *NOT*). As a reminder, the *OR* Boolean Connector instructs Fastcase to find results that include one or the other keyword (or both), while the *NOT* Boolean Connector instructs Fastcase to exclude one (or more) keywords from your results.

The **Boolean Search Tips** menu (Figure 9.6), provides **Syntax** (ways to arrange your words) examples so you can create more targeted searches than just connecting your words with the *AND* Boolean Connector. In addition to Boolean Connectors, the menu shows syntax examples for phrase searching, proximity searching, wild card searching, etc.

However, to view this menu, you must first click the **Jurisdiction & Sources** tab (Figure 9.3), then the **Advanced** tab (Figure 9.3), and then the **Guided Search** tab (Figure 9.6).

Another way to search Fastcase is by entering your keywords into one or more of the five **Guided Search** fields shown in Figure 9.6.

To see how Fastcase's Keyword Search syntax works, let's start by searching for cases.

**Figure 9.6** Guided Search and Boolean Search Tips on the Search Options Page. Screenshot from Fastcase used with permission.

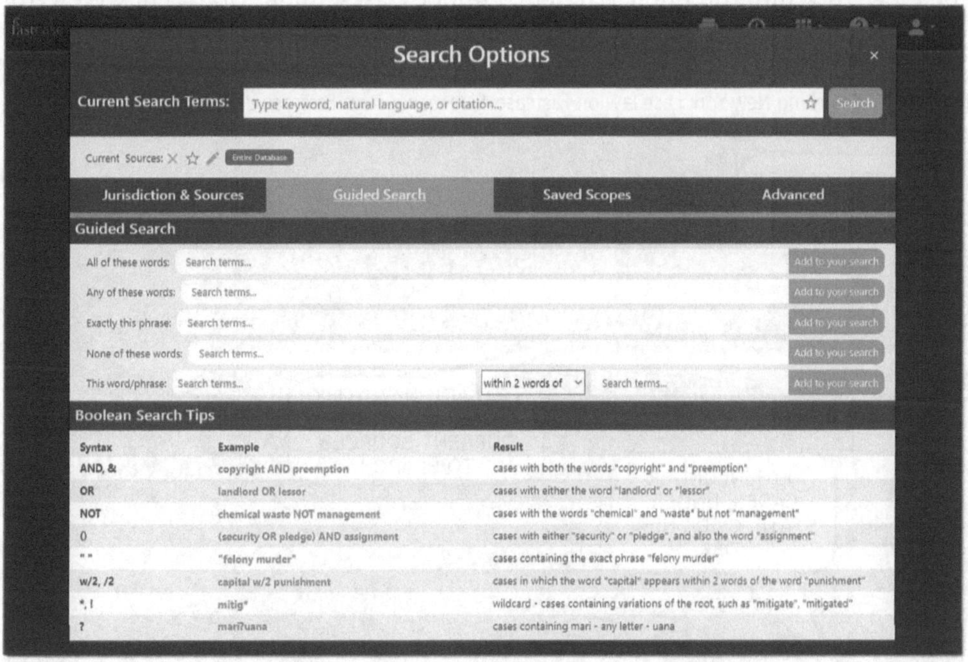


## CASE LAW

Fastcase has the same content on both Fastcase 6 and Fastcase 7. For most states, Fastcase's coverage of case law goes back at least to 1950, and for many states it goes back further, even to the 19th century for some jurisdictions. Fastcase has a full run of all U.S. Supreme Court decisions, and federal cases going back to the start of the West National Reporter System reporters for federal courts of appeal cases (the *Federal Reporter*, now in its third series) and for federal district courts (the *Federal Supplement*, also now in its third series). A complete list of the resources available on Fastcase, with the scope of coverage for case law in state and federal courts, is available at http://www.fastcase.com/coverage. Fastcase frequently adds additional cases, so consult that page if you are curious whether older cases have recently been added in any specific jurisdiction.

Here's an example of a case law search on Fastcase 7. Say you are an attorney in New York and you need to find cases about the liability of a landlord for injuries sustained when a tenant's dog bit someone. First, you will need to select the correct Library, or Libraries. There are several ways to do this. The easiest way is to click the

Jurisdiction & Sources button to open the Filter Sources drop-down menu and type New York into the Filter Bar. Then under Cases, under State, click New York to add all the New York case libraries to your Current Sources.

**Figure 9.7** Searching New York case law on Fastcase. Screenshot from Fastcase used with permission.

A good keyword search for this issue would be something like *landlord /7 "dog bite"*; this proximity search looks for the word landlord within seven words—the /7 in this search query—of the two-word phrase "dog bite." (Using quotation marks requires Fastcase 7 to search for those words as a phrase.) Click the search button to run this search in the selected New York case Libraries. (See Figure 9.7.)

Figure 9.8 shows the results list for this search, with thirteen cases from New York. By default, the cases are listed by relevance. The relevance of each search result is shown as a percentage, listed to the left of the case name and citation. Note two other things on the Search Results page. First, look at the small arrows between, and on the edges of, the various parts of this, and other, Fastcase pages; these Re-Sizing Arrows can be used to display, or hide, parts of any Fastcase page. Second, notice the small Star icon to the right of your search: clicking on that icon will save your current search to your Favorite Searches. Retrieving Favorite Searches will be mentioned later in this chapter.

**Figure 9.8** Search Results List on Fastcase 7. Screenshot from Fastcase used with permission.

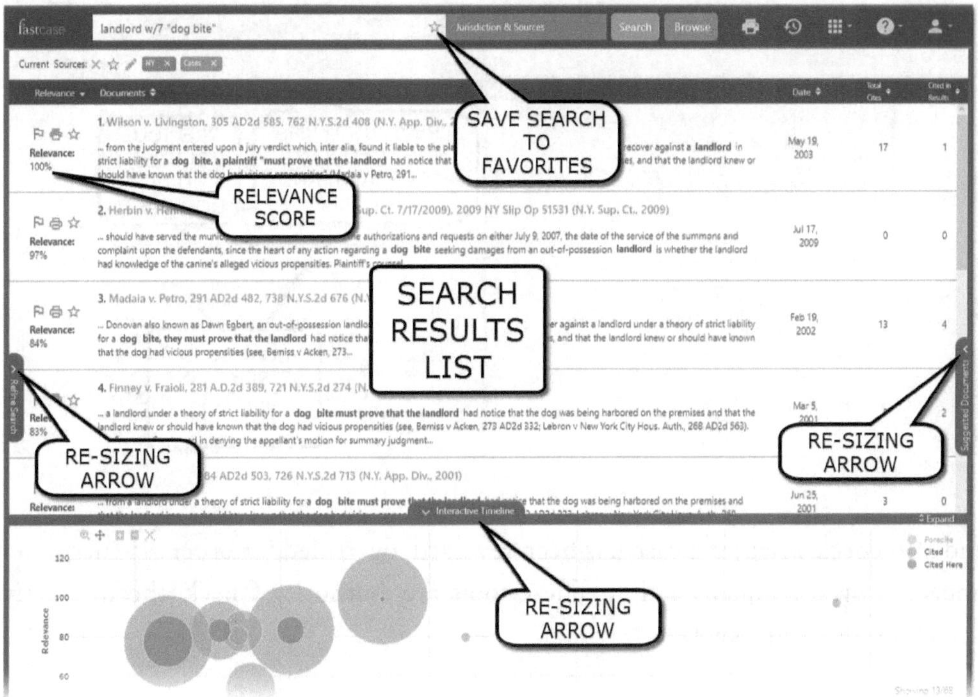


Click any case in the search results to view the full text of the opinion. Figure 9.9 shows case from these results. Notice a few features about this page:

- The case is shown on the right side, and you can still see your list of search results on the left.
- Your search terms are highlighted in the opinion, and you can navigate forward and backwards among the instances of the search terms with the **Previous Term** and **Next Term** arrows, found at the top of the court opinion.
- The icon that looks like a sheet of paper with highlighted text, between the **Previous Term** and **Next Term** arrows, is the **Most Relevant Paragraph icon.** Click it to go to the part of the opinion with the most instances of your search terms.
- The **Previous Document** and **Next Document** arrows will take you forward and backward through the documents in your search results.

Fastcase provides some additional tools to help you work with case law. These tools can help you determine which cases are the most relevant and authoritative,

**Figure 9.9** Viewing a case on Fastcase. Screenshot from Fastcase used with permission.

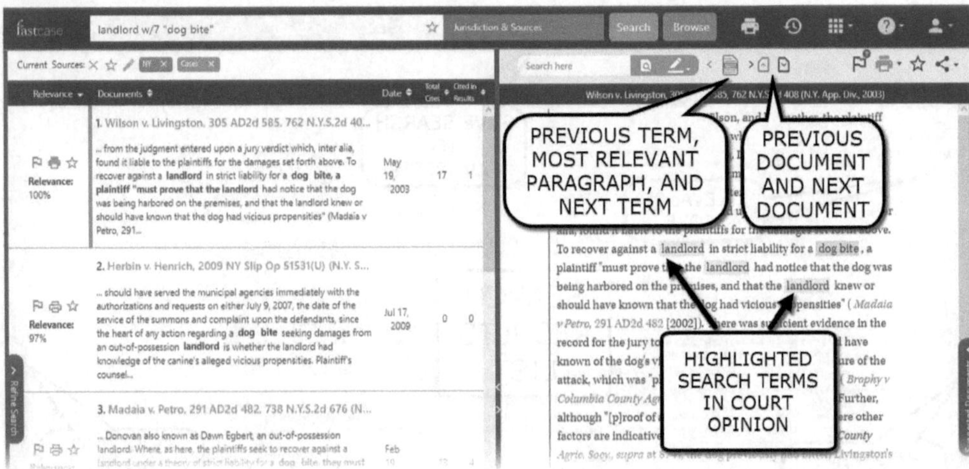


and also check whether a case has been reversed, overruled, or otherwise negatively impacted by subsequent action. These tools are Authority Check, the Interactive Timeline, and Bad Law Bot.

## AUTHORITY CHECK

The first of these tools is **Authority Check.** Authority Check tells you how many other cases have cited to the cases in your search results. Back on the search results page with New York cases about landlords and dog bite injuries, to the right of each case's name and citations, past the case date, notice the two numbers: Total Cites and Cited in Results; these are the Authority Check statistics (see Figure 9.10). "Total Cites" is how many times a case was cited in all the cases on Fastcase, and "Cited in Results" is how many times a case was cited within the other cases in these search results.

**Figure 9.10** Case search results and Authority Check statistics. Screenshot from Fastcase used with permission.

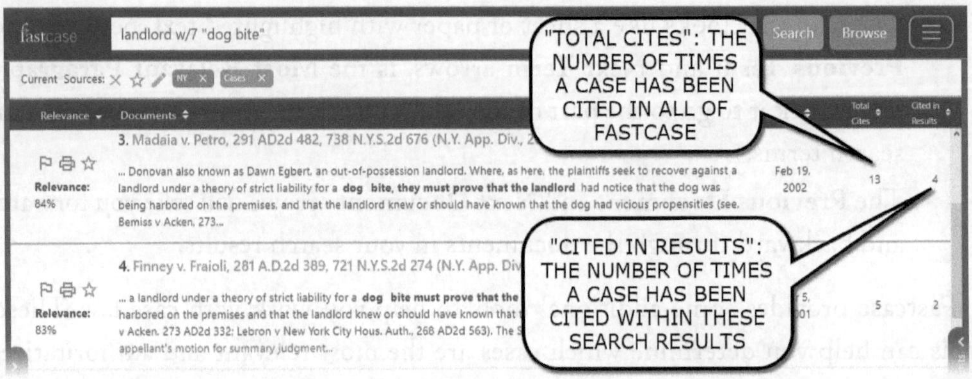

If you want to re-order the search results so that the top of the list shows the cases that were most cited by other cases in these search results, click on "Cited in Results" at the top of that column of numbers.

Figure 9.11 shows this re-sorted list, now with *Bemiss v. Acken* at the top. As the Results number for this case shows, it has been cited by nine of the other cases in these search results. Cases can be cited for many reasons, but this is a strong indication that *Bemiss* may be particularly relevant to this issue. If a case in your search results has been cited by a large number of cases in all of Fastcase, but only by a few cases within your search results, it may not be as relevant for your purposes because it was likely cited for some issue other than the one you are researching.

**Figure 9.11** Cases sorted by "Cited in Results." Screenshot from Fastcase used with permission.

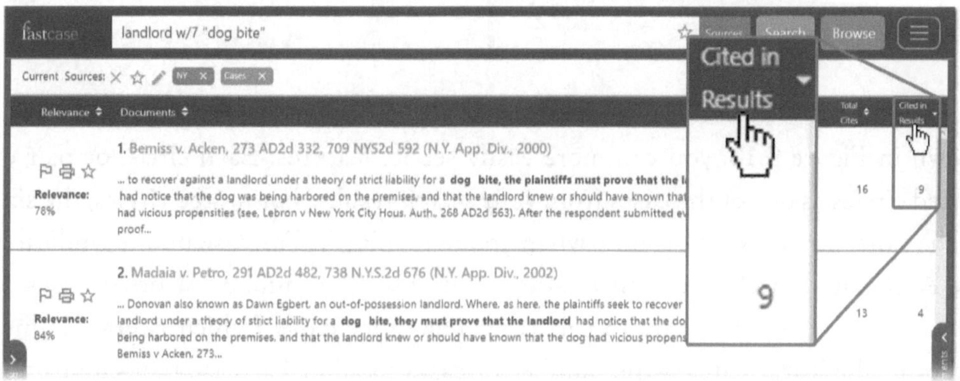

You can also get a full Authority Check Report, listing all cases that cite to the case you are viewing. Click the small Authority Check **Flag icon** on the toolbar above the opinion, as shown in Figure 9.12.

## INTERACTIVE TIMELINE

The **Interactive Timeline** takes the Authority Check citation statistics for a group of search results and presents them in a graphical format. You can more easily visualize each case's weight of authority, as well as see other relevant details about the cases, with the Interactive Timeline. Figure 9.13 is an expansion of the small Interactive Timeline (the group of different-sized circles) that you might have noticed below the list of search results back in Figure 9.9. As mentioned earlier, like with any part of the Fastcase screen, you can use the Re-Sizing Arrows to make the Interactive Timeline larger. Once you have expanded the Interactive Timeline, as

**Figure 9.12** Authority Check Report. Screenshot from Fastcase used with permission.

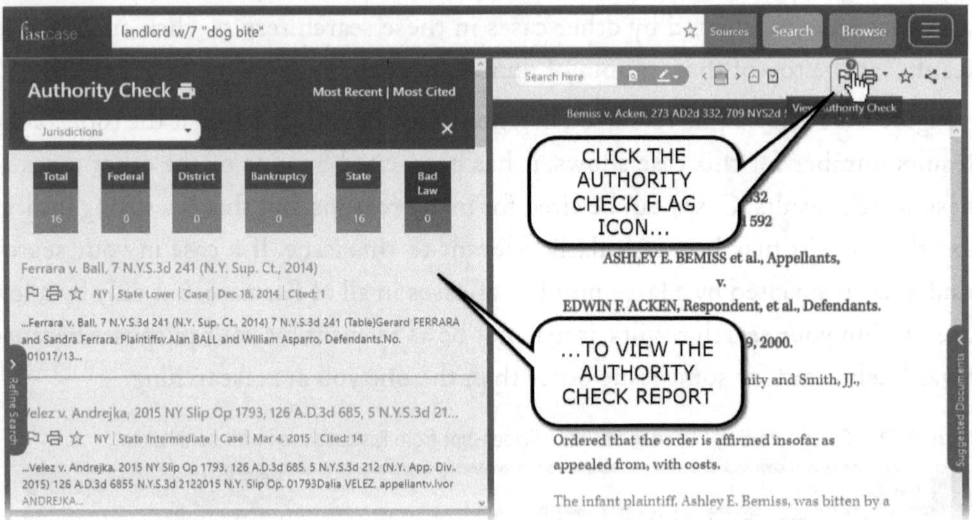


shown in Figure 9.13, you can more easily see its features. Each circle, or pair of nested circles, is one of the cases from your search results. For nested circles, the size of the inner circle (which is blue when you're looking at Fastcase online) indicates the Authority Check **Cited in Results** citations—the number of other cases in these search results that cite to this case. The outer circle (which is gray online) indicates the **Total Cites**—the number of cases in all of Fastcase that cite to this case. For both circles, the bigger they are, the more cases that cite to that case.

The cases in the Interactive Timeline graph are placed chronologically along the horizontal axis shown at the bottom, with older cases to the left, and newer cases to the right. Vertically, cases are placed with the most relevant cases at the top and less relevant cases at the bottom. You can change the default vertical display by using the **Y-Axis** menu at the bottom right corner of the Interactive Timeline. You can use this drop-down menu to arrange the cases vertically by **Authority**, i.e., by court level. Displaying the cases by Court Level is primarily useful when researching federal cases. Using the **Authority** display lets you easily see which cases are from Federal District Courts, Federal Appellate Courts, and which, if any, are from the U.S. Supreme Court.

To see information about any of the cases on the Interactive Timeline, just hover your cursor over it. A pop-up will appear showing the name and citation of the case, as well as an excerpt of the case where your search terms appear the most, and the two Authority Check statistics: the number of times that case has been cited within these search results (the "Cited Here" number), and the number of times it has been

**Figure 9.13** The Interactive Timeline. Screenshot from Fastcase used with permission.

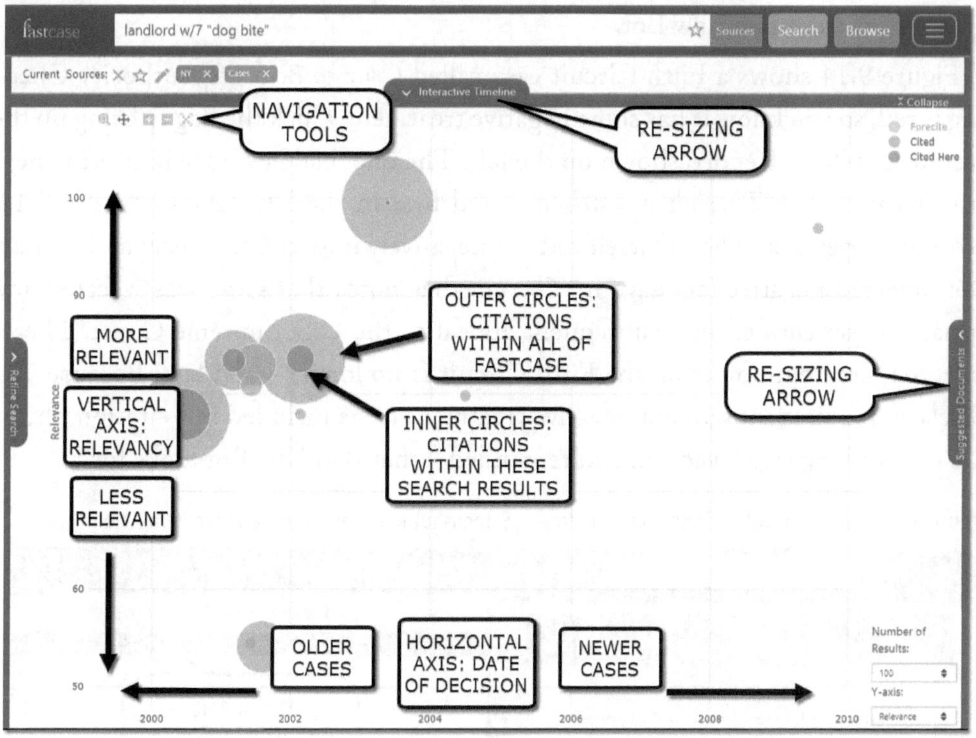


cited in all cases on Fastcase (the "Cited" number). If you have a lot of cases on the Interactive Timeline, you can use the navigation tools in the upper left corner to zoom in, pan, and zoom out (see Figure 9.13). This will let you focus on only part of the Interactive Timeline, which can be helpful when there are many cases in it that overlap each other.

## BAD LAW BOT

Fastcase's citator tool, which is used to check whether a case you have found is still good law, is called Bad Law Bot. Bad Law Bot isn't a full citation service like Shepard's or KeyCite. Instead, Bad Law Bot uses citation analysis algorithms to look for text indicating that a case has been reversed, overruled, or negatively impacted by subsequent judicial proceedings, and even whether a case has been affected by subsequent legislation.

Bad Law Bot is integrated into Fastcase in several ways. First, if you see a red flag to the left of a case in the list of search results, that is Bad Law Bot's signal that the case has received some sort of negative treatment. If the Authority Check Report flag on the toolbar above the text of the opinion is red, that is also a negative treatment signal from Bad Law Bot.

Figure 9.14 shows a Fifth Circuit case called *Cruz v. Beto*; its Authority Check flag is red, so you know it has some negative treatment. Click the flag to bring up the Authority Check Report, shown on the left. The one "bad law" case indicating negative treatment is *Therialt v. Carlson*, listed first in the left pane of Figure 9.14. Note, however, that *Therialt* itself did not negatively impact *Cruz*. Instead, Bad Law Bot detected negative language in *Therialt* that notes that *Cruz* was "vacated and remanded *per curiam*" in a subsequent appeal to the U.S. Supreme Court. Therefore, the *Cruz* opinion from the Fifth Circuit is no longer "good law." Because *The Bluebook* requires subsequent negative treatment to be included in a citation, this is the type of language ("vacated and remanded") that Bad Law Bot looks for.

**Figure 9.14** Bad Law Bot finds negative treatment. Screenshot from Fastcase used with permission.

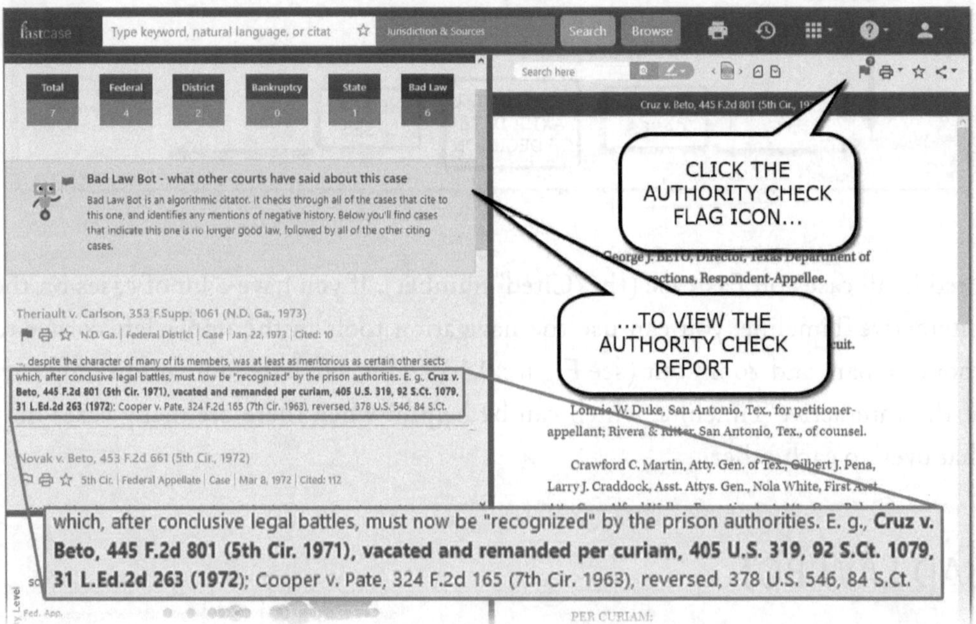


# STATUTES

Fastcase has the U.S. Code and current statutes for all states. It also has the session laws and copies of superseded statutes for many jurisdictions. To find statutes and other legislative resources for a given state, use the Jurisdiction & Sources Tab on the Search Options page. For example, to find the current Arkansas statutes, type

Arkansas to filter and display only resources from Arkansas. Then, under Statutes, click the link for the Arkansas Code to add it to the Current Sources to search (see Figure 9.15).

**Figure 9.15** Using Search Options to select a statutes Library. Screenshot from Fastcase used with permission.

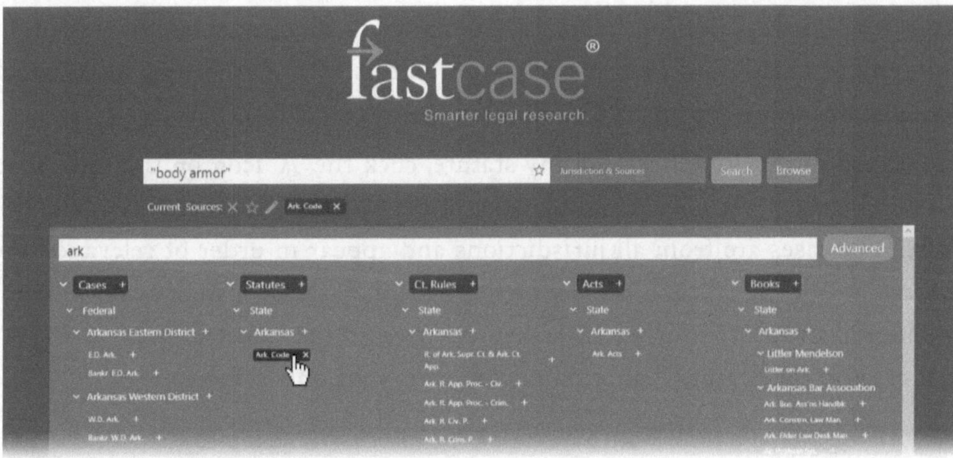


Say you need to find the criminal statute in Arkansas about possessing body armor. With the library for the Arkansas Code selected, enter the phrase, "*body armor*" and click the Search Button. The left side of Figure 9.16 shows the first of the two search results; the first is Ark. Code § 5-79-101, Criminal possession of body armor (the second search result is just the chapter heading for the part of the code containing this section). After you click the first result, its full text is displayed on the right side of the page.

**Figure 9.16** Statutes search results. Screenshot from Fastcase used with permission.

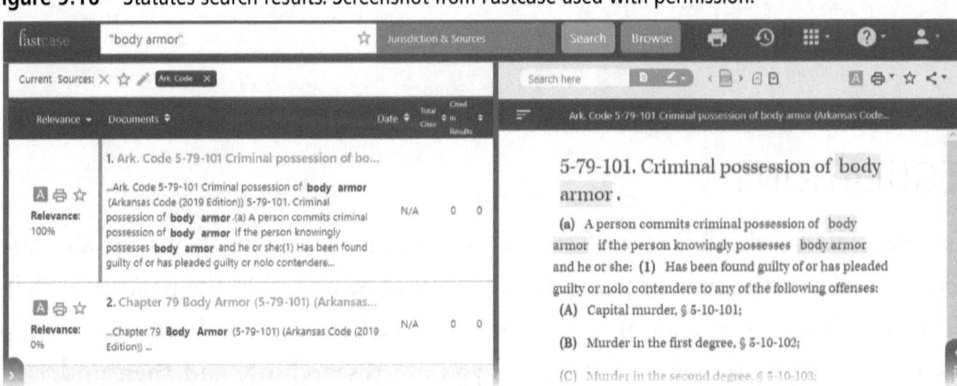

## AUTHORITY CHECK FOR STATUTES

One final tool for researching statutes on Fastcase 7 is worth mentioning. As detailed as any given statute might be, legislators cannot anticipate every fact situation in the real world, and often courts are required to decide cases involving a statute where its application is not straightforward. Finding cases that discuss a statute can be useful, and Fastcase helps you do this with Authority Check, which works just like using Authority Check with cases, as shown earlier.

To access Authority Check for any statute, click the "A" icon on the toolbar, as shown in Figure 9.17. This brings up a list of cases in the left column that cite this statute. The cases are from all jurisdictions and appear in order of relevance, but there are no additional tools to sort or filter them. Fastcase also does not provide any editorial signals to indicate how the cases treated the statute. So, browsing the list of cases in the Statute Annotations Report is your only option.

**Figure 9.17** Statutes Annotations Report on Fastcase 7. Screenshot from Fastcase used with permission.

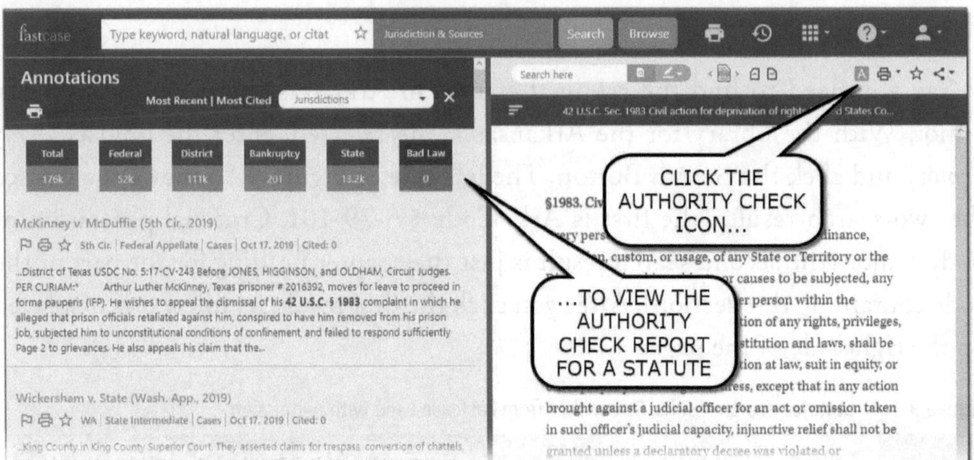


## REGULATIONS

Fastcase provides the full text of federal regulations and regulations for all states except Arkansas (the Arkansas regulations should be added in the near future). To select the Library for the set of regulations you need, go to the Filter Sources drop-down menu, type the name of the state you are researching, and then under the regulations category look for that state's regulations. The state compilations of regulations have various names such as the Ohio Administrative Code, the Code of Vermont Rules, and the California Code of Regulations. The compilation of federal regulations are published in the Code of Federal Regulations ("CFR"); type federal into the Filter Sources drop-down menu to sort for federal resources, and under the regulations category you'll see the link for the Code of Federal Regulations Library.

Regulations are searched the same way as you search other Libraries on Fastcase (e.g., by keyword or citation). Note that Fastcase has not enabled Authority Check for regulations, though they have said they will do so in the future. Instead, for the time being, if you want to find cases that cite to a regulation, you will need to conduct a search for that regulation's citation in the case law Library for the jurisdiction you are researching. For example, to see if the U.S. Supreme Court has ever cited 29 CFR § 516.2 in one of its decisions, select the Library for Supreme Court cases and run a keyword/phrase search such as *"29 CFR" /3 516.2*. Notice that this search uses the proximity connector with the number three - /3 - to find any instance of the phrase *"29 CFR"* within three words of *516.2*, the CFR section we are looking for. Courts do not necessarily cite regulations like the CFR using a consistent format; for example, sometimes they spell out the word "section," and sometimes they use the section symbol (§). A search like this should find the CFR section, no matter what format was used to cite it. Figure 9.18 shows a Supreme Court case that cited the section, found by running this search.

**Figure 9.18** Finding a case that cites to a regulation. Screenshot from Fastcase used with permission.

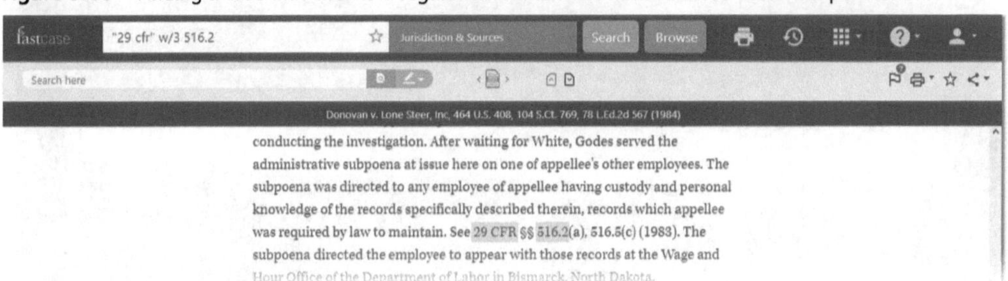


## SECONDARY RESOURCES

Besides primary resources like cases, statutes, and regulations, Fastcase provides users with access to a good number of secondary resources like law journals, treatises, and practice guides. However, access to many of these secondary resources requires a separate subscription to companies that Fastcase has partnered with. Also, some state-specific secondary resources are only available to members of that state's bar association.

## TREATISES

Fastcase users can access over a hundred treatises, but most of them require an additional subscription fee. Some of these treatises are specific to certain jurisdiction, and some are not.

To find treatises on Fastcase 7, click Jurisdiction & Sources, type in the name of the jurisdiction you're working in into the Filter Bar, then scroll down the resulting categories of resources to see if one of these categories is named Books: that is where Fastcase will list any treatises it has available for that jurisdiction. (If there is NOT a category named Books, then Fastcase doesn't have any treatises for that jurisdiction.)

Figure 9.19 shows how to use this technique to look for treatises from California: if you are defending a DUI cases in California, Fastcase provides a title called California Drunk Driving Law, from James Publishing.

**Figure 9.19** Selecting a state-specific treatise. Screenshot from Fastcase used with permission.

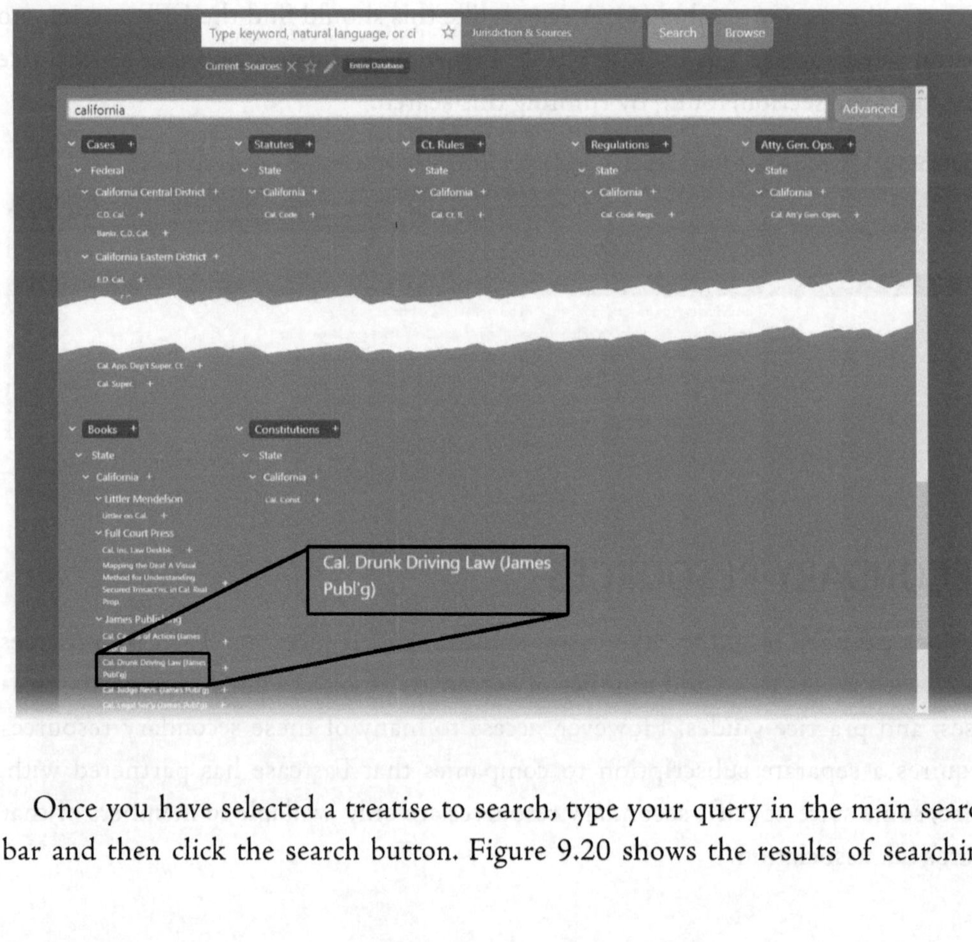


Once you have selected a treatise to search, type your query in the main search bar and then click the search button. Figure 9.20 shows the results of searching

California Drunk Driving Law for the word breathalyzer. Note that access to most treatises like this require an additional subscription on Fastcase: if you try to access one of these search results and you haven't subscribed to the treatise, you'll get a notice that it is outside your subscription.

**Figure 9.20** Search Results from a treatise. Screenshot from Fastcase used with permission.

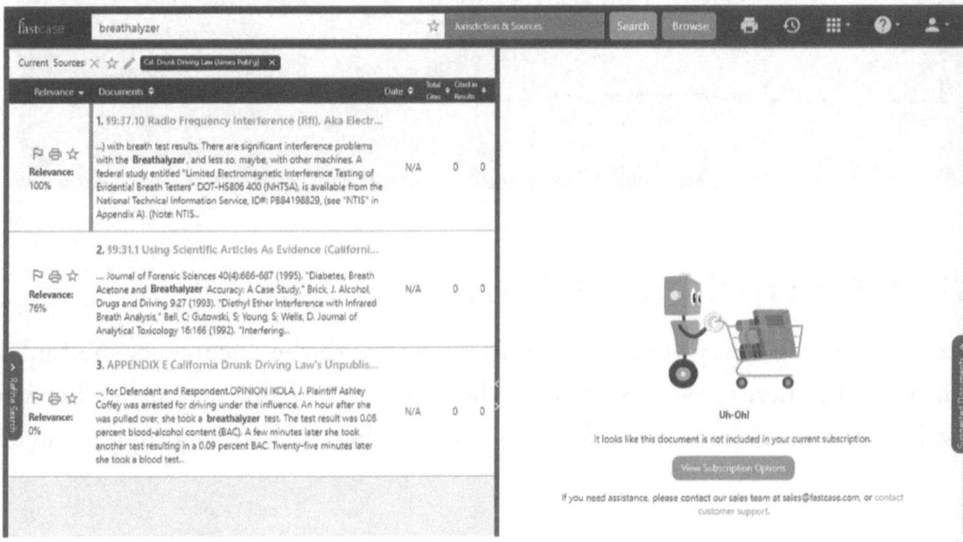


## LAW REVIEWS

Fastcase has partnered with HeinOnline to integrate its database of articles from law review articles into Fastcase's search tools. To access the full text of the articles on HeinOnline, however, you or your firm will need to have a subscription, or pay for short-term access.

As of this writing, Fastcase doesn't let you search within only specific law reviews, but you can search all 2,000+ journals at once. To search all of HeinOnline, click Jurisdictions & Sources and then filter by the word Journal. This brings up the sources shown in Figure 9.21. Under Other is listed HeinOnline, and below that is the link for Hein Journals (abbreviated "Hein Js"): click that to load all HeinOnline law reviews and journals into the Current Sources so you can search them.

When you find a useful article, if you have a HeinOnline subscription or pay for short-term access, you can then get a full-text PDF copy of the article. (See the Articles section in Chapter 1 to learn how to obtain certain law—and non-law—journal articles for free.)

**Figure 9.21** Finding law review articles from HeinOnline on Fastcase 7. Screenshot from Fastcase used with permission.

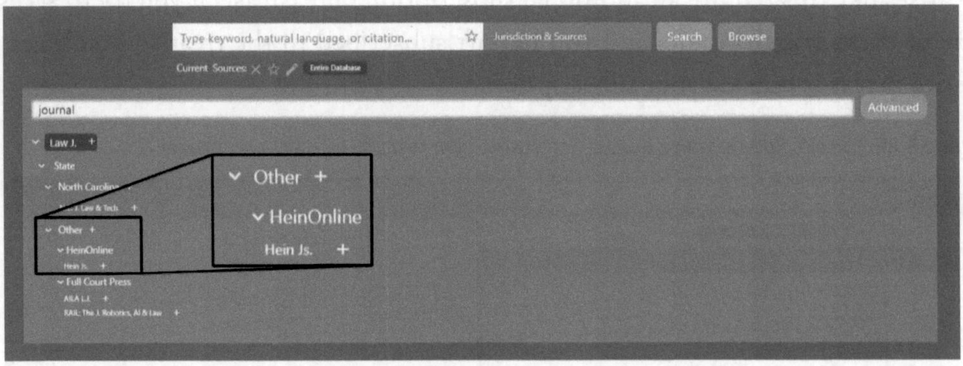


## WORKING WITH DOCUMENTS

Fastcase gives you a very good set of tools to work with the documents you find in your research. There are several icons on the toolbar above any document when you view it from a list of search results that will let you do just about anything you need.

### Printing

Two printing options are available under the Print Icon (see Figure 9.22). You can either print a single document when you find it ("Print Now"), or add a document to a print queue to print later ("Add to Print Queue"). You can also add documents to your print queue directly from the search results list by clicking the printer icon to the left of the name and citation of the document.

**Figure 9.22** Printing Options under the Printer Icon. Screenshot from Fastcase used with permission.

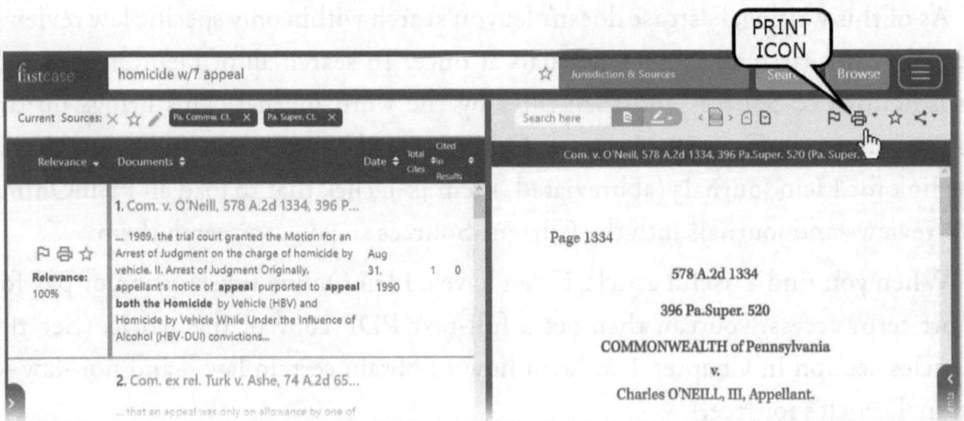

When you click **Print Now**, you get a pop-up window with the options shown in Figure 9.23. By default, dual-column printing is already checked, and you can choose to highlight your search terms by clicking that checkbox. There is also a pull-down menu: if you don't want to create a PDF of your document, then you can specify Microsoft Word. After making these selections, click **Print** for Fastcase to configure your document. You'll get a notice that your document is prepared, and then, depending on your browser and computer configurations, you might either get an Open/Save dialogue box as shown in Figure 9.24, or your computer might start to download the document in the background and notify you when it has downloaded it to the default folder.

**Figure 9.23** Print Options. Screenshot from Fastcase used with permission.

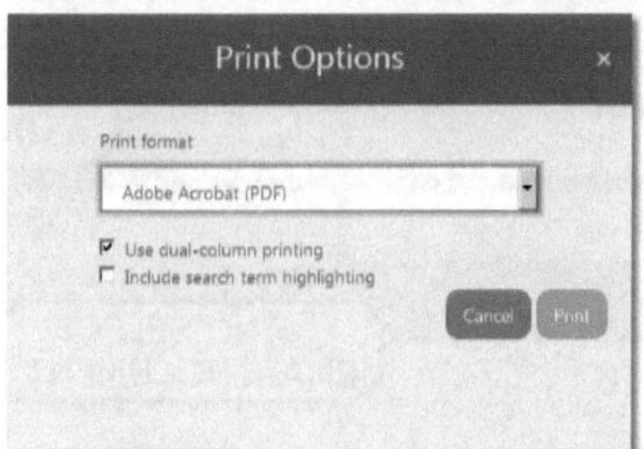


The Print Queue options are similar to the ones for printing a single document, with the additional step allowing you to either select all the documents in your queue or select only some of them. Then Fastcase asks you to name the document queue, set the other options, and specify whether you want to print them to a single document, or zip the files together to download.

**Figure 9.24** Open/Save Dialog Box. Screenshot from Fastcase used with permission.

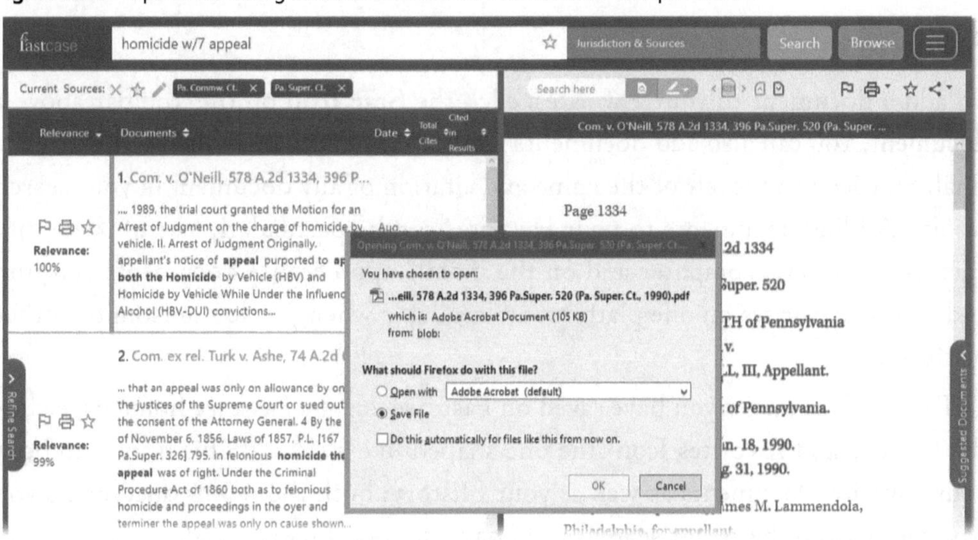

## Emailing Documents

Fastcase provides several other options to save and share your research. Using Fastcase's rudimentary email option, you can email a document to someone by selecting the Share this Document icon from the Toolbar and clicking Email Document (see Figure 9.25). However, the Fastcase email feature only allows you to email one document at a time. You also cannot add a message to the document, and you can't email the document as an attachment: the text of the document is actually displayed in the body of the email. Additionally, the email shows Fastcase as the sender and not you, which might confuse a client or co-counsel. So, if you need to email documents, it is probably better to download and then email them from your own email account as an attachment.

**Figure 9.25** Emailing a document. Screenshot from Fastcase used with permission.

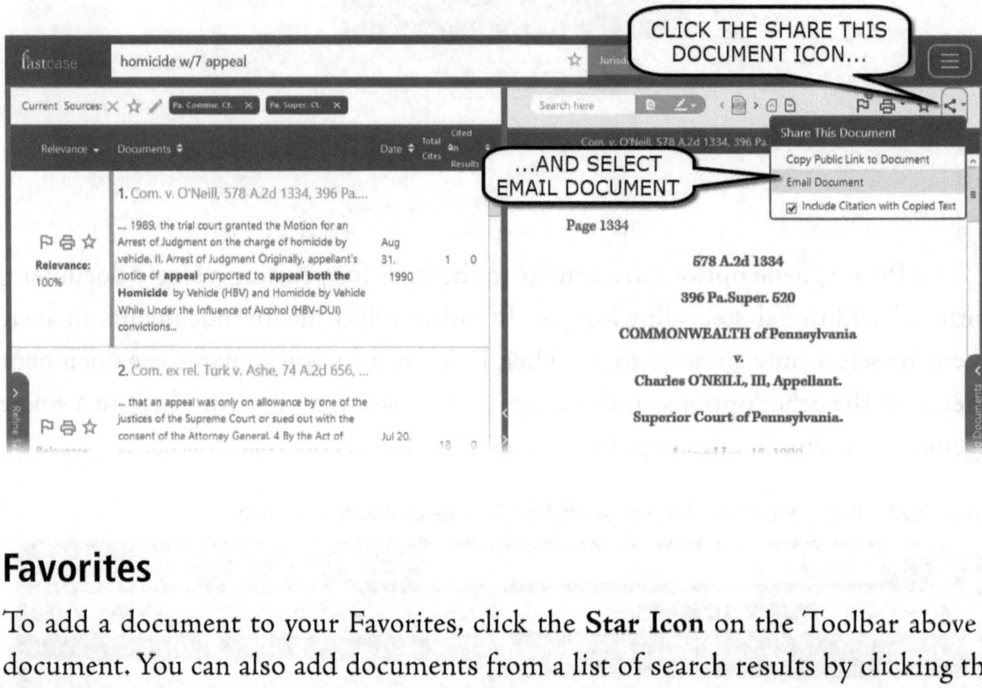


## Favorites

To add a document to your Favorites, click the **Star Icon** on the Toolbar above a document. You can also add documents from a list of search results by clicking the small Star Icon to the left of the name and citation of any document in your search results. Adding documents to your Favorites can be particularly useful if you use Fastcase both on a computer and on the mobile app because documents you find and save as Favorites on one platform are available when you log in from the other platform.

To view documents you have saved on Fastcase, on the Fastcase home page click the History and Favorites Icon (the one shaped like a clock). This brings up both your Favorite Documents as well as your History: both the recent documents you have viewed and the recent searches you have run (see Figure 9.26).

**Figure 9.26** History and Favorite Documents on Fastcase 7. Screenshot from Fastcase used with permission.

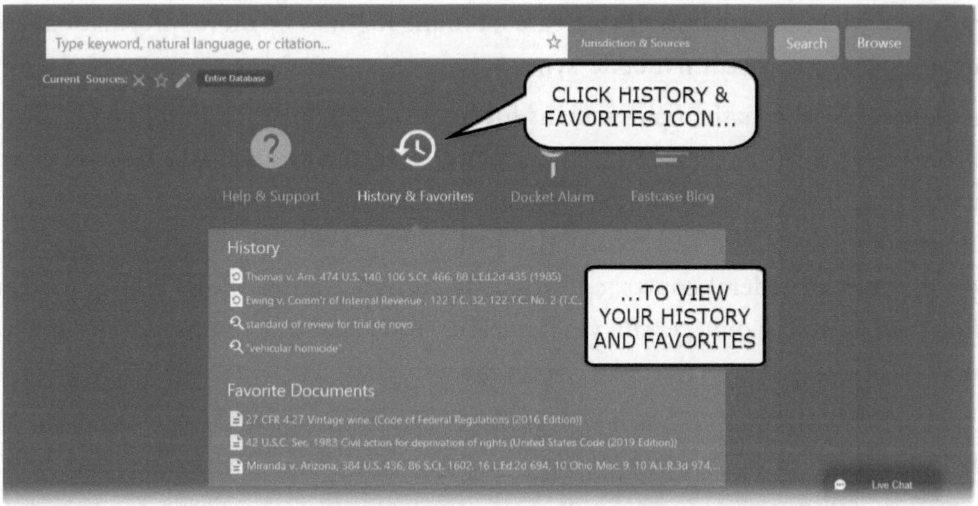


## Share Documents with Non-Fastcase Users

Finally, Fastcase lets you share documents and search results. Under the Share this Document Icon (where the Email Document link shown in Figure 9.25 is located), when you click **Copy Public Link to Document**, Fastcase displays a unique public URL for that document. You can then copy and paste the URL for that document and share it by email, blog post, or in a brief or other document. Anyone can then view that document through the URL, even if they do not have a Fastcase account; and because the link is static, it will not expire. Fastcase also uses unique, static URLs for each set of results generated by every search you conduct on Fastcase. You can copy and paste those URLs into an email, word processing document, etc. However, anyone with whom you share your search results URLs will need their own Fastcase account to access those documents.

# THE FASTCASE MOBILE APPS

Fastcase has free mobile apps for both Apple and Android devices (and an app for Windows mobile devices is in the works). You can only work with cases and statutes on the mobile version of Fastcase, but if you need to a read a statute or look up a case while away from your office, the Fastcase mobile app is the way to do this. You can also sync the mobile app with your existing Fastcase account to access recent searches and saved documents. Just log into the mobile app with the same credentials you use to log in to the web version of Fastcase. Or, if you use the web version through a portal such as your bar association's web page or your firm's intranet, you can use Fastcase's Mobile Sync option to create a unique log-in. For more information, see http://www.fastcase.com/mobile-sync.

Figure 9.27 shows the main screens for both the Apple and Android apps. Both screens have three options: **Search Caselaw**, **Search Statutes**, and **Browse Statutes**. Click **Search Caselaw** to view the case law search options for both apps (shown in Figure 9.28). You can use the **Jurisdiction** option to search for cases from specific state or federal courts, and the **Date Range** option allows you to further limit your search to only certain years of cases. You can use the same search connectors on the Fastcase app that you use on the web platform.

Figure 9.29 shows a case as it appears on the Android app and Figure 9.30 shows that same case on the Apple App.

One major difference between the two apps is that you can rotate Apple mobile devices so the Fastcase app's display will show both the text of a case and the list of search results, as shown in Figure 9.31. The Android app does not do this when you rotate the screen.

Unlike with the web version of Fastcase, you cannot search multiple state statutes (or multiple case law Libraries) at the same time. To search for statutes, return to the main screen on the app and select that option, then click **Source** to select either the U.S. Code or the statutes for a specific state. Figure 9.32 shows how to select the latest edition of the Arkansas Code on the Apple Fastcase app. First click **Source**; then click **Arkansas**, and then **Arkansas Code (2017 Edition)**, the latest edition of the Arkansas Code on the Fastcase app (as of this writing). If you then want to find the section of the Arkansas Code that mentions body armor, type those words as a phrase (with quotation marks around them) and click **Search**, as shown in Figure 9.33.

Figure 9.34 shows the resulting document, Ark. Code §5-79-101, on the Apple app, and Figure 9.35 shows this same section on the Android app. Note that both apps provide the same basic functionality as the web version when viewing documents. You can save the document you're looking at, you can search within the text of the document, and you can move to the previous or next document in a list of results.

**Figure 9.27** Fastcase mobile apps: Apple (left) and Android (right). Screenshots from Fastcase used with permission.

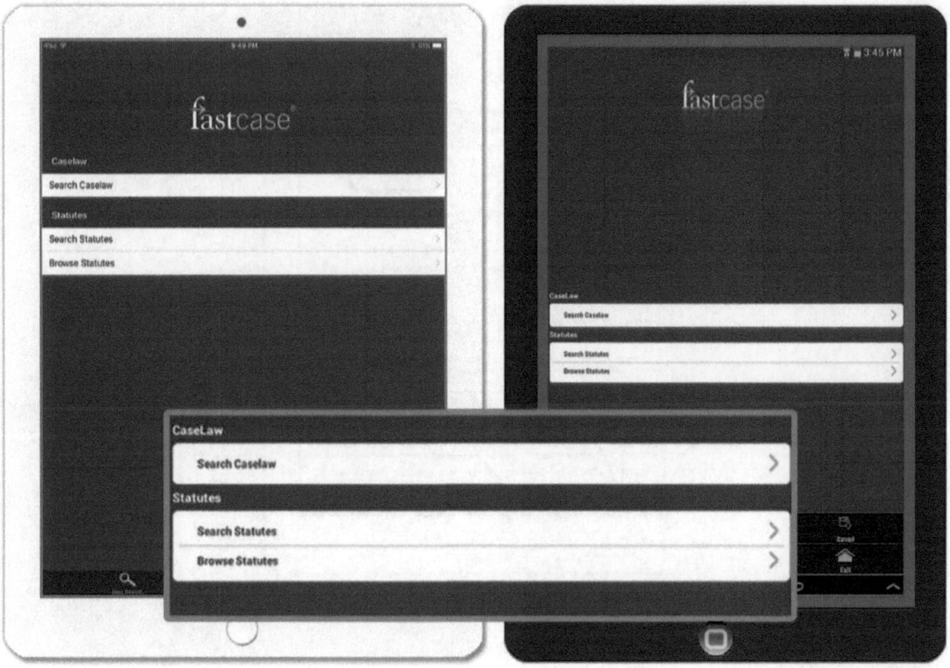


**Figure 9.28** Searching for cases on the Fastcase mobile app. Screenshots from Fastcase used with permission.

Figure 9.29 Viewing a case on the Fastcase Android app. Screenshot from Fastcase used with permission.

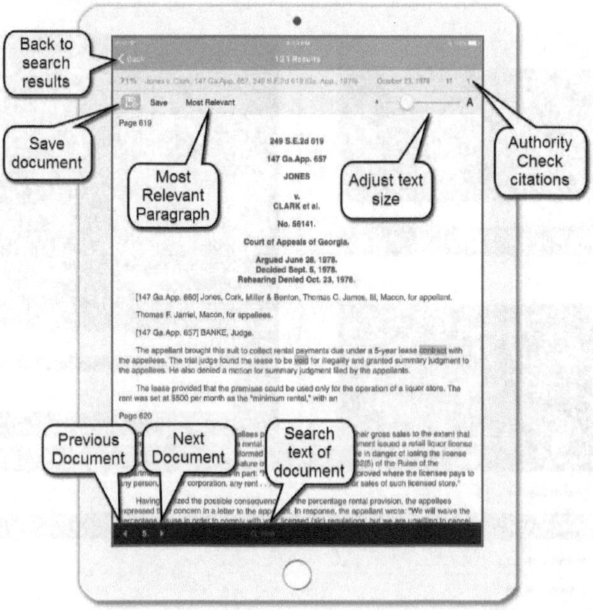


Figure 9.30 Viewing a case on the Fastcase Apple app. Screenshot from Fastcase used with permission.

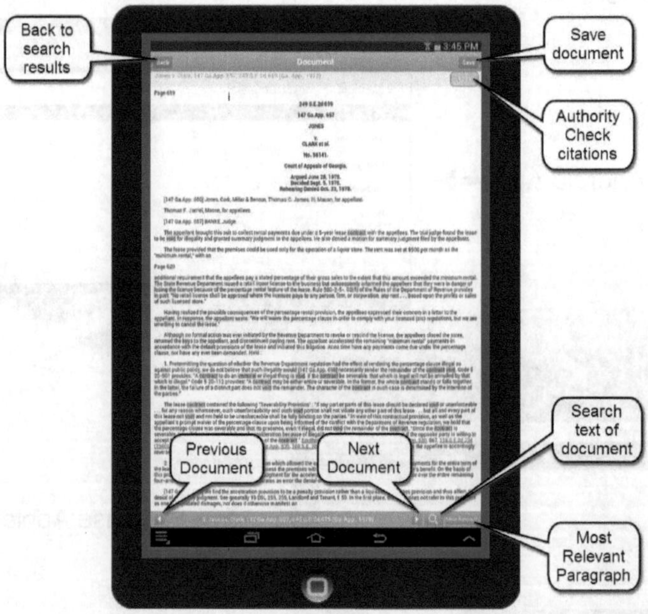

**Figure 9.31** Search results and a case opinion on the Apple app. Screenshot from Fastcase used with permission.

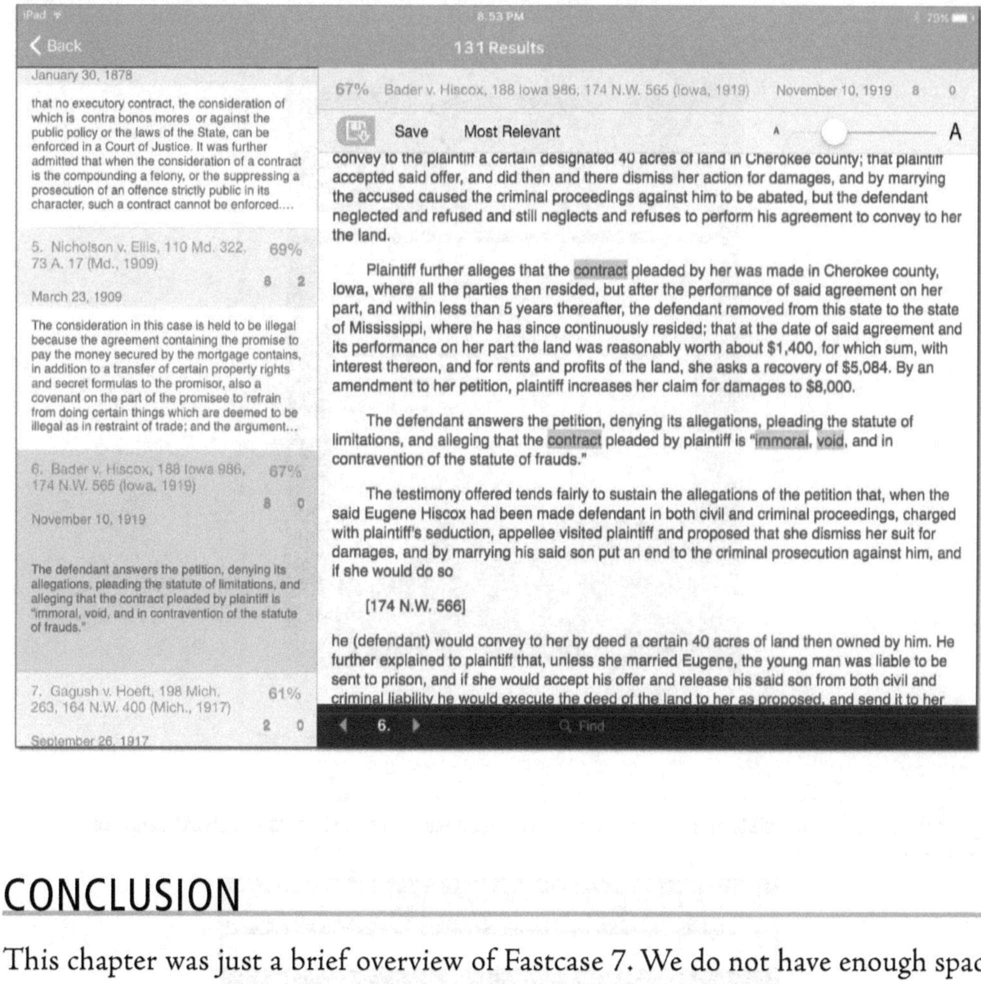

## CONCLUSION

This chapter was just a brief overview of Fastcase 7. We do not have enough space here to cover court rules, constitutions, and some other types of resources, nor to go into more detail about some of the research tools and advanced techniques that can help you make full use of Fastcase 7, but this chapter should give you a running start. To learn more about Fastcase, click the Question mark on the upper right-hand side of the homepage (or on any search results page). A **Help & Tutorials** menu will drop down and offer you links to **Changelog** (What's New), **User Guide, Tutorials,** and **Webinar Schedule, Hotkeys** (Shortcuts), and **More Support** (Email or Call). If you prefer to chat, click the **Live Chat** button on the lower right side of any search results page.

**Figure 9.32** Selecting state statutes to search on the Fastcase app. Screenshot from Fastcase used with permission.

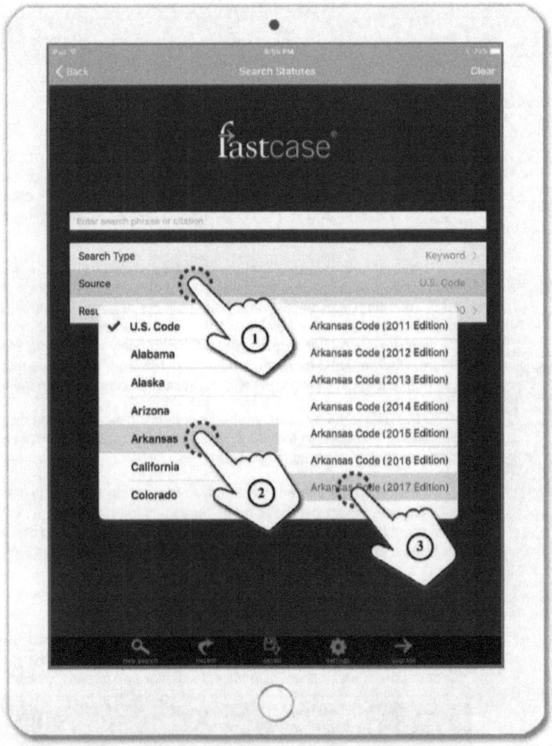


**Figure 9.33** Searching state statutes on the Fastcase mobile app. Screenshot from Fastcase used with permission.

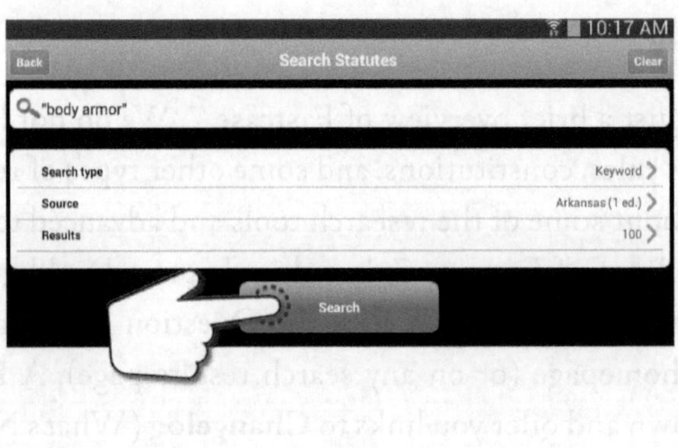

**Figure 9.34** A state statute on the Apple Fastcase app. Screenshot from Fastcase used with permission.

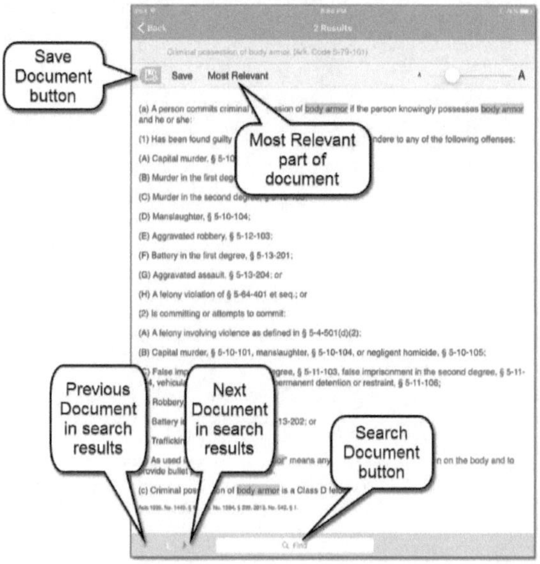


**Figure 9.35** A state statute on the Android Fastcase app. Screenshot from Fastcase used with permission.

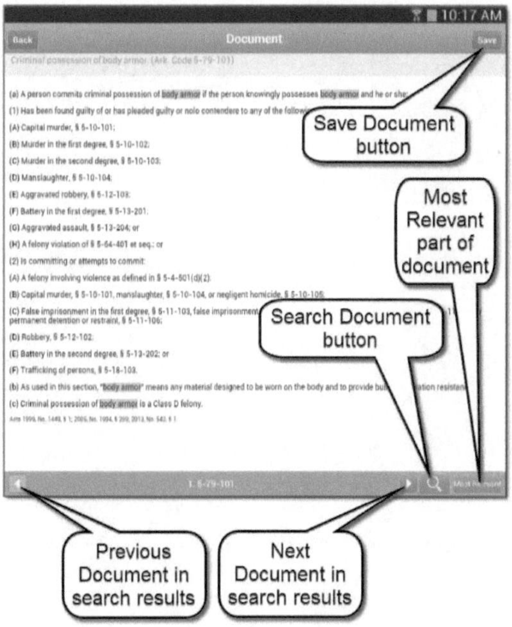

# Chapter 10

## FEDERAL STATUTORY RESEARCH

A great deal of federal statutory information is available online through free websites. We've arranged this chapter by first discussing where to find and research the U.S. Constitution at two sites: **govinfo** (http://bit.ly/govinfoConstitutionAnn) and Cornell Law School's **LII** site (https://www.law.cornell.edu/constitution). Next, we discuss the Declaration of Independence, found at the Library of Congress's **Primary Documents in American History** page (http://bit.ly/LOCDeclaration). Then, we will explain where to find and research the United States Code at three sites: **govinfo** (https://www.govinfo.gov/#advanced), Cornell's **Legal Information Institute** (http://bit.ly/LII_USC), and the Office of the Law Revision Counsel's **United States Code** (http://uscode.house.gov).

This chapter deals primarily with statutory research. The next chapter will focus on finding and using sites that track the federal legislative process, from newly introduced and recently signed bills, to bills that never made it out of committee, and more.

## UNITED STATES CONSTITUTION AND THE DECLARATION OF INDEPENDENCE

The **govinfo** website provides access to a useful document for researching the U.S. Constitution: the **Constitution of the United States of America: Analysis and Interpretation** (known as the "Constitution Annotated"), which consists of the

U.S. Constitution, along with analysis and interpretation in the form of in-text annotations based on cases decided by the U.S. Supreme Court (http://bit.ly/govinfoConstitutionAnn). The analysis is provided by the Congressional Research Service (CRS) at the Library of Congress.

The Constitution Annotated page displays links to PDFs of the 1992, 2002, 2012, 2013, 2014, 2015, 2016, and 2017 editions of the Constitution, along with eight supplements. If they are not displayed, click the plus sign to the left of the link to the Constitution Annotated, and they will appear (see Figure 10.1). The supplements are cumulative, so you only need to read the most recent one for any edition of the Constitution you are browsing through. For example, if you are browsing the 1992 edition of the Constitution, you need open only the 2000 Supplement (Figure 10.1).

**Figure 10.1** The Constitution Annotated page on govinfo.gov.

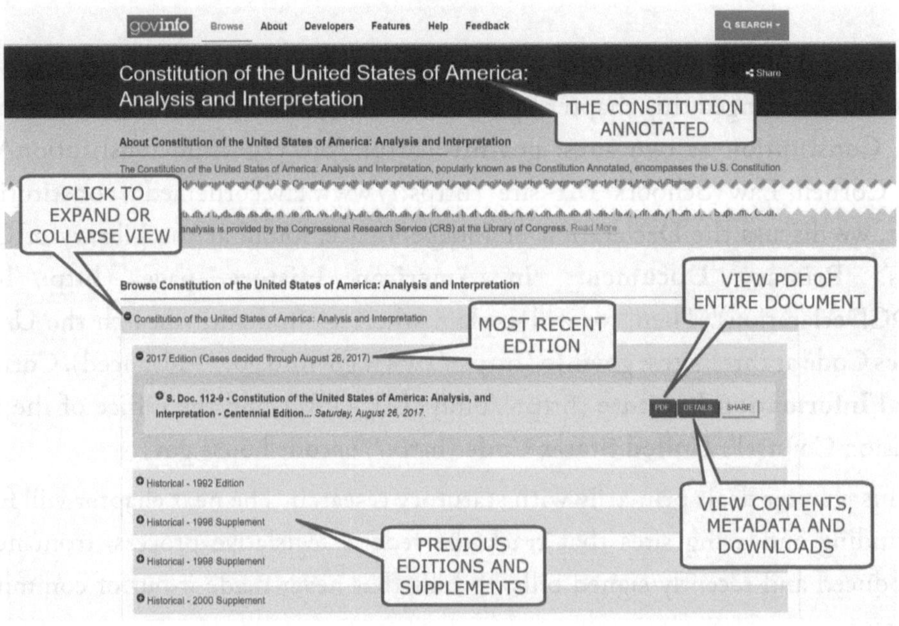


To keyword search the PDF of an individual edition or supplement of the Constitution Annotated, use the Find function (Ctrl+F if you are a PC user or Command+F if you have an Apple device). But, to keyword search all editions and supplements of the Constitution Annotated together, you would use govinfo's Advanced Search feature. From the govinfo homepage (https://www.govinfo.gov), follow these steps, illustrated counterclockwise in Figure 10.2:

1. Click the **Advanced** tab near the top of the page.

2. In the center column, titled **Refine by Collection**, select **Additional Government Publications** from the menu if you don't see the collection you want to search.
3. In the right-hand column, click the **+Additional Criteria** link beneath the **Full-Text** default search criterion. A new set of search criteria will appear, also with the **Full-Text** default.
4. Click the **down arrow** to the right of the new **Full Text** criterion and choose **Publication Name** from the drop-down menu.
5. Now a second drop-down menu will appear beneath **Publication Name**, titled **Choose Value**. Click the **down arrow** beside **Choose Value** and select **Constitution of the United States of America: Analysis and Interpretation** from the drop-down menu.
6. Your screen should now look similar to Figure 10.2. You are ready to keyword search the Constitution Annotated, using the search box below the **Full-Text** criterion.

**Figure 10.2** Searching the Constitution Annotated with govinfo.gov.

See Chapter 5 to learn about general govinfo search protocols that apply to all collections.

Another searchable database of the Constitution can be found at **Cornell Law School's LII** site (https://www.law.cornell.edu). LII's search engine allows you to connect your search terms and phrases with Boolean connectors (*AND, OR,* and *NOT*). You can also perform a wildcard search with an asterisk (*) and search phrases by using quotation marks. If you enter your terms into the search box that appears in the upper right corner of each page on the site, you would be searching LII's entire site rather than individual databases, and then you must filter to the individual database (such as the Constitution) you are interested in. However, to restrict your search to the Constitution specifically, first click **Get the Law** (from the upper left side of the homepage). A drop-down menu appears from which you can click **Constitution.** Then enter your terms into the search box that appears in the upper right corner of the **U.S. Constitution** page. (See the discussion in Chapter 5 for more information on searching LII.)

Instead of having to download the entire Constitution and analysis as you do at govinfo (see above), on the LII site you can browse just one specific **Article, Section,** or **Amendment** of the Constitution. From its Table of Contents (http://bit.ly/LIIConstitution), click a specific **Article, Section,** or **Amendment** to read its text. To read an analysis of the text, return to the Table of Contents and click the **(see explanation)** link next to the **Article, Section,** or **Amendment** that interests you. The analysis is the same one prepared by the **CRS** on the govinfo site.

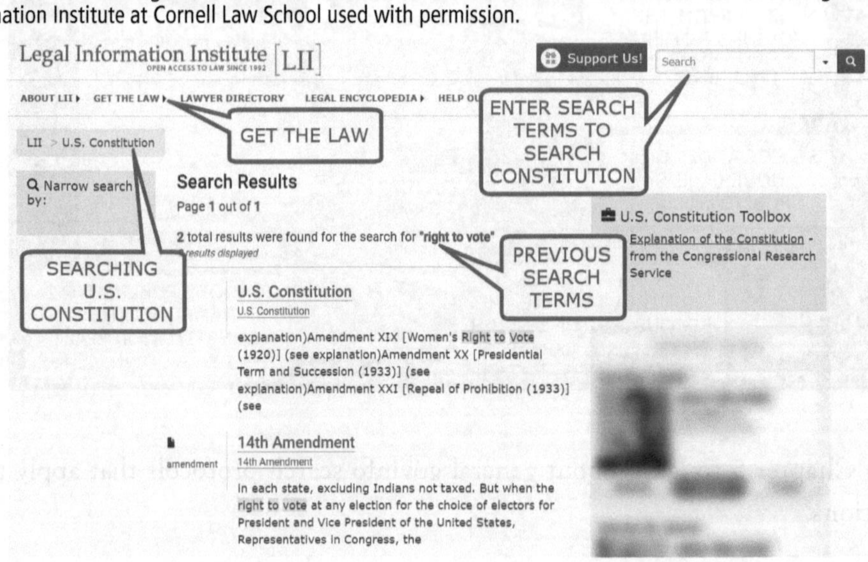


**Figure 10.3** Searching the Constitution with Cornell Law School's LII site. Screenshot from the Legal Information Institute at Cornell Law School used with permission.

To read the Declaration of Independence and related documents, visit the Library of Congress's **Primary Documents in American History** page (http://bit.ly/LOCDeclaration). To keyword search the Declaration, use your browser's Find function (Ctrl+F or Command+F).

## UNITED STATES CODE (U.S.C.)

Three helpful websites—**govinfo** (https://www.govinfo.gov), **Office of the Law Revision Counsel (OLRC) United States Code** (http://bit.ly/HouseUSCode), and **Cornell Law School's LII** (http://bit.ly/LII_USC) offer free online, searchable versions of the United States Code. **govinfo** also provides additional legislative material (which we will discuss in Chapter 11). **Cornell's LII** lacks much of the legislative material that the govinfo and OLRC contain, but it is still useful, especially for its **Parallel Table of Authorities**, which we'll detail soon.

Of the three online U.S.C. websites, only the OLRC site is the "official" one. Cornell and govinfo both use the online OLRC version of the U.S.C. to create their online searchable databases. Although it may seem redundant to have three databases, each is unique in terms of its search and updating features and dates of coverage. Which database you decide to search may change from time to time, depending on your needs.

If you want to use the most up-to-date U.S.C., the OLRC United States Code is a better choice over govinfo and Cornell. The OLRC site states that it updates the U.S.C. throughout each congressional session on an ongoing basis instead of delaying the update process until the end of the session. Cornell and govinfo make no representations about their currency. OLRC's currency information is found by selecting the **Currency and Updating** tab in the left-hand column of any page on the OLRC site. (Currency and Updating are discussed later in this chapter.)

For those who want to conduct a retrospective U.S.C. search, the OLRC site or govinfo are the best choices because they date back to the 1994 edition. Cornell has only the current version of the U.S.C.

For those who prefer to jump back and forth between sections (offering the look and feel of browsing a book), the OLRC or Cornell versions will work best.

For those who want to search the U.S.C. and then quickly link to related federal regulations, Cornell Law School's LII (http://bit.ly/LII_USC) is the best option.

Sometimes a researcher only knows the popular name of an act—e.g., the Racketeer Influenced and Corrupt Organizations Act (RICO)—rather than the citation or other information. The best choices for those who prefer to browse through lists of popular names would be **Cornell's Table of Popular Names** feature (http://bit.ly/LIIPopularNames; see Figure 10.4) or the **OLRC's Popular Name Tool** (http://bit.ly/OLRCPopularNames). For those who prefer to keyword search popular names, the best choice is govinfo, which offers a **Short Title** search criteria option for its **United States Code** collection on the Advanced Search page (https://www.govinfo.gov/#advanced).

**Figure 10.4** Cornell Law School LII's Table of Popular Names. Screenshot from the Legal Information Institute at Cornell Law School used with permission.

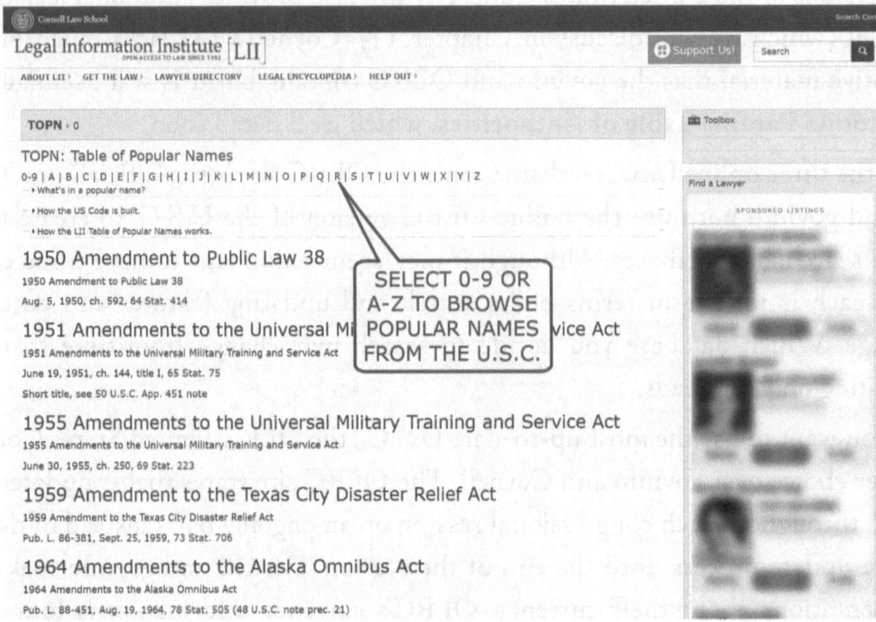


## THE OLRC UNITED STATES CODE

The **ORLC's United States Code** website has many helpful search features. The homepage (http://uscode.house.gov/browse.xhtml) provides search boxes to search the U.S.C. by keyword or by title and section number (see Figure 10.5). Underneath the search boxes is a table of contents with links to browse the U.S.C.

You can perform a citation search by using the **Jump To** boxes on the home page (see Figure 10.5). To do this, leave the keyword search box empty and fill in the title and section number that you want to retrieve. Even if you know only the section number but not the title, you can enter just that number in the Section box to retrieve any section with that number found within the Code. You cannot do the reverse; searching for just a title number without a section number will retrieve no results. When you enter keywords into the search box and click **Search**, the search function ignores anything in the Jump To (citation) boxes. You also cannot use the homepage search boxes to only keyword search a specific title or section of the U.S.C.

**Figure 10.5** OLRC United States Code homepage features.

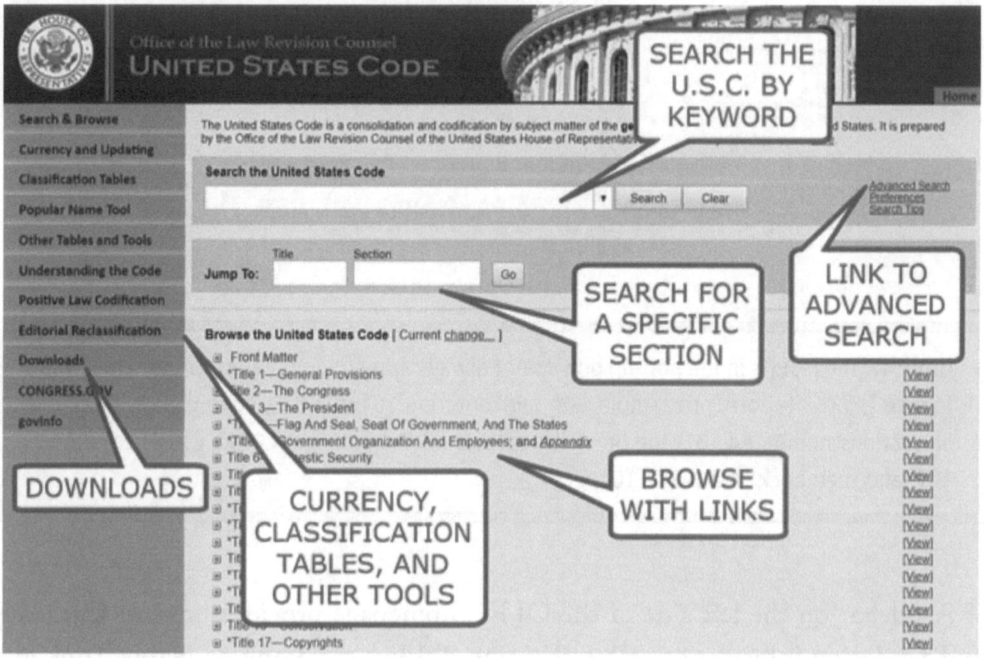


Your keyword search results list will appear on a regular web page, but if you click a link for a result, the full text of that code section will appear in a pop-up box, as shown in Figure 10.6. (Citation search results will always appear in a pop-up box.) Once you have opened the full text of one section, you can browse the different sections in your search results by using the small arrow tools at the top of the screen, as shown in Figure 10.6. Note that the forward and backward arrows serve a different function than the **Next** and **Previous** links underneath them. The forward and backward arrows allow you to browse through your search results (22 U.S.C. 6201, 22 U.S.C. 6215, etc.). **Next** and **Previous** jump to the next/previous section within the code (22 U.S.C. 6201, 22 U.S.C. 6202, etc.), regardless of whether your search terms appear in these sections. **Next** and **Previous** allow you to browse the code just as you might if you were browsing the print edition. You can use these links, along with the Title number and Chapter number links, to browse the code.

**Figure 10.6** Viewing search results from the OLRC United States Code.

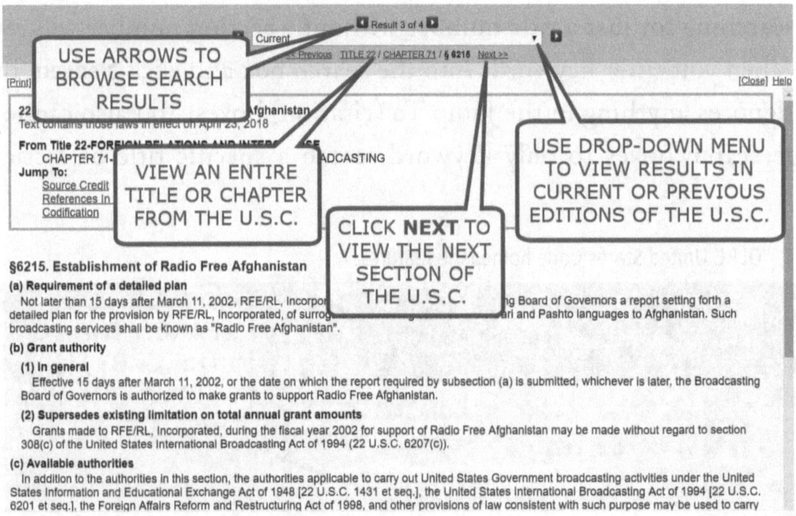


> **CAVEAT:** the results in the pop-up box do not always appear in numerical order with regard to their U.S.C. citation. For example, although entering 101 into the Section box will retrieve all sections numbered 101, the browsing arrows might jump from 1 U.S.C. 101 to 4 U.S.C. 101, and then back to 3 U.S.C. 101, etc.

A sidebar on the left side of the OLRC homepage provides links to **Currency and Updating** information, **Classification Tables**, the **Popular Name Tool**, and **Other Tables and Tools**, as well as resources to help understand various aspects of the U.S.C. and the functions of the Office of the Law Review Counsel (Figure 10.5). A **Downloads** link (Figure 10.5) goes to a page with downloadable files for the most current updates or "release points" of the U.S.C. At the bottom of the sidebar are links to Congress.gov and **govinfo**.

OLRC United States Code also provides a handy **Advanced Search Options** page; click the link to the right of the main page search box (Figure 10.5), or go directly to http://bit.ly/OLRCAdvanced (see Figure 10.7). Among other options, you can choose which version of the U.S.C. to search back to 1994, which **Title**(s) or **Section**(s) to search within, which **Fields** to search, including Statutory Text, Citation, Heading, Future Amendments, and more. A link in the upper right corner of the page allows the user to specify **Preferences** such as the number of search results per page, the search results view (context or citation), and the sorting order (code number or relevance).

**Figure 10.7** OLRC Advanced Search Options page.

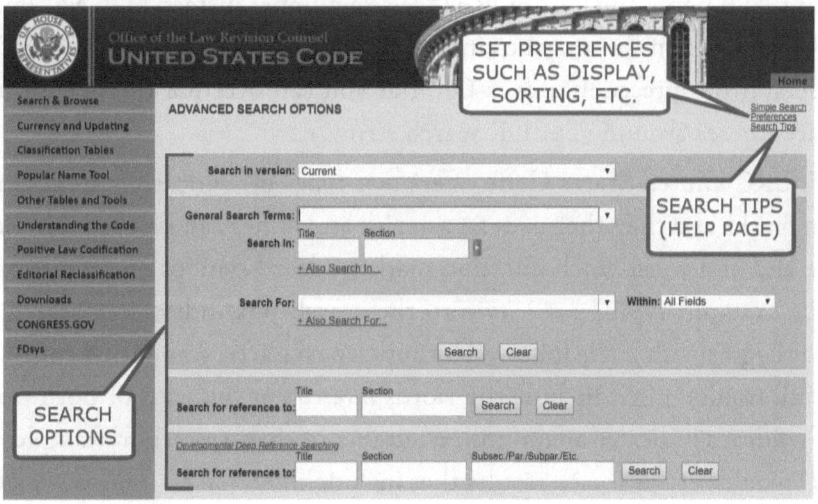


The OLRC **Help Searching the United States Code** page (http://bit.ly/OLRCHelp) explains specific searching and browsing options available on this site (see Figure 10.8). For example, **Simple Searches** search the entire text of the code for the best match containing all your search terms. Phrases may be searched by enclosing them in quotation marks.

**Figure 10.8** OLRC Help Searching the United States Code page.

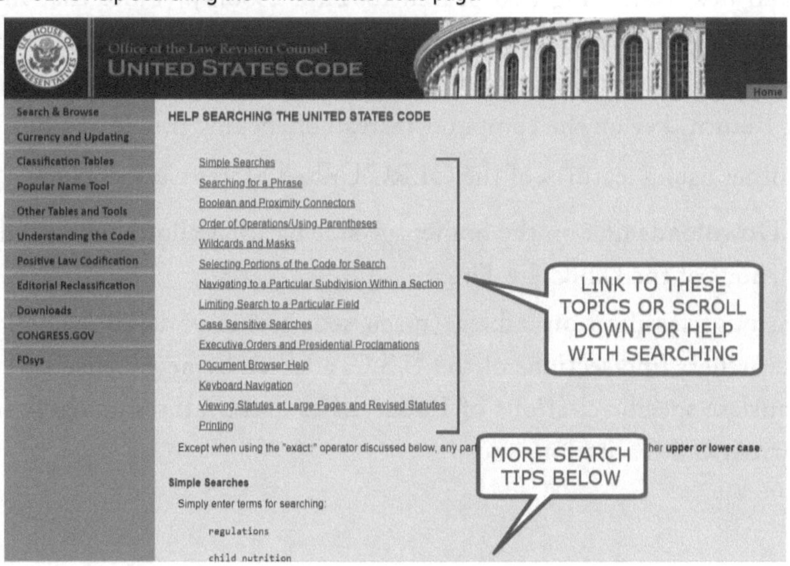

The help page also describes the operation of the site's search engine and includes tips for the use of Boolean connectors, wildcards, and order of operations. Boolean connectors—*AND, OR, NOT*—and proximity connectors—*NEAR/#* (use a number instead of #; e.g., immigrant NEAR/3 homeland), *ADJ* (adjacent; e.g., immigrant ADJ homeland), *BEFORE/#* (use a number instead of #; e.g., immigrant BEFORE/6 homeland)—may be employed to refine the search. (The *AND* operator by default has precedence over *OR*, but you can override the default order by using parentheses around your *OR* search string.)

The OLRC United States Code offers two types of wildcard searches; one uses question marks and the other uses an asterisk and either can be used within a word or at the end of a word. Each question mark wildcard symbol represents one character. For example, typing *int??city* into the search box indicates a search for any word that begins with *int,* is followed by any two characters, and then ends with *city.* The search results might include the words *intercity* or *intracity,* or both words. An asterisk wildcard indicates an unlimited number of characters. For example, a search for *child** would return search results that include *child, child's, children, childish,* and so on. Other helpful hints explain things such as case-sensitive searches, locating executive orders and presidential proclamations, document browser help, and special keyboard navigation functions.

If researchers do not want to conduct a keyword search of the entire U.S.C., they can use the **Advanced Search Options** page (http://bit.ly/OLRCAdvanced) to search within a particular Title, Section, etc., or within a combination of any of the available criteria. For example, in Figure 10.9, the number *29* was entered into the Title search box, restricting that search to Title 29 only. (Note that in our test searches, clicking the **Search** button on this page sometimes returned an error message, especially if we were editing a previous search. We fixed this by hitting the Enter (or Return) key on the computer instead of clicking the Search button.)

Some other useful features of the OLRC United States Code include:

- A **Downloads** link on the homepage side bar that allows users to download portions of the U.S.C. by Title;
- Various classification tables (discussed in more detail below) to help researchers find sections of the U.S.C. affected by newly enacted laws or to translate specific citations of Public Laws and Statutes at Large into their current U.S.C. citation; and

- An **Advanced Search** feature that includes the ability to find sections referring to a specific title and section (although this is a very imprecise type of search).

**Figure 10.9** Example of an Advanced Search in OLRC United States Code.

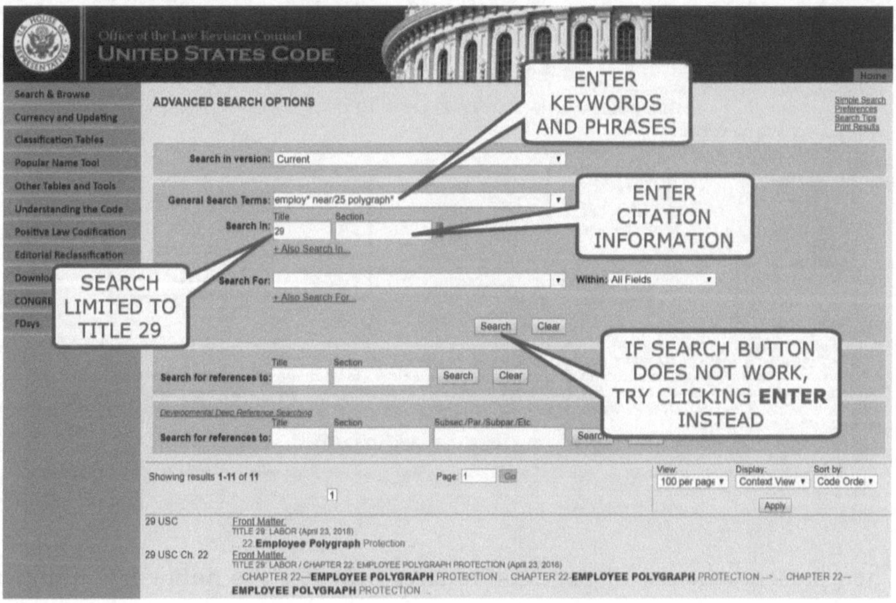


## Updating the OLRC United States Code

The OLRC's **Currency and Updating** page (see left-hand column in Figure 10.9 or go to http://bit.ly/OLRCCurrency) states that: "If the section has been affected by any laws enacted after [the currency] date, those laws will appear in a list of 'Pending Updates.' If there are no pending updates listed, the section is current as shown." According to the OLRC United States Code Currency and Updating page, as of December 11, 2019, all Titles in the OLRC United States Code (http://uscode.house.gov) are current through Pub. L. 116-78 (12/05/2019). The currency information on this page is updated as the code is updated. You can also consult the **United States Code Classification Tables** at http://bit.ly/OLRCClassification (see Figure 10.11) to be sure of the latest laws that affect the U.S.C.

Also, near the top-left corner of the screen in every section of the OLRC United States Code is a date and a statement that the text contains those laws in effect as of the date shown (see Figure 10.10). (This date may not be the same as the date on the Currency and Updating page.) If the section has been affected by any laws enacted after that date, those laws will also appear in a list of "Pending Updates" (see Figure 10.10). If there are no pending updates listed, the section is current as shown.

Figure 10.10 Currency date and pending updates for an OLRC United States Code section.

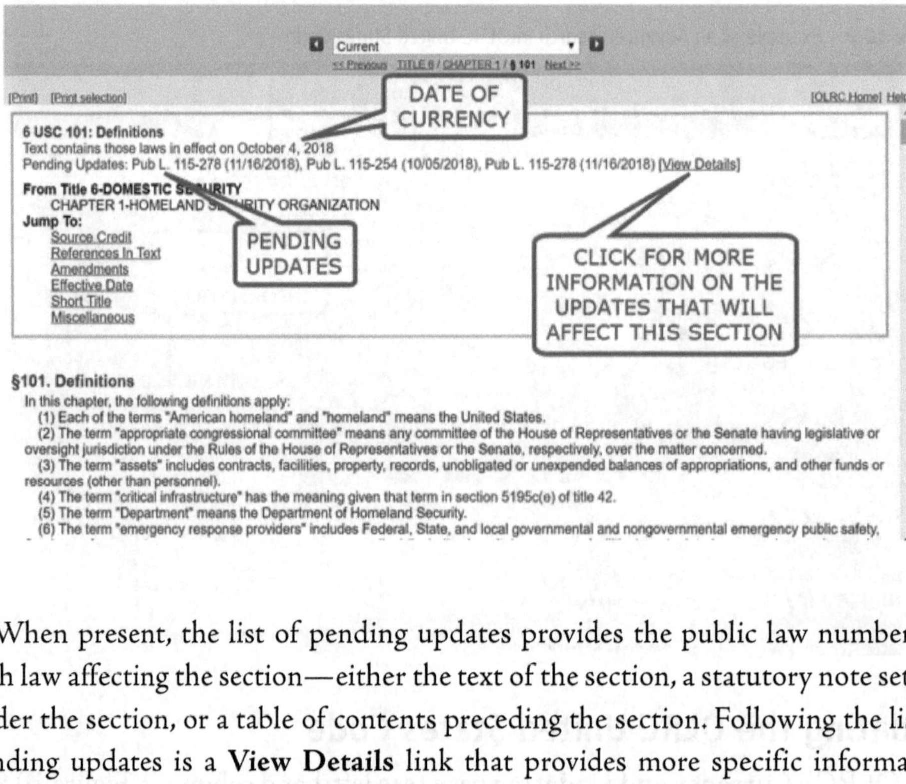


When present, the list of pending updates provides the public law numbers of each law affecting the section—either the text of the section, a statutory note set out under the section, or a table of contents preceding the section. Following the list of pending updates is a **View Details** link that provides more specific information about how each new law has affected the section.

Figure 10.11 OLRC United States Code classification tables.

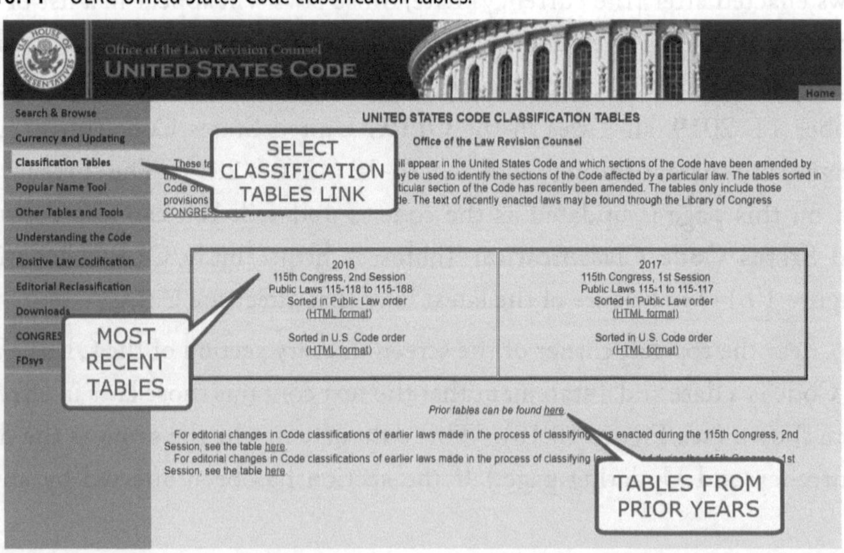

The **Classification Tables** (http://bit.ly/OLRCClassification), shown in Figure 10.11, can also be used to find the latest laws affecting the U.S.C. The Classification Tables indicate which sections of the Code have been affected by recently enacted laws, and they show where the recently enacted laws and amendments will eventually appear in the U.S.C. Users can view the tables either in Public Law order or in U.S.C. citation order. The text of public laws listed as Pending Updates or appearing in the Classification Tables can be found in a number of sources, such as govinfo or Congress.gov.

## THE CORNELL LII U.S.C. DATABASE

You can access **Cornell LII**'s U.S.C. database by direct link (http://bit.ly/LII_USC) or from the LII homepage (https://www.law.cornell.edu) by first clicking **Get the Law** in the menu bar across the top of the page, and then selecting **U.S. Code** from the available options. In addition to browsable links for the different titles in the U.S.C., the **U.S. Code** page features a citation search (see Figure 10.12). The right-hand column of the page has a section titled **U.S. Code Toolbox**. This section includes links to the **Table of Popular Names** and **Parallel Table of Authorities**, as well as to Wex (LII's legal dictionary and encyclopedia).

**Figure 10.12** LII's U.S. Code page. Screenshot from the Legal Information Institute at Cornell Law School used with permission.

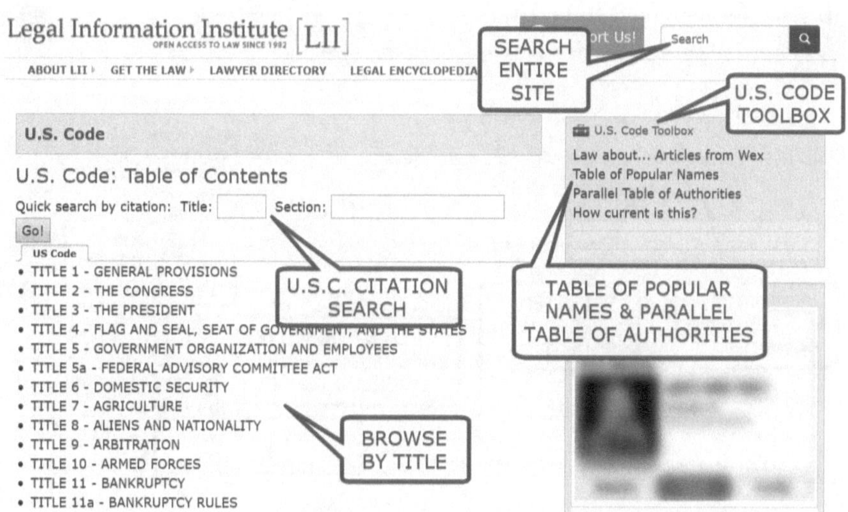

## How to Keyword/Phrase Search Cornell LII

To keyword search the U.S. Code, follow a procedure similar to the one described earlier in this chapter for searching LII's version of the U.S. Constitution. Click **Get the Law** (from the upper left side of the homepage at https://www.law.cornell.edu) and select **U.S. Code** from the drop-down menu. Then enter your terms into the search box that appears in the upper right corner of the **U.S. Code** page (see Figure 10.12). For more information on searching LII, see the discussion in Chapter 5.

## How to Navigate Cornell LII's U.S.C. Pages

Once you have located the section of the U.S.C. you need, your screen will look similar to the page shown in Figure 10.13. The text of the statute is displayed under the default **US Code** tab. Selecting the **Notes** tab will provide historical and background information about the section you are reading (46 U.S.C. §30102, for example). To browse other sections of the U.S.C., use the **prev** and **next** links to the upper right of the statute text. Some terms may be hyperlinked, such as "vessel" in Figure 10.13. These hyperlinks will take you to additional information about the terms, such as definitions.

**Figure 10.13** United States Code section on LII. Screenshot from the Legal Information Institute at Cornell Law School used with permission.

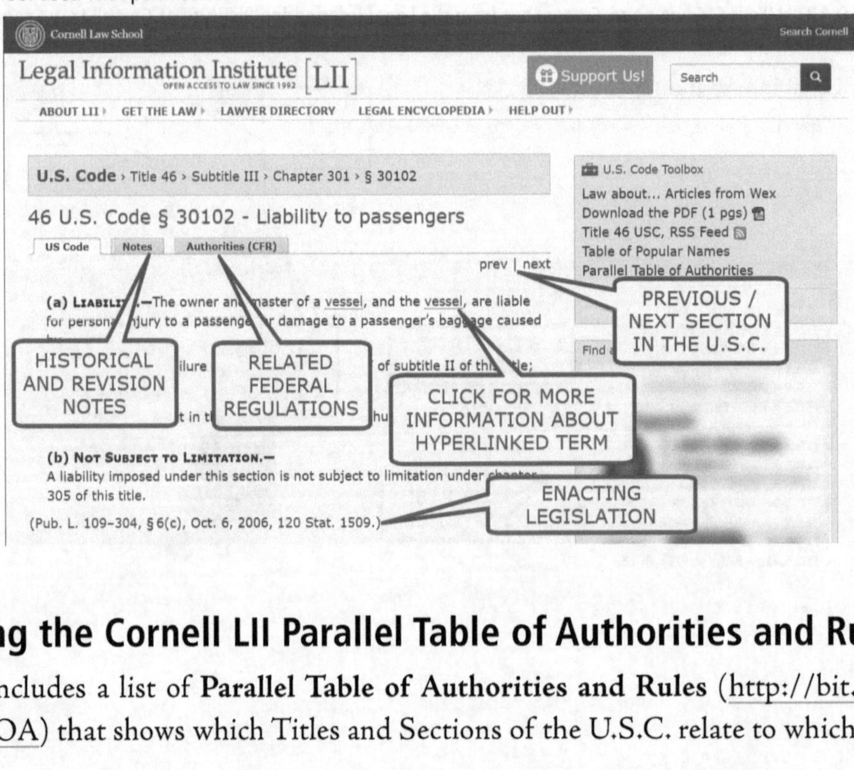


## Using the Cornell LII Parallel Table of Authorities and Rules

LII includes a list of **Parallel Table of Authorities and Rules** (http://bit.ly/LII_PTOA) that shows which Titles and Sections of the U.S.C. relate to which Titles and Parts of the CFR. The list used by LII is provided by the GPO (Government Publishing Office), but LII explains that it "is not guaranteed to be accurate or up-to-date, though we do refresh the database weekly" (http://bit.ly/LII_PTOA). To use this list, click one of the U.S.C. Titles, such as 46, and then scroll down the results list to find the U.S.C. section you are interested in, such as Section 2 (see Figure 10.14). To the right of Section 2, the related CFR Title and Part(s) are listed: 33 CFR 125. Click the CFR Part number (125) to view this CFR Part that is related to 46 U.S.C. 2 (see Figure 10.14).

**Figure 10.14** LII's Parallel Table of Authorities. Screenshot from the Legal Information Institute at Cornell Law School used with permission.

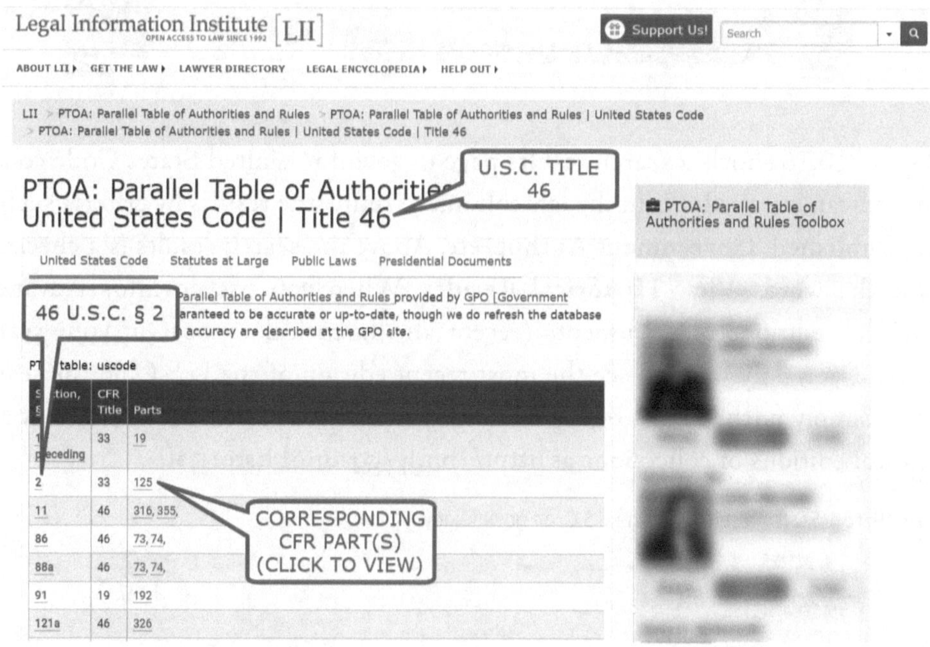


# THE GOVINFO UNITED STATES CODE DATABASE

The govinfo website allows users to keyword search or browse the United State Code. As noted earlier, a major difference between various govinfo collections is their search criteria, so when you choose the **United States Code** collection from the **Advanced Search** page (https://www.govinfo.gov/#advanced) and click the downward arrow to the right of the **Full-Text** criterion, you see search criteria specific to the United States Code collection (see Figure 10.15). Also, as noted earlier in this chapter, all govinfo collections follow the same search protocol, so be sure to review the search protocol discussed in Chapter 5.

**Figure 10.15** United States Code search criteria on the govinfo website.

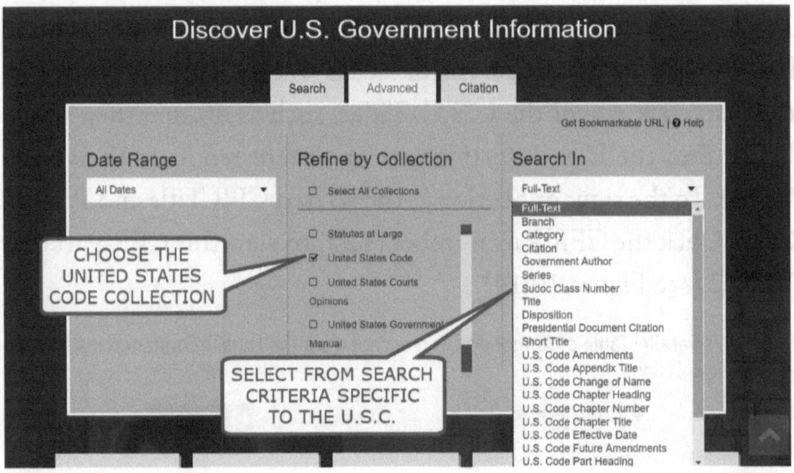


Figure 10.16 shows a search results page in govinfo's United States Code collection. You can use the links in the left column to refine the results by criteria such as **Date Published, Government Author**, etc. Above the search results is a checkbox beside the words **View Historical Results.** When you use govinfo's Advanced Search, all editions of documents (recent and historical) appear in your search results. If you only want to see the most recent edition of the U.S.C. in the search results, simply uncheck this box. govinfo provides more information on recent and historical editions of collections at http://bit.ly/govinfoHistorical.

**Figure 10.16** Search results from the U.S.C. on govinfo.gov.

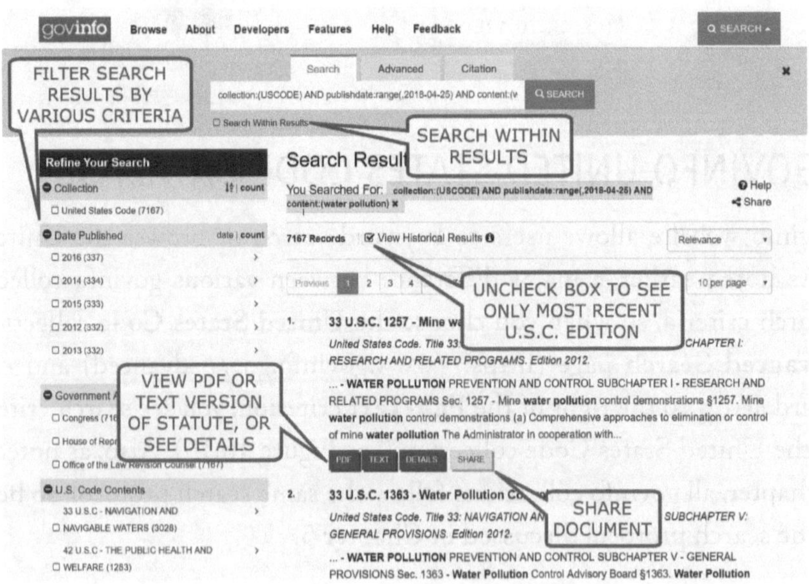

Below each search result are links to full-text **PDF** and **Text** (HTML) versions of that U.S.C. section. Next to the PDF and Text links is a link titled **Details.** Clicking Details will display **Content Details** for each search result (see Figure 10.17). Content Details (or metadata) are information about the document. For example, the Content Details for the U.S.C. section shown in Figure 10.17 give us the SuDoc (Superintendent of Documents) Class Number for this statute, the effective date, and the Statutes at Large and Public Law citations, among other things. There is also a link called **Share** below each search result (see Figure 10.16). Clicking it will allow you to share a link to the document via email or social media. (Note, however, that certain security settings on your browser, such as anti-tracking settings, may prevent the **Share** link from working.)

**Figure 10.17** Content Details about a U.S.C. section on govinfo.

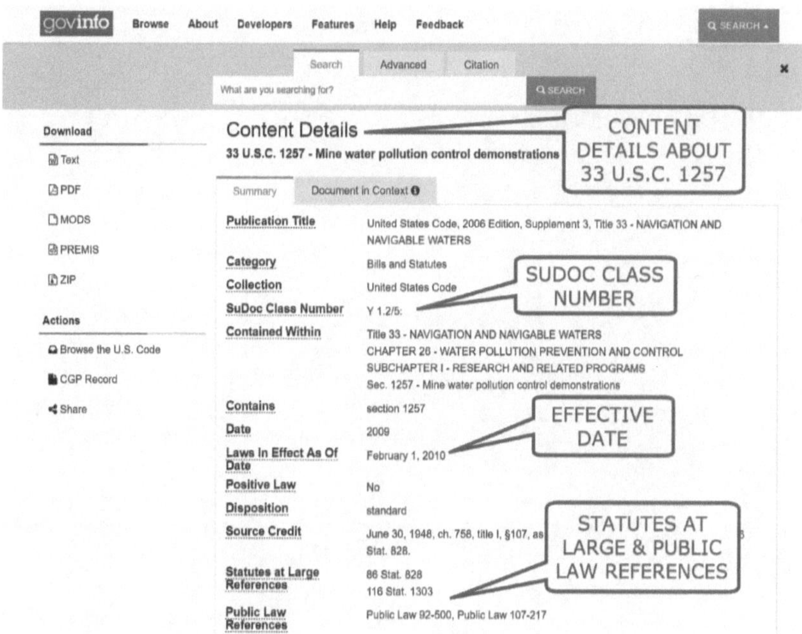

Below each search result are links to full-text PDF and Text (HTML) versions of that U.S.C. section. Next to the PDF and Text links is a link titled **Details**. Clicking **Details** will display **Content Details** for each search result (see Figure 10.17). *Content Details* (or metadata) are information about the document. For example, the Content Details for the U.S.C. section shown in Figure 10.17 gives the SuDoc (Superintendent of Documents) Class Number for this statute, the effective date, and the Statutes at Large and Public Law citations, among other things. There is also a link called **Share** below each search result (see Figure 10.16). Clicking it will allow you to share a link to the document via email or social media. (Note, however, that certain security settings on your browser, such as anti-tracking settings, may prevent the *Share* link from working.)

Figure 10.17 Content Details about a U.S.C. section on govinfo

# Chapter 11

## FEDERAL LEGISLATIVE AND CONGRESSIONAL MATERIALS

Searchable databases of federal legislative and congressional materials (other than the United States Code discussed in Chapter 10), such as public laws, bills, resolutions, hearings, congressional reports, and committee reports can be found at the governmental sites we describe in the upcoming sections. (For non-federal legislative research (state, local, territorial, and tribal law), see Chapter 13.)

Legislative and congressional materials are valuable research tools because they can:

- Track a current bill as it is proceeding through the legislative process (e.g., lawyers track bills when a client would be affected by this bill or if the lawyer was lobbying on behalf of or against the bill).
- Discern the legislative intent of a bill (e.g., when there are no court opinions on a topic to support their client's side, lawyers will research legislative history to find support).
- Conduct research about the history of a bill that never passed (and, thus, would not be contained in a Public Law database or the U.S.C.).
- Read a public law in its entirety (instead of trying to piece it together once it has been scattered throughout various sections of the U.S.C.).

## CONGRESS.GOV

In 2012, the Library of Congress introduced a website called **Congress.gov** (https://www.congress.gov), which presents the Library of Congress's congressional information system in a modern and user-friendly format. Congress.gov replaced THOMAS.gov, the site that previously provided the federal government's legislative information; THOMAS was retired in July 2016. Congress.gov contains the sections listed below. These will be discussed in greater detail in this chapter.

1. **Legislation** (https://congress.gov/legislation) is available from the 93rd Congress (1973) to the present.
2. The **Congressional Record** (https://www.congress.gov/congressional-record) is available from the 104th Congress (1995) to the present.
3. **Committees** (https://congress.gov/committees). Profile pages are available for all House and Senate committees for the current Congress, with links to specific Committee pages.
4. **Members** (https://congress.gov/members) Congress member profiles are provided for all members since 1973 and selected members from 1929–1972 (if the member was still serving as of 1973).
5. **The Legislative Process** (https://www.congress.gov/legislative-process) provides basic information on the legislative process and is a good resource for the general public.
6. **Committee Reports** (https://congress.gov/congressional-reports) are available from 1995 to the present.

Links to the first four sections outlined above are available from a menu near the upper right corner of any page on the Congress.gov site (see Figure 11.1). You can also keyword search the first four sections outlined above directly from the Congress.gov homepage. A **Browse** link at the top of the page goes to a page where you can also browse information by categories such as Congressional Activity, Committees, Laws, and more.

**Figure 11.1** Congress.gov homepage search options.

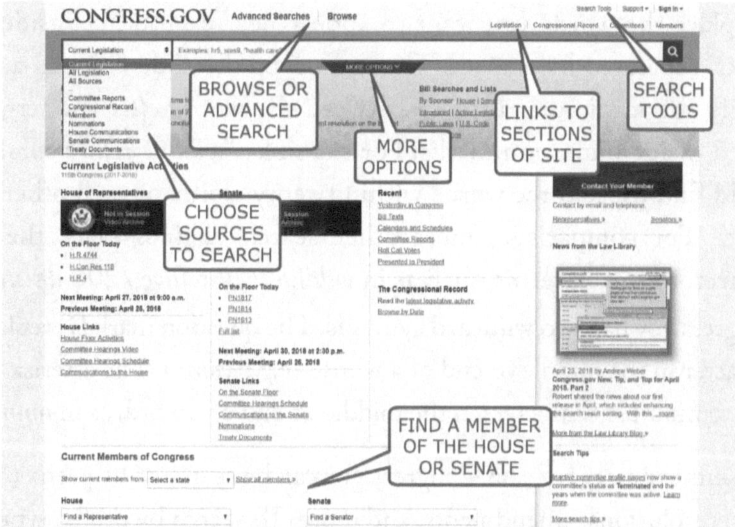


## Searching Congress.gov for Legislative Information

All the legislative materials on Congress.gov can be searched using the same methods. For the simplest search, start from the homepage (see Figure 11.1), and choose which source to search from a drop-down menu to the left of the search box. Sources include **Current Legislation, All Legislation, All Sources, Committee Reports, Congressional Record, Members, Nominations, House Communications, Senate Communications,** and **Treaty Documents.** After you have selected a source, enter your search terms into the box and click the magnifying glass icon.

Although you can search Congress.gov with keywords and phrases (enclosed in quotation marks), the site's search engine also accepts sophisticated queries. We will summarize more sophisticated search methods for Congress.gov and point out further resources on the site where you can find additional information.

Congress.gov's search engine accepts many Boolean operators. In addition to the connectors *AND* and *OR* (must be in capital letters), you can use the following operators:

- **Plus sign** (+) to require a term and **minus sign** (-) or the word *NOT* to exclude a term.
- **Parentheses** () to group search terms when you are using the connectors *AND, OR,* or *NOT* (-).
- **Proximity connector tilde** (~) to find words within a specified distance from each other. Congress.gov's proximity connector is placed differently

than proximity connectors of some other search engines. On Congress.gov, you place the words you want to appear near each other inside quotation marks, separated by a space. Then you type the tilde (~) and a number to specify the maximum distance between the words *after* the terms you just placed inside quotation marks. For example, *"wildlife refuge subsistence"~20* would find those three words within twenty words of each other in a document. (For comparison, most other search engines place the proximity connector *between* terms, such as in *wildlife /20 refuge /20 subsistence.*)

- Congress.gov has two **wildcard symbols.** The question mark (?) replaces a single character in the middle or end of a word—e.g., *wom?n.* The asterisk (*) replaces zero to multiple characters in the middle or end of a word, as in *immigr*.*

Many document categories on Congress.gov can be searched by prefix (or citation), such as bills, resolutions, amendments, and more. To search by prefix, type the alphabetical prefix for your document category (such as *hr* for House Bills or *hrept* for House Report), along with the specific document number for the item you want. For example, to search for House Report 113-202, your prefix search could look like this: *hrept113-202.* You could also search for this house report by its citation: *113hrept202.* Congress.gov will accept many prefix and citation searches in varying formats. Figure 11.2 illustrates some formats for searching, as described on Congress.gov's **Search Tools** page. For the complete list of prefix and citation search options, see the Search Tools page at http://bit.ly/CongressSearchTools, or click the **Search Tools** link at the top right corner of the homepage, as shown in Figures 11.1 and 11.2.

**Figure 11.2** Congress.gov Search Tools for prefix and citation searching.

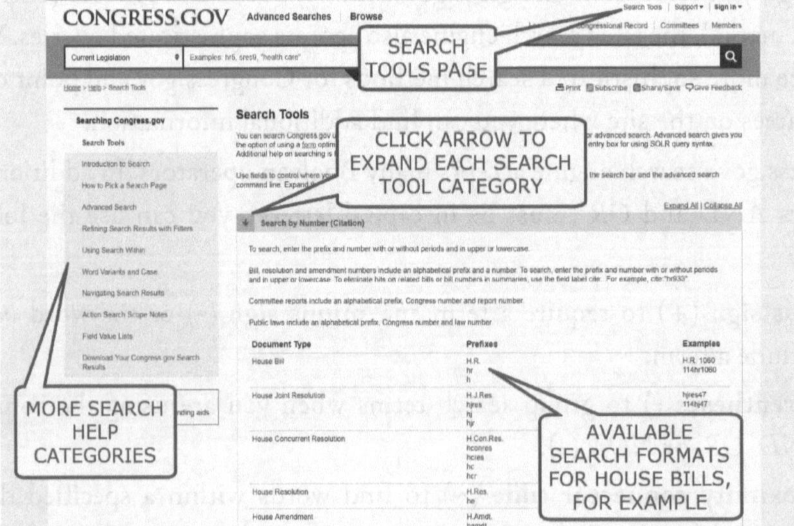

Congress.gov also allows field searching. To search a field, type the field label (*title* or *chamber*, for example) followed by a colon, and then type your search terms. For example, *title:"income tax"* would find documents with "income tax" in the title. Figure 11.3 shows the field searching section (titled **Fields Across Search Collections**) on the **Search Tools** page. The chart in the Fields Across Search Collections section provides a list of searchable fields and their labels, the collections in which you can search them (if applicable), and one or more search examples for each field.

**Figure 11.3** Search Tools for field searching on Congress.gov.

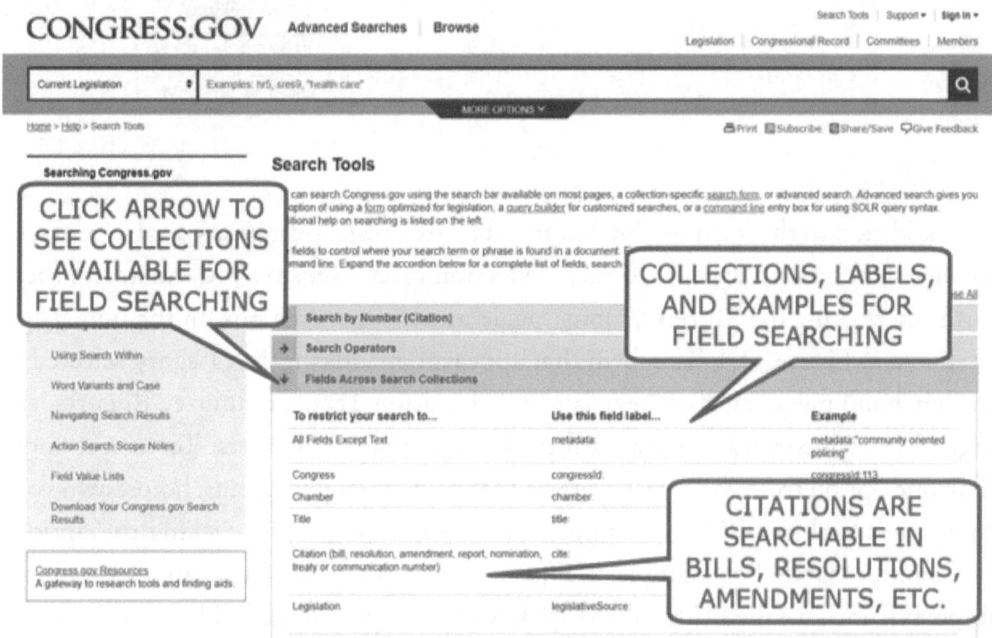


You can also search fields for **Legislation** by using the form on the **Advanced Search** page, found by clicking the **Advanced Searches** link at the top of the homepage, or going directly to http://bit.ly/CongressLegislationAdvanced (see Figure 11.4). Many search criteria are available, such as session of Congress, Legislation and Law Numbers, Words and Phrases (full text), and more.

Figure 11.4 Congress.gov's Advanced Search page for legislation.

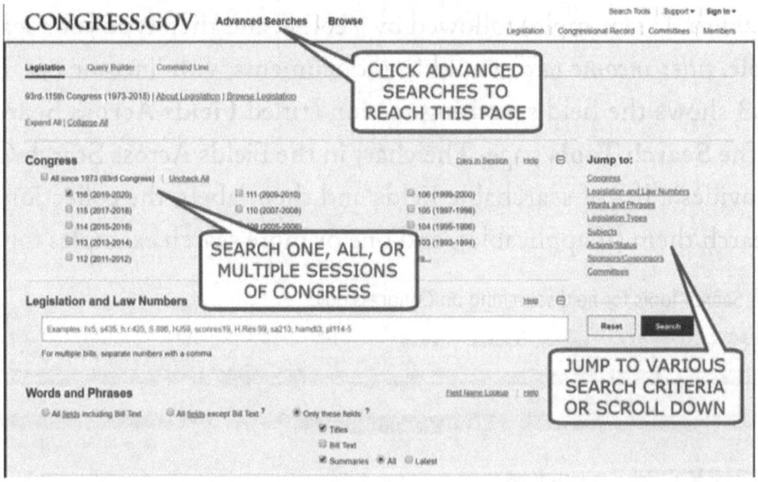


In addition to the form on the Advanced Search page, Congress.gov also provides smaller search forms specific to each collection on its website. You can access these forms by clicking the **More Options** toggle under the search box on the homepage, as shown in Figure 11.1. The form that appears depends on the category selected in the left-hand menu, such as Legislation, Legislation Text, Committee Reports, etc. Figure 11.5 illustrates the search form for Committee Reports. To choose more than one option from the search criteria that have scrollable menus, hold down your computer's Ctrl (for PC) or Command (for Apple) key while clicking the options you want to search. For example, in Figure 11.5, if you wanted to search Committee Reports from both the 115th and 114th Congresses, you would hold Ctrl/Command and click **115 (2017–2018)** and then click **114 (2015–2016)** before releasing the Ctrl/Command key.

Figure 11.5 Congress.gov search form for Committee Reports collection.

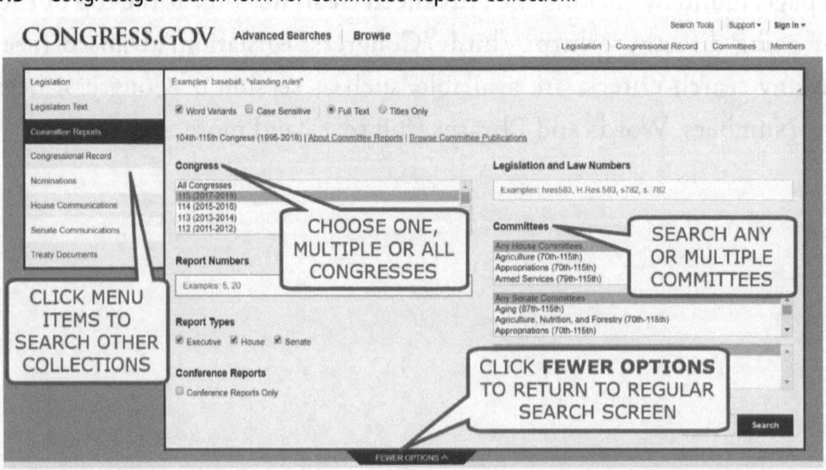

Congress.gov provides even more complex search options than the ones we have described. From the Advanced Search page, you can also select **Query Builder** or **Command Line** from tabs at the top of the page. Query Builder lets you build complex searches by using multiple rows of drop-down menus for collections, fields, dates, etc. (see Figure 11.6). Command Line searching is essentially one large search box that allows you to build your own custom search in any combination of collections, using any combination of Boolean operators and fields. Command Line searching differs from the Congress.gov homepage search box in that the homepage search only allows you to search one collection at a time.

**Figure 11.6** Congress.gov's Query Builder search feature.

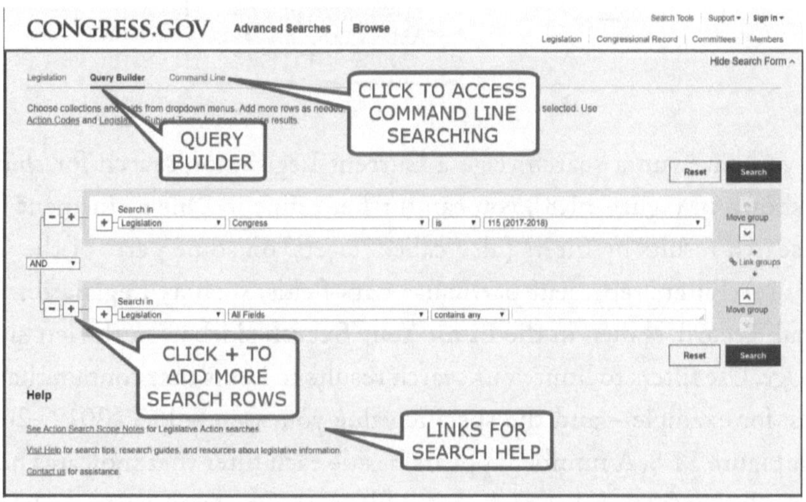


The main help page at Congress.gov has a wealth of information to assist you with both basic and advanced searches. The main **Help** page is at https://www.congress.gov/help#, or you can click **Support** in the upper right corner of most pages of the site and then choose **Help** from the drop-down menu that appears. The Help page is divided into several topics, such as **Get Started**, **Search Guides**, and **About** (see Figure 11.7). Although not shown in Figure 11.7, if you scrolled down the Help page, you would also find useful resources such as **FAQs**, a **Glossary** of terms used on the site, and a link to a **Contact Us** page where you can contact a law librarian for research help. In the lower right-hand corner of the Help page is a link titled **Congress.gov Resources**. This link goes to a comprehensive A–Z directory of help pages, research guides, and more.

**Figure 11.7** Congress.gov Help page.

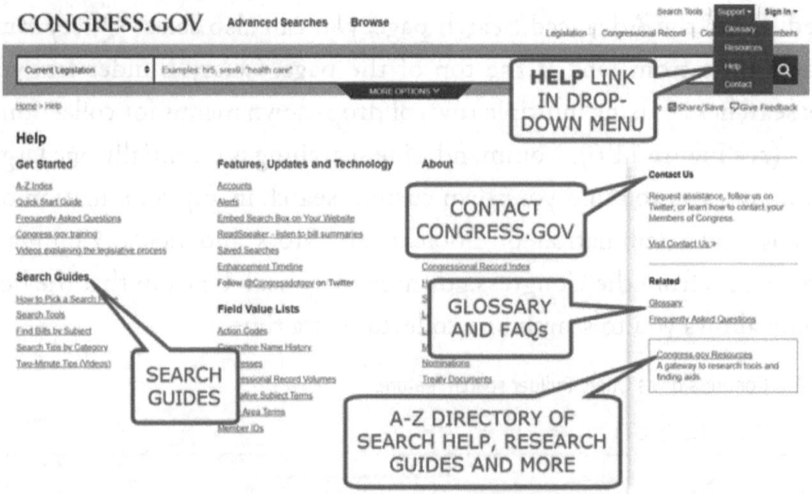


Once you have run a search (e.g., a Current Legislation search for *china AND trade* as shown in Figure 11.8), you can further refine it. One refinement option is to limit search results by filters (also called "facets" on some parts of the Congress .gov website). Filters represent particular data fields, such as **Legislation** or **Congressional Record**, shown in the **Limit Your Search** sidebar on the left side of the results page. Use filters to limit your search results to items that contain that filter—Congress, for example—and the specific value you want—115 (2017–2018)—as shown in Figure 11.8. A number appears beside each filter that indicates how many results match that filter. A list of the main filters on Congress.gov is available on the **Refining with Filters** page at http://bit.ly/CongressFilters.

**Figure 11.8** Search results on Congress.gov.

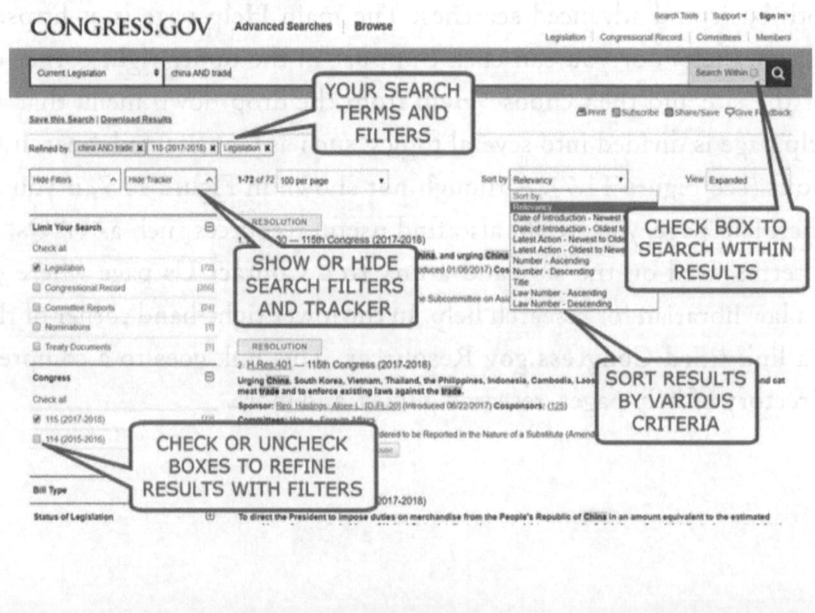

You can also refine search results by searching within those results. From the results page, check the **Search Within** box next to the search box (see Figure 11.9). Then clear your original search terms, and type in additional search terms. This will narrow your original set of results. All search terms and filters, including the new ones, will appear near the top left side of the new search results page. To remove any of the terms (or filters), just click the "x" beside the term. If you added a filter by clicking it in the left column, clicking it again will also remove it.

**Figure 11.9** Search within results on Congress.gov.

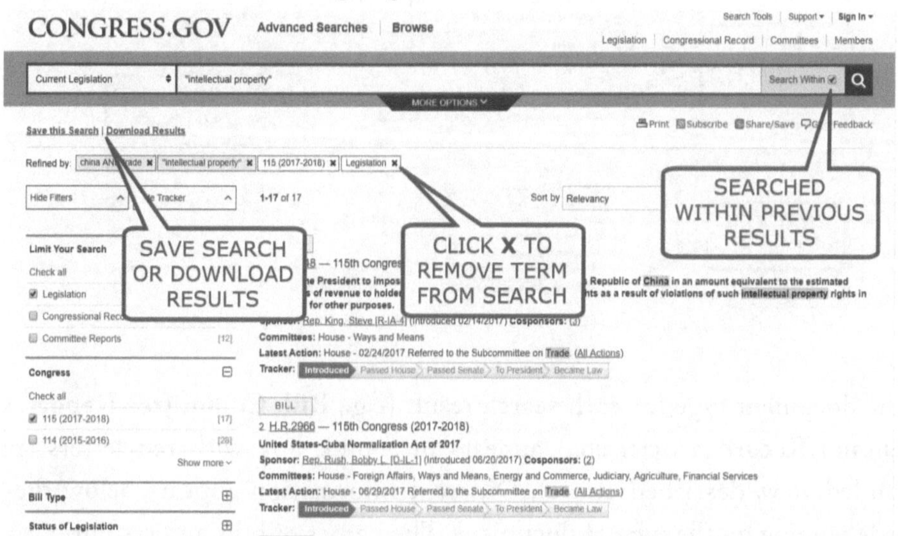


## Navigating Search Results on Congress.gov

The search results list gives brief information about each item. You can use the drop-down menu just above the search results to sort the list by **Relevancy, Date of Introduction, Latest Action, Number, Title** (alphabetically), and **Law Number** (see Figure 11.10). Next to the sorting menu is a **View** option that allows for **Expanded** or **Compact** view. The only difference we found is that the Expanded view shows the document type, and the Compact view hides it.

**Figure 11.10** Navigating search results on Congress.gov.

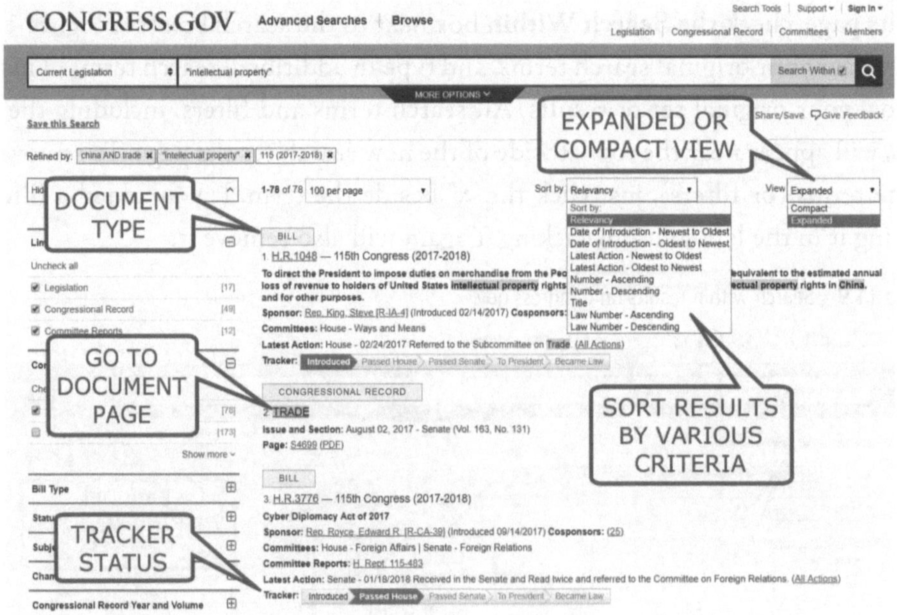


The document type for each search result (e.g., **Bill, Committee Report, Congressional Record** article, etc.) appears in a pink box with red letters (in the Expanded view, described above). Different information appears below the item link, depending on the type of document. The names of bills and resolutions are in boldface type. Below that is a link to the sponsor of the legislation (*Rep. King* for Result #1 in Figure 11.10), along with a link for information on any co-sponsors. Underneath that is the Latest Action taken (*Referred to the Subcommittee on Trade*). Finally, a graphic **Tracker** indicates where the item is in the legislative process (*Introduced*). Below the document type box is a blue link with document title or citation information (e.g., *H.R.1048* for result #1 in Figure 11.10). Click this link to go to the page for the item.

Resolutions have similar features to bills, including the Tracker timeline. Congressional Record Articles have a link (for HTML and PDF) to the page in the Congressional Record where the article appears.

## Viewing Legislation Pages on Congress.gov

Click an item link to view the full content for each item. Figure 11.11 shows the landing page for a law. Pages for other legislation types have features similar to the ones described here.

**Figure 11.11** Document view page on Congress.gov.

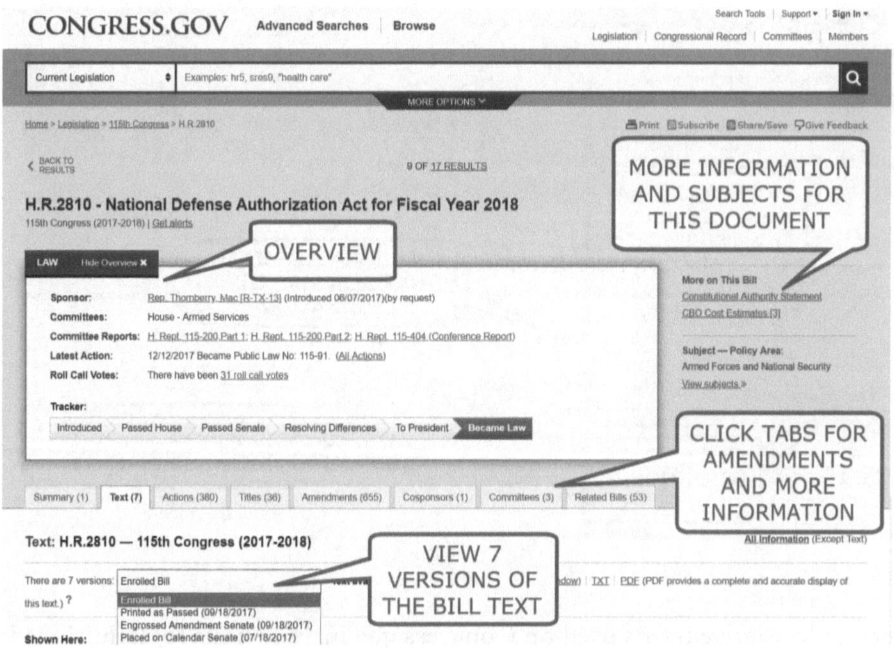


The top part of the page repeats the brief information that appeared in the item results list. The bottom of the page is arranged into tabs to help researchers quickly find key information about the document. The tabs for a law include a **Summary** of the law, the full **Text, Actions** taken, **Titles, Amendments, Cosponsors, Committees,** and **Related Bills.** Each tab shows the number of items available for that category. If you select **Text** (7) as shown in Figure 11.11, you can read seven versions of the bill. You will most likely be interested in the Enrolled Bill because it is the final copy that was passed by both chambers.

Another useful feature on the page includes subject information, as assigned by legislative analysts. Click the **View subjects** link in the right-hand column to see all subjects assigned to the legislation. From there, you can click a link for the **Policy Area** (the one term that best describes the legislation) to retrieve other legislation in the same subject category (see Figure 11.12).

**Figure 11.12** Subjects assigned to legislation on Congress.gov.

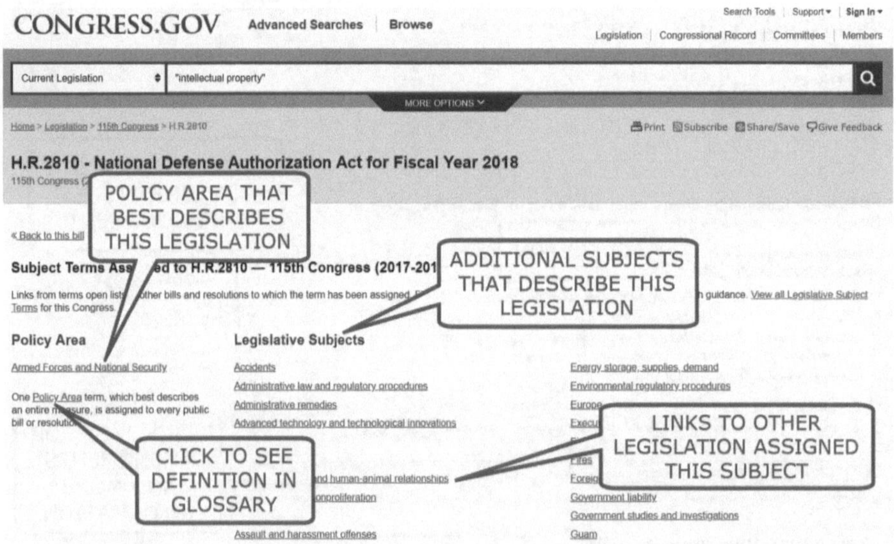


Certain legislative terms used on Congress.gov include links to definitions in the site's **Glossary**. (See **Policy Area** in Figure 11.12, for example.) When there is no link for a word you need to define, however, you can go directly to the **Glossary** (http://bit.ly/CongressGlossary) to check for a definition.

## The Congressional Record on Congress.gov

Congress.gov has several additional features that are worth mentioning here. For example, besides keyword searching the Congressional Record from the homepage, you can also keyword search it at its own landing page, found at http://congress.gov/congressional-record. The default display for the Congressional Record page is the most recent issue available, but you can retrieve any other issue back to 1995 by date; a drop-down menu next to the **Date** search box allows you to select a date from the calendar without typing it. You can also use a combination of year and page number (see Figure 11.13). Information about the Congressional Record App (for the iPhone and the iPad) is also available on this page.

**Figure 11.13** Congressional Record page on Congress.gov.

When you retrieve older issues of the Congressional Record on this page, they appear in the same format as the most current issue, illustrated in Figure 11.13, along with the same links and tabs. You can also view the complete issue in PDF by clicking the **Entire Issue** link under the date.

## Committee Information on Congress.gov

The **Committees of the U.S. Congress** page (http://congress.gov/committees) provides information about committees in general and links to individual pages for all current congressional committees. The individual committee pages include an **Overview** section that lists legislation the committee has considered recently, as well as links to meeting schedules, live video for House committees, and the official committee website. Below the Overview is a results list of legislation and reports associated with the committee. You can sort and refine this list with the same filters you've seen elsewhere on Congress.gov (see Figure 11.14).

**Figure 11.14** A committee page on Congress.gov.

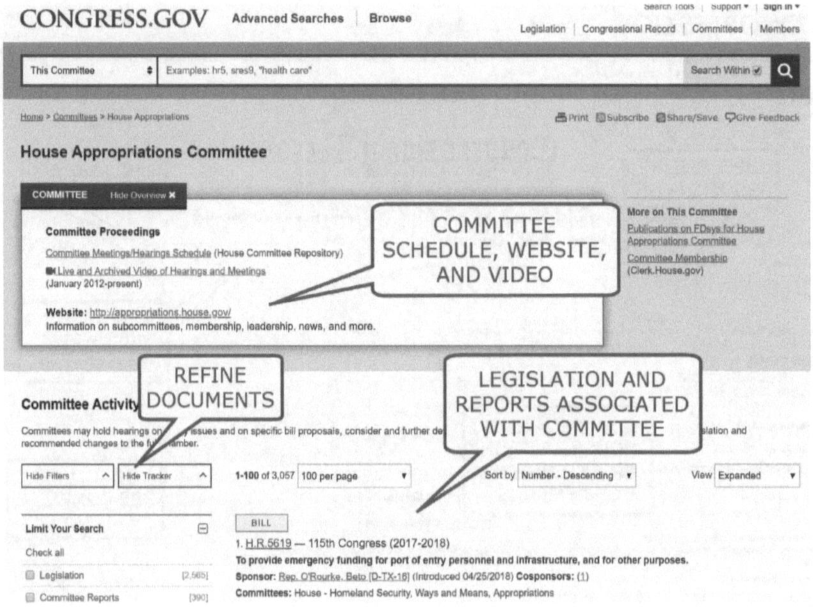


## Committee Reports on Congress.gov

Committee reports are searchable from the homepage of Congress.gov, although their separate landing page has been pared down compared to landing pages for other categories (see http://congress.gov/congressional-reports). You can reach the same page by changing the default **Current Legislation** search field on the homepage to **Committee Reports** and clicking the magnifying button next to the main search box (without entering any search terms). This retrieves every committee report in Congress.gov's database. This page has the same filtering and sorting options discussed previously in this chapter (see Figure 11.15). One difference between this page and a regular search results page is the link to **About Committee Reports** that appears near the upper left corner. If you click the link and go to the About Committee Reports page, you can learn about committee reports, but you can also browse three lists of committee reports by type: **House Reports, Senate Reports,** and **Executive Reports.**

**Figure 11.15** Searching Committee Reports on Congress.gov.

## Finding Members of Congress on Congress.gov

Like the other categories discussed above, members of Congress can be searched from the homepage of the site. Drop-down menus near the bottom of the homepage also allow users to browse members of Congress by name and filter them by state. The **Members of the U.S. Congress** landing page (https://www.congress.gov/members) provides an **Overview** that also contains drop-down menus to browse members of Congress. In addition, it provides contact information for all members of Congress, Member Guides, a Biographical Directory for the U.S. Congress from 1774, a link to a video on how to create email alerts for members of Congress, and other Congress.gov resources (see Figure 11.16).

Below the Overview section is a results list of current and former members, listed alphabetically. This list can be filtered by **Congress, House** or **Senate, Party,** or **US State or Territory.**

Figure 11.16 Members of the U.S. Congress page on Congress.gov.

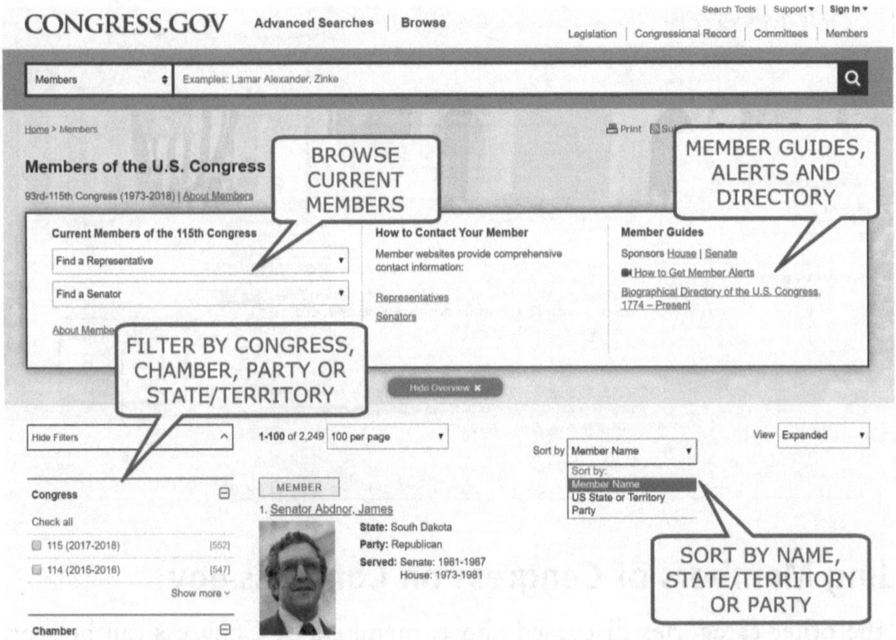


Each member of Congress's individual page contains the member's photograph and a brief Overview, including their website address and contact information. Below the Overview is a list of all legislation that the member has sponsored or cosponsored. Users can sort the list by date and use the list of refinements in the left column to filter by **Sponsorship** (sponsored or cosponsored), **Congress, Chamber, Legislation Type, Subject, Status** (current legislation only), and **Committee.**

### Learn about the Legislative Process on Congress.gov

Congress.gov includes a page called **The Legislative Process** (https://congress.gov/legislative-process) that provides educational videos to help the general public and students understand the legislative process. The videos are short (mostly under five minutes) and include a written transcript of the narration. A **Diagram of the Legislative Process** is also provided (underneath the list of videos) in JPG and PDF formats.

## GOVINFO LEGISLATIVE AND CONGRESSIONAL MATERIALS (COLLECTIONS)

The govinfo website (https://www.govinfo.gov) has many legislative and congressional collections, including Congressional Bills, Congressional Record, Congressional

Reports, and more. You can browse these collections, search them, or look up a specific document with its citation. We explain all three methods in this section and then describe some govinfo collections that may be especially useful for researching legislative and congressional materials.

To browse govinfo's collections, hover your cursor over the **Browse** link on the left side of the menu bar that runs across the top of any page on the site (see Figure 11.17, upper left corner). A drop-down menu will appear and you can choose a link to an **A to Z** list of resources, **Category, Date, Committee,** or **Author.** Each option will take you to a page with additional links or options where you can continue browsing.

**Figure 11.17** govinfo's Advanced Search page.

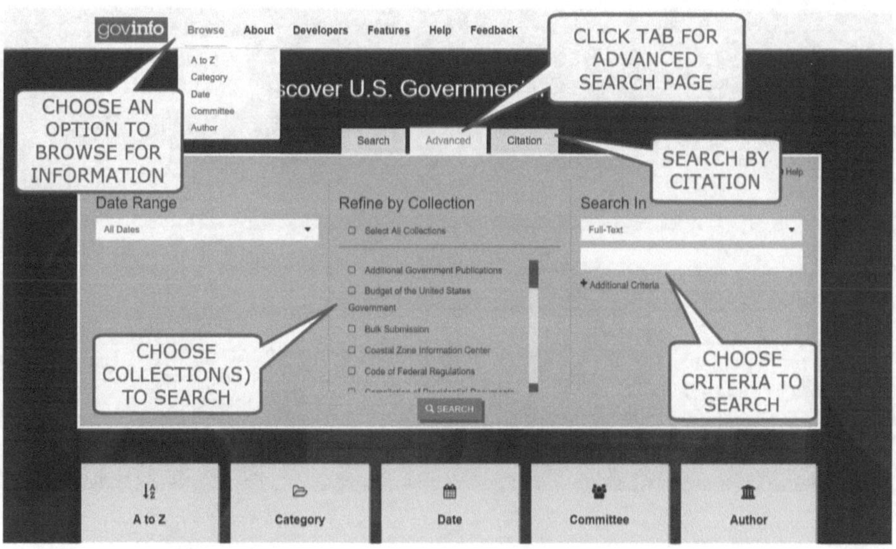


Often, searching will be more useful for your research than browsing. You can enter keywords into the main search box on the homepage and search the entire site. However, we recommend using govinfo's **Advanced Search** page, found at https://www.govinfo.gov/#advanced (see Figure 11.17), because it allows you to perform more specific searches than the main box. To use the Advanced Search page, click the **Advanced** tab that appears below the **Discover U.S. Government Information** heading (Figure 11.17). Then, in the **Refine by Collection** menu in the center column, select the collection(s) you wish to search by using the checkboxes next to the collection names. Finally, select search criteria such as **Full-Text, Citation, Congress Session,** or **Sudoc Class Number** from the **Search In** drop-down menu in the right column (Figure 11.17). (You can also choose a **Date Range** from the left column.) We provide more detailed instructions for using govinfo's Advanced Search feature in Chapter 5; please refer to it for additional information.

You can also retrieve documents by citation. Click the **Citation** tab (to the right of the **Advanced** tab) or go directly to https://www.govinfo.gov/#citation (see Figure 11.18). A drop-down menu with the words **Select Collection** appears in the center of the page, use it to choose a collection from the available options (Congressional Bills, Congressional Reports, Congressional Record, etc.). Additional menus and/or search boxes will then appear, depending on the collection you selected. You can use them to enter the citation information for the document you want.

**Figure 11.18** Searching by citation on govinfo.

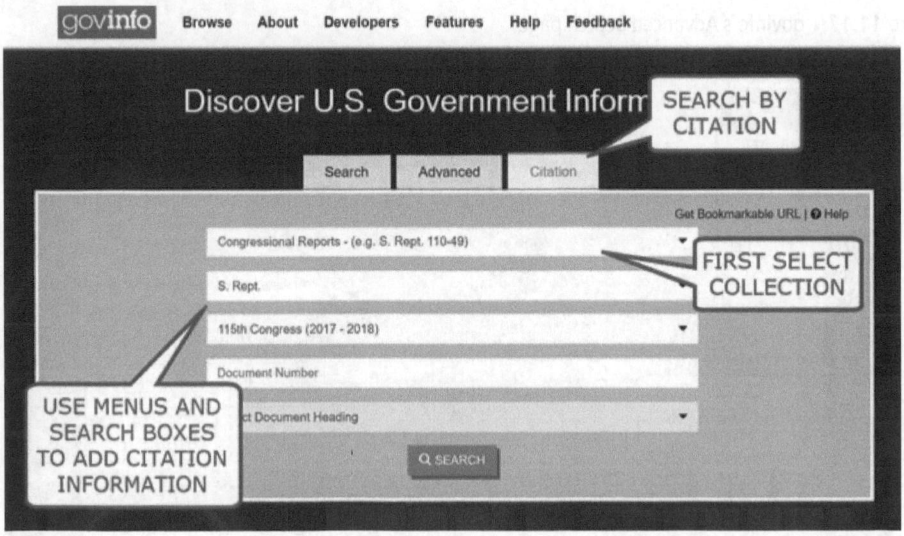


Below are several of govinfo's collections that may be useful for researching legislative and congressional information. Locate each collection by choosing its title from the **Refine by Collection** menu on govinfo's **Advanced Search** page (https://www.govinfo.gov/#advanced).

- **Congressional Bills** can be keyword searched back to 1993. Use the drop-down menu in the **Search In** column on the right side of the **Advanced Search** page to choose among nineteen criteria by which to search. To limit Congressional Bills to a specific Congress or multiple Congresses, choose the **Congress Number** criterion from the **Search In** menu and then use the **Choose Value** drop-down menu to select a Congress number. You can search by up to five criteria, so you could select five different Congresses to search or you could select one Congress and add up to four other criteria to search by, such as Bill Number. To search Congressional Bills by sponsor, you would select the **Sponsors and Co-sponsors** criterion. There is no drop-down menu to search Sponsors and Co-Sponsors, however, so you would need to type in the sponsor's name. We prefer Congress.gov for these searches because we can go directly to the member's landing page to see a list of legislation she or he sponsored.

- **Congressional Reports** go back to 1995 and offer 23 criteria by which to search. Although there is not a separate govinfo collection for committee reports, this is where you can find them. If you are looking for a report from a specific committee (Ways and Means, for example), choose **Committee** from the **Search In** menu, and type *ways and means* into the search box that appears. You can then refine your search further to look for specific reports.
- **Conference Reports** are among the most helpful documents for researching legislative history. Congress.gov's **Glossary**, mentioned earlier in this chapter, defines a *conference report* as, "The document presenting an agreement reached by a joint temporary committee (a conference committee) appointed to negotiate a compromise between the House and Senate" (https://www.congress.gov/help/legislative-glossary#c). They are not a separate collection, but they are so useful that we have listed them here. To search them, first choose the Congressional Reports collection (described above) and then select the **Conference Report** search criterion from the **Search In** menu. Coverage goes back to 1995.
- The **Congressional Record** can be searched by thirty-five criteria back to 1994. Searchable criteria include **Full-Text, Sudoc Class Number, Congress Member Speaking, Congress Member Voted No,** etc.
- **History of Bills** offers fifteen criteria by which to search. While this collection is not available at the **Citation** search page, **Bill Number Citation** is one of the fifteen criteria that can be searched in **History of Bills.** If you don't know during which Congress a specific bill number was introduced, you can search all Congresses back to 1983. Select **Bill Number Citation** from the **Search In** menu and enter just the bill number. For example, entering *s.9* will search for the history of every Senate Bill Number 9 in every Congress back to 1983. (For house bills, you would follow the same procedure, but with a house bill number—*h.r.1,* for example.)

- The **Public and Private Laws** collection goes back to 1995. (For earlier years, see Congress.gov's **Legislation** section, which goes back to 1973.) Public and private laws, also known as slip laws, can be useful when doing legislative history research. Choose this collection from the **Refine by Collection** list on the **Advanced Search** page, and you can search by fifteen criteria, such as **Full-Text, Citation** (of the public or private law—e.g., Pub. L. 111-202), **United States Code Citation** (to find all the public or private laws that reference a specific section of the U.S.C.), and **Associated Bill Citation** (to locate public or private laws associated with a certain bill). Note that govinfo has modernized its citation search feature so you no longer have to enter a citation with precise punctuation; e.g., entering *22 usc 6208* will return the same results as *22 U.S.C. 6208*.
- Statutes at Large are the bound volumes into which slip laws are compiled chronologically. Statutes at Large can be searched back to 1951 by twenty-two criteria, including **Full-Text, Statutes at Large Citation, Associated Bill Citation,** and **Public or Private Law Citation.**

## ADDITIONAL RESOURCES

The **Congressional Research Service** (CRS) is a public policy research division of the United States Congress that is part of the Library of Congress (http://www.loc.gov/crsinfo). As part of its mission to provide Congress research and analysis on current and developing issues of national policy, the CRS provides reports, called Congressional Research Service Reports, to Congress. These in-depth reports cover a wide range of topics and clearly explain and define issues in a legislative context. The reports often contain legislative history information in addition to other information. Unfortunately, as a matter of policy, CRS reports are not available to the public, except in limited circumstances. (You can try contacting your member of Congress or submitting a FOIA request for a specific report.) Until recently, the reports that were public tended to be sporadically available on various web archives. In 2002, as a public service, the Government Documents Department at the University of North Texas (UNT) began archiving the publicly available CRS reports into a searchable collection in its digital library. To search, browse, or read more about the scope of UNT's **Congressional Research Service Reports** collection, see http://bit.ly/UNT_CRSR. (The search and browse features appear near the bottom of the page, so you must scroll down to find them.)

For more information on the legislative process in general (or even just to find your Senator or Representative), use the **United States Senate** website at https://www.senate.gov and the **United States House of Representatives** website at https://www.house.gov.

# Chapter 12

## FEDERAL EXECUTIVE AND ADMINISTRATIVE LAW

The executive branch of the federal government is responsible for enforcing the laws of the land. This branch includes the president, the vice president, the cabinet, and various agencies. Agencies help execute policy by creating regulations based on laws. This chapter will explain several resources to help you locate and research executive (also known as administrative) law.

govinfo is useful as a starting point to conduct research about the executive branch of the federal government because govinfo allows you to access all the executive branch's collections (https://www.govinfo.gov/#advanced) in one place, from regulations in govinfo's Federal Register (FR) to presidential materials in the Compilation of Presidential Documents. In the next pages, we will also discuss the Code of Federal Regulations (CFR), the publication into which the FR is codified annually. Next, we will look at the White House site. Finally, we will discuss government agencies and methods for locating and using them in your research.

## THE FEDERAL REGISTER

The **Federal Register** (FR) is the official daily publication (printed Monday through Friday) of proposed and final rules, notices of federal agencies and organizations, and executive orders and other presidential documents. To browse the govinfo FR database by **year, month, date,** or **agency**, visit http://bit.ly/govinfoFR.

**Figure 12.1** Browsing the Federal Register on govinfo.

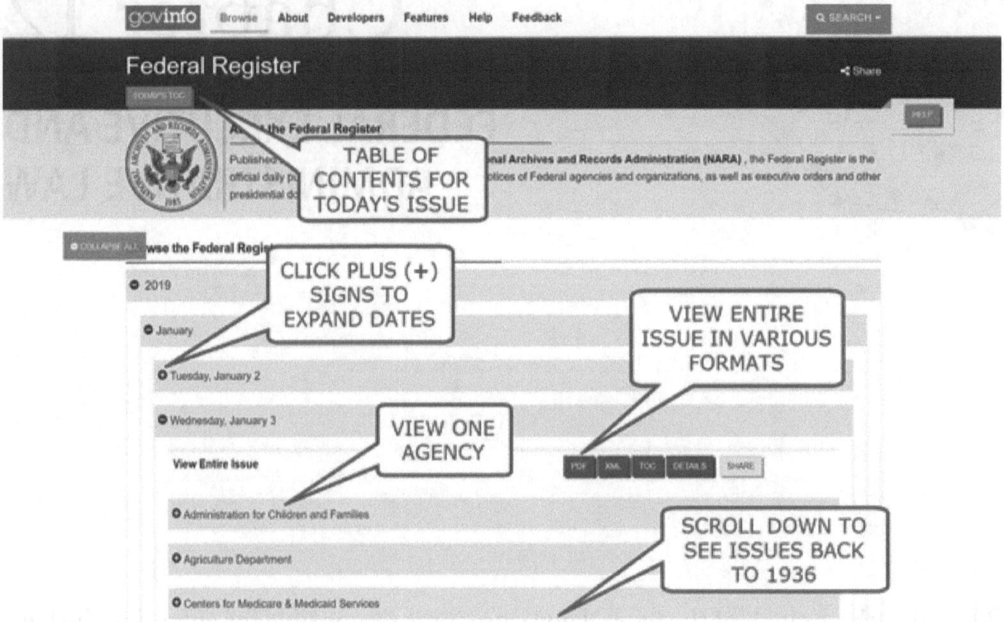


A link to the table of contents of the current day's issue (**Today's TOC**) of the FR is displayed on the homepage. You can use the table of contents to browse the full text. You can also browse issues from 1936 to the present (see Figure 12.1). Once you select a specific issue, you can view the entire issue in **PDF** or **XML** (back to 2001), view just the **Table of Contents,** view the **Details** (metadata), or select just one agency for which to view information (back to 1994). For issues older than 1994, you can view the entire issue as a PDF and see the Details. To receive a daily e-mail alert of the FR Table of Contents, sign up at http://bit.ly/FRemail or see **Justia's Regulation Tracker** (https://regulations.justia.com).

To search the Federal Register by keywords and other criteria, visit the **Advanced Search** page (https://www.govinfo.gov/#advanced), enter a date (or leave the default date as **All Dates** in the **Date Range** drop-down menu), choose the **Federal Register** from the **Refine by Collection** menu, then choose how to search (by choosing criteria such as **Citation, Action,** etc. from the **Search In** drop-down menu), and finally, enter keywords or citations into the search box. Because all govinfo collections follow the same search protocol, be sure to review the search protocol discussed in Chapter 5. You can search the FR via **Full-Text** and **Citation** from govinfo's Federal Register collection back to 1936 (Volume 1).

You can also download bulk data from the FR in XML format at https://www.govinfo.gov/bulkdata/FR. (Downloading in the XML format "allows developers to grab large sets of rich, structured XML data more easily for their own mashups" according to govinfo (http://bit.ly/govinfoxml).)

## THE CODE OF FEDERAL REGULATIONS

The **Code of Federal Regulations** (CFR) is the annual codification of the general and permanent rules and regulations that are first published in the FR by the departments and agencies of the federal government. The CFR is divided into fifty Titles—distinct areas subject to federal regulation (e.g., Title 1 is Energy, and Title 26 is Internal Revenue). One-quarter of the CFR Titles are updated at a time on a rolling quarterly basis, until the full CFR has been updated each year. Presidential documents and executive orders from the FR are compiled annually into Title 3 of the CFR.

Search the CFR database at govinfo by first selecting the **Code of Federal Regulations** from the **Refine by Collection** menu on the **Advanced Search** page (https://www.govinfo.gov/#advanced) as shown in Figure 12.2.

**Figure 12.2** Advanced search of the CFR or govinfo.

After you choose the collection, the search criteria appropriate to that collection will be available in a drop-down menu in the right-hand column, under the **Search**

**In** heading. In Figure 12.3, we have searched by the **CFR Title Number** criteria and **CFR Section Number** criteria. This search differs from a **Citation** search. A Citation search limits you to one year while our search allows us to search through all years from 1996 to the most current print version, if you need to see if and how a specific section of the CFR has changed over time. (**Citation** searches are discussed later in the chapter.)

**Figure 12.3** Searching the CFR by title number and section number on govinfo.

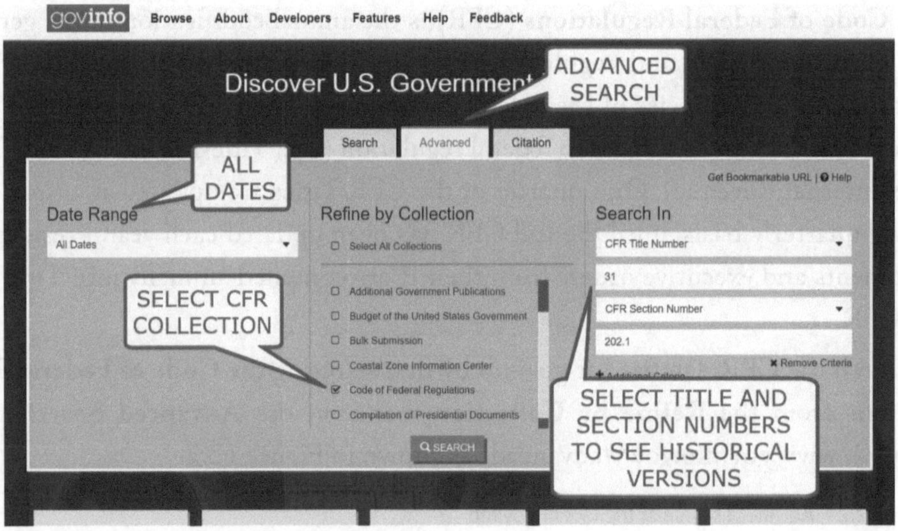


Figure 12.4 shows the search results page for *Title Number 31* and *Section Number 202.1* in govinfo's CFR collection. In the left column of the page, under **Refine Your Search**, are checkboxes and links to several editions (years) of the full text of the CFR Title and Section. There is also a checkbox to **View Historical Results** (checked in Figure 12.4); to view only the current version, you could uncheck it. You can refine your search by clicking links in the left-hand column, such as **Government Author**, **Location**, and **Date Published**. You can also view the individual search results in **PDF** or **XML**, view the **Details** (metadata) or **Share** it via email, social media, printing, etc. (Note that if you have ad blockers or anti-tracking extensions installed on your browser, the **Share** feature may not work on your computer.)

**Figure 12.4** CFR Title Number and Section Number search results.

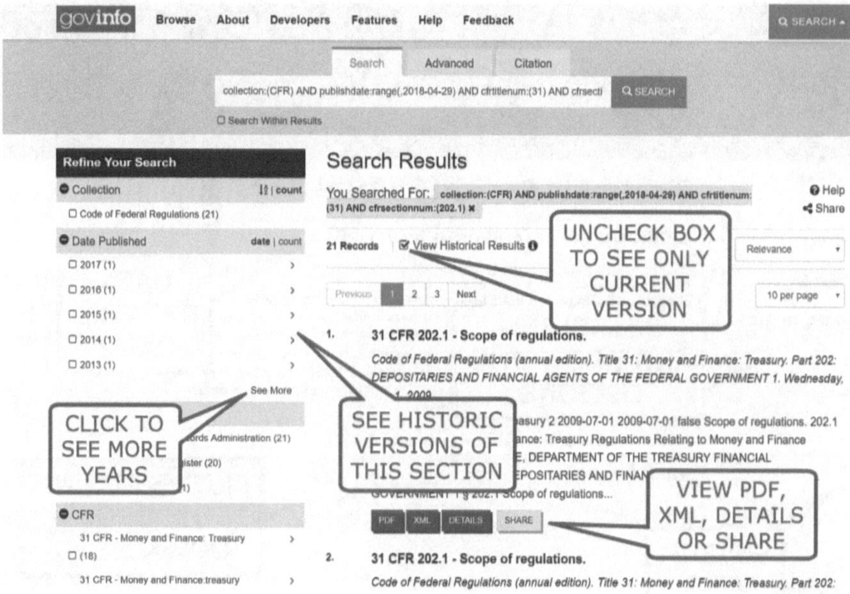


You can keyword search the CFR from the **Advanced Search** page (https://www.govinfo.gov/#advanced) by choosing **Full-Text** from the **Search In** drop-down menu (shown in Figure 12.2) and then entering keywords into the search box. Instructions on govinfo's keyword search protocol are discussed in Chapter 5. govinfo also allows you to browse the CFR at http://bit.ly/govinfoCFR by (1) selecting a year; (2) clicking the plus signs to drill down to a specific **Title, Part, Chapter**, or **Section**; and (3) viewing the document in **PDF** or **XML**. The PDF will look just like the print document while XML will be only the document text.

## THE E-CFR

Although the **e-CFR** website (https://www.ecfr.gov) displays some branding of the Government Publishing Office (GPO), it has always run on a separate platform. Therefore, e-CFR (see Figure 12.5) remains online, even though GPO Access has been taken offline and replaced by govinfo. However, it is still not deemed to be the "official" CFR and is described as an "an editorial compilation of CFR material and *Federal Register* amendments produced by the National Archives and Records Administration's Office of the Federal Register (OFR) and the Government Publishing Office" (https://www.ecfr.gov).

Figure 12.5 Searching and browsing on the e-CFR.

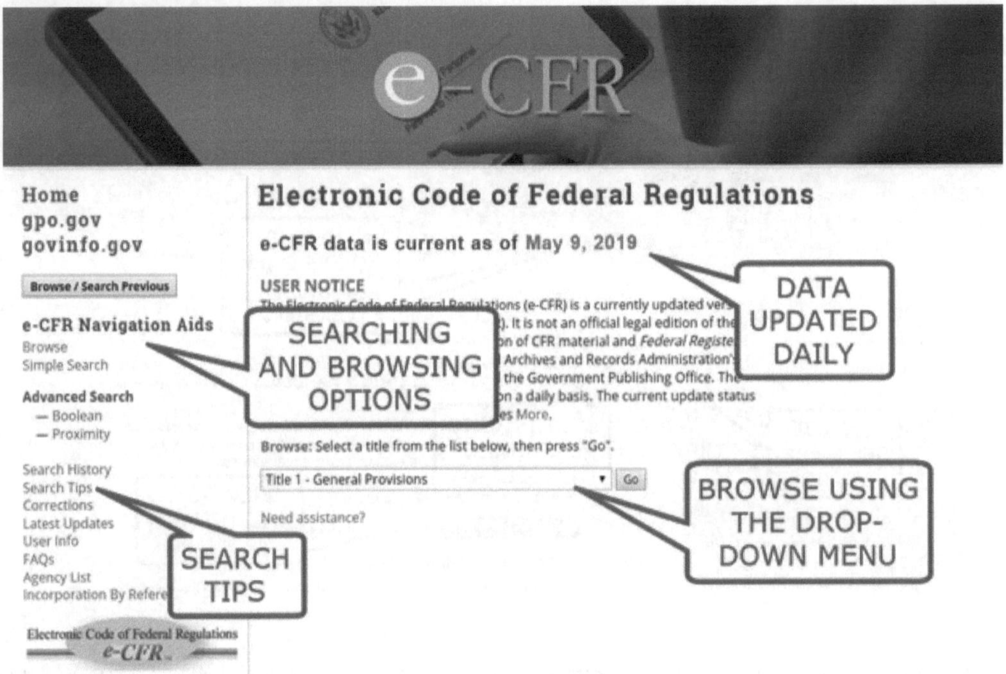


While the govinfo CFR database discussed in the previous section is updated only annually, the e-CFR is updated every day, which is the reason we use it more than the govinfo version. As amendments become effective, the Office of the Federal Register adds the changes to the current CFR database, so you can view the full text of the updated CFR in one place instead of having to run a search in both the CFR and FR (or in both the CFR and LSA, discussed in the next section). Note that the e-CFR only searches the current CFR. For historical searching back to 1996, use govinfo's CFR database (discussed in the previous section), along with the List of CFR Sections Affected and its Compilation (discussed in the next section).

You can browse the e-CFR database numerically by **Title**, or you can keyword search the database using the **Simple Search** option or the **Advanced Search** option (in the left-hand column). The Simple Search option allows you to search the entire CFR (current) or just one CFR Title (current). You can search for your term anywhere within the text or within a specific field, such as a Part or a SubPart. The Advanced Search option offers a Boolean and a Proximity search. Detailed **Search Tips** can be found at http://bit.ly/eCFRHelp or from the **Search Tips** link in the left column of the homepage (see Figure 12.5).

# SEARCHING THE LIST OF CFR SECTIONS AFFECTED (LSA) AND THE LIST OF CFR PARTS AFFECTED

The **List of CFR Sections Affected** (LSA) is a list of new revisions to the CFR, such as proposed, new, and amended federal regulations published in the FR since the most recent revision date of a specific CFR Title. Researchers use it to determine if a particular CFR section has been revised by material published in the FR but not yet incorporated into the CFR. The LSA is issued monthly, but each LSA issue is cumulative, so there is no need to read each issue; just read the most current. (Or as discussed shortly in this chapter, there is no need to read monthly LSAs for the years 1986 to 2000, because the **LSA Compilation** consolidates the LSA into a single resource for those years, organized by Title.)

To browse the LSA from 1997 forward by date, visit http://bit.ly/govinfoLSA (see Figure 12.6) and select a year listed beneath **Monthly LSA** (below the link for LSA Compilation), select a month, and then click on the **PDF** or **Text** link of any **Title** to view the list of CFR parts and section numbers of that Title that have been affected. There will be a description of how it has been affected (e.g., amended, removed, or revised) and the FR page number will be listed where the change(s) can be found. You would need to then visit the **FR collection** (discussed earlier in this chapter) to retrieve the text of the change.

**Figure 12.6** Browse the List of CFR Sections Affected (LSA) on govinfo.

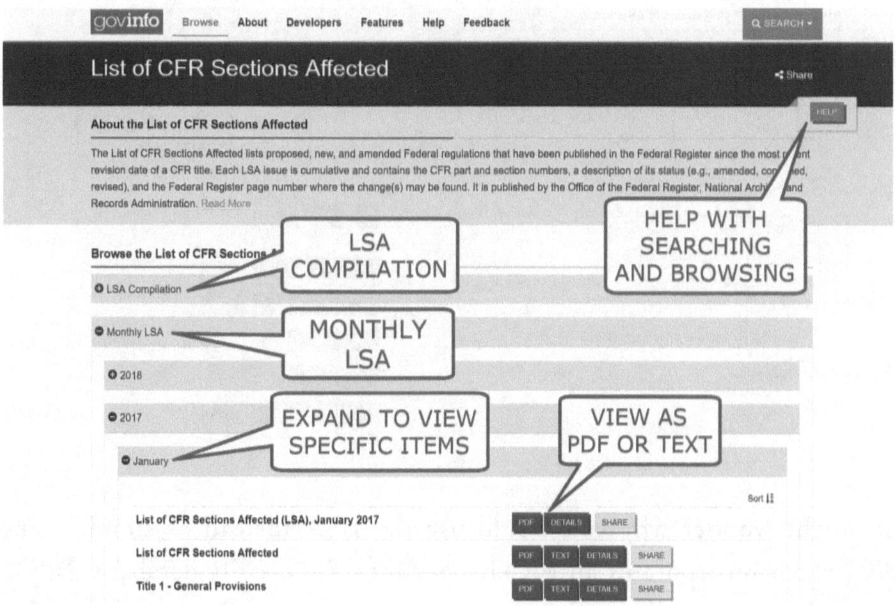

The **LSA Compilation** consolidates the LSA from the years of 1986 to 2000 into a single resource organized by Title. (This goes back one year further than the LSA monthly issues.) The LSA Compilation cannot be keyword searched, but to browse it by Title, visit the **List of CFR Sections Affected** page at http://bit.ly/govinfoLSA (see Figure 12.7). The LSA Compilation link appears above the Monthly LSA link. To view the LSA Compilation, open the links for **LSA Compilation,** then **2002** (where the compilation is located), and then **April.** Each CFR Title is listed individually and will include a list of changes from 1986 to 2000. Choosing Title 4, for example, will return a list beginning with the year 1986 (and ending with 2000) and any chapters of Title 4 affected during each of those years. There will be a notation of how they were affected (amended, revised, or removed), and the volume and page number of the FR where the change occurred will be included. You would need to then visit the FR Collection to retrieve the text of the change.

**Figure 12.7** The LSA Compilation on govinfo.

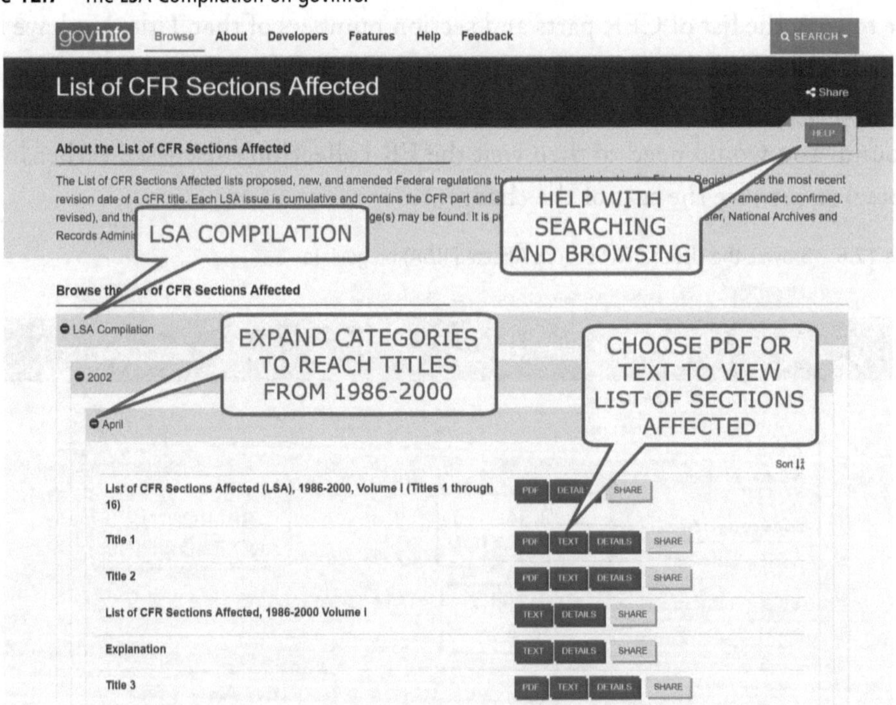


You might wonder why you would use the LSA instead of simply using the e-CFR (which incorporates all FR changes into the e-CFR database daily). The answer is this: There are searches at the LSA that cannot be accomplished at the e-CFR site, such as conducting historical research (by browsing the 1986–2000 LSA Compilation or searching older volumes back to 1997).

To search the LSA by keywords and other criteria, visit the **Advanced Search** page (https://www.govinfo.gov/#advanced), choose **List of CFR Sections Affected** from the **Refine by Collection** menu, and select which part of the collection to search (from the **Search In** drop-down menu on the right side of the page). The default is **Full-Text**, so this is where you can enter keywords (e.g., *ocean*). If you want to add other criteria to your **Full-Text** search, click **Additional Criteria.** You can then limit your search results to **Annual Compilations**, for example, and then choose a **Value** (in this case you are offered ranges of **Titles**, e.g., **Titles 28 to 41**). Or, you could change the **Full-Text** default to another criteria, such as **Branch, Citation**, or **Title**.

Although the LSA is not listed on the **Citation** search menu at https://www.govinfo.gov/#citation, you can conduct a citation search of the LSA using the **Advanced Search** page (https://www.govinfo.gov/#advanced), choosing the **List of CFR Sections Affected** from the **Refine by Collection** menu, then choosing **Citation** from the **Search In** drop-down menu, and entering the citation in this format: *LSA, January, 2012, Title 1*. To learn the correct LSA citation format and to see a list of other Field operators (including Citation) unique to the LSA collection, see the **Help** page for the List of CFR Sections Affected, 1997 to Present at https://www.govinfo.gov/help/lsa (or click the Help link in the upper right corner of the **List of CFR Sections Affected** page, as shown in Figures 12.6 and 12.7).

govinfo also allows users to browse **CFR Parts Affected from the Federal Register** (http://bit.ly/govinfoCFRParts) to find final and proposed rules that affect the CFR (and that are published in the FR). This approach saves an extra step versus using the List of CFR Sections Affected, which requires you to find the rule that has been changed and then visit the FR collection to retrieve the text of the change. To browse the CFR Parts Affected from the Federal Register, select one of the following from the menu in the left column: **Past 24 Hours, Past 7 Days, Past 30 Days, Past 180 Days,** or **Past 365 Days;** or **Select a Date Range** from the right column (see Figure 12.8). Then choose the **Title** and then the **Part** in which you are interested. Clicking the **PDF** or **Text** link will bring back the full text of the rule.

Figure 12.8 CFR Parts Affected from the Federal Register on govinfo.

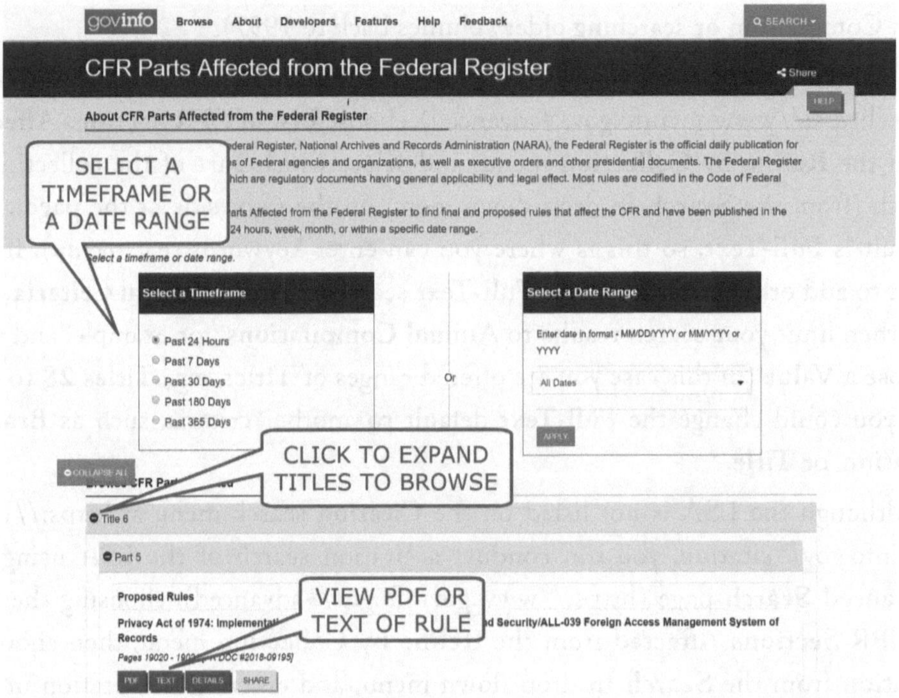


## U.S. REGULATION TRACKER

Justia's free **Regulation Tracker** allows researchers to search for and track regulations through the Federal Register back to 2005. You can search all federal agencies and departments together, search a specific one (by **Department/Agency**), add a date range (**Regulations Filed**), show one or multiple types of regulatory law (i.e., notices, rules), add keywords into the **Full Text** search box, or use any combination of these search options (see Figure 12.9). The full-text search is powered by Google so it can search by keywords and phrases and with the Boolean and proximity connectors Google allows (described in Chapter 4). Results can be sorted by date or by relevance. Search results can also be filtered by type of regulatory law—e.g., **Rules, Administrative Orders,** and so on. From the homepage you can also select the option to **Browse by Government Agency** or **Browse by Date** while filtering by type of regulatory law. To use the Regulation Tracker, select **Regulations** near the bottom of Justia's homepage, or visit https://regulations.justia.com.

**Figure 12.9** Search and Track the Federal Register on Justia. Screenshot from Justia used with permission.

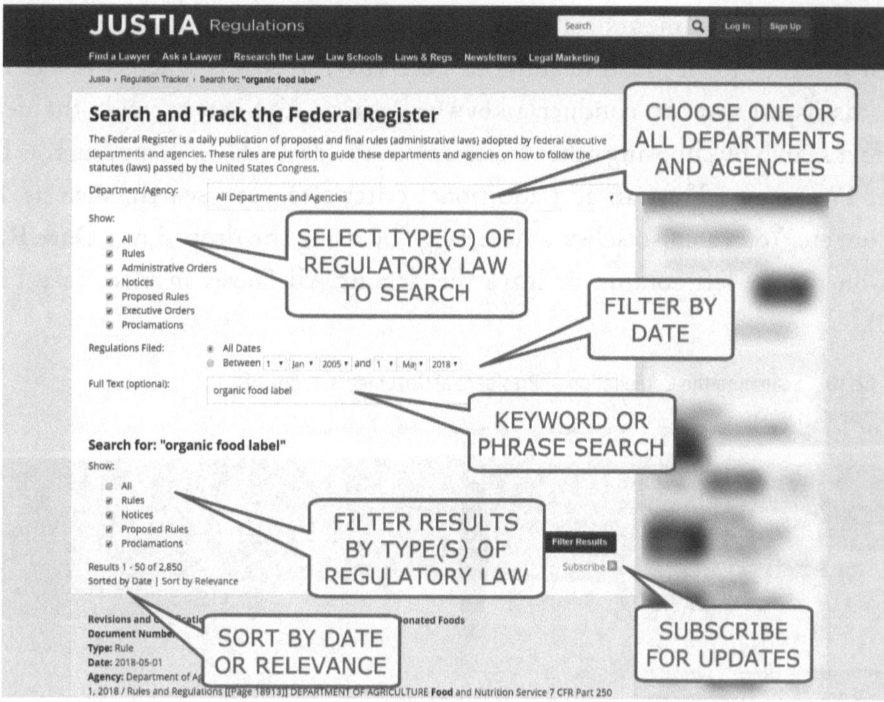


Researchers can subscribe to news feeds (e.g., RSS and others) for daily regulation alert updates (see Figure 12.9). The Federal Register's own alert service (for the Table of Contents only) is also available and described earlier in this chapter.

## GOVINFO AND PRESIDENTIAL MATERIALS

govinfo offers several collections relating to the President, including the **Compilation of Presidential Documents** and the **Public Papers of the Presidents of the United States.** The Compilation of Presidential Documents comprises the **Daily Compilation** (January 2, 2009, to date) and its predecessor, the **Weekly Compilation** (1993 through its change to a daily on January 20, 2009). The Compilations include Presidential statements, messages, remarks, executive orders, State of the Union Addresses, and so on, released by the White House Press Secretary. At govinfo, you can browse the Weekly and the Daily Compilations at http://bit.ly/govinfoPresidential, or **Advanced Search** them at https://www.govinfo.gov/#advanced.

To Advanced Search the Weekly or Daily Compilation, select the **Compilation of Presidential Documents** collection from the **Refine by Collection** menu. The **Search In** drop-down menu defaults to **Full-Text**, so this is where you can enter keywords if you want to conduct a keyword search. You can override the default Full-Text search by choosing other criteria from the drop-down menu, such as **Document Frequency**. You can add additional criteria to your search, such as Title, Citation, etc. You can also select a date range by using the drop-down **Date Range** menu on the far-left column or leave the default **All Dates** in place (see Figure 12.10).

**Figure 12.10** Searching the Compilation of Presidential Documents at govinfo.

The **Public Papers of the Presidents of the United States** collection consists of Presidential writings, addresses, and remarks of a public nature. The collection can be browsed back to 1991 (http://bit.ly/govinfoPPP) or searched by choosing it from the **Refine by Collection** menu at https://www.govinfo.gov/#advanced and then selecting additional criteria and/or dates to search.

You can also conduct a **Citation** search for both the Public Papers of the Presidents of the United States and the Weekly and Daily Compilations on govinfo's **Citation** page (https://www.govinfo.gov/#citation).

govinfo allows you to browse the **State of the Union Addresses** collection, although the feature is unlike most other browsable collections on the site. If you go to the **Browse by A to Z** page (https://www.govinfo.gov/browse-a-z) and click the link for **State of the Union Addresses, 1994 to Present,** you are taken to a search results page. By examining the text near the top of the page, you can determine that the site has just run a search in the **Compilation of Presidential Documents** collection for documents with the title, "Address Before a Joint Session of the Congress on the State of the Union" (see Figure 12.11). The results are displayed in order of relevance, which doesn't seem useful, so use the **Relevance** drop-down menu to re-sort by **Date New to Old** or **Date Old to New.** You can then select a State of the Union Address to browse through, or you can filter these results by any criteria in the left column, such as **Date Published** or **President.**

If you want to conduct a keyword search, you can do so from the Advanced Search page (https://www.govinfo.gov/#advanced) by choosing **Compilation of Presidential Documents** from the **Refine by Collection** menu. The **Search In** drop-down menu defaults to **Full-Text,** so enter the phrase "*Address Before a Joint Session of the Congress on the State of the Union*" (with the quotation marks to signal a phrase search) into the search box beneath the **Search In Full-Text** drop-down menu. You can then add more keywords (e.g., "*north korea*") by clicking **Additional Criteria** to open another Full-Text Search box.

**Figure 12.11** Browsing State of the Union Addresses on govinfo.

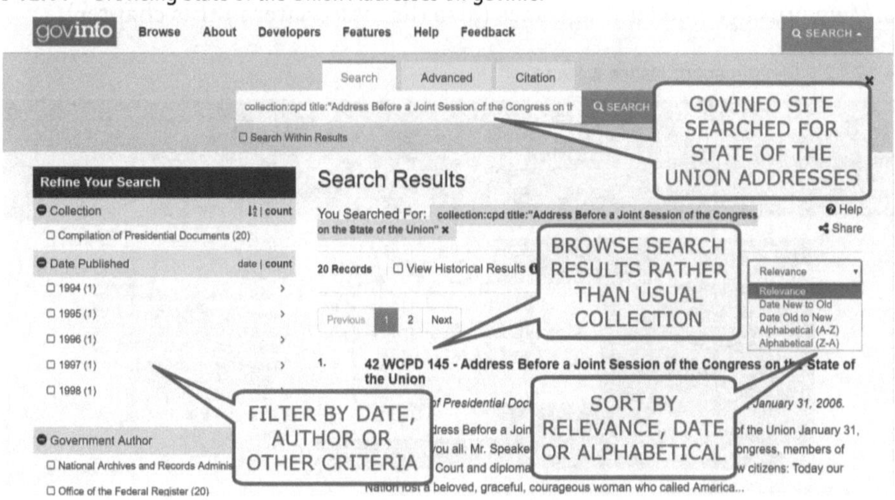

## THE WHITE HOUSE

The White House's site is at https://www.whitehouse.gov. There you can take a virtual tour of the White House, get biographical information about current and past presidents and vice presidents (and first ladies), e-mail the current ones, read press briefings, and more. All documents on the White House site are keyword searchable by clicking the magnifying glass in the upper-right corner of the page.

You can even view the President's speeches on YouTube (https://www.youtube.com/whitehouse) and follow the White House (along with millions of other followers) on Twitter (https://twitter.com/whitehouse) or a host of other social media sites.

## FEDERAL AGENCIES

The executive branch also includes numerous federal agencies whose websites can be useful for legal research. Their sites can include a wide range of information, from staff directories, rules, regulations, and reports, to administrative decisions, laws, and forms. Sometimes it is easier to pinpoint a rule, regulation, or law at an agency's website instead of searching through the CFR, FR, or U.S.C. For an example of an agency website, see the U.S. Department of Justice site shown in Figure 12.12 (https://www.justice.gov). For a complete list of U.S. departments and agencies, see USA.gov at https://www.usa.gov/federal-agencies (also discussed later in this chapter).

**Figure 12.12** Department of Justice website.

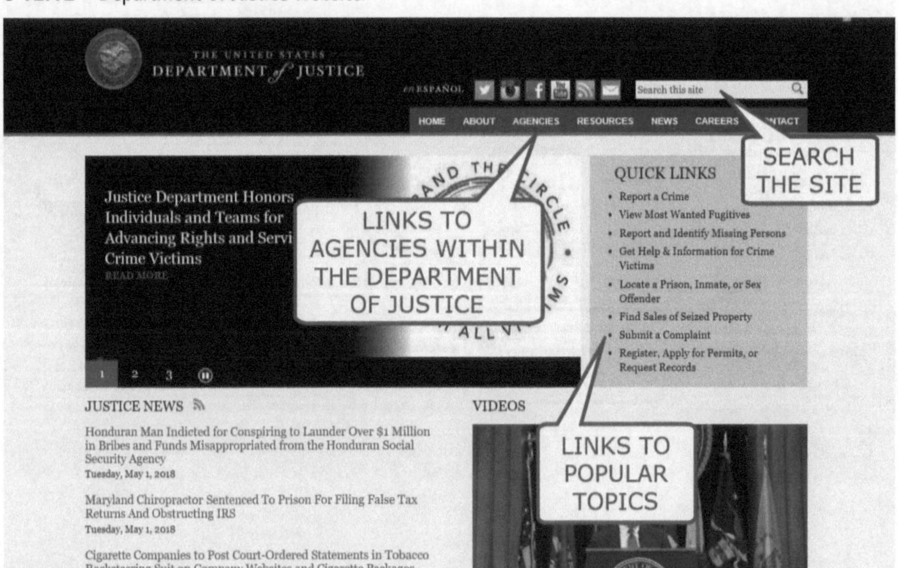

# UNITED STATES GOVERNMENT MANUAL

To locate even more government websites, we also recommend the **United States Government Manual**, in addition to the USA.gov website mentioned above. The manual is the official handbook of the federal government (https://www.usgovernmentmanual.gov). This resource provides information about executive branch agencies and staff; legislative, judicial, and quasi-official agencies; international organizations in which the United States participates; boards; commissions; and committees.

The manual is available at two sites, both of which provide the full text of the manual and links to the various agencies: (1) the **United States Government Manual** site (https://www.usgovernmentmanual.gov), which is jointly administered by the Office of the Federal Register (OFR) and GPO; and (2) the **govinfo** site (http://bit.ly/govinfoGovtManual). At the United States Government Manual site, you will find only the current manual. You can browse the manual by category or search it by keywords. To find archived versions of the manual back to 1995 as well as the current version, visit govinfo, where the manual can be searched or browsed. You can only browse by year (http://bit.ly/govinfoGovtManual); either download the entire year's manual as a PDF or XML text file, or view an individual section as a PDF or XML file (see Figure 12.13).

**Figure 12.13** Browsing the United States Government Manual on govinfo.

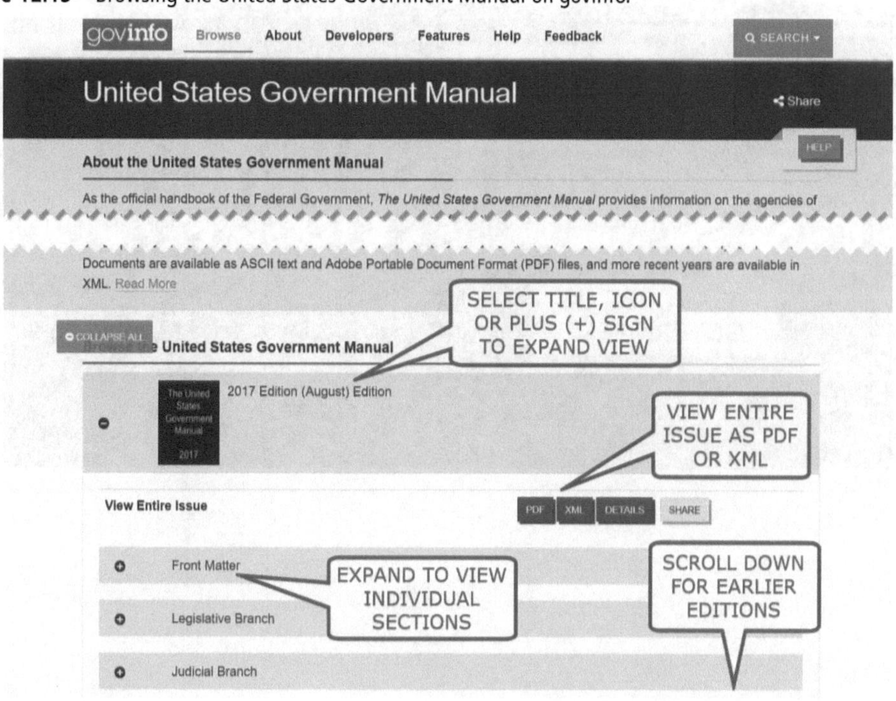

To search the manual by **Full-Text, Citation,** etc., choose **United States Government Manual** from the **Refine by Collection** menu on the **Advanced Search** page (https://www.govinfo.gov/#advanced). More details on how to search govinfo are provided in Chapter 5.

## USA.GOV

**USA.gov** (https://www.usa.gov) is useful for locating federal agencies. At its **Government Agencies and Elected Officials** page (https://www.usa.gov/agencies), you can use the search box to keyword search by agency name. You can also follow the link to **USA.gov's A–Z Index of U.S. Government Agencies** (https://www.usa.gov/federal-agencies) where you can browse an alphabetical list of all federal government departments and agencies by name. Under the **Branches of Government** heading, you can learn more about the federal Legislative, Executive, and Judicial branches (see Figure 12.14).

**Figure 12.14** Government departments and agencies at USA.gov.

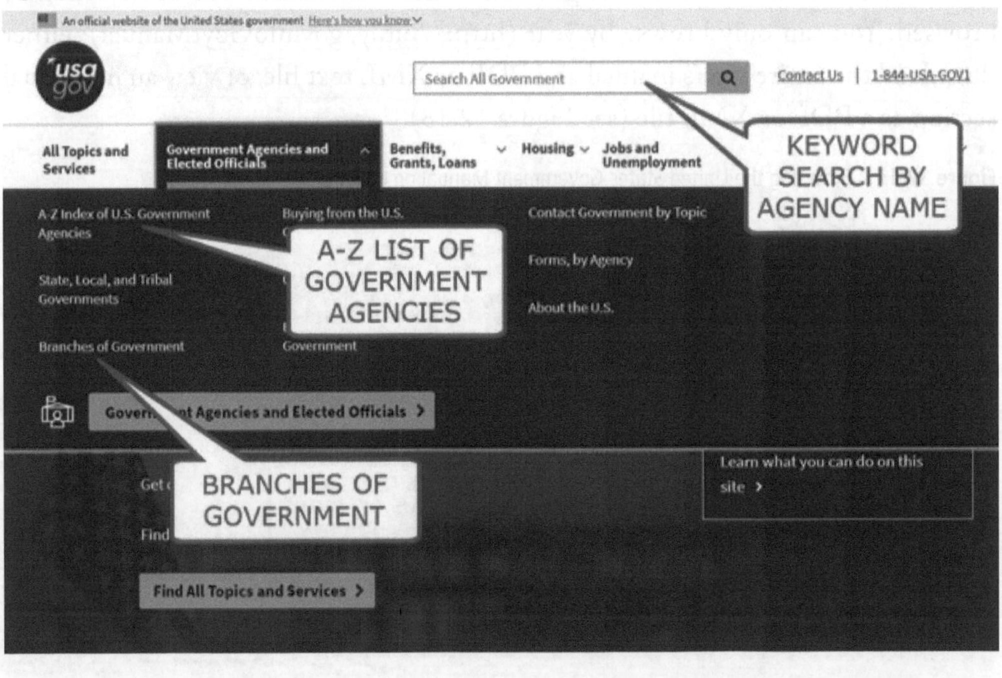

# FINDING DEFUNCT FEDERAL AGENCIES' AND COMMISSIONS' WEBSITES

If you ever need to research a government agency that no longer exists, you may still be able to conduct your research by using a website called the **CyberCemetery** (https://govinfo.library.unt.edu), which is the product of a partnership between the University of North Texas Libraries and the GPO. It provides permanent public access to defunct federal government agencies' and commissions' websites and publications.

You can search or browse the site. The **Search the CyberCemetery** page (http://bit.ly/CyberCemSearch) allows keyword searching and also accepts: quotation marks for phrase searching, the asterisk (*) wildcard symbol, and the plus or minus sign (+, -) which requires or excludes a term from the search, respectively. The search page explains each feature (see Figure 12.15).

**Figure 12.15** Find administrative websites that don't exist anymore at Cybercemetery.

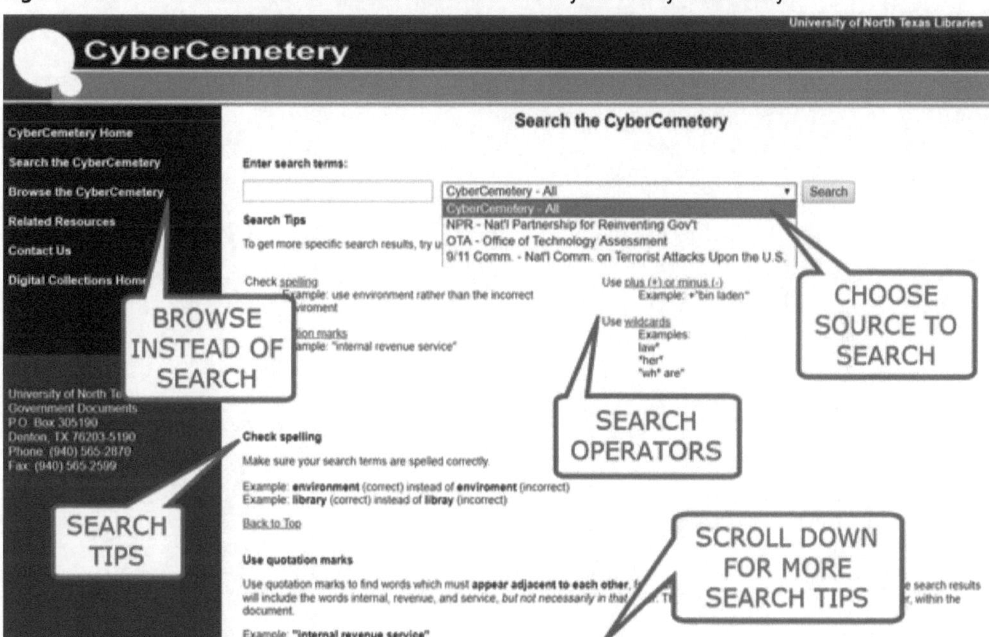

A drop-down menu to the right of the search box lets you search within one of the following:

- All of CyberCemetery
- NPR (the National Partnership for Reinventing Government)
- OTA (the Office of Technology Assessment)
- The 9/11 Commission

The **Browse the CyberCemetery** page (http://bit.ly/CyberCemBrowse) allows the researcher to choose from a list of links to browse agencies by **Branch of Government**, by **Date of Expiration**, or by **Name.**

# Chapter 13

## STATE, LOCAL, TERRITORIAL, AND TRIBAL LAW

Although it is not feasible for us to provide specific instruction on researching the individual resources of every state, county, territory, and tribe in the United States, we will discuss free directories and portals that assemble links to official government websites that serve as starting points to research them. These are helpful to determine if the jurisdiction you are researching makes its statutes, ordinances, courts, opinions, and other resources available on the Internet.

In other chapters we have discussed how to find state case law using free commercial case law sites (Chapter 6); free governmental case law sites (Chapter 7); and databases that are free to certain bar association members—Casemaker (Chapter 8) and Fastcase (Chapter 9)—so please refer to those chapter for state case law research.

## USA.GOV

USA.gov is a useful site not only for federal government links, but also for links to state, territorial, local, and tribal government websites (http://bit.ly/USAStateTribal). USA.gov's **State Government** page (Figure 13.1) at http://bit.ly/USAStates, provides a drop-down menu (in alphabetical order) to links to the official websites of all fifty states, the District of Columbia, and U.S. territories and sovereign states (American Samoa, Federated States of Micronesia, Guam, Northern

Mariana Islands, Puerto Rico, Republic of Palau, Republic of the Marshall Islands, and the U.S. Virgin Islands).

**Figure 13.1** USA.gov's State Government page.

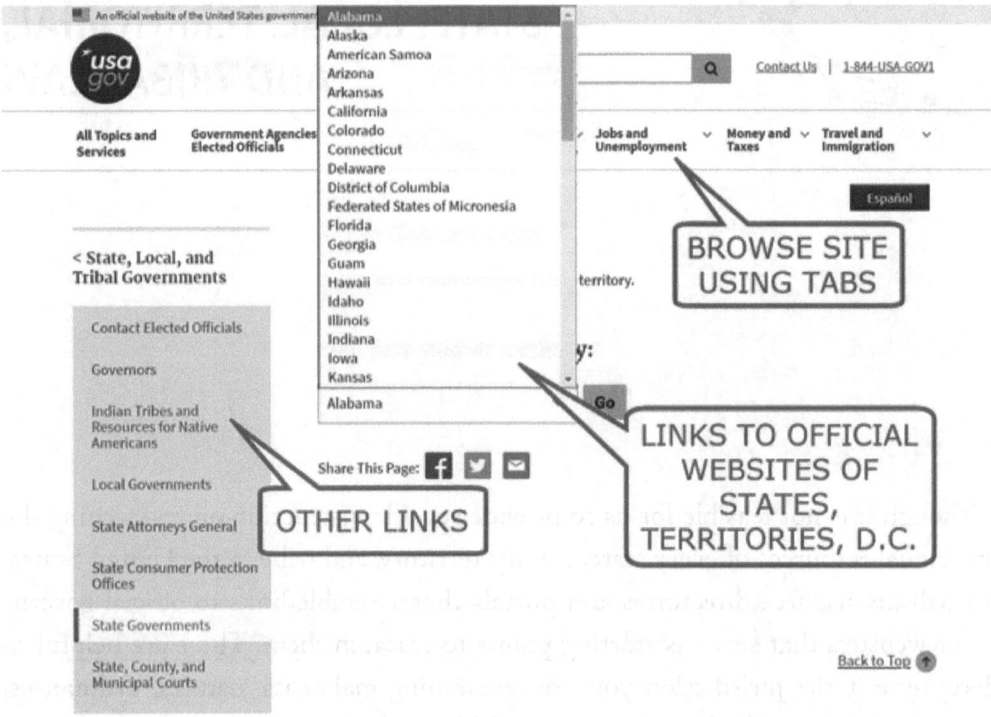


Other useful links are provided on the left side of the page, such as the:

- **Governors** link, which goes to a list of the official website of each state's governor.
- **State, County, and Municipal Courts** link, which goes to further resources for state, county, and municipal courts.
- **Local Governments** link, which goes to a drop-down menu with a link for each state. Each state then links to local government and agency information for that state.
- **Indian Tribes and Resources for Native Americans** link, which goes to a page with legal topics and resources for researchers of tribal law that provides links to the Bureau of Indian Affairs, the BIA's Tribal Leaders Directory, Tribal Constitutions and Codes, and more.

Besides using the links on USA.gov's state, local, territorial, and tribal government pages, you can search the USA.gov website with keywords to find legal and government information for these jurisdictions. For example, in Figure 13.2, the search term was *puerto rico court*. You can also browse the site by using the tabs across the top of the homepage (Figure 13.1), or by clicking the **Browse site** link with three horizontal bars that appears in the upper right corner after you run a search (Figure 13.2).

**Figure 13.2** USA.gov keyword search results page.

See Chapter 5 on Government and Academic Portals for details on how to use USA.gov's internal search engine, which is powered by Bing.

## LII'S LAW BY SOURCE: STATE

We discussed Cornell's Legal Information Institute (LII) in Chapter 5's discussion of Portals, but we would also like to point out its section on state law here. Titled **Law by Source: State** (http://bit.ly/LIIStates, see Figure 13.3), the section compiles Internet sources for state constitutions, statutes, case law, and regulations for all fifty states, D.C., U.S. territories, and affiliated jurisdictions.

**Figure 13.3** LII's Law by source: State page. Screenshot from the Legal Information Institute at Cornell Law School used with permission.

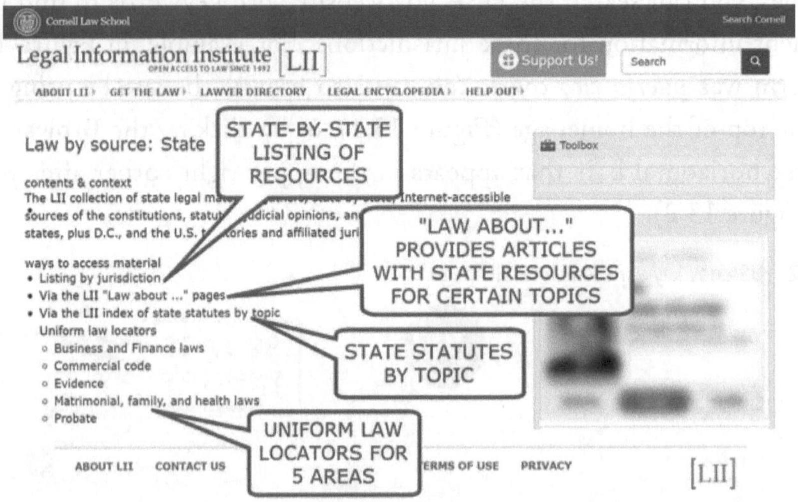


The **Law by source: State** page (Figure 13.3) provides four ways to access state legal materials:

- A **Listing by jurisdiction** link goes to a page with an alphabetical list of links for all fifty states, the District of Columbia, U.S. territories, and affiliated jurisdictions (http://bit.ly/LIIJurisdiction). Each link goes to a page for the relevant jurisdiction, and that page contains additional links to sites with statutory and legislative information, judicial sites, administrative law, and more. Figure 13.4 shows the page for Texas.

**Figure 13.4** LII's Law by source: State page for Texas. Screenshot from the Legal Information Institute at Cornell Law School used with permission.

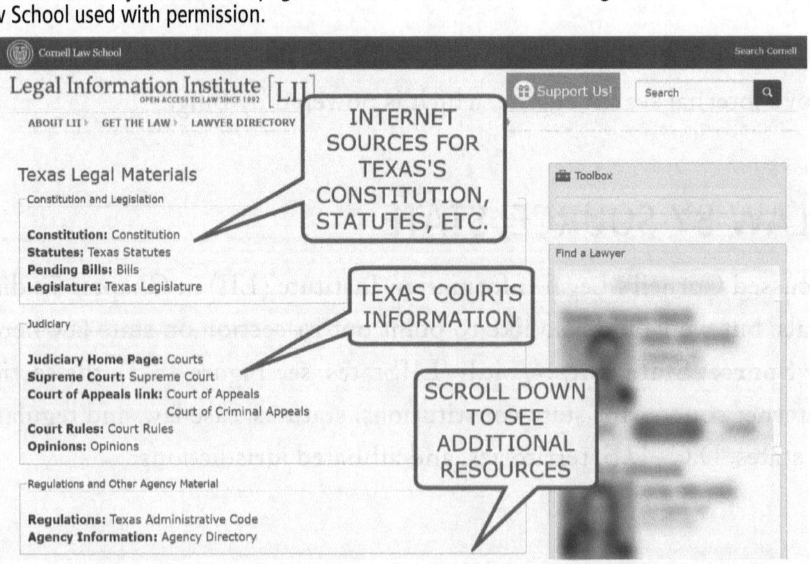

- A "**Law about. . .**" link (see Figure 13.3) goes to Wex (http://bit.ly/LII_Wex), LII's legal dictionary and encyclopedia. You can browse Wex or search it using the Search link near the center of the Wex page. Some (but not all) of its topics, such as Divorce laws and Labor and Employment laws, list resources for all fifty states, D.C., and U.S. territories.
- A link for LII's **index of state statutes by topic** (see Figure 13.3) goes to an alphabetical listing of links for forty-three topics such as Agriculture, Education, Taxation, and much more (http://bit.ly/LIIStateStatutes). Each topic link goes to a page with an alphabetical listing of state links to statutes for that topic. (This resource is discussed in Chapter 5.)
- Beneath the Uniform law locators label (see Figure 13.3) is a list of links to five uniform law locators for the subject areas of **Business and Finance laws, Commercial code, Evidence, Matrimonial, family, and health laws,** and **Probate.** Each locator is on a separate page with links to state statutes that correspond to Uniform Laws for the relevant subject areas. Figure 13.5 shows the locator page for the Uniform Rules of Evidence (http://bit.ly/LIIEvidence).

NOTE: When we tested LII's state pages, we found that not all of the links worked.

**Figure 13.5** LII's Uniform Rules of Evidence page. Screenshot from the Legal Information Institute at Cornell Law School used with permission.

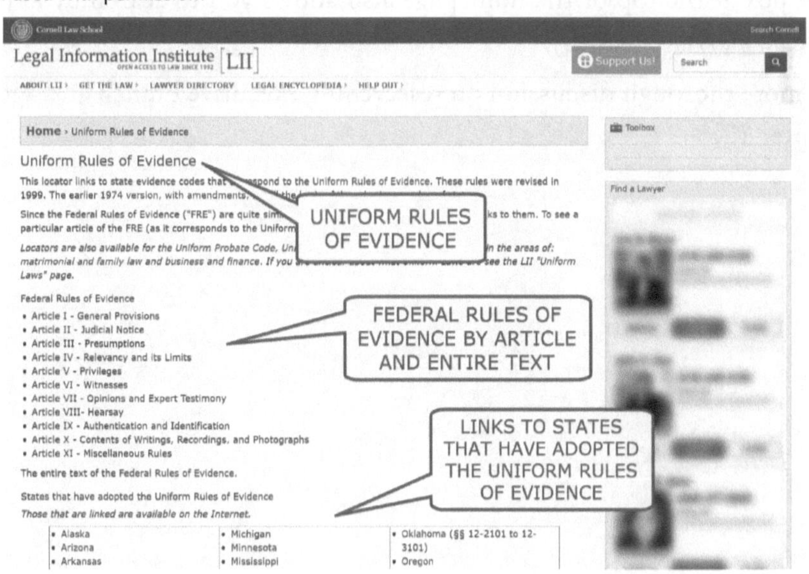

## STATE AND LOCAL GOVERNMENT ON THE NET

The **State and Local Government on the Net** (http://www.statelocalgov.net) directory provides access to the websites of thousands of state agencies as well as city and county governments. Drop-down menus on the left side of the homepage allow you to view directory pages for any state or local government website. You can also link by topic, such as Legislature or Education (see Figure 13.6). The drop-down menus are labeled: (1) **Select State** (which also includes territorial and tribal choices), (2) **Select Topic**, and (3) **Local Govt**. After selecting from a drop-down menu, you must click the **Go** button. You cannot select more than one drop-down menu at a time.

To access state or territorial executive branches, agencies, and so on, first click the **Select State** drop-down menu on the left. Then choose a state or territory, and click **Go**. Next, scroll down to **Executive Branch** (which will list agencies) or scroll down to **Boards and Commissions**. Browse through the list to link to the appropriate entity's website. To find links to local executive branches and agencies, use the **Local Govt** drop-down menu.

The **Select State, Select Topic,** and **Local Govt** drop-down menus on the left side of the page go to the same place as the **State Government, Local State Government,** and **Topic Pages for All 50 States** labels farther down on the page (shown in Figure 13.6). So, you will get the same results no matter which search you choose. A search box at the top of the homepage also allows you to search by keyword or phrase (e.g., *marriage records*).

For a more thorough discussion on researching executive branch and agency law, see Chapter 12.

**Figure 13.6** State and Local Government on the Net Home Page.

# LIBRARY OF CONGRESS

The Library of Congress's **State Government Information** page (http://bit.ly/LOCState) provides links to all fifty states' homepages and to some local government pages. Click the state you want on the map at the top of the page or select from the list of state links below the map (see Figure 13.7).

**Figure 13.7** Library of Congress State Government Information page.

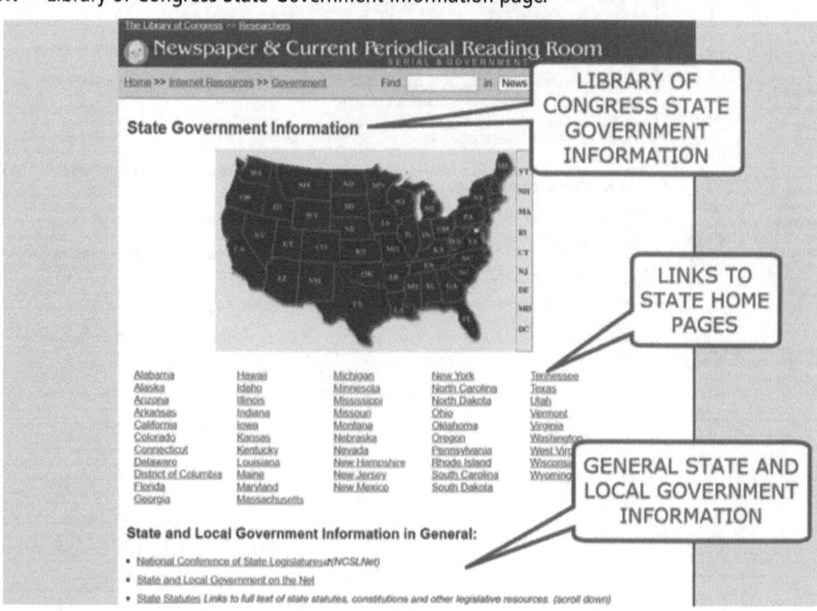

## WASHLAW LEGAL RESEARCH ON THE WEB

Washburn University School of Law provides a legal research website titled **WashLaw Legal Research on the Web.** This site's **State Resources** section (http://bit.ly/WashLawStates) is comprehensive. It provides many links to official state sites as well as resources for local city and county sites. Although our tests indicate some links are broken and no updating information is provided, we have included it here as an additional resource. The site appears to be the only one of its kind that goes beyond just government sites, with links to resources such as **Law Libraries, Law Schools, Practitioner Resources,** and more.

Information on the site is arranged by jurisdiction, with a menu in the left column from which you can choose a link to a state (see Figure 13.8). Once you choose a state, each state page is organized by topic—**Agencies, Executive Branch, Judicial Branch, Law Libraries, Law Schools,** and so on. You can also choose from the multi-jurisdictional material in the main section of the homepage to see resources that apply to all jurisdictions (see Figure 13.8).

**Figure 13.8** Washburn Law's State Resources page.

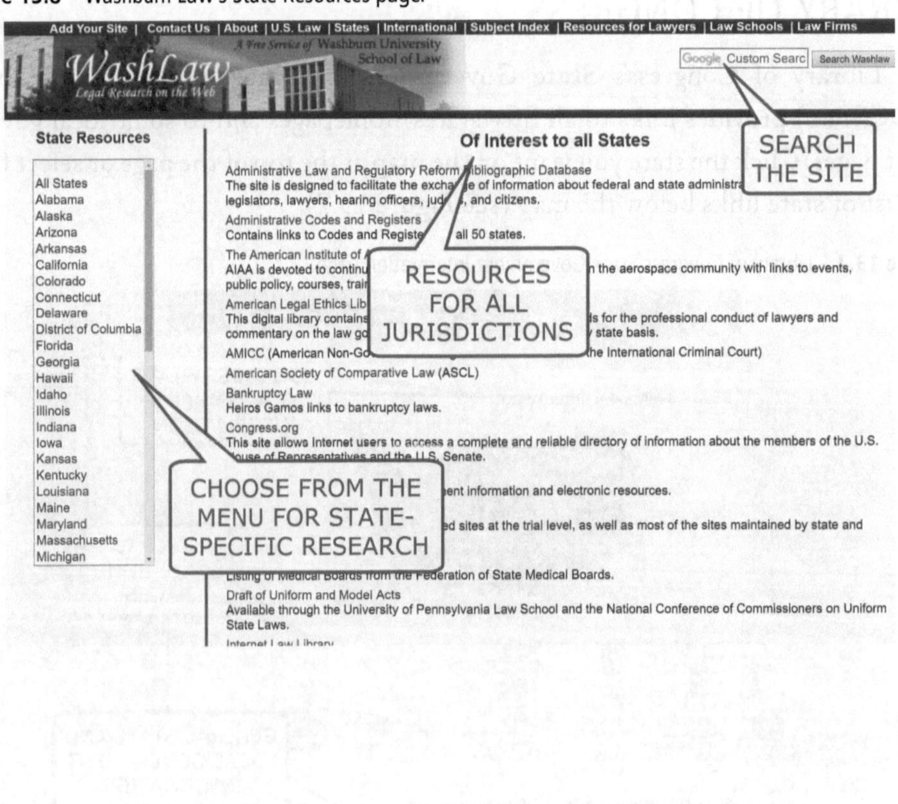

## FULL-TEXT STATE STATUTES AND LEGISLATION ON THE INTERNET

The **Full-text state statutes and legislation on the Internet** site (http://bit.ly/FTStatutes) provides access to all states', D.C.'s, and U.S. territories' (American Samoa, Guam, Puerto Rico, and the U.S. Virgin Islands) statutory codes, administrative codes, regulations, bills, constitutions, and local ordinances. The site arranges the material by state name, in alphabetical order. Links for sites maintained by governments appear in bold type.

## FINDLAW

Chapters 4 and 6 discuss **FindLaw** as a useful portal and tool for researching case law, but it also provides a directory of state statutory materials (http://www.findlaw.com/casecode). Scroll down to **State Resources** and select a state or territory (see Figure 13.9). The site offers links to all states, the District of Columbia, and to the territories of Guam, American Samoa, the U.S. Virgin Islands, Puerto Rico, and the Northern Mariana Islands (at the end of the list of states). By using the directories provided by FindLaw and Full-text State Statutes and Legislation on the Internet (discussed above), you don't have to remember the title of any state's (or territory's) statutory or regulatory material (e.g., New York Consolidated Laws or Arizona Revised Statutes) because the directories make it easy for you to browse through each state's list.

**Figure 13.9** FindLaw's State Resources. Originally appeared on FindLaw.com. Used with permission.

## OPEN STATES

**Open States** (https://openstates.org) began in 2009 as a project of the Sunlight Foundation, but it has been independently run since 2016. The site provides various tools that allow researchers to search and track past and present state legislation. You can browse or search bills, see legislators' voting records, contact your representatives, and more. Open States aggregates information from all fifty states, the District of Columbia, and Puerto Rico.

Figure 13.10 Open States homepage.

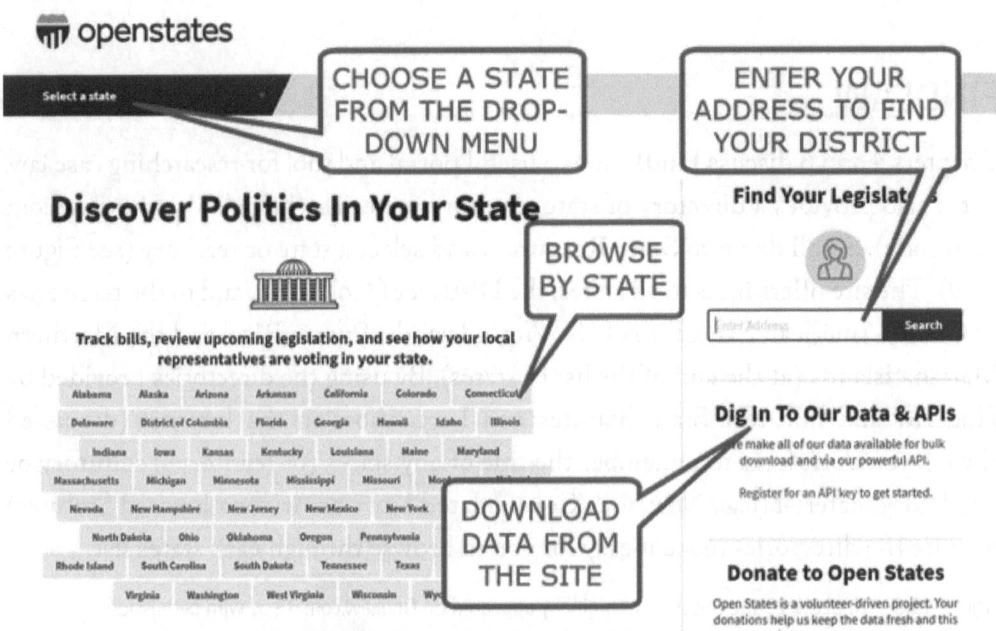


To browse legislation, select a state from the drop-down menu in the upper left corner of the homepage, or choose from an alphabetical list of links farther down the page (see Figure 13.10). You will be taken to that state's **Overview** page. The Overview page provides an interactive map of the state's districts, information about legislators and committees, and a summary of recent legislation. Use the links at the top of the page to also visit pages for the state's **Legislators, Bills,** and **Committees.**

California's **Bills** page is shown in Figure 13.11. From this page you can research California legislation by browsing or searching. Toward the bottom of the page (not shown in Figure 13.11) is a list with links to all available legislature sessions. You can choose a session to browse and then filter results by various criteria on the right side of the page, including **Status, Session, Chamber of Origin, Type, Status,**

**Sponsor**, and **Subjects**. A **Search text** box near the upper right side of the page also allows you to filter legislation by keyword or phrase (see Figure 13.11). You can also use the **Search text** box to keyword or phrase search for legislation. Clicking a search result takes you to the page for that bill. Each bill page includes the text, sponsor(s), voting records, a list of actions taken, and a status tracker.

**Figure 13.11** Open States state bills page.

Open States also provides contact information for current legislators, committees on which they serve, a list of bills they have sponsored, and their voting record. On the homepage, enter your address or zip code into the box under the **Find Your Legislators** heading to locate your legislative district and your legislator (see Figure 13.10). All data on Open States is available via API and bulk download (see Figure 13.10) and a video tutorial is provided to learn more about the site (http://bit.ly/OpenStatesTutorial).

## LEGISCAN

**LegiScan** (https://legiscan.com) monitors current legislation in all 50 state legislatures and the U.S. Congress. Although some of LegiScan's services involve a fee, some are free. With the site's OneVote feature, you can set up a free account and track legislation from one state. (You choose the one state when you set up your account.) You can also search the full text of legislation by state. LegiScan's search engine is more robust than that of Open States and accepts the Boolean connectors *AND*, *OR*, and *NOT*, as well as the plus sign (+, require a term) and the minus sign (-, exclude a term). You can also group terms with quotation marks and parentheses, and search by field. For more features and search tips, see LegiScan's **Full Text Search** page at https://legiscan.com/fulltext-search. The legislation pages for state bills provide the status, latest action, sponsors, history, and more. Links to the full text of legislation go to the official website of the state.

## STATE CASE LAW DATABASES

As mentioned at the outset of this chapter, state case law databases are discussed more extensively in Chapters 6, 7, 8, and 9, but we will mention one portal here to help you quickly link to official state courts and their case law databases.

**Justia** has a directory of state court links (http://bit.ly/JustiaStateCourts). It provides links to all fifty states. When you click a link to a state, you are taken to a page listing all the courts in that state, including federal courts. Selecting a court takes you to a page where you can browse opinions from that court by date.

## STATE AND LOCAL COURTS: DOCKETS

Some state and local courts have placed dockets online. See Chapter 15 for more information.

## TRIBAL GOVERNMENT AND LAW

USA.gov, discussed above, provides resources for U.S. tribal law and government. Another website that provides some helpful links to tribal information is that of the **Wisconsin State Law Library**. The library's **Tribal Law** page (http://bit.ly/WisconsinTribalLaw) provides links to several official and unofficial sites with tribal law and government information. Much of this page is Wisconsin-specific, but some of the links—**Tribal Court Decisions** and the **Tribal Directory**, for example—lead to information about tribes nationwide.

The website of the **National Indian Law Library (NILL)**, located at http://bit.ly/NILLibrary, provides federal Indian and tribal law, as well as Indian Law Bulletins and Online Research Guides. NILL's **Tribal Law Gateway** (http://bit.ly/NILLGateway) provides online access to tribal law materials, organized alphabetically by tribe. The **Directories** page (http://bit.ly/NILLDirectories) lists links to the Federal Register's annually published list of **Federally Recognized Tribes and Native Villages** (back to 2008), links to **Tribal Governments and Courts**, and more.

Also, see Chapter 8, An Introduction to Casemaker, to learn about Casemaker's new Tribal Library, which offers a searchable database of court opinions from 62 tribes. You can search all the tribes together or just one tribe (but not multiple tribes). There are 525 recognized tribes, so Casemaker has a way to go until the Library is complete, but they assure us it's a growing collection.

## COUNTY AND CITY LEVEL

The **NACo** (National Association of Counties) website (http://www.naco.org) is devoted strictly to counties. To find basic information about each county, such as demographics and government contact information, with links to each county's website, hover your mouse over **What We Do** (as shown in Figure 13.12) and choose **Find a County**. From the **NACo County Explorer** page, you can click a county from the interactive map, or enter the name of a county in the search box in the upper right corner of the page. Once you retrieve the county you want, a **County Information** box appears. From there, you can learn about the county and link to the county's website.

**Figure 13.12** Find a County on the National Association of Counties homepage. Screenshot from the National Association of Counties (NACo) used with permission.

The **State and Local Government on the Net** site (discussed earlier in this chapter) also provides links to both county and city websites, in addition to the states' sites. Select a state from the **Local Govt** drop-down menu on the upper left side of the homepage (see Figure 13.6).

## LOCAL CODES AT THE COUNTY AND CITY LEVEL

Many local jurisdictions' codes can be found online for free either at the jurisdiction's website or at the websites of one of the three publishers of local codes (noted below). Most of the local codes are full-text and keyword-and-phrase-searchable, although some only offer the ability to browse by title or chapter.

**American Legal Publishing** offers hundreds of keyword-and-phrase-searchable local codes in thirty-six states (http://bit.ly/AmLegalCodes; see Figure 13.13). It is the only vendor that offers a free search of all of the city and county codes from all states in its database together. The option is listed in the middle of the homepage (click **View All State Codes**). You can also select just one state from the map or from the list of states on the homepage, and then choose a city or county within that state.

**Figure 13.13** Search state and local codes on American Legal Publishing's site. Screenshot from American Legal Publishing used with permission.

You can also search all available local codes in one state. First, click **View All State Codes** to go to a browse and search page. From this page, you can click the **Search** link near the top of the page, which takes you to the **Advanced Search** page. You can now enter keywords and phrases into various pre-set Boolean and phrase search boxes (see Figure 13.14). In addition, you can check the **Find alternate word forms (stemming)** box or the **Find synonyms (thesaurus)** box. The Boolean Search page (not shown) allows you to enter keywords and phrases into a single search box and connect them with Boolean and also proximity connectors. Study the **Search Syntax Summary** listed at the bottom of the Boolean Search page because some of the syntax may be unfamiliar to you.

**Figure 13.14** American Legal Publishing's Advanced Search page for local codes. Screenshot from American Legal Publishing used with permission.

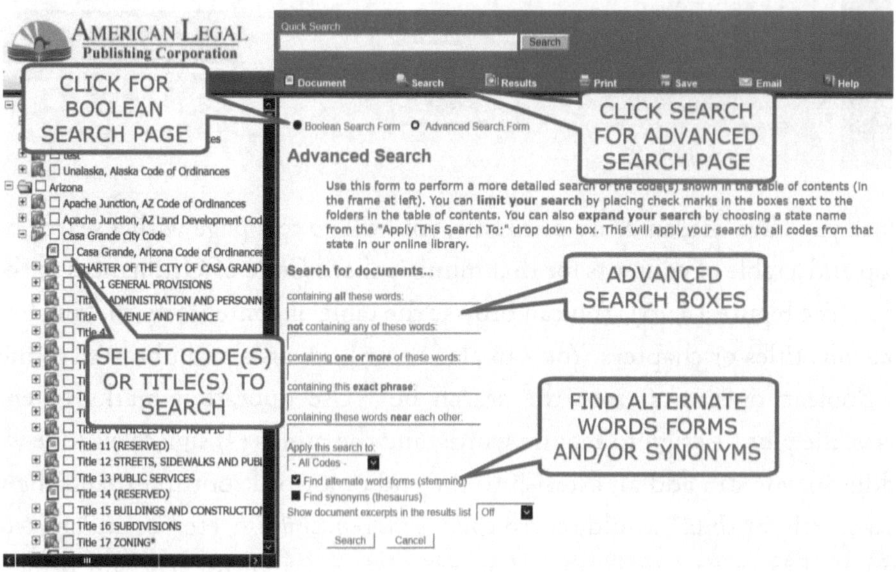


American Legal Publishing allows you to create slightly more complex searches than you can at most other municipal code sites (discussed below). You can also search an entire code or just a specific chapter or title, and you can browse the codes instead of searching (see left-hand column in Figure 13.14).

**Municode** offers keyword-and-phrase-searchable codes for over 4,200 local governments in fifty states (https://www.municode.com). Individual codes can be browsed and searched for free, but there is an annual fee to search multiple codes at once. To begin a search, click the **Library** link at the top of the homepage. You will then go to a page where you can choose a state from a list of links, and then to another page where you can choose a city or county. (The alphabetical list of states also provides a Tribes and Tribal Nations option, with three tribes listed: Fort McDowell Yavapai Nation, Mohegan Tribe, and Poarch Band of Creek Indians.)

**Figure 13.15** Search or browse local codes on Municode.

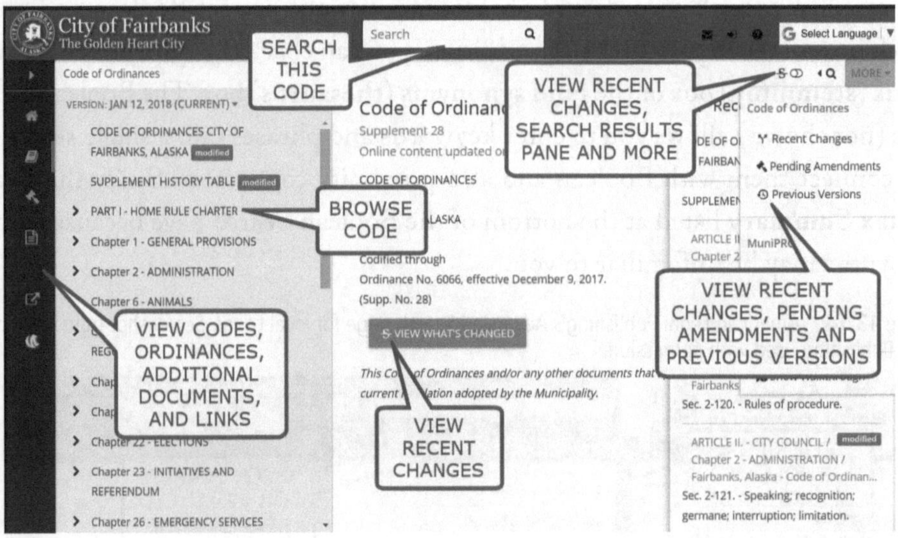


Once you have chosen a city or county, you will go to a page with a search box at the top and a table of contents for that municipality's Code of Ordinances in the left column (see Figure 13.15). You can browse the table of contents by clicking links to the various titles or chapters. You can also enter keywords and phrases (connected with Boolean operators) into the search box. Use quotation marks to enclose phrases, the plus (+) sign to require words, and the minus (-) sign to exclude words. In addition, you can add an asterisk to the end of a word root to expand the word (e.g., a search for *child** would return *child, children, childish,* etc.) or add an asterisk within a word to find variations of words (e.g., a search for *a*n* will bring back results that include *addition, assign,* etc.). You can search an entire code and then filter results to specific titles or chapters afterward (see Figure 13.16). For additional search help, see Municode's Advanced Search Options page at http://bit.ly/MunicodeSearchHelp.

Municode's search page has several additional features (see Figure 13.15). To the left of the table of contents is a menu of linked icons that allow you to browse codes (book icon), browse individual ordinances (gavel icon), view additional municipal documents (document icon), view additional municipality links (link icon), and view Municode links (Municode icon). Near the upper right corner of the page is a **Show Changes** link. Clicking it makes a column appear on the right side of the page where you can view recent changes to the code, see your search terms highlighted, and view additional options including Pending Amendments and Previous Versions of the code.

Once you have searched a code on Municode, you can filter the results to specific chapters or titles, sort by **Relevance** or **Document Order**, and view **Codes, Ordinances,** or **Documents** (see Figure 13.16). Your search terms will be highlighted in the results list. There is an **Options** link at the right side of the search box that explains the search function and provides a link to an article on **Advanced Search Options,** or use this direct URL: http://bit.ly/MunicodeHelp.

**Figure 13.16** Viewing search results on Municode.

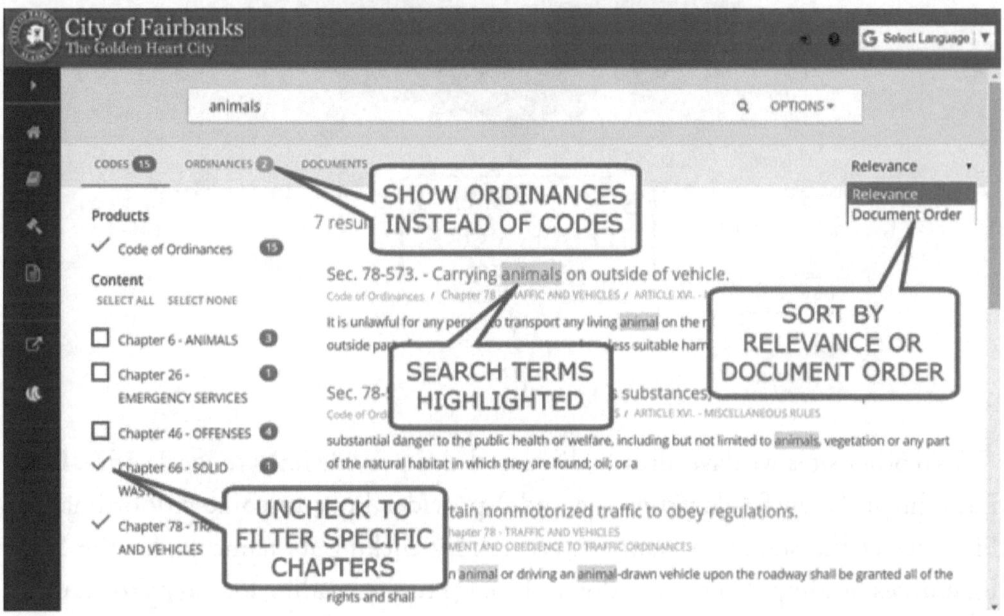


**General Code** provides its **eCode360 Library,** which contains local codes for twenty-four U.S. states and one city in Canada (http://bit.ly/eCode360Library). Individual codes can be searched for free, but searching multiple codes simultaneously requires an annual fee. In addition to keyword and phrase searching of local codes (connected by Boolean connectors), you can open an entire chapter or just portions of one and also search by a specific section number. To begin a search, choose a state from the map or choose a local government from the list below the map (alphabetized by state; see Figure 13.17). You can also browse codes by their Tables of Contents or Indices.

**Figure 13.17** Search local codes on eCode360 Library. eCode360 © 2009 General Code, LLC. eCode360 is the property of General Code, LLC and its affiliates. All rights are reserved. Image used with permission.

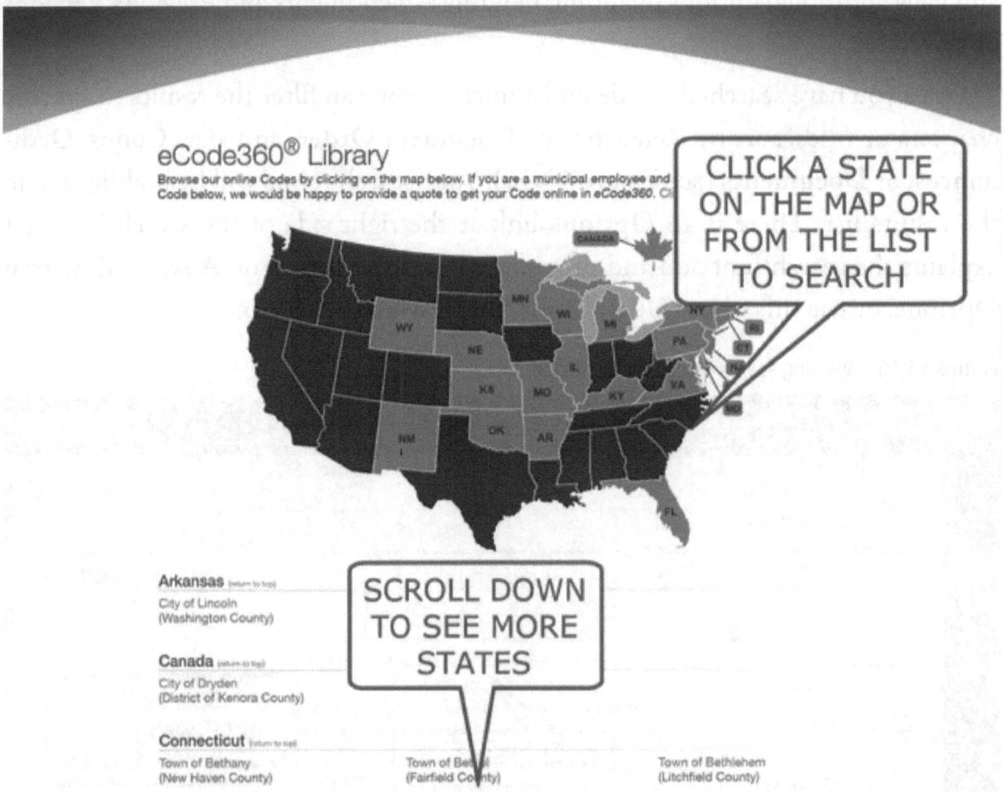


Two other sites we have already discussed also provide links to local codes. **FindLaw** (http://www.findlaw.com/casecode) provides links to some city ordinances. First, select the state you want to research by clicking its name under the **State Resources** heading. Then scroll down the page to the heading for **City Ordinances.** Some local codes are also available on **Full-text State Statutes and Legislation on the Internet** (http://bit.ly/FTStatutes). Scroll down to the relevant state and look for a link such as city codes, municipal codes, or local ordinances; the exact title can vary from state to state.

# Chapter 14

## FOREIGN, INTERNATIONAL, AND COMPARATIVE LAW RESOURCES

Foreign law and international law are two separate but related categories. Foreign law is the national or internal law of any individual nation except the United States. International law concerns the relations between different countries and their governments, organizations, and so on (e.g., treaties). Comparative law is the study of similarities and differences among the law and legal systems of different countries around the world. This chapter will provide guidance for researching all three of these.

The body of information that includes foreign and international laws is large and has no centralized structure or organization. We will therefore provide several starting points for research that, when combined, cover the majority of the most useful foreign and international resources. We have evaluated the sites discussed here from among the many that are available and believe these will be especially helpful to you in beginning your research.

This chapter outlines several portals, directories, and academic sites we have discussed in other chapters, but here we will focus on their foreign and international sections. These sources provide guides and other background materials to help researchers understand the basics of foreign and international legal research. They will also lead you to, and explain, the primary sources of foreign and international law. We will look at several useful resources, such as the websites of the United Nations and the European Union, and official sources of the law for many individual countries.

Some of the sources in this chapter may be in languages other than English. To overcome this language issue, you can use **Google Translate** for a rudimentary translation of an entire website by typing its address into https://translate.google.com (or by copying and pasting selected text from a web page or document into Google Translate). If you're using the Google Chrome browser, you can install an extension that will automatically translate a page for you.

## THE LAW LIBRARY OF CONGRESS

The **Law Library of Congress** provides several helpful resources for researching foreign and international law. Its **Guide to Law Online** (http://bit.ly/LLOCGuide) is a well-known and frequently used website for legal research generally. From the Guide's homepage, you can also link to additional guides for foreign law, international law, and several how-to guides for researching law in specific countries (see Figure 14.1).

**Figure 14.1** The Law Library of Congress's Guide to Law Online.

For help researching international law, click the **International** link near the center of the homepage to go to the LOC's **International** page (see Figure 14.1). (The **International and Multinational** link, farther down the page, under the **Select a Link** heading, also goes to the same page.) The International page contains links to sources too numerous to name here, but examples include the LOC's Global Legal Information

Catalog, the websites of the United Nations and Organization of American States, guides for Treaties and Multinational Reference, and links to guides produced by other organizations, such as the law schools of Columbia, Georgetown, and Harvard.

Another useful resource linked from the homepage of the **Guide to Law Online** is the **Nations** page (http://bit.ly/LLOCNations). You can reach it by clicking the **Nations** link near the center of the page, or the **Nations of the World** link, farther down under the **Select a Link** heading (see Figure 14.1). The Nations page provides an alphabetical list of links for many countries, territories, regions, and other locations. The links lead to a page for each location. Each location's page contains additional links to resources such as constitutions, the country's branches of government, additional guides, and "general" sources, such as country profiles and more.

A third useful section of the Guide is harder to locate. The **Legal Research Guides** link is roughly in the center of the Guide's homepage (see Figure 14.1). That link goes to the **Legal Research Guides** page which lists titles and brief descriptions of nine research guides, ranging from Administrative Law to Judicial Decisions. As you scroll down the page, you will notice the **Foreign and International Law Guides** title. Click the **Read More** link under the guide description to go to the guide page, entitled **Foreign and International Law** (see Figure 14.2). You can also go directly to it at http://bit.ly/LLOCForeign.

**Figure 14.2** The Law Library of Congress's Foreign Law Research Guides.

The Foreign and International Law page differs from the Nations page because it provides country-specific research guides, while the Nations page is a list of links. Also, the Nations page covers many countries, territories, regions, and other locations, while the country-specific research guides are for only fourteen individual nations (see Figure 14.2).

Above the country-specific guides is a **View Guide** link to a 2007 PDF guide titled "Researching Foreign, International & Comparative Law" (see Figure 14.2). Below the country-specific guides are two sections (not shown in Figure 14.2). The first is labeled **Foreign Law Bibliographies**; it lists two bibliographies: (1) Personal Status Laws in Arab Countries and (2) Islamic Law: A Bibliography of Recent Works. The second section is labeled **Customary Law Research Guides**; it lists research guides to the customary law in Africa, India, and the Māori culture.

## THE AMERICAN SOCIETY OF INTERNATIONAL LAW

The **American Society of International Law** (ASIL) is a respected nonprofit educational organization that aims to support the study of international law and promote international relations. ASIL's website (https://www.asil.org) contains two important resources for researching international law.

ASIL's **Electronic Resources Guide** (**ERG**), found at http://bit.ly/ASIL-ERG, is a user-friendly guide to current, important online resources that concern the most relevant areas in international law. (You can also find the ERG from ASIL's homepage by clicking **Resources** and then clicking the **ERG** link inside the **Library** box.) The ERG covers topics such as the European Union, International Organizations, and commonly researched subjects, including international commercial arbitration, international criminal law, international environmental law, and international human rights. For the complete list of topics covered, see the guide at http://bit.ly/ASIL-ERG.

The second resource that ASIL provides is its **Electronic Information System for International Law** (**EISIL**), located at http://www.eisil.org. (Like ERG, EISIL can also be found by clicking **Resources** on ASIL's homepage and then clicking the **EISIL** link inside the **Library** box.) EISIL is a free online database that provides information about, and links to, resources that include all aspects of international law. EISIL includes high quality primary sources, research guides, and reliable websites. The resources are arranged in an easy-to-use list on EISIL's homepage (see Figure 14.3).

**Figure 14.3** Homepage of Electronic Information System for International Law (EISIL). EISIL is the property of the American Society of International Law. Image used with permission.

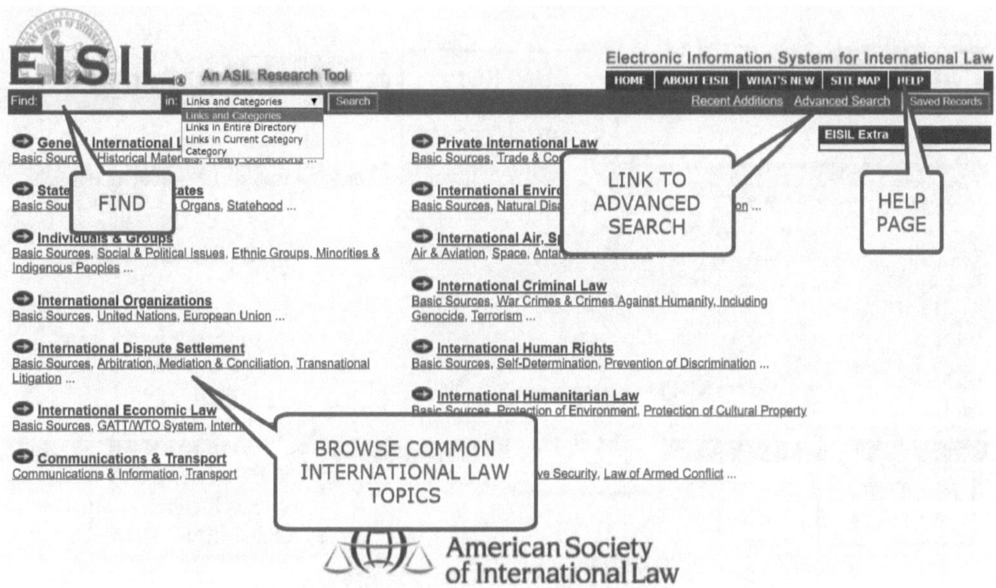


Unlike many foreign and international law resources, EISIL is also keyword searchable. The homepage has a **Find** box in the upper left corner (see Figure 14.3) where you can enter your keywords. A drop-down menu (to the right of the **Find** search box) allows you to restrict your keyword search to **Links and Categories, Links in Entire Directory, Links in Current Category,** or **Category.**

Click the **Advanced Search** link in the upper right corner of any page to go to a page similar to Google's advanced search (see Figure 14.4).

> **CAVEAT**: Our test searches indicated that EISIL's Advanced Search feature may not always work. EISIL acknowledges that the site has issues and told us that the site will be updated in the future, but likely after this book is published. Until then, you may need to rely on the browsing and Find (search) features, which are still helpful. Nevertheless, we will explain how the site's Advanced Search should work in case the problems are resolved after this book is published.

The different boxes on the Advanced Search page allow you to search **all** words, with an **exact word, phrase or acronym,** with **any of the words,** or **without** specific words. A **Find in** drop-down menu allows you to restrict your search terms to **any field,** or to the **Title, Description, Keyword,** or **Citation** (see Figure 14.4).

**Figure 14.4** EISIL's Advanced Search page. EISIL is the property of the American Society of International Law. Image used with permission.

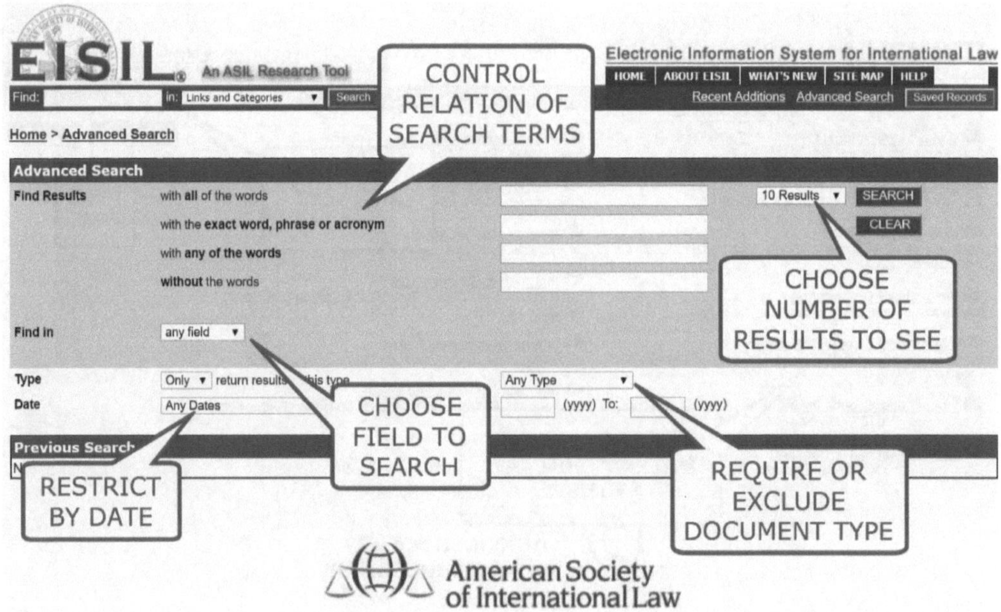


On the Advanced Search page, you may also restrict your search by **Type** of document. A drop-down menu on the right side of the page allows you to choose **Any Type** of document or restrict to **Primary Document, Web Site,** or **Research Resource.** You may also include or exclude these types of documents by an additional drop-down menu on the left side of the page that works in conjunction with the **Type** selection. Choose **Only** to return only results of a specific type, or **Don't** to exclude results of a specific type (see Figure 14.4).

You can also restrict the dates of your search. First, on the left side of the Advanced Search page, select one of the following from the **Date** drop-down menu: **Any Dates, Last Updated, Entry into Force (EIF) Date,** or **Conclusion Date.** Then use a set of two range boxes on the right side of the page to enter the year(s) to which you wish to restrict your search (see Figure 14.4).

Finally, you can choose how many search results you receive. From a drop-down menu near the upper right corner of the Advanced Search page, you can select 10, 20, 30, 50, or 100 results. Once you have constructed your search, click the blue **Search** button on the far-right side of the page (see Figure 14.4) or to start over, use the **Clear** button just beneath the **Search** button.

The EISIL site also allows you to save your search results during a search session. Unlike the Advanced Search described above, this feature works, although the saved results are not retained once you leave the site. Once you have a list of search results, **Save All (#) Records?** appears at the top of the results list, next to a check box. If you check the box, a pop-up will ask you to confirm that you want to add all the records to your saved records list. If you click **OK**, EISIL will save your results. To retrieve them later (but before you leave the site), click the gray **Saved Records** link in the upper right corner of the screen. You will go to a screen like the one in the Figure 14.5, where you can use checkboxes on the right side of the screen to select specific records to retain or discard. You can also print, download, or e-mail your finalized list of results. You can also switch between a brief or complete display of all search results. Click the **Display Complete Record** link above the search results to show the complete records; click **Display Brief Record** to return to the brief view. To clear all saved search results, use the **Clear All Records** link.

**Figure 14.5** Saved search results in EISIL. EISIL is the property of the American Society of International Law. Image used with permission.

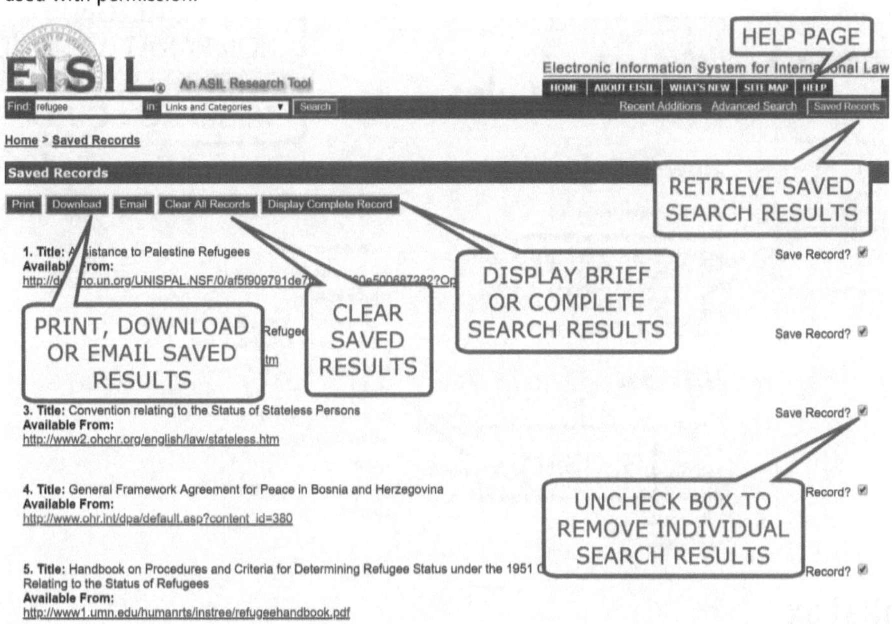


EISIL also provides a **Help** page (http://bit.ly/EISILHelp) to assist users with the site's features. Click the **Help** link in the upper right corner of any page on the site (see Figure 14.5), and you will be taken to the Help page. It assists with the following topics: **Browsing, Quick Search, Advanced Search, Search Results,** and **Saving Records.**

## GLOBALEX AND OTHER NYU LAW RESOURCES

New York University School of Law provides some useful resources for foreign, international and comparative legal research at its **Research Guides** page at http://bit.ly/NYUGuides (see Figure 14.6). Specific research guides exist for topics such as **Chinese Law Online, Finding Foreign (non-US) Law in English, NAFTA,** and more. NYU's **Global Research Tools** page (http://bit.ly/NYUGlobal) also contains links to research guides (near the bottom of the page) and to several databases, such as **Multi-jurisdictional databases, Foreign databases organized by topic,** and more.

**Figure 14.6** NYU's research guides for foreign, international, and comparative law and GlobaLex.

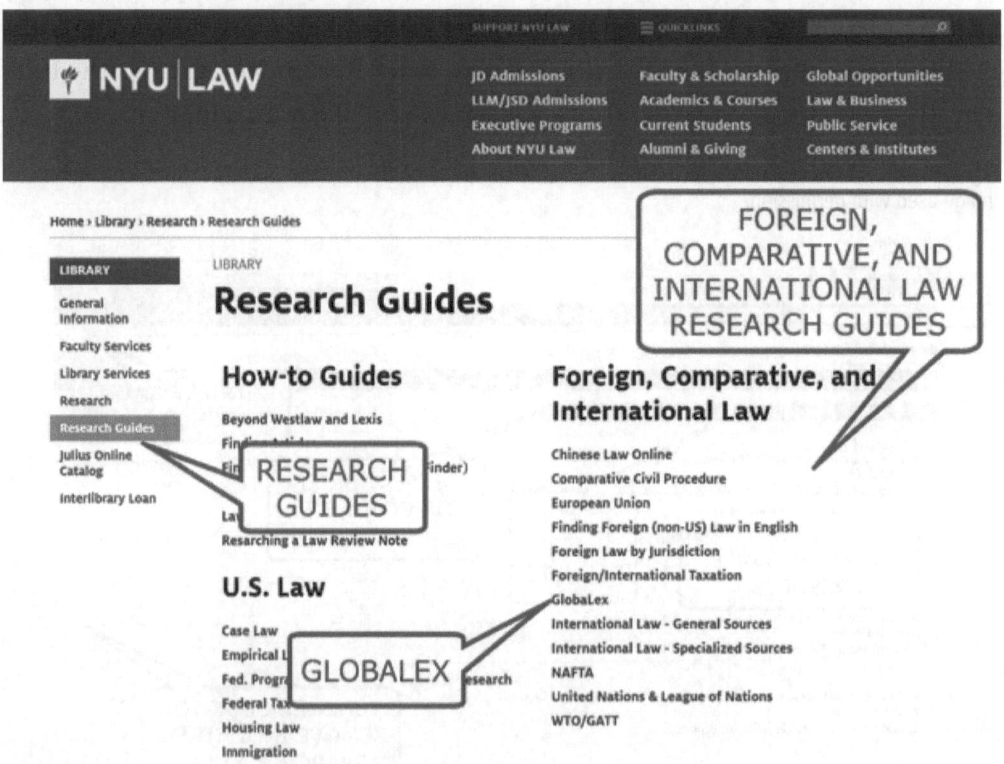


### GlobaLex

One resource on NYU's website is especially noteworthy, and we will describe it briefly here. **GlobaLex** is a well-known online publication that the NYU School of Law produces to assist in researching foreign and international law. Access it at http://bit.ly/GlobaLex or from links available on both the Global Research Tools page and the Research Guides page (see Figure 14.6). GlobaLex's homepage displays links to different areas for research:

- **International Law Research**
- **Comparative Law Research**
- **Foreign Law Research**

Clicking any one of the links will open a directory of research guides on many subtopics, written by experts whose credentials are described at the beginning of each guide. International Law Research guides include areas such as the **Council of Europe, Human Trafficking, International Criminal Law, NAFTA and CAFTA,** and the **United Nations**. The Foreign Law Research section includes guides for researching 161 countries, from Afghanistan to Zimbabwe.

## WorldLII

The World Legal Information Institute (WorldLII) is a free legal research resource developed by several Legal Information Institutes and other organizations from around the world (http://www.worldlii.org). The WorldLII website has over 1,800 searchable databases from 123 jurisdictions. Databases include foreign and international case law, legislation, treaties, and more.

**Figure 14.7** WorldLII homepage. Screenshot from WorldLII used with permission.

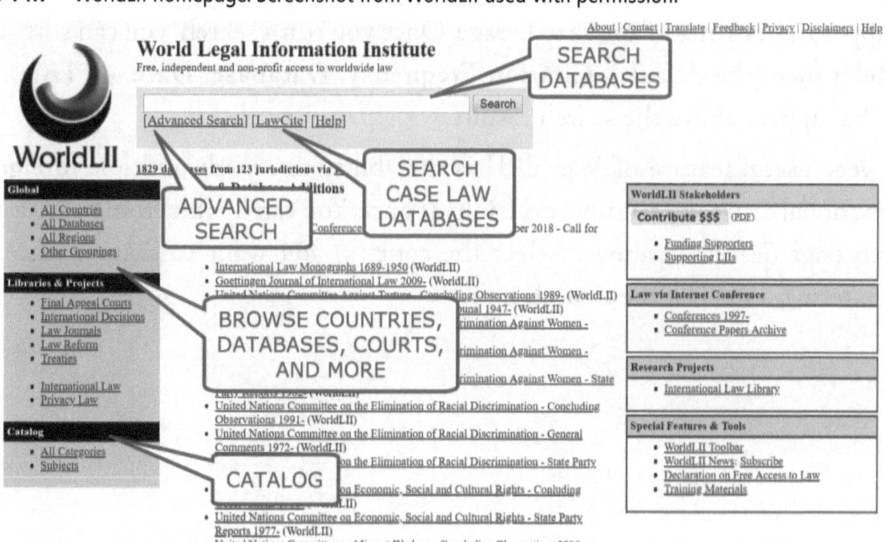

You can search WorldLII from the homepage or from an advanced search page accessed by clicking the **Advanced Search** link under the homepage search box (see Figure 14.7). From the homepage, you can also browse links to databases, country information, and more. NOTE: In the lower left corner of the homepage is a category titled **Catalog** (see Figure 14.7). Links in this category go to two search pages for All Categories and Subjects. Our test searches with both these pages were problematic, however, and the only search feature on these two pages that seemed to work was a Google web search. Your best option for searching this site is probably using the homepage search box or the advanced search feature, which we will now describe.

If you click the **Advanced Search** link on WorldLII's homepage, you are taken to the site's **Advanced Search** page (see Figure 14.8). You can choose one, several, or all databases from the list to search. (To choose more than one database but not all, hold down the Ctrl key or Command key on your computer while clicking the titles of the databases you want.) You can use a drop-down menu to the left of the search box to choose the type of search. The default search type is **Boolean**, but you can also choose **autosearch** (similar to natural language), **any of these words, all of these words, this phrase, this document title, this case name**, or **this legislation title**. Four additional options are available at the bottom of the page to control how the search results are displayed. You can get help with searching by clicking the **Help** or **Boolean operators** links, which appear both below the search box and in the upper right corner of the search page. Once you run a search, you can sort results by **Relevance** (the default), **Citation Frequency, Database, Date**, or **Title**, using tabs that appear above the search results.

A very useful feature of WorldLII is the ability to search multiple foreign and international court and tribunal decisions at once. You can do this from the Advanced Search page described above. Select the court(s) you want to search, enter your search terms, and click the **Search** link.

**Figure 14.8** Advanced searching on WorldLII. Screenshot from WorldLII used with permission.

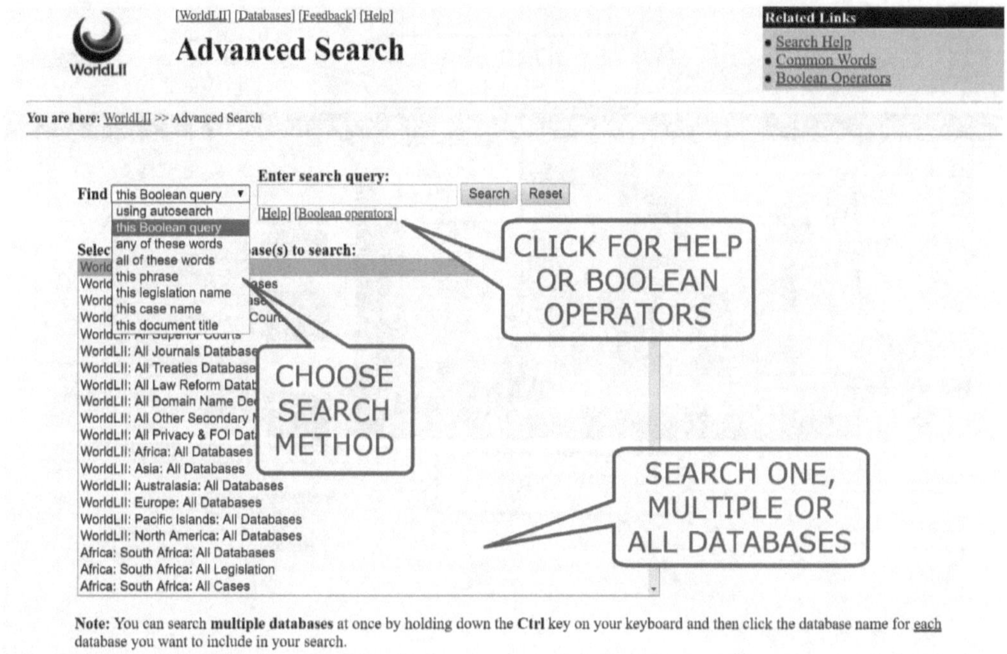


WorldLII also has a citator feature called **LawCite** (http://www.worldlii.org/LawCite). It is discussed in Chapter 18 Cite-Checking Cases.

## HIEROS GAMOS

**Hieros Gamos**, or "HG" (https://www.hg.org), was founded in 1995 by Lex Mundi, a large network of law firms, and was one of the first websites designed to provide information on law and government. In addition to its general collection on law and government, HG also provides resources for foreign and international legal research.

**Figure 14.9** HG homepage with links to foreign and international resources. Screenshot from HG.org used with permission.

HG's homepage has a Google-powered search box in the upper right-hand corner that can keyword search the site (see Figure 14.9). For example, when we searched the words *uae real estate,* we found an article titled "Buying Property in Dubai." (We had to sift through several ads and listings for real estate attorneys to get to the article, however.) From the homepage (see Figure 14.9) you can also access two links to pages on the HG site that provide tools for researching foreign and international law.

## International Legal Articles

When you hover your mouse over the **Legal Articles** link in the menu bar across the top of the homepage (see Figure 14.9), a drop-down menu with three links appears. Clicking **Articles for 260 Areas of Law** from the menu takes you to HG's **Articles for 260 Areas of Law** page (http://bit.ly/HG260), which provides an alphabetical list of legal topics. Scroll down and click the link for **International Law,** or for one of its subtopics, such as **Customs Law** or **International Trade.** You will then be taken to a page with a list of recent articles on that topic (or subtopic) and a search box where you can search the HG website (see Figure 14.10).

**Figure 14.10** Recent international law articles on HG. Screenshot from HG.org used with permission.

## United Nations–World Organizations

HG's **United Nations–World Organizations** page can be accessed at http://bit.ly/HG-UN. This page provides a list of relevant links for UN research, including the **United Nations** website itself and its **Treaty Collection, UN Law Reports,** and many others. In addition, this page provides a section on **NAFTA** with several related links. Farther down the page are sections with links to **Useful United Nations Publications** and **Other UN and International Government Sites.**

## European Union

Access HG's **European Union** page at http://bit.ly/HG-EU. The EU page is divided into five sections:

1. **European Union Institutions** provides links to the websites of important organizations, such as the European Parliament and Europa, the official portal to the European Union.
2. **European Law** links to sources of European case law, legislation summaries, and other useful resources.

3. **European Union Activities** provides subject-specific links to Europa for thirty-two subject areas such as Agriculture, Environment, and Taxation.
4. **European Central Banks** lists links for the European Central Bank and the national banks of twenty-seven member nations (Croatia is omitted).
5. **Law Firms Directory** links to a country-by-country directory of EU law firms generally, and also those that work in international trade.

### International Law

HG's **International Law** page can be accessed at http://bit.ly/HGInternational. The International Law page has several sections that provide links to useful guides, publications, treaties, organizations, and other resources. Examples of linked resources include important websites such as the **ABA International Law Section** and the **International Court of Justice**, and law journals such as the ***European Journal of International Law*** and the ***Stanford Journal of International Law***.

## JUSTIA'S LATIN AMERICAN RESOURCES

In Chapter 4, we discussed **Justia** (http://www.justia.com), a useful legal portal. Besides the U.S. resources already discussed, Justia also provides sources for researching Latin American law. About halfway down the middle of Justia's homepage (it is a long page, so it takes considerable scrolling) is a section entitled **Latin America** (see Figure 14.11). This section has three sub-headings: **Mexico, Central American & Caribbean**, and **South America**. Under each sub-heading are links to various jurisdictions in Latin America.

**Figure 14.11** Latin America resources on Justia's homepage. Screenshot from Justia used with permission.

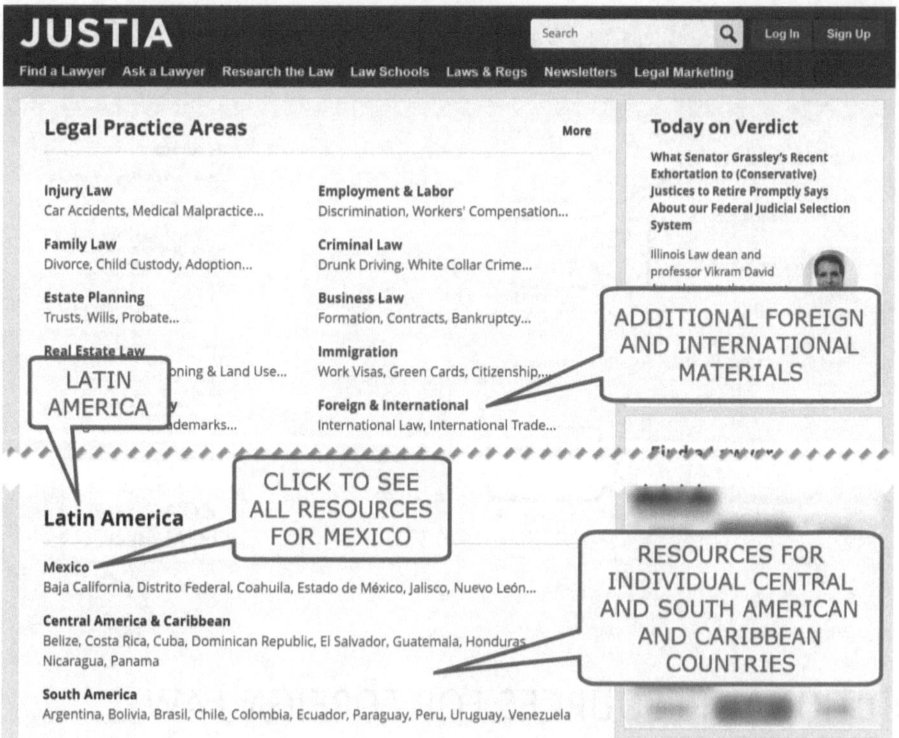


The **Mexico** subheading, which is also a clickable link, has links underneath for individual states in Mexico. Clicking **Mexico** will take you to a page (in Spanish) for Mexican federal and state laws (shown in Figure 14.12). Farther down on the page are several legal blogs in Spanish. The other two headings under the Latin America section of the homepage list links for the countries of Central and South America and the Caribbean. They go to similar Justia pages with law for those countries. To access additional foreign and international resources on Justia, click the **Foreign and International** link, near the top of the site's homepage, under the **Legal Practice Areas** heading (see Figure 14.11).

Figure 14.12 Justia's Mexico page. Screenshot from Justia used with permission.

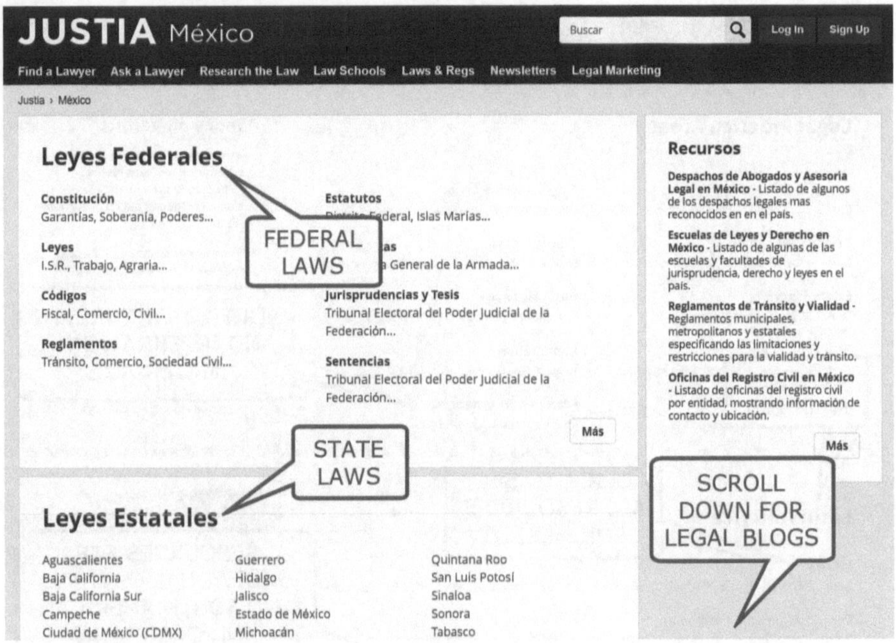


# ADDITIONAL RESOURCES FOR FOREIGN LAW

## CommonLII

The Commonwealth Legal Information Institute (CommonLII) provides over 1,400 searchable legal databases from 60 commonwealth and common law jurisdictions (http://www.commonlii.org). The site aggregates databases from these organizations:

- Australasian Legal Information Institute
- British and Irish Legal Information Institute
- CyLaw (Cypriot databases)
- Hong Kong Legal Information Institute
- Institute of Advanced Legal Studies (University of London)
- New Zealand Legal Information Institute
- Pacific Islands Legal Information Institute
- Southern African Legal Information Institute
- Ugandan Legal Information Institute

CommonLII's search features function similarly to those of WorldLII, described earlier in this chapter. The site also uses the same LawCite citator that we describe in Chapter 18 Cite-Checking Cases.

### The World Law Guide

**The World Law Guide** (http://bit.ly/WorldLawGuide) provides over 70,000 links to national information for more than 180 countries. The homepage lists several categories to choose from, including Legislation, Courts & Cases, and Law Journals. A link to Articles also allows you to keyword search legal articles by country and topic.

### Cornell LII's Law by Source: Global

Cornell Law School's Legal Information Institute (LII) is discussed more extensively in Chapter 5, but its **Law by Source: Global** page (http://bit.ly/LIIGlobal) is worth mentioning here. The page is divided into two primary categories—National Law Material and International Law. Links under each heading go to sites with primary sources such as constitutions, statutes, court opinions, and more. National coverage varies by country.

## ADDITIONAL RESOURCES FOR SUBJECT-SPECIFIC INTERNATIONAL LAW

Washburn University School of Law (WashLaw) provides a legal research website titled **WashLaw Legal Resources on the Web.** We discuss this site in more detail in Chapter 13, State, Local, Territorial, and Tribal Law. The site also has a useful foreign and international resource, however, so we will mention it here. The **International Resources** page of WashLaw's site (http://bit.ly/WashLawInternational) provides an extensive A–Z list of subject-specific international law topics with links to various sources for each. You can browse the topics list or you can choose the geographic region you wish to research from a menu in the left sidebar of the page.

For additional resources on specific international law topics, see ASIL's **Electronic Resources Guide** (http://bit.ly/ASIL-ERG) and **GlobaLex** (http://bit.ly/GlobaLex), both discussed earlier in this chapter.

## FOREIGN CONSTITUTIONS

Many resources discussed earlier in this chapter can lead you to foreign constitutions for individual countries but, if you want to compare two or more foreign constitutions, you may find the **Constitute Project** useful (https://www.constituteproject.org). Funded by a grant from Google to the University of Texas, this free online resource provides a growing number of constitutions from various countries that researchers can compare across a wide range of categories. To begin your search, click **Explore Constitutions,** which is located at the bottom of the page.

# Part IV

## ADDITIONAL RESEARCH SOURCES

Most of this book has focused on "pure" legal research resources—statutes, codes, cases, etc., but a lawyer's job often involves more than legal research. For instance, most lawyers need to conduct investigative (background/due diligence) research about clients, opposing parties, witnesses, and others. The next two chapters will focus on how to use dockets and social media sites to meet a lawyer's need for that type of research. In addition, once you identify cases with similar issues to yours, you can use docket research to find that case's docket and then use its pleadings as samples and the citations in its memos and briefs to jump-start your research.

# Chapter 15

## DOCKETS AND CASE DOCUMENTS

All federal appellate, district, and bankruptcy courts (including multi-jurisdictional litigation cases), the United States Court of International Trade, and the United States Federal Claims Court have placed their docket sheets online. For the most part, case documents (pleadings, opinions, orders, and transcripts) are also included online. Some state and local courts have also placed docket sheets online, but not necessarily the case documents, so you must obtain them in person.

If you must retrieve copies of docket sheets or case documents that are not available online, you can hire someone from the **Public Record Retriever Network (PRRN)** at http://bit.ly/PRRNSearch to visit a court to retrieve them. Some fee-based online docket database companies (such as **Bloomberg Law Dockets**, **Thomson Reuters Court Express**, and **LexisNexis CourtLink**), all noted later in this chapter, will also retrieve documents that are not available online.

Some docket databases can only be searched by docket number, while others can be searched by party or attorney names (and other options). Fee-based commercial docket databases (noted above and some others) usually offer better search options than free docket sites (whether an official court site or a free site sponsored by a commercial company). For example, fee-based commercial docket databases often offer full-text keyword searching, alert services, and litigation history reports.

## HOW DOCKETS AND CASE DOCUMENTS CAN BE USED FOR LEGAL AND INVESTIGATIVE RESEARCH

Docket searching and reviewing the case documents can be useful for legal research and also investigative (background/due diligence) research. Searching dockets by a person's or company's name could provide you with this background/due diligence information:

- How litigious a person or company is
- Whether someone has a criminal background
- Whether someone has declared bankruptcy
- What type of allegations have been lodged against a party
- A good address to use for service of process, if you are reviewing a recent complaint

Some attorneys use dockets for legal research purposes. For example, instead of drafting a complaint or an answer from scratch, some attorneys search dockets to find sample pleadings for cases that are similar to their case. If you are using PACER, there are a few ways to identify a similar case. For instance, you can find sample pleadings if you either know the party name or case number of a similar case. Or, if you don't, you can search **PACER** by its **Nature of Suit (NOS)** codes. The NOS is a classification system for federal civil litigation cases. When a complaint is filed, the court assigns it a numerical code and topic (such as *1110 Insurance*). This provides an easy way to identify and search for civil dockets with the same or similar issues across federal courts.

An alternative, and better, method to search for similar cases is by full-text keyword searching through case documents at the free **CourtListener Recap Archive** (and some pay databases), as explained later in this chapter.

## FEES

The federal courts offer docket searching by party name and case number (and other options) for a fee at PACER. The fees are complicated, and they are described in more detail later in this chapter. The fee-based databases must be contacted for pricing information.

Some state and county courts charge a fee for a party-name docket search. For instance, the Los Angeles Superior Court (LASC) (http://bit.ly/lasuperbyname)

charges registered users $1.00 to $4.75 per search (depending on number of searches per month) and guest users $4.75 per search. However, a case-number search is free (http://bit.ly/lasuperbyno). The LASC also charges a fee for civil case documents (beginning at $1.00 per page, for up to five pages, then $0.40 for pages six and on, with a cap of $40 per document).

On the other hand, the dockets of New York State and local courts can be searched many ways (depending on the court) at its **eCourts** site (http://bit.ly/nycourtsfree), all for free. For instance, you can search **WebCivil Supreme** (this is New York's trial level) cases for active and disposed Civil Supreme Court case in all 62 counties and search **WebCivil Local** (all the local Civil Courts in New York State—61 City Courts, the District Courts in Nassau and Suffolk Counties, and the New York City Civil Courts) by **Index Number, Party Name, Justice Name, Attorney Name,** or **Firm Name. WebCriminal** only provides information on pending criminal cases for selected New York State Courts and can only be searched by Case Number or Party Name. **WebFamily** provides information on active Family Court cases in all 62 counties of New York State and Integrated Domestic Violence (IDV) Court cases in those counties with IDV Courts and can only be searched by File or Docket Number. Some docket results also include access to decisions and other case documents. Some courts have mobile sites, besides web-based sites.

## FEDERAL, STATE, AND LOCAL COURT DOCKET DIRECTORY

**Legaldockets.com** (https://legaldockets.com) is a useful, free directory of federal, state, and local court dockets. Select a state and then browse the list of federal and state courts to link to that jurisdiction's docket database.

## DOCKET WEBSITES

While some pay investigative databases (e.g., **TLOxp** at https://www.tloxp.com, **Accurint** at http://www.accurint.com, and **Thomson Reuters's PeopleMap** at http://bit.ly/TRPeopleMap) indicate if someone has declared bankruptcy and sometimes provide criminal record information, they do not include the docket sheets or case documents, so we will not include these resources in our discussion of docket websites.

## PACER

**PACER** (http://www.pacer.gov) is the federal government's court docket database, covering over 51 million cases, from all the Circuit Courts of Appeals, District Courts, Bankruptcy Courts, and National Courts (Judicial Panel on Multidistrict Litigation, U.S. Court of Federal Claims, and U.S. Court of International Trade). **PACER** was rolled out in 1988 and it took many years for all federal courts to become participants. Most lawyers use **PACER's CM/ECF** (Case Management/ Electronic Case Files) to electronically file and manage their cases (**CM/ECF** is being replaced by **Next Generation (NextGen) Case Management/Electronic Case Files**). However, this discussion will not cover how to file documents on **PACER**. Instead, our focus is how to search for dockets and case documents primarily for investigative research purposes and secondarily how to find pleadings to use as samples and how to use others' memos and briefs to jump-start your research on similar issues.

### PACER Content

**PACER** includes the case's docket sheet and its case documents (but not necessarily for all cases). Case documents include pleadings, transcripts, written opinions, and orders. As of January 31, 2018, there were 310 million case documents in PACER. It's important to know that some documents may be completely unavailable to the public, including pre-2003 bankruptcy case documents and any criminal case documents older than November 1, 2004. However, we have regularly come across documents from these "unavailable" dates in **PACER**.

Besides missing documents, certain "personal identifiers" are "missing" from some case documents. This would include Social Security numbers, financial account numbers, the name of a minor, dates of birth, and in a criminal case, home addresses. These personal identifiers are supposed to be redacted (or truncated in the case of Social Security numbers) by the attorney or whoever files the documents at **PACER**.

An October 25, 2015 Federal Judicial Study found 16,811 separate instances of unredacted Social Security numbers among the 3,900,841 PACER documents filed in November 2013 in federal district and bankruptcy courts. Upon closer examination, the study found that these 16,811 instances involved Social Security numbers for just over 5,000 different individuals (*Unredacted Social Security Numbers in Federal Court PACER Documents*, by Joe S. Cecil, George Cort, Ashley Springer, and Vashty Gobinpersad, Federal Judicial Center, October 25, 2015;

http://bit.ly/noredactionssn). This failure to redact continues to occur despite the Federal Rules of Procedure (Civil, Criminal, and Bankruptcy) requiring redaction (or truncation) of full Social Security numbers (and other information) by attorneys before filing a pleading. However, from an investigative research standpoint, this unredacted information can prove to be useful.

## PACER Costs

No annual or monthly fee is imposed; you pay only for actual use. PACER charges $0.10 per page (capped at $3.00 for most documents). You are entitled to $30.00 worth of free documents per quarter as of January 1, 2020. Users will see this reflected in the April 2020 billing statement. This will result in more than 75 percent of users accessing court records paying no fee in a given quarter.

This pricing explanation is from PACER at http://bit.ly/pacercharges (click **What are some examples of per-page charges**):

> The $.10 per page charge is based on the number of pages that result from each search and each requested report or document. The charge is not based on printing. Here are some examples that may be helpful to understanding how the charges are generated:
>
> - Enter party name "johnson, t" and receive 2 pages of matches. The charge is $.20.
> - Enter case number 01-10054 and select Docket option. The docket is 10 pages, so the charge is $1.00. (You may enter a date range to limit the number of pages by displaying entries for the date range rather than all entries in the report.)
> - Select the link within the docket report to view a document. The scanned document is 5 pages, so the charge is $.50.
>
> Please note that there is a 30-page cap for documents and case-specific reports (i.e., docket report, creditor listing, claims register). You will not be charged more than $3.00 when you access documents or case-specific reports that are more than 30 pages. However, the 30-page cap does not apply to name search results, lists of cases, or transcripts (when available online).

## Registering or Logging In

PACER's home page (http://www.pacer.gov), shown in Figure 15.1, offers the following three options:

- You can **Register** for an account. Anyone can open a PACER account. For same-day registration, you must provide a credit card.

- If you already have an existing account, and you wanted to e-file, you would click the **Login** tab.
- If you wanted to begin a docket search, you would click the **Find A Case** tab.

Figure 15.1 Register for PACER or log into PACER.

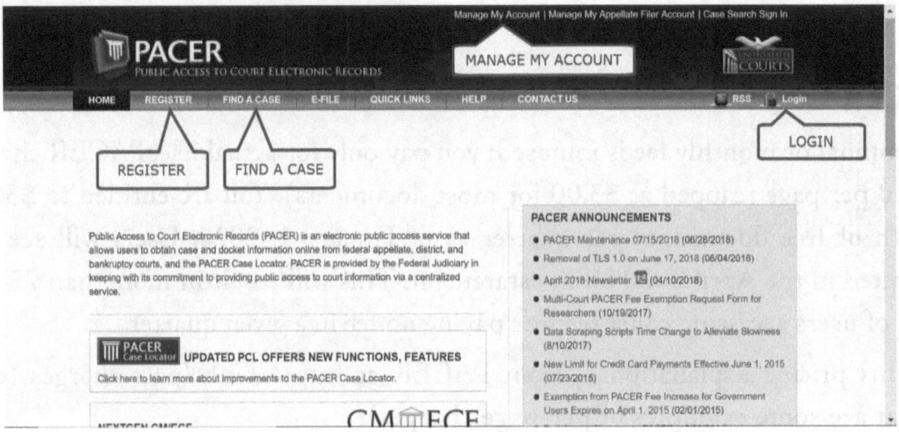


## Dates of Coverage

Although PACER began in 1988, dates of coverage will vary for each court because the courts came online at different times and some courts even uploaded dockets back to the 1950s. Coverage dates are indicated at each court's PACER site and on the Court Information page, but that page (see Figure 15.2) is only accessible after you log into PACER and click **Court Information** from the top of the page. Newly filed cases will usually appear on PACER within 24 hours.

Figure 15.2 PACER Date Coverage.

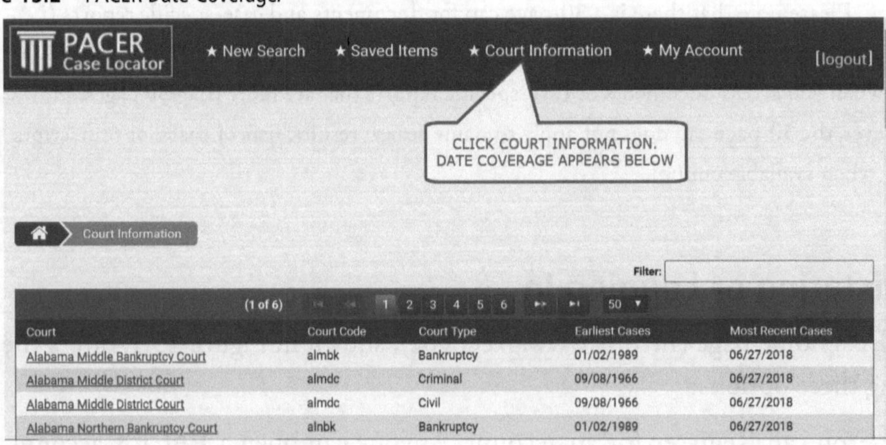

## Search the Case Locator

After 29 years of very few updates to **PACER**, major changes were made to the **PACER Case Locator**, effective December 9, 2017, beginning with adding **Quick Searches** (see Figure 15.3).

**Figure 15.3** Quick Searches.

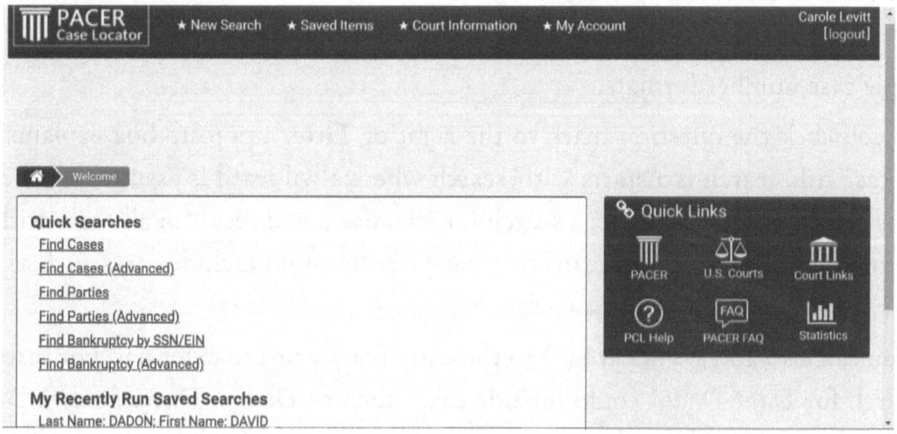


The **Find Cases** and **Find Cases (Advanced)** options (see Figure 15.3) are used when you know the case number or the case title.

After you click **Find Cases** you can perform a basic search (Figure 15.4), which allows you to enter a **Case Number, Title,** or a **Court Type** (or a combination of any of these). Notice you can switch to an **Advanced Case Search** by clicking the link on the right.

**Figure 15.4** Case Search (Basic).

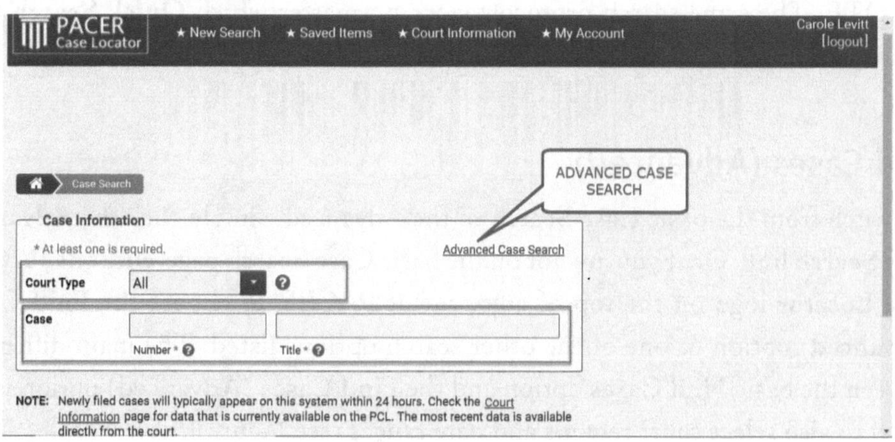

If you click the question mark to the far right of **Court Type**, a pop-up box explains that **All** is the default setting for court types, but that you can narrow your search to one federal Court Type (Appellate, Bankruptcy, Civil, Criminal, or Multi-district). To make the choice, click the down-arrow to the right of **All**. You cannot search two, three, or four Court Types together; you can only search one Court Type or all five Court Types together.

If you click the question mark to the right of **Number**, a pop-up box shows sample case number formats.

If you click the question mark to the right of **Title**, a pop-up box explains that "the case title search is a 'starts with' search where a wildcard is assumed at the end of the search string. Example: a search for *john doe v* will result in all cases with the case title *John Doe v.*" This means that your results could include cases such as *John Doe v. Acme, John Doe v. Brown*, etc.

You can also add a wildcard (*) to the end of any word to extend it. For instance, a search for *Dav* Dado** could include cases such as *Dadon, Dave; Dadon, David; Dadon, David J; Dadones, David J; Dadoun, David J*; etc. In this example the wild-card extended beyond the first name and brought back results including middle initials. This is a very broad search and could bring back irrelevant results (and could be a costly search because the $3.00 cap does not apply to name search results). You can also use the * to replace a character (e.g., *Sm*th* will bring back *Smith* and *Smyth*). Remember, a wildcard is assumed at the end of the search string, so our *Sm*th* example will also bring back *Smithers* or *Smethers*, etc.

Names are not case sensitive, so it doesn't matter if you use upper or lower case.

NOTE: The same search protocols work no matter which **Quick Search** (See Figure 15.3) option you select.

## Find Cases (Advanced)

To switch from the basic Case Search to the Advanced, simply click the **Advanced Case Search** link. Or, if you are not on the basic Case Search page, click the **PACER Case Locator** logo on the top of any page at PACER to choose the **Find Cases (Advanced)** option or one of the other search options listed. The main difference between the basic **Find Cases** option and the **Find Cases (Advanced)** option is the ability to also select court regions and date ranges (see Figure 15.5).

You can enter specific date ranges into the **Date Filed** or **Date Closed** search box or you can click **Prior Month, Prior Six Months,** or **Prior Year** (as shown in Figure 15.5). You could enter a start date only and results will include dates from that date to the present. Another option is to enter an end date only, and results will include dates on or before that date.

**Figure 15.5** Find Cases (Advanced).

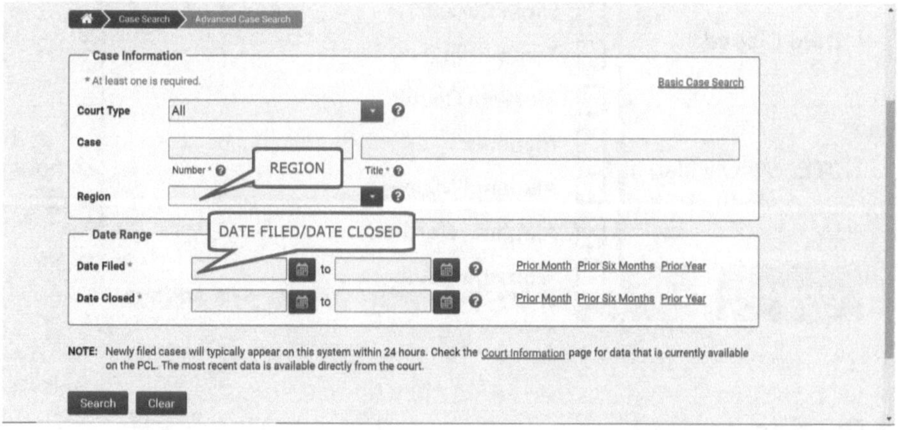


Depending on which **Court Type** you choose, different **Region** options appear in a drop-down list when you click the down-arrow to the right of the Region search box. For instance, if you choose **Appellate Court Type,** the Region list of choices is limited to the 1st to the 11th Circuit, the Federal Circuit, and the District of Columbia Circuit, but if you leave the Court Type at the default **All** (as shown in Figure 15.6), the Region drop-down list expands to also display: the **Federal Claims Court**; each **District Court** (e.g., the **Alabama Middle District Court**), and the name of each **State,** which allows you to search all the federal Court Types in a specific state. To choose one Region, simply click into the check-box to the left of that Region and to add more Regions, click into each of the check-boxes to the left of their Region (as shown in Figure 15.6). This **Region** choice also applies to the **Find Parties (Advanced)** search we'll discuss later.

Figure 15.6 Region.

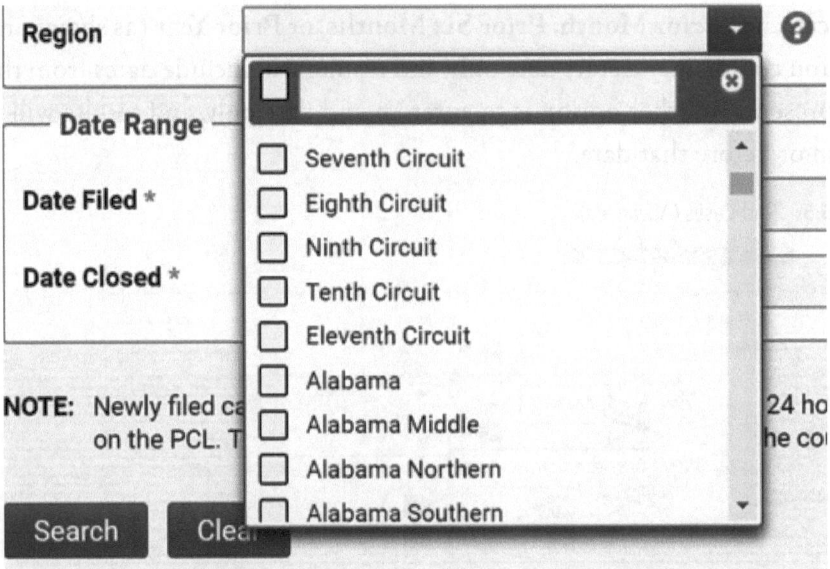


## Find Parties

If you wanted to locate a case but didn't know its case number or full case title but you knew one of the party's names, or if you wanted to conduct background or investigative research about a specific party, you would choose the **Find Parties** option (as shown in Figure 15.7) to search by a name.

Figure 15.7 Find Parties.

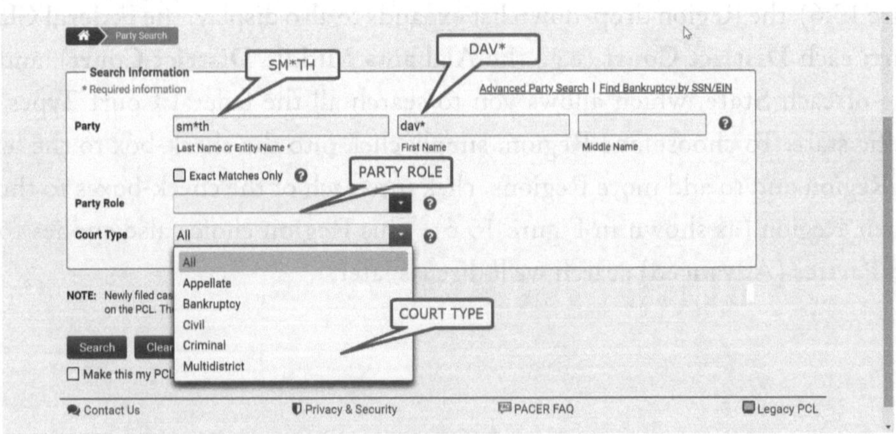

If we use the basic **Party Search** form (Figure 15.7), we typically leave the Court Type set to its default (All) to find cases involving our subject in any and all federal jurisdictions. But to narrow the search, you could select just one Court Type.

Conducting a **Party Search** is similar to the **Title** search explained in the **Find Cases** section (above). Like the **Find Cases Title** search, you can add a wildcard (*) to a name in a **Party Search** as shown in Figure 15.7 (*sm*th dav**). While the **Find Cases Title** search offers one search box to search by case title (Figure 15.4), the **Party Search** offers three search boxes to search by name: **Last Name or Entity Name, First Name,** and **Middle Name** (Figure 15.7). (For those of you familiar with the older PACER **Party Search** protocol, you no longer enter *Last Name, First Name* (e.g., *levitt, joseph*) into one search box and you no longer must separate them by a comma.)

If you are unsure of your subject's first or middle name (or its spelling) or if you want to create a broad search, you would search by last name only. If you check off the **Exact Matches Only** box (not offered in the **Find Cases' Title** search), you will be overriding the automatic wildcard (*) search and will be searching only the name entered (see Figure 15.7).

To conduct an **Entity Name** search when you are unsure of the full name, use one or more wild cards. For example, to search for an entity you think begins with the word *Stevens* and contains the word *Lake*, you could enter *Stevens* Lake** into the **Last Name or Entity Name** search box. Our search produced these two results:

- *Stevensville Lake Hotel* (adding the wildcard * after *Stevens* extended Stevens* to *Stevensville* and a wildcard was assumed at the end of the search string, adding an additional word, *Hotel*, after *Lake*.)
- *Stevens Lakeshore RV Center* (adding the wildcard * after *Lake* extended *Lake** to *Lakeshore* and a wildcard was assumed at the end of the search string, adding two more words, *RV Center*, after *Lakeshore*.

You can limit your search in advance to one of the thirty **Party Roles** (including attorney) once you click the down-arrow to the right of Party Role (see Figure 15.7) to view the drop-down list (not shown).

## Find Parties (Advanced)

To create an even more targeted party name search, you can click the **Advanced Party Search** link on the upper right side of the basic search form (see Figure 15.7).

Or, if you are not on the basic Party Search page, click the **PACER Case Locator** logo on the top of any page at PACER to choose the **Find Parties (Advanced)** option (see Figure 15.3).

The **Find Parties (Advanced)** option offers additional search boxes just like the **Find Cases (Advanced)** option does, such as **Region, Date Filed,** and **Date Closed** (see Figures 15.5 and 15.6).

However, the **Find Parties (Advanced) Region** search is different from the **Cases (Advanced) Region** search because when you choose the **Appellate** or **Civil** Court Type in a **Find Parties (Advanced) Region** search, another drop-down menu appears (see Figure 15.8). This menu offers you a way to narrow your search even further—by **Nature of Suit (NOS)**, as discussed earlier in this chapter. You can choose more than one **NOS**.

**Figure 15.8** Find Parties (Advanced): Civil or Appellate and Nature of Suit.

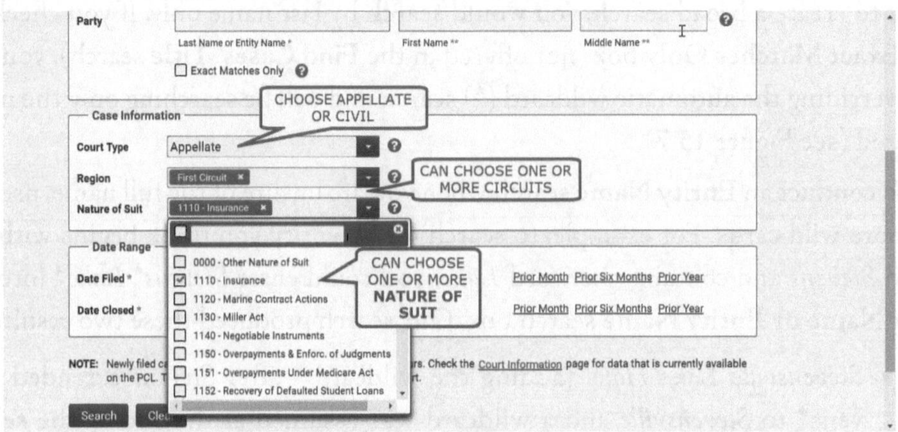


If you choose **Appellate,** the **Region** drop-down menu allows you to narrow your search to one or more Circuits (Figure 15.8).

If you choose **Civil** (not shown), the **Region** drop-down menu allows you to narrow your search to one or more courts (e.g., *First Circuit, Alabama Middle District Court*) or regions (e.g. *Alabama*).

If you choose the **Bankruptcy** Court Type, you are offered these additional search options: (1) a **Four Digit SSN** (Social Security Number), which must be combined with a Last Name; (2) a full **SSN or EIN** (Employer Identification Number); (3) a **Chapter** search; and (4) two more Date Ranges: **Date Dismissed** and **Date Discharged** (see Figure 15.9). When you are unsure where a subject might have filed bankruptcy, **PACER** is useful because you can search all the bankruptcy courts together.

**Figure 15.9** Find Parties (Advanced): Bankruptcy Court Type.

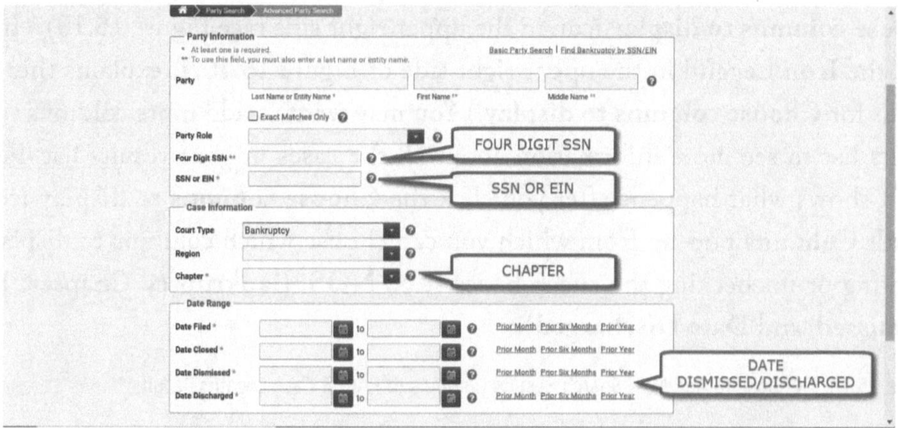


## PACER Case Locator Search Results

Figure 15.10 is the **PACER** Case Locator list of twenty-one results from a Party Search of Last Name *Dadon* and First Name *David*. Results are sorted by party name and displays five more columns of information. Even though we did not add a wildcard (*) to the end of *Dadon*, our results brought back more than *Dadon* (e.g., *Dadones*) because a wildcard is assumed at the end of the search string (*Dadon* and *David* are each a "search string"). If we had checked off **Exact Matches Only**, then our results would have been limited to *Dadon, David*.

**Figure 15.10** PACER Case Locator Search Results.

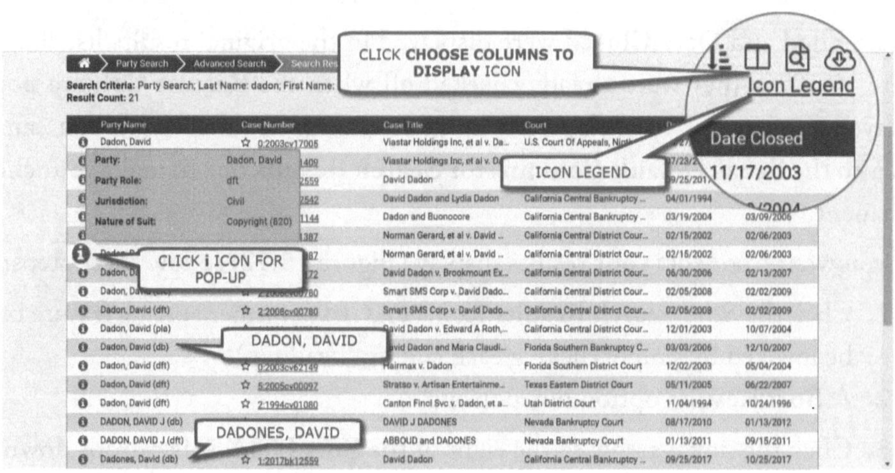


If you click on the **i** (information) Icon (see Figure 15.10), a pop-up shows you it's a **Civil** case and that the **Nature of Suit** is **Copyright (820)**. To avoid clicking the **i** Icon for each case to learn more information about the case, you can click the **Choose columns to display** icon in the upper right side (see Figure 15.10). (If you click the **Icon Legend** in the upper right side of Figure 15.10, it explains this Icon stands for **Choose columns to display.**) You may want to add more columns to the results list to see more information about all the cases in your results list. Figure 15.11 shows what happens after you click the **Choose columns to display** icon: a **Result Columns** pop-up from which you can choose which columns to display by checking or unchecking the check-boxes (e.g., **NOS, Bankruptcy Chapter, Date Dismissed,** and **Date Discharged**).

**Figure 15.11** Choose to Add New Search Results Columns to PACER Case Locator Results.

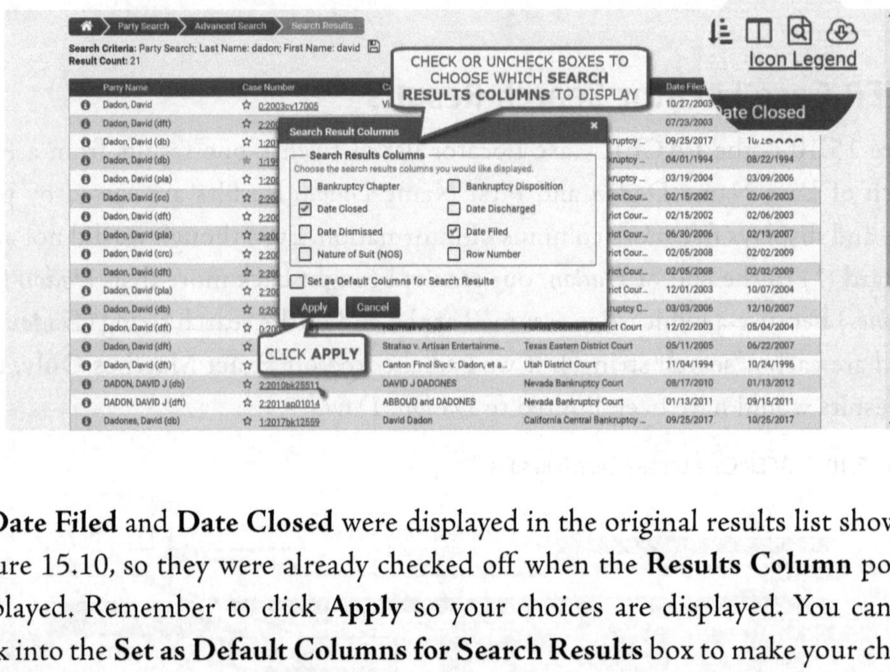


**Date Filed** and **Date Closed** were displayed in the original results list shown in Figure 15.10, so they were already checked off when the **Results Column** pop-up displayed. Remember to click **Apply** so your choices are displayed. You can also click into the **Set as Default Columns for Search Results** box to make your choices permanent.

If you want to re-sort your results display (Figure 15.12) follow these steps:

1. Click the **Sort Search Results** Icon. (**PACER's** former sorting feature could be invoked by simply clicking each column heading.)
2. A **Sort Results** option box pops up.
3. Click the down arrow to the right of the **Sort Field.** A list drops down for you to choose one of the following to sort by: **Party Name** (which is the default), **Case Title, Court, Nature of Suit, Bankruptcy Chapter, Date Filed,** etc.

4. Choose the display **Direction: Ascending** (alphabetically A–Z or oldest to newest if by date) or **Descending** (alphabetically Z–A or newest to oldest if by date).
5. NOTE: You are informed that **Sorting search results executes a new search for which a fee is charged.** (Previously, re-sorting had been free.)
6. Click **Apply.**

**Figure 15.12** Sort PACER Case Locator Search Results.

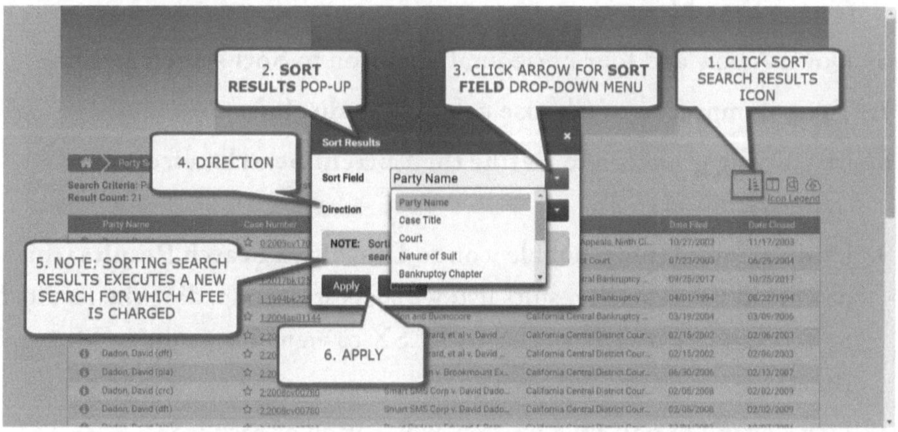


Many new Case Locator features were introduced in December of 2017 (see Figure 15.13 and the numbered call-outs) and an **Icon Legend** (see lower, right-hand corner of Figure 15.13) was also added to help interpret the Icons.

**Figure 15.13** New Features and Icon Legend for PACER Case Locator Search Results.

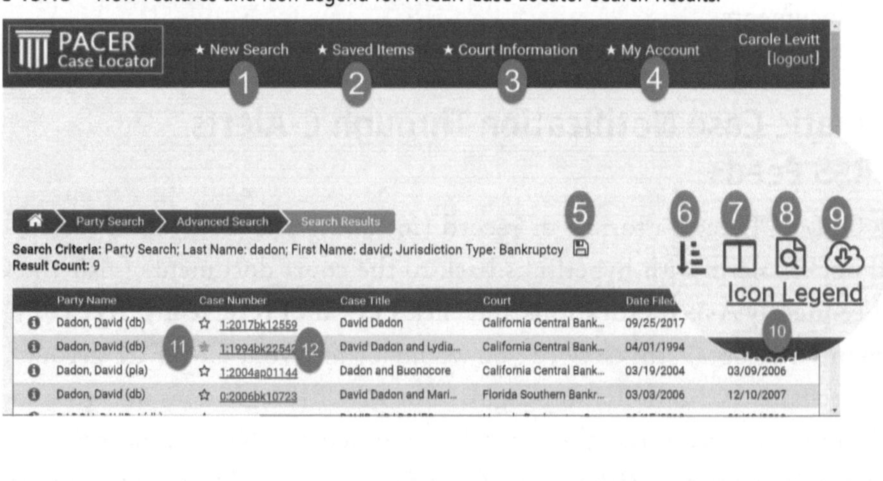

To invoke these features, click:

1. **New Search** to begin a new **Case** or **Party** search (a fee will be charged)
2. **Saved Items** to view your saved searches and saved cases
3. **Court Information** to learn date coverage of each court
4. **My Account** to: **Change Client Code, Manage my account, Billing History**, and **User Options**
5. **Disk** icon to save your search (e.g., your search string and other parameters) to **Saved Items**
6. Down Arrow and four horizontal lines icon to **Sort search results**
7. Two columns icon to **Choose columns to display**
8. Magnifying glass icon to **Refine the Current Search** (a fee will be charged)
9. Down arrow within a bubble icon to **Download Search Results** (this will download your search results list; we suggest downloading the results list to CSV and then save as XLS or XLSX to view the results in Microsoft Excel)
10. **Icon Legend** to pop-up a written explanation of each icon
11. **Star** to save a case to **Saved Items** (the star will turn from white to yellow) or click a starred case again to remove it from your **Saved Items** (the star will turn back to white)
12. Click any case number to view the docket and, if available, its case documents

## Automatic Case Notification Through E-Alerts and RSS Feeds

Using CM/ECF, each attorney of record (including *pro se* litigants) receives free e-mail docket alerts with hyperlinks back to the court documents (visit the CM/ECF **Frequently Asked Questions** and click **How do I receive my "free copy" of a document?**). To obtain this service, you would log into your CM/ECF account with your court-issued CM/ECF filing login. (The PACER login does not work for this e-mail notice service, unless the court has adopted the **Next Generation (NextGen) Case Management/Electronic Case Files** system.) Then, you would supply your e-mail address and the docket number of your case. You can also supply additional e-mail addresses for others to receive alerts. You can choose to receive an e-mail alert for each new event related to a filing or a daily summary notice of all filings. One free copy of each document is provided to each attorney of record and to any secondary addressee listed under the e-mail information screen.

If you are a non-party who is following a case for research purposes, you can also receive alerts (for free), but you must register for both a PACER ID and password and a CM/ECF filer ID and password, and be an approved registrant in a federal court. To view any case documents, the non-party would be assessed the same fees as other PACER users. Later in this chapter we'll discuss **RECAP's** free **Alerts** and case documents.

Some courts now provide free automatic case notification through RSS feeds. To learn which courts have implemented RSS visit http://bit.ly/pacerrss, click the **Court Links** link and then select the court's RSS feed icon, if there is one for the court you are interested in. Once you subscribe to a court's RSS feed you will receive notice of all activity in all cases from that court (not just a case that you specify), a summary of the documents filed, links to the documents, and the docket report. You can sort the feed results by date or case title. You must log into PACER and pay the usual costs to retrieve the document or docket report.

## Audio Recordings

Digital audio recordings of court proceedings are available online for twenty-six federal district and bankruptcy courts (http://bit.ly/pacerrecording). The cost is $2.40 per proceeding (it used to cost $26.00 to order a CD).

## Free Federal Court Opinions

Even though court opinions are free at **PACER**, you still need an account to search for the opinion, and you are charged for the initial docket search. If you are only looking for a free opinion (or if you need to run a keyword search), you should search Google Scholar (see Chapter 6) or bar association member-benefit databases (such as Fastcase in Chapter 9 or Casemaker in Chapter 8).

## PACER Public Access Terminals

PACER public access terminals are provided free at federal courthouses (but only for filings in the courthouse where the terminal is located). Viewing documents is free, but printing is priced at the usual $0.10 per page (http://bit.ly/pacerfreeview). The charge for copies from paper case files at the clerk's office is $0.50 per page.

### Mobile Access to PACER

To search the **PACER Case Locator** via mobile devices, such as iOS devices (iPads and iPhones) and Android devices (with version 2.2 and higher), you can go directly to pcl.uscourts.gov. The search interface mirrors the web-based interface.

### Firm Billing Now Available

PACER now offers a **PACER Administrative Account** (PAA) so firms can receive just one invoice for multiple users' accounts (http://bit.ly/paceradmin). The administrator of a PAA can:

- Choose whether to add existing users to the PAA (or leave some users outside the PAA)
- Set up new users and receive their login information immediately
- Activate and deactivate users
- Update user information
- Set the Client Code field as a requirement before a user can begin a search

### Help

If you need help, visit http://www.pacer.gov/help.html to find out how to call or e-mail the PACER Service Center. A link to **Frequently Asked Questions** is also available from that URL. PACER also offers a free **User Manual** (http://bit.ly/PACERUserManual), which was updated June 2018. There are free training modules on how to use the basic functions of CM/ECF (http://bit.ly/pacertrainingmod) and a training site populated with actual case documents filed between Jan. 1, 2007 and July 1, 2007 from the New York Western District Court (http://bit.ly/pacertraining). Unfortunately, the training modules and training site do not include the Case Locator, but the free User Manual does.

## RECAP (PACER SPELLED BACKWARDS) ARCHIVE FREE FEDERAL COURT DOCKETS AND CASE DOCUMENTS DATABASE

In 2009, to provide free access to millions of U.S. Federal District and Bankruptcy Court PACER case documents, a team at the Center for Information Technology

Policy at Princeton University and Harvard University's Berkman Center created a software extension that volunteers could add to their browser which would automatically transfer any U.S. Federal District and Bankruptcy Court (and now expanded to U.S. Courts of Appeals) dockets and case documents that they paid for from PACER to a free alternative archive that provides access to anyone. The extension and alternative archive were named RECAP (now renamed as RECAP Archive) and the site's tag line was: "Turning PACER Around" (https://www.recapthelaw.org).

Besides offering free documents, RECAP also created more user-friendly file names than PACER by including the PACER court, case number, and docket entry number as the file name (https://free.law/recap/features). Despite providing free access to millions of federal court dockets and case documents, RECAP is more limited than PACER because its collection does not include every docket for those courts and does not include every case document of included dockets. Before downloading a particular case document from your results list at PACER or another pay docket database, check to see if it is available at RECAP for free.

In May of 2014, the Free Law Project took over RECAP. (The Center for Information Technology Policy at Princeton University remained as a partner.) In August 2016, the Free Law Project retired the recapthelaw.org website and moved all the old content to a new site, with a new URL: https://free.law/recap.

Then, in November of 2016, the **RECAP Archive** was relaunched by **CourtListener** and given a new URL: https://www.courtlistener.com/recap. The Free Law Project and the Center for Information Technology Policy at Princeton University remained as partners.

## CourtListener Enhancements to the RECAP Archive (2016 and 2017)

In 2016, CourtListener made several enhancements to the RECAP Archive, such as:

- converted many scanned case documents into keyword-searchable documents by applying Optical Character Recognition (OCR) software,
- added more robust search features, including full-text keyword searching (noted above) and field searching (discussed later in this chapter),
- and, expanded the RECAP Archive coverage to U.S. Courts of Appeals' dockets and case documents (originally, the Archive included only federal district and bankruptcy dockets and case documents).

In 2017, RECAP Archive made more changes and enhancements, which they explain below:

> After nearly a year of work, and with support from the U.S. Department of Labor and Georgia State University, we have collected every free written order and opinion that is available in PACER. To accomplish this, we used PACER's "Written Opinion Report," which provides many opinions for free. This collection contains approximately 3.4 million orders and opinions from approximately 1.5 million federal district and bankruptcy court cases dating back to 1960. More than four hundred thousand of these documents were scanned and required OCR, amounting to nearly two million pages of text extraction that we completed for this project. All of the documents amassed are available for search in the RECAP Archive of PACER documents and via our APIs. New opinions will be downloaded every night to keep the collection up to date. As a backup and permanent repository, we are continuing our partnership with the Internet Archive, where we are in the process of uploading a copy of every opinion that we download. (See http://bit.ly/recapfreectops.)

On February 16, 2018, we learned that RECAP was no longer uploading to the Internet Archive daily. Instead, it had switched to quarterly uploading. Unless that changes, be sure to search dockets at the RECAP Archive and not the Internet Archive.

## How to Add the RECAP Extension to Donate PACER Documents

To donate PACER documents to RECAP, you must download the RECAP extension to your Firefox or Chrome Web browser by clicking the appropriate link at https://free.law/recap (shown in Figure 15.14).

**Figure 15.14** RECAP: Add RECAP Extension. Screenshot from RECAP used with permission.

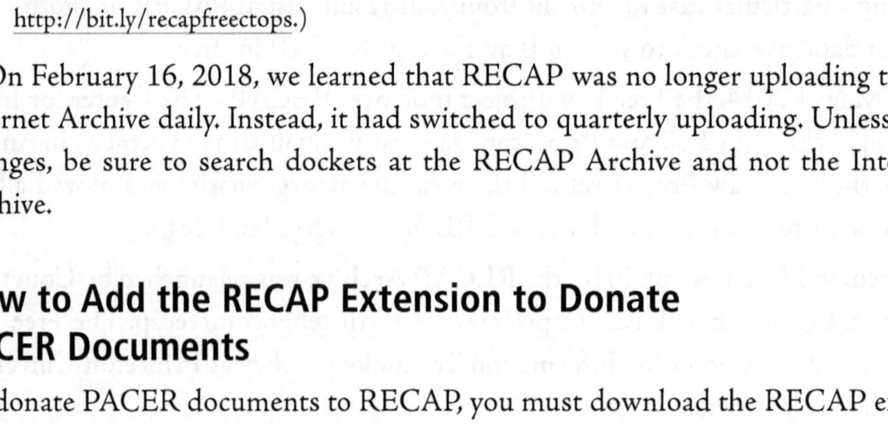

Once you have downloaded the RECAP extension, each time your search results are displayed at PACER, RECAP will display a small "R" icon next to the document link if a free version of any of the documents is already available from the RECAP Archive. Over time, this can save you considerable fees. And, once you pay for a PACER docket sheet or case document, it is automatically transferred to the **RECAP Archive** for free public use. The Free Law Project also requests monetary donations (https://free.law/donate) to support The RECAP Archive and its other projects (e.g., "Gather and curate the latest opinions from more than 200 courts daily, making them searchable in our collection of nearly 4M opinions. Host the largest archive of oral argument audio in the world, with nearly 1,000,000 minutes of recordings.")

## How to Search RECAP

To reach the RECAP Archive, use this direct URL: https://www.courtlistener.com/recap. Although RECAP requires you to use Firefox or Chrome to upload a document, you are not required to only use those browsers to search the RECAP Archive.

At the **Advanced RECAP Search** page (https://www.courtlistener.com/recap), you can conduct a full-text, keyword search of the RECAP Archive case documents that have been OCR'd. At **PACER** (and many of the other free or hybrid docket databases discussed in this chapter), you *cannot* full-text keyword search case documents; you can only keyword search through short descriptions of each case document listed on the docket sheet. So, it should be apparent why RECAP provides a huge advantage to researchers. However, not all RECAP Archive documents have been OCR'd yet.

To search the RECAP Archive, enter one or more keywords (or phrases) into the top search box and click **Search** on the top right-hand side of the search menu (see Figure 15.15).

**Figure 15.15** Advanced RECAP Search. Screenshot from RECAP used with permission.

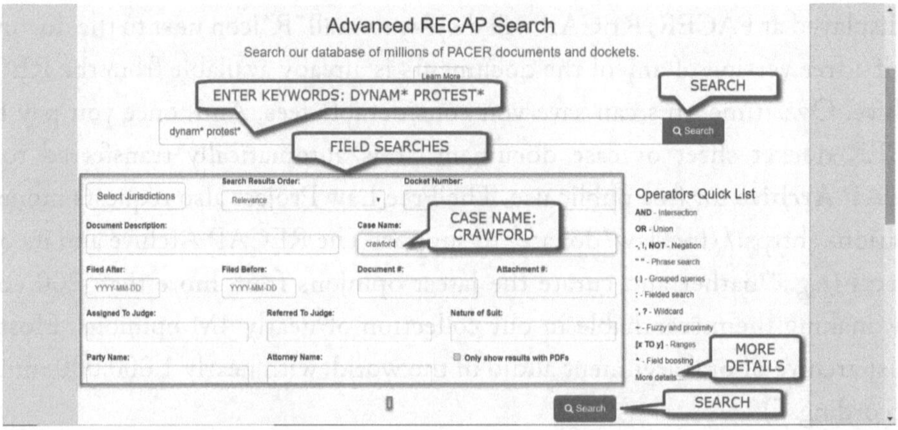


You can create a more sophisticated keyword/phrase search by using one or multiple advanced query techniques displayed in the **Operators Quick List** found on the right side of the search menu shown in Figure 15.15. To learn how to invoke these operators (often called "connectors" at other websites and search engines), wildcards, fielded queries, and other search techniques, click the **More details** link beneath the **Operators Quick List.**

You can also enter more information into one or more of the various field search boxes located below the large keyword/phrase search box if you want to refine your search (see Figure 15.15). The field searches allow you to refine your keyword/phrase search by adding more information, such as **Docket Number, Document Description, Case Name, Filed After:YYYY-MM-DD, Filed Before:YYYY-MM-DD, Document #, Attachment #, Assigned To Judge, Referred To Judge, Nature of Suit, Party Name,** and **Attorney Name** (this can also include firm name). Click either the **Search** tab on the bottom right-hand side of the search menu (see Figure 15.15) or the one on the top right-hand side. They both work.

Instead of refining your keyword/phrase search by adding information into field boxes, another search option is to leave the keyword/phrase search box empty and conduct a field or fields-only search. For example, entering an attorney name (or law firm name) into the **Attorney Name** field search box is a good way to do background research about the cases handled by attorneys (or law firms) whom you may be opposing or considering hiring. You could refine this search even more by entering dates into the **Filed After** or **Filed Before** field search boxes. After you are done using the field boxes, click **Search** on the right-hand side at the bottom of the page to run the search.

In addition to field searching, the Advanced RECAP Search page also allows you to display **Search Results Order** by: **Relevance, Newest First,** or **Oldest First** (these options appear once you click the down-arrow to the right of **Search Results Order**); or you can check the box to **Only show results with PDFs** (see Figure 15.15).

In our sample search (see Figure 15.15), we are trying to find a case discussing the dynamics of protesting and the party name Crawford. Instead of entering the word *dynamics* and *protesting* into the full-text keyword search box, we'll enter the root of each word and add the asterisk (*) as a wildcard to retrieve cases with words beginning with the letters we entered. You can see in Figure 15.15 that we entered *dynam** (this could retrieve *dynamic/dynamics/dynamically/dynamite*) and then *protest** (this could retrieve *protest/protests/protested/protesting,* etc.). The asterisk will also work in the beginning or middle of a word. To find Smith or Smyth, you would enter: *sm*th*.

After entering our keywords, we then used the field boxes and entered the party's name (*Crawford*) into the **Case Name** box. (We could have used the **Party Name** field box instead.) However, if we had entered the party name into the top full-text keyword search box, our results could have included anyone named Crawford anywhere in the document, from a judge to an attorney, to a witness, so it's much better to use the Case Name or Party Name field box if you want to limit the results to a party to the suit. You can only enter one party name into the Party Name field box, but you can enter multiple party names (e.g., *crawford sussman*) or the full case title (e.g., *crawford v sussman*) into the Case Name field box. (The **Party Name** and **Attorney Name** fields were added in March 2017.)

Figure 15.16 shows our search result, **Sussman v. Crawford.** Keywords are highlighted in yellow. Notice the variations of the words **protest*** and **dynam***. You can **Refine Your Query** by using the options on the left-hand side column and then clicking **Search** (not shown) at the bottom left-hand side of the page to re-run the query. These are the same options as noted earlier in our description of Figure 15.15 (**Docket Number, Document Description,** and so on).

When searching the RECAP Archive, you are warned that the docket is unofficial and may be incomplete or out-of-date, so if you must view complete dockets, check PACER.

**Figure 15.16** RECAP Search Results and Refine Your Query. Screenshot from CourtListener used with permission.

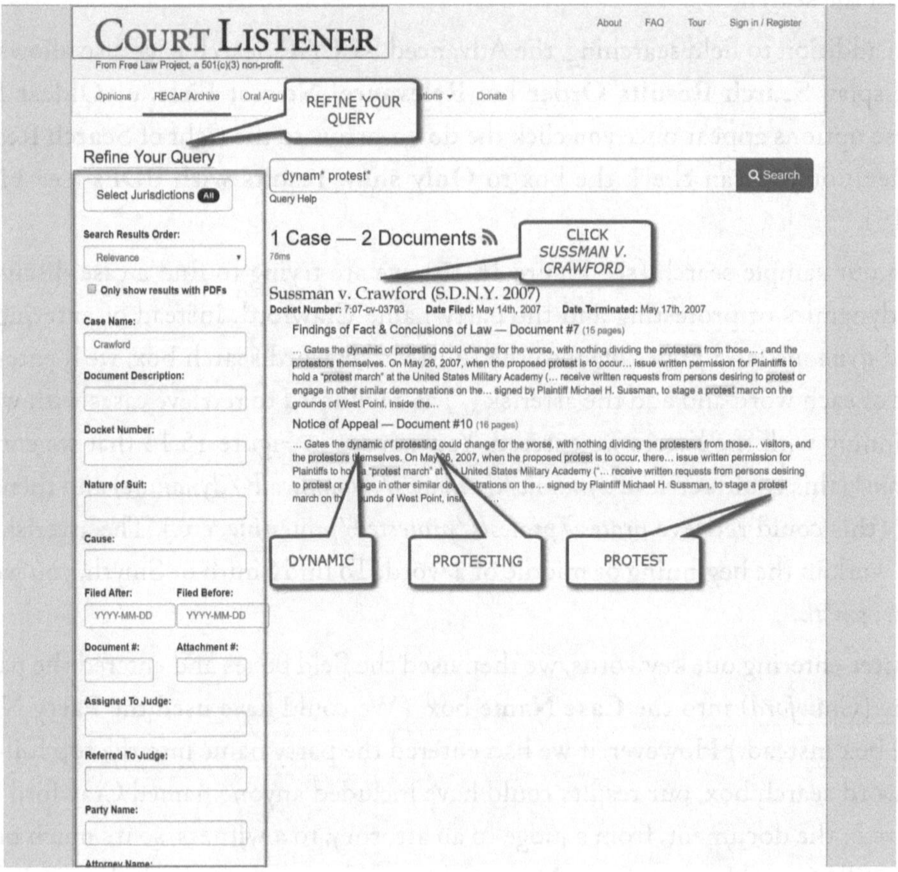


To view a particular docket sheet, click the case name (see Figure 15.17). A list of all the case documents will be displayed, but you can display the list of documents in a many other ways, such as by:

- **Date Filed:** Enter the date(s) into one or both of the boxes to the right of **Filed.**
- **Documents:** Enter one or more document number(s) of only the documents you are interested in displaying into the boxes to the right of **Documents** (we chose to display only documents 10 and 11).
- **Ascending** or **Descending** order: Click the **Ascending** or **Descending** tab (to the right of the **Documents** boxes).

Notice the tabs to the right of the document description. The **Download PDF tab** indicates this document is available on RECAP and can be downloaded for free by clicking the tab. But, if you see a **Buy on PACER** tab, this indicates this document is not available on RECAP and must be purchased at **PACER**.

**Figure 15.17** RECAP Docket Sheet. Screenshot from RECAP used with permission.

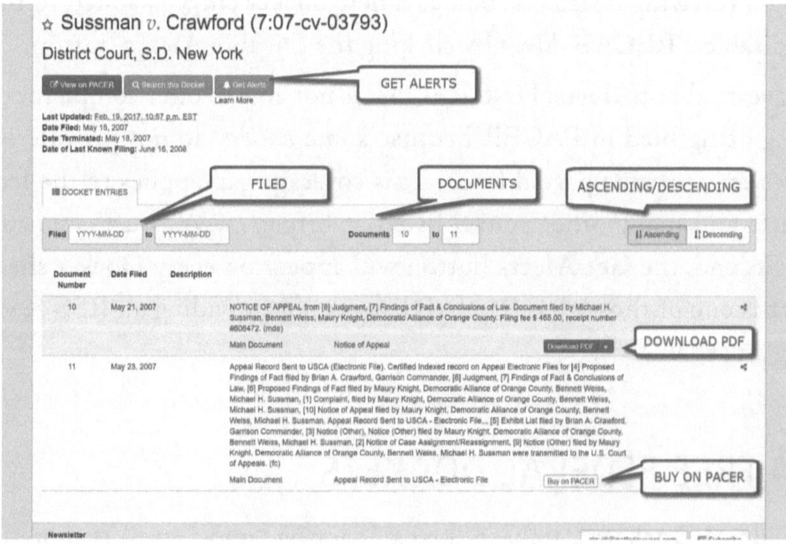


Notice the **Get Alerts** tab on the top of the page. Before CourtListener relaunched the RECAP Archive in 2016, users had the option to set up alerts for specific cases to be advised via e-mail or RSS feeds every time a new document was added to that case's docket sheet. This option disappeared for two years but returned in June 2018.

CourtListener explains its Alert service this way (https://www.courtlistener.com/help/alerts):

> RECAP Alerts are a way of keeping up with cases in the PACER federal court filing system. These alerts monitor tens of thousands of cases across the country for new docket entries and send an email whenever new entries are acquired. In the last 24 hours, 66,801 dockets and 73,906 docket entries were updated [these numbers are from November 5, 2018]. For active cases, this means that alerts will come any time from about a minute after the content is posted to PACER (for a case of national importance), to an hour or two, for a case of lesser importance in a jurisdiction that does not regularly provide public updates via their RSS feed. For closed cases, we get new content and can send alerts when we do client work on those cases or when a RECAP extension user shares a docket with us.

To create a **RECAP Alert** once you have retrieved a docket from RECAP, click the **Get Alerts** button on the top of the page. If you don't already have a free account you will be prompted to register for one before you can actually set up for an Alert. You'll begin receiving Alerts as soon as a new docket entry is added to the docket. You can disable a **RECAP Alert** by clicking the **Disable Alerts** Button.

Two caveats about **Alerts:** First, RECAP is not able to offer complete coverage of everything being filed in PACER because some courts do not provide RSS feeds and others only provide partial feeds. This coverage gap applies to the federal Circuit Courts and many other courts listed at https://www.courtlistener.com/help/alerts/. Second, the **Get Alerts** button will appear on every Docket sheet, even if that court is one of those that RECAP lists as not providing an RSS feed (or only providing a partial feed).

## JUSTIA FREE FEDERAL DOCKETS

Justia's **Federal Dockets** database (https://dockets.justia.com) is more limited in scope than PACER and RECAP because it does not provide access to bankruptcy dockets. It provides access to the dockets of the U.S. Federal District Court, the United States Court of International Trade, the United States Federal Claims Court, and the U.S. Courts of Appeals (including the U.S. Court of Appeals for Veterans Cases). Another difference is that case documents are only available for some dockets (and even then, some documents may be missing from a docket). However, Justia was the first site to offer free federal dockets. Its database goes back to 2004. The database is no longer displayed prominently on Justia's home page but can be accessed by scrolling all the way to the bottom of the home page (http://www.justia.com) and selecting **Dockets and Filings** from the left-hand column titled **US Federal Law.** Or, use the direct URL (https://dockets.justia.com/; see Figure 15.18).

**Figure 15.18** Justia's Federal Dockets. Screenshot from Justia used with permission.

The database is poorly documented (possibly because it is still in beta mode, and has been for many years), so we have run many test searches to assist you in using it. At the **Search** page (see Figure 15.18), you can search by one or more of the following criteria:

- **Party Name**
- **Judge**
- **Filed In**: select **Federal Appellate & District Courts - All, Federal Appellate Courts - All, Federal District Courts - All,** one specific circuit court of appeals (e.g. **Ninth Circuit**), one specific circuit court of appeals along with all its district courts (e.g., **Ninth Circuit Appellate and District Courts - All** ), or one or all of a state's federal district courts (e.g., **California Central Federal District Court** or **California Federal District Courts - All**), or one of the national courts (e.g., **U.S. Court of Federal Claims**)
- **Type** (this refers to PACER's NOS designation, such as **Contract**)
- **Show** (choose either **All Case Filings** or **Only Case Filings with Downloadable Opinions or Orders**)
- **Cases Filed** (select **All Dates** or enter a date range)

Besides searching, you can scroll past the search menu to browse by: **Type of Lawsuit** (PACER's NOS designation), **Cases by Circuit, Cases by State,** or **Most Recently Filed** (not shown in Figure 15.18).

Our search for the **Party Name** *Rich Yi* and **Filed In** *Seventh Circuit* brought back one result (as shown in Figure 15.19), where *Rich Yi* is one of many defendants in *Brown v. City of Chicago et al.* While many of Justia's docket results provide only a summary of the docket sheet, some include the full docket sheet. Also, if you see a gavel icon (as shown in Figure 15.19), this indicates its full docket sheet and a link to its available documents will be displayed for free. (see Figure 15.20). Some dockets include all the case documents, this would be indicated by a yellow star icon.

**Figure 15.19** Justia's Docket Search Results. Screenshot from Justia used with permission.

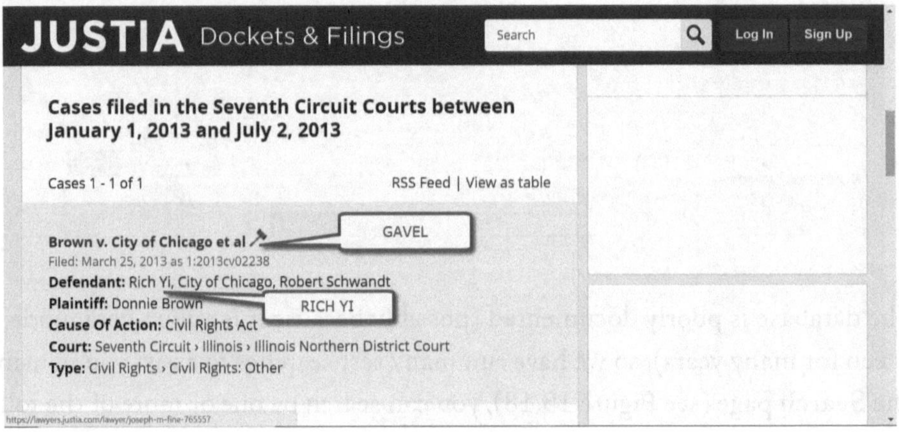


In this example (see Figure 15.20), Justia has only one case document (#5) available. To download this document, click its docket entry number (e.g., #5). You can also opt to receive free RSS feeds of filings that meet your search criteria by clicking the RSS icon to the left of **Follow case documents by RSS.** When Justia does not have the complete docket sheet or any (or less than all) of the case documents, you can scroll down past the available case document(s) and Justia points (not shown in Figure 15.20) users to PACER (discussed earlier in this chapter).

**Figure 15.20** Justia Docket Search Results With Case Details and Link to Case Document. Screenshot from Justia used with permission.

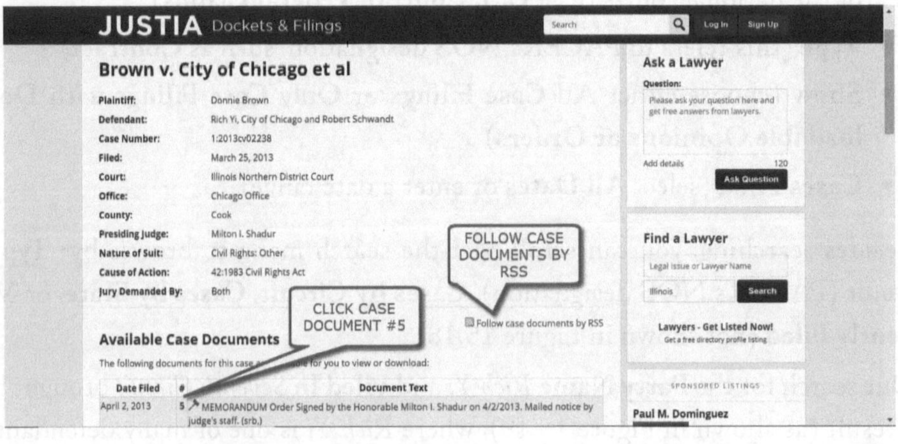

# U.S. SUPREME COURT DOCKETS AND CASE DOCUMENTS (ORAL ARGUMENTS—AUDIO RECORDINGS AND TRANSCRIPTS, AND MERIT AND AMICUS BRIEFS)

## Dockets

The U.S. Supreme Court (https://www.supremecourt.gov) does not participate in PACER's CM/ECF system or the Case Locator, but the Court has had its own docket database (see Figure 15.22) for some time. However, electronic filing was *not* required until November 13, 2017 when the Court amended Supreme Court Rule 29:

> 7. In addition to the filing requirements set forth in this Rule, all filers who are represented by counsel must submit documents to the Court's electronic filing system in conformity with the "Guidelines for the Submission of Documents to the Supreme Court's Electronic Filing System" issued by the Clerk. (See http://bit.ly/sctrule29.)

The Court explained:

> The Supreme Court's new electronic filing system is now in operation. While paper remains the official form of filing, all parties who are represented by counsel must also submit electronic versions of filings through the system. Most documents that are submitted electronically will be made available on the Court's public docket free of charge. Filings from pro se parties are submitted only on paper, but will be scanned and made available electronically on the Court's docket. (See http://bit.ly/sctelecfile.)

The Supreme Court's docket system provides the status of cases filed since the beginning of the 2001 Term (both pending and decided). Until November 2017, the U.S. Supreme Court's docket database did not include any case documents (e.g., petitions, motions, briefs, etc.) unless it was an important/controversial case. But, as of November 2017, it began including copies of all briefs in the docket report.

**Figure 15.21** U.S. Supreme Court Home Page.

To search, click **Docket Search** located near the top, right-hand side of the home page (Figure 15.21). Once you click Docket Search, you are presented with a simple search box and informed that you can search for a docket by: docket number, a case name, or even other words or numbers included on a docket report. Searching with other words that might be included on a docket report comes into play when you don't know the case name or docket number of a case, but you know something about the case. For example, let's say you knew that the Hudspeth County Conservation and Reclamation District was involved in a water rights case, but you didn't know the case title. You could search "Hudspeth County Conservation" to see if a docket entry included those words. The search results retrieved the docket sheet for *Texas v. New Mexico and Colorado,* which included this docket entry: **Brief amicus curiae of Hudspeth County Conservation and Reclamation District No. 1 filed** (see Figure 15.22).

**Figure 15.22** U.S. Supreme Court Docket Search Results.

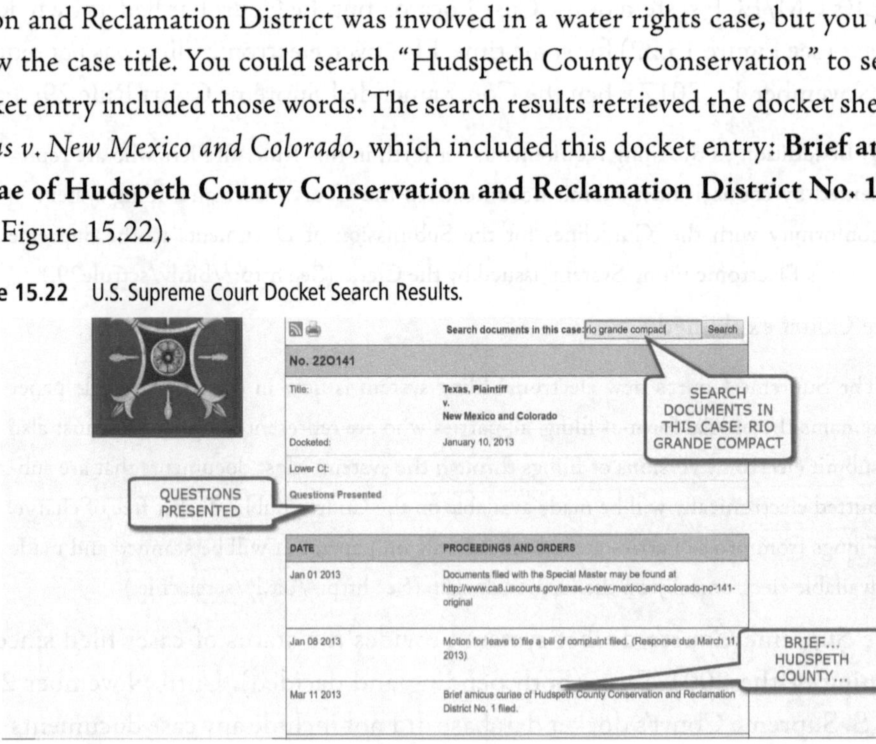


Once you retrieve the relevant docket report, notice you are offered the ability to enter keywords into the **Search documents in this case** search box (Figure 15.22). This is a full-text search of any of the documents in the docket report that are available for this case, but remember, very few case documents are available in the Court's docket database. Our search for *Rio Grande Compact* retrieved four documents, including a **Motion for Divided Argument.**

The **Questions Presented** can be found using either of two methods: If you already retrieved the docket you were searching for, the first method is to simply click the blue **Questions Presented** hyperlink on the docket report (shown in Figure 15.22). Once the hyperlink is clicked, a PDF file setting forth the Questions Presented in the case will appear.

The second method is to click **Advanced Search** on the homepage (see Figure 15.23). Then a search menu appears where you can enter keywords into the **Search for** box, and then place a check mark into the **Questions Presented** check-box (see Figure 15.23). This will retrieve all **Questions Presented** that include those keywords.

**Figure 15.23** U.S. Supreme Court Docket Questions Presented Search Results.

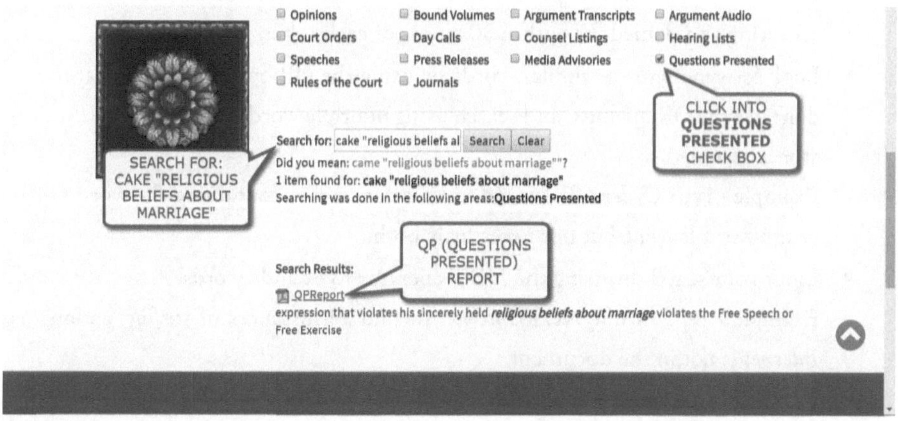


Many other options are on this menu to keyword search, such as **Opinions**, **Argument Transcripts**, etc. You can click into one or more of the check boxes to expand your search to other documents. Not all documents are full-text searchable, however. For instance, our search for *cake* to find the **Argument Audio** for *Masterpiece Cakeshop, Ltd. v. Colorado Civil Rights Comm'n* did not work. A search for *Masterpiece Cakeshop* worked.

To learn how to create a sophisticated **Advanced Search**, click the **Search Tips** link on the homepage (see Figure 15.21); or use this URL: https://www.supremecourt.gov/search_help.aspx, where you will be instructed:

> To use this search page, you can look for a single word. Or, use the tips below to refine your search to find more specific results. In all these examples please note that the searches are case insensitive, so searching for *Supreme Court* is the same as searching for *SUPREME COURT*.
>
> - Look for two or more words at once by just separating them by a space or using the *AND* operator.
>
>   Example - type *Supreme AND Court* or simply *Supreme Court* to find documents that have both the word supreme and the word court anywhere.

- Look for a phrase.
  Example: type "*Supreme Court*" in quotes to find the exact phrase Supreme Court. The search is not case-sensitive.
- Look for words close to each other by using the *NEAR* operator instead of the *AND* operator. When you use *NEAR*, the closer together the words are, the higher the rank of the page, so the higher it appears in the list of search results.
  Example - type *Rehearing NEAR denied* to match documents where the word rehearing and denied are within 50 words of each other.
- Look for synonyms or similar words by using the *OR* operator. Note that if you don't use the *OR* operator and search using multiple words, a boolean *AND* operator is assumed.
  Example - type *Order OR Journal* to find documents containing the word *Order* or the word *Journal*, but not necessarily both.
- Limit your search by using the *NOT* operator to exclude words.
  Example - type *surfing NOT Internet* to find all instances of *surfing*, as long as *Internet* is not in the document.
- Use double quotes if you want to use *AND*, *OR*, *NOT*, or *NEAR* literally.
  Example - type "*Search will not find*" to find documents with the phrase *Search will not find*. Without the double quotes, this query would use the *NOT* operator to exclude the word find.
- Look for words that begin with the same letters by using a single asterisk (*).
  Example - type *cert** to find *certify*, *certiorari*, *certification* and so on.

More advanced searches

You can combine many of the above tips to create more specific searches such as:

- Using multiple operators: Use parentheses around each combination of *NEAR* and combine them into a more complicated search such as: (*Supreme NEAR Court*) *AND* (*Capital NEAR Case*) would return items where the word *Supreme* is near the word *Court* and where *Capital* is also near the word *Case*. This would differ from *Supreme NEAR Court NEAR Capital NEAR Case* because that would require all four words to be in close proximity to each other.

## Oral Arguments (Transcripts): Supreme Court of the United States

While the Court's site has included oral argument transcripts (http://bit.ly/sctoralargtran) back to 2000 for some time, Heritage Reporting Corporation took over the project beginning in the October Term 2017. They are all archived on the

Court's website. Oral argument transcripts are posted on the same day an argument is heard by the Supreme Court. Note that "Same-day transcripts are considered official but subject to final review. . ." The transcripts are browsable by **Term** and then by **Date Argued** but can also be full-text keyword searched using the **Advanced Search** feature offered on the Court's home page (see Figures 15.21 and 15.23).

## Oral Arguments (Audio Recordings): Supreme Court of the United States

The Court's site includes audio recordings of all oral arguments back to 2010 to the present; these are provided to the public on Fridays after Conference of each argument week. (http://bit.ly/sctoralargaudio). You can either download the audio files or listen to them on the Court's website. The audio recordings are browsable by **Term** and then by **Date Argued** but can also be full-text keyword searched using the **Advanced Search** feature offered on the Court's home page (see Figures 15.21 and 15.23).

Oyez (http://www.oyez.org/cases) provides free access to the audio recordings of many of the Supreme Court's oral arguments from 1955 to the present; these can be accessed by **Court term** or **Issue**. However, the **Issue** choice is not displayed until you click the down-arrow to the right of **View by: Court term.** If you choose **Court term,** a list of court terms is then displayed. After you choose a specific court term (e.g., 2000-2001), a list of cases is then displayed alphabetically by plaintiff. If you choose **View by: Issue,** an **Issue** tab appears. Click its down-arrow and choose an issue from the drop-down menu. Just like the **View by: Court term** choice, a list of cases is then displayed alphabetically by plaintiff. In both cases, you must click on the case name to view an information page about the case and then click the **Oral Argument** speaker icon in the left-hand column of the page to listen to the argument.

## Oral Arguments (Audio Recordings): Supreme Court of the United States and Other Federal Courts

CourtListener also downloads the latest oral arguments from the Supreme Court of the United States at the end of each day to create a searchable archive (https://www.courtlistener.com/audio). It goes back further in time than the official Supreme Court's archive and offers a different search experience than that of the Supreme Court site. (In addition, CourtListener downloads the latest oral arguments from the Courts of Appeals, First through the Ninth Circuits, the D.C. Circuit, and the Federal Circuit.) You can locate the audio version of an oral argument by entering full or partial party names into the **Advanced Oral Argument Search** box (https://www.courtlistener.com/audio) and/or by entering information into one (or multiple) of the following field search boxes: **Jurisdictions, Docket Number, Case Name, Argued After:YYYY-MM-DD, Argued Before:YYYY-MM-DD,** and **Judge.** Dates of coverage are not detailed, but when we conducted an **Argued Before 1969-01-01** field search we retrieved no results. When we revised the search to **Argued Before 1970-01-01**, we retrieved three oral arguments from 1969.

### Merit and Amicus Briefs

As of November 2017, the Supreme Court finally began hosting its merit and amicus briefs. Before that, **FindLaw** and the **ABA** hosted them on their site, but they recently removed them from their sites. This is unfortunate because they went back further in time than November 2017. There is no obvious access to the briefs hosted on the Court's site. Instead, they are listed on each opinion's docket report. To retrieve a brief, visit the **Docket Search** page (https://www.supremecourt.gov/docket/docket.aspx), enter a docket number or a case name into the docket search box, and then select the case you are interested in from the list of retrieved cases if there is more than one. Scroll through the docket report until you find the brief that interests you and click the blue **Main Document** link to view the brief.

### Opinions, Orders, and Other Resources on the U.S. Supreme Court Website

For a discussion of opinions and orders and other resources on the U.S. Supreme Court website, please see Chapter 7. See Chapters 5, 6, 8, and 9 for other free websites that have better search options and date coverage for Supreme Court opinions than the U.S. Supreme Court's website.

## STATE, FEDERAL, AND LOCAL COMPLAINTS

**Courthouse News Service** (http://www.courthousenews.com), while not a full-fledged docket database, offers access to selected civil complaints filed in over 1,600 federal, state, and local courts—but only to paid subscribers. (Even though access to complaints are not free, we mention it here because many law librarians find this service useful.) For information about which courts are covered and for subscription information, you must call (909) 483-6165, or e-mail csage@courthousenews.com, or submit their online form found at https://www.courthousenews.com/information.

# Chapter 16

## SOCIAL MEDIA

This chapter is not geared to teaching lawyers how to have a social media presence and how to manage and schedule their own accounts. Instead, it is geared towards teaching you how to research a few of the most popular social media sites to quickly find social media profiles of people you need to gather information about. Besides searching for people, you can also search for companies or even governmental agencies, because entities can also create accounts on many of the social media sites. Because social media profile owners often "overshare," you might find the following types of information to use as evidence or as background about:

- an opposing party in a personal injury lawsuit who claimed extensive injuries but posted photos of a very active lifestyle;
- a potential or current client who failed to tell you something which has an important bearing on their case or transaction;
- a potential hire or expert witness who said or did something on social media that might give you pause in hiring or retaining them.

Information in social media profiles can also be useful for conducting due diligence about a client's potential business partner; deciding whether to retain or challenge a potential juror; discrediting an expert witness; or learning about a judge's biases for disqualification purposes. In addition, information found in social media profiles could help you find an address of a missing party for service of process, a witness you need to subpoena, or even a missing heir.

We hope by now you know about the ABA's 2012 change to Comment [8] of its *Model Rules of Professional Conduct*, Rule 1.1 (http://bit.ly/ABACommentRule1-1), which says that lawyers "should keep abreast of changes in the law and its practice, *including the benefits and risks associated with relevant technology*" [emphasis added]. (As of this writing, thirty-six states have adopted this comment.) Seeing that social media sites are "technology" and that information from them has become a useful source of evidence, it comes within "relevant technology." Thus, lawyers should have an ethical duty to be familiar with the benefits and risks of using social media—at least lawyers in the thirty-eight states that have adopted Comment 8 and in jurisdictions that have issued ethics opinions on this topic, such as New Hampshire and the District of Columbia. For example, the New Hampshire Bar Association Ethics Committee issued an Advisory Opinion that specifically advises lawyers that they "have a general duty to be aware of social media as a source of potentially useful information in litigation, to be competent to obtain that information directly or through an agent, and to know how to make effective use of that information in litigation" (Advisory Opinion 2012-13/05, *Social Media Contact with Witnesses in the Course of Litigation*, June 20, 2013, available at http://bit.ly/NHBarEthicsOp2012-13-05). The DC Bar Association's Ethics Opinion 371 (2016) states, "Because of society's embrace of technology, a lawyer's ignorance or disregard of it, including social media, presents a risk of ethical misconduct" (http://linkon.in/2qOJl96). Using these two ethics opinions as guidance, lawyers should be advised that ignoring relevant evidence from social media could likely be an ethical breach. And, they cannot use ignorance of social media as a defense to failing to search social media sites for relevant information.

**Ethics Alert!** Three social media sites, **LinkedIn**, **Twitter**, and **Classmates** have the ability to alert your subject when you've searched his or her profile. This could cause an ethical violation of MRPC Rule 3.5 Impartiality and Decorum of the Tribunal (a lawyer shall not communicate with a member of the venire or jury before and during trial, except during official proceedings) and MRPC Rule 4-2 (no communication with a represented party). There are ways to avoid this alert feature, which we'll discuss in more detail in the upcoming **LinkedIn** and **Twitter** sections.

We will only touch briefly on researching social media profiles, and doing so ethically, because it would take another book to cover every detail of social media research (and ethics). (In fact, one author of this book has written a seventy-five-page social media research and ethics chapter in another book. Some of this chapter is excerpted from Chapter 20 of that book, *The Cybersleuth's Guide to the Internet: Conducting Effective Free Investigative & Legal Research on the Web*, 14th edition, available at http://bit.ly/cyberabalp.)

## FACEBOOK

Facebook is the social media site that most lawyers search for evidence because it has the most users and contains the most amount of information about users. In fact, our search at Google Scholar for case law in the first quarter of 2019, using the keywords *facebook* and *evidence*, produced 691 case results.

Without being logged into your own account, it is impossible to search on Facebook (https://www.facebook.com). However, if a Facebook account is public, you can use search engines to find someone's profile. The easiest way to find these public Facebook profiles is by searching at a search engine like this: *site:facebook.com carole levitt*. Then, when you click the search results link for the profile of the person who set their profile to public, you will be able to view their profile at Facebook, unless they've tinkered with some other settings, in which case you can only view their primary profile page and photo.

If you log into your account, you can conduct a simple name search by using the search box at the top, left-hand side of the Facebook screen (Figure 16.1). (Facebook users do not know that you have searched their profiles.) This will often turn up the profile of your investigation target because most people use their real name to set up their profile. However, if it's a common name, you may get too many results to cull through, so the best way to search is by entering your target's name into the search box and adding a relevant keyword (e.g., their city, profession, or an interest). Using only keywords to search Facebook is possible, but the results are very hit or miss (mostly miss).

Although not widely known, you used to be able to enter the e-mail address or phone number of your target into the search box. That was very useful when your target had a common name or used a pseudonym. As of April 2018, Facebook disabled this search, so it's become more difficult to find your hard-to-find targets.

**Figure 16.1** Mark Rosch's Facebook Profile. Screenshot from Facebook used with permission.

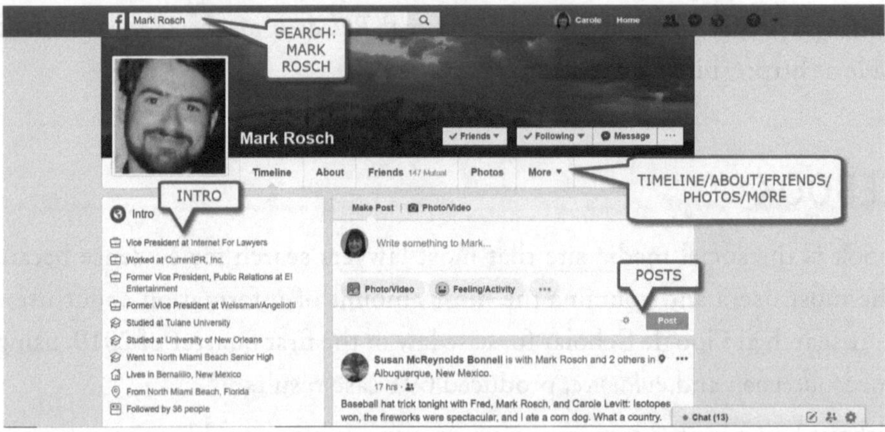


If you can view someone's full profile, this means it is public, or you are his or her Friend, or a Friend of a Friend. Here (Figure 16.1), I am Mark's friend. The first thing I see on Mark Rosch's Facebook profile is his primary Facebook photo on the top of the page (and you will see this even if a profile is private) and his **Intro** on the far left side (Figure 16.1). The search result defaults to his **Timeline**, which displays **Posts** he wrote or ones his friends posted to him. And by clicking on the tabs to the right of **Timeline** (**About**, **Friends**, **Photos**, and **More**), I can see more information.

If you can't see the full profile, then it is a private profile, available only to their Friends or Friends of Friends. However, you can always see their Facebook profile name and primary photo, and if they made individual posts or photos public, you could see those.

Private lawyers cannot subpoena someone else's profile from a social media site because the 1986 Stored Communications Act (SCA), 18 U.S.C. § 2701 et seq. prevents it (http://bit.ly/nofbsubpoena). However, they may be able to subpoena the "customer records"—the name and email address of the profile owner who opened the account. This is helpful if a profile displays a pseudonym and you must prove who owns the account, which we'll discuss later.

Since you can't subpoena a profile from a social media site, you must request production via discovery. We suggest you try to find your target's profile before requesting it via discovery, just in case they decide to delete it after you request it. If your target refuses to produce, judges will typically compel them to turn over their profile if it's relevant to the matter. Facebook provides a method to download an entire profile. The account owner (your target) must be logged into his/her account and enter this URL (http://bit.ly/downloadfbinfo) into the browser (not into the Facebook search box). Then, the account owner would click the link labeled: **Download Your Information.** You will probably want to ask the judge to have the account owner download his/her profile *in camera,* so your target does not delete or change anything.

Now we'll discuss how you might subpoena the "customer records" from Facebook. Their Help page (http://bit.ly/yesfbrecsub) reads in part:

> Account Information
>
> Facebook may provide the available basic subscriber information (not content) where the requested information is indispensable to the case, and not within a party's possession upon personal service of a valid subpoena or court order and after notice to affected account holders.
>
> If you are domiciled within the U.S. or Canada, the subpoena must be a valid federal, California or California domesticated subpoena, addressed to and served on Facebook, Inc. If you are domiciled outside the U.S. or Canada, the subpoena or court order must be addressed to and served on Facebook Ireland Limited.
>
> Any such subpoena or court order should be limited in scope to seek basic subscriber information only, and set out the specific accounts at issue by identifying them by URL or Facebook user ID (UID). Names, birthdays, locations, and other information are insufficient.

It is unclear if you must provide Facebook with the numerical UID or if the vanity URL (which Facebook allows people to create to replace the numeric UID) is good enough. Once you find your target's Facebook page, their numerical UID (or their vanity URL) is displayed in the browser. If a Facebook user's UID looks like this:

*https://www.facebook.com/profile.php?id=52188973194*

the string of numbers that follow ***?id=*** (in this example *52188973194*) is the number you must supply to Facebook. If the Facebook user's URL looks like this:

*https://www.facebook.com/ElPintoRestaurant*

this means they have created a vanity URL. Copy this URL, then visit **Find Your Facebook ID** (http://findmyfbid.in) and paste it into the search box. After you click **Find numeric ID** this site will retrieve the Facebook user's numerical UID. (Despite the site's name, you can use it to retrieve anyone's Facebook ID number.)

## YOUTUBE

YouTube (http://www.youtube.com) is a free video-sharing website where anyone can create and upload their own videos to share with others or view the videos created and shared by others. From its launch in 2005, YouTube has grown into one of the most popular sites on the Web, with an estimated 1.3 billion users. Our search at Google Scholar for case law in the first quarter of 2019, using the keywords *youtube* and *evidence*, produced 124 case results. Because the site is meant to publicly display and share video, you can search it without having an account of your own. The search box at the top of the YouTube homepage allows you to search the site's billions of videos by keywords. Google acquired YouTube in 2006.

Just as with Google, there are a number of specific search operators and instructions you can use in the search box to narrow down your search results. For example, you can limit your search to:

- an exact phrase by enclosing your keywords in quotation marks (e.g., "street racing");
- a specific time range by including the instructions hour, today, month, week, or year along with your keywords (e.g., *"street racing", today*).

You can enter a target's name into the search box as a keyword (or phrase) but in order to be displayed in search results, their name has to be included in the title or description of a video, or in the name of a YouTube channel. Note that there can be some false positives for these types of searches, where videos are returned in the results even when the name you've searched does not appear in the title or description. This can occur when the name does appear in the title or description of an associated video (e.g., one that is next on a playlist or is recommended in the right-hand side bar). You can eliminate some of these false positives by instructing YouTube to limit your keyword to appearing only in the title of returned search results by using the **allintitle** search instruction this way: *allintitle:"Mark Rosch"*.

## TWITTER ACCOUNTS

You can use **Twitter** (https://twitter.com) to conduct investigative research about a person (or to figure out the best people to follow on Twitter who write about your practice area). Our search at Google Scholar for case law in the first quarter of 2019, using the keywords *twitter* and *evidence*, produced 97 case results.

If you have an account and have logged into it, a search box appears in the upper right corner to search by a person's name or by keywords. However, if you do not have an account (or you have one, but have not logged into it), you can't simply visit **Twitter's** homepage to search because there is no search box on **Twitter's** homepage. If you don't wish to set up a **Twitter** account, but still wish to search it, visit **Twitter's Advanced search** page (https://twitter.com/search-advanced) and there you will be able to search through the millions of individual tweets. Even if you have an account, you might prefer to use the **Advanced search** because it allows you to create more sophisticated searches than the homepage's simple search box. For that reason, we'll focus only on the **Advanced search** box.

A Twitter profile displays two names: the **Profile** name (also called display name), which could be the person's real name or a pseudonym and a **Username** (also called account name or handle). For example, my profile name is *Carole Levitt* and my username is: *@carolelevitt*. (Many usernames are the person's first and last name mashed together.) If your subject is using their real name as their profile name, you can enter it into the **All the words** search box to find their profile. Once you do that, you will see their username displayed on their profile. From there, you can go to the **Advanced search** menu and enter their username into the **People** search boxes to locate tweets: **From these accounts, To these accounts**, or **Mentioning these accounts**. Entering their profile name won't work.

Besides searching by a person's profile name or username, you can also enter keywords into the various Boolean search boxes. (You can also add a date range or a place.) For example, you could search for people who tweet about criminal law in the UK and restrict the tweets to specific dates by entering: *uk* into the **All of these words** search box, *criminal law* into the **This exact phrase** search box, and *2018-11-06 to 2018-11-08* into the **From this date** search box.

By default, **Twitter** accounts are public, so you can read almost all tweets. (In contrast, **Facebook** accounts, by default, are not public; they are set to "friends," so you may not be able to read certain posts unless the Facebook account holder has taken the step to change the account default to public or made an individual post public.) Twitter alerts a user you are following them only if you proactively click **Follow**, so don't click **Follow** if you are doing clandestine research, because, as noted earlier, this could be tantamount to an ethical violation. (See also the **LinkedIn** section of this chapter for ethical violation examples.)

## INSTAGRAM

Instagram (http://www.instagram.com) is a social networking site focused on sharing images and video. Account owners or visitors can add comments to the images. Our search at Google Scholar for case law in the first quarter of 2019, using the keywords *Instagram* and *evidence*, produced 83 case results.

By default, all photos posted to Instagram are public. Users can also make their accounts private, so that only people who follow them on Instagram will be able to see their photos. If they have made their profiles private, their photos are not returned in search results. You must be logged into your own Instagram account to be able to search, but its search capabilities are not as robust as other social networking sites we've discussed. You can use the search box at the top of the Instagram site to search by keyword, username, hashtag, or place of interest. Because there is very little text associated with Instagram accounts, we do not find this site to be that useful for gathering detailed background information about a person. But it could be useful as a source of evidence if you are, for example, trying to tie a gun used in a crime to a certain person who is pictured with that gun in his or her Instagram account.

## LINKEDIN

**LinkedIn** (or **Linkedin**; it's spelled both ways at their site) is a professional networking site (http://www.linkedin.com) and can be used by attorneys in much the same way that they use Facebook and other social media sites. LinkedIn users typically want to be found—thus, they use their real names. This makes the LinkedIn site an ideal tool for finding people, especially professionals. Our search at Google Scholar for case law in the first quarter of 2019, using the keywords *linkedin* and *evidence*, produced 44 case results.

LinkedIn allows you to search when you're not logged into an account by entering a first and last name into the **Find a colleague** search boxes. But then, a pop-up asks you to join or sign in. If you do neither, but just click **Search**, LinkedIn does one of two things: (1) it might show you a results list, but it won't let you see any profiles or (2) it won't even show the results list but just asks you to sign in or join. (LinkedIn used to show you a results list and let you view profiles, but now it doesn't.) To view profiles, you must be logged into your account. But even then, you might not see much because individual profile owners can set their LinkedIn privacy settings to limit the information people to whom they are not directly connected to can see.

Once you log into your account, you can search for others' profiles by entering a name (person or company) or even keywords or phrases into the **Search** box on the top left side of the page (Figure 16.2). When you click into the **Search** box, a drop-down menu (not shown in Figure 16.2) allows you to narrow down your search by using **People, Jobs,** or **Post** filters and also shows your recent searches if you want to click on one to re-run it.

**Figure 16.2** Carole Levitt's LinkedIn profile and search box. Screenshot from LinkedIn used with permission.

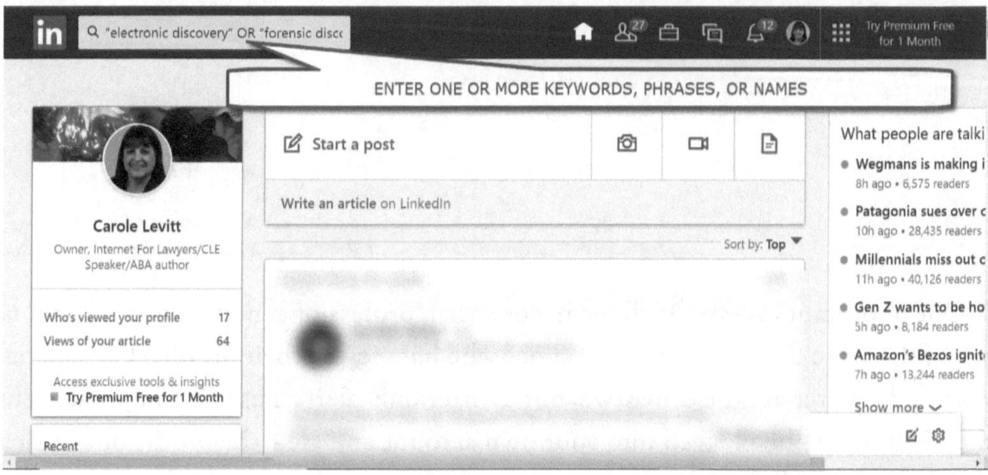


Like at Google, the LinkedIn search box allows you to search with keywords or phrases and allows you to connect your keywords or phrases using three Boolean connectors (*AND, OR,* and *NOT*). LinkedIn's Boolean connector default is AND, so there is no need to type it in between your keywords or phrases. In Figure 16.3, we conducted a phrase search (*"electronic discovery" OR "forensic discovery"*) to locate an expert in this field. The OR and the NOT Boolean connectors must be capitalized for LinkedIn to recognize them as connectors, while the keywords and phrases can be upper or lower case.

Our search results brought back too many results, so we used the **Location** filter and narrowed our results to **San Francisco Bay Area** (Figure 16.3). To narrow our search further, we can use the **Connections** or **Current Companies** filter tabs or we can click **All Filters** for even more ways to narrow the search, such as by: **Title, Industries, Profile language, Schools,** etc. For instance, you could filter by adding the word *attorney* into the **Title** filter box and adding a school name into the **Schools** filter box. Alternatively, if the person you are searching for hasn't designated their

**Title** as "attorney" but the person has noted somewhere in his/her profile the word "attorney" you'd find them by putting all these keywords into the original search box instead of using the filter search boxes.

**Figure 16.3** LinkedIn Search Results. Screenshot from LinkedIn used with permission.

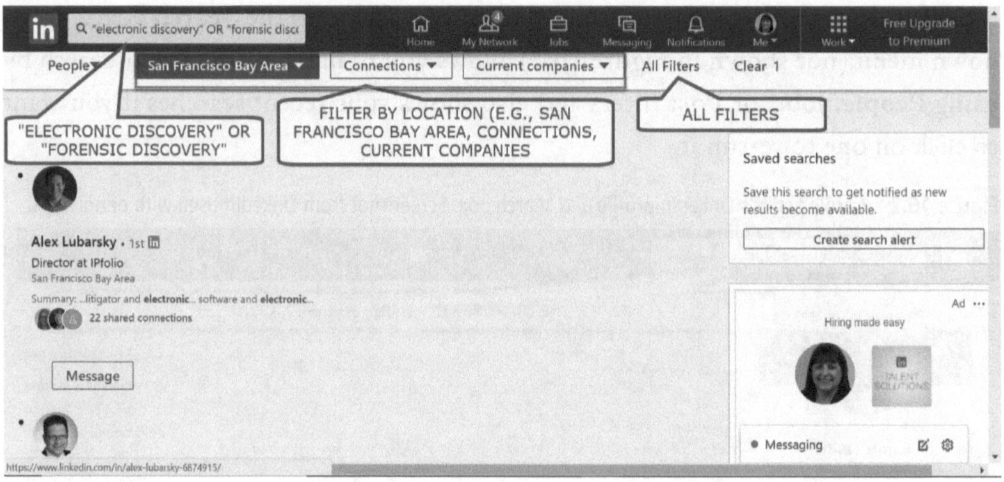


One important caveat: Of all the major social/professional networks, LinkedIn is one of the three that alerts its users about who has viewed their profile. (Classmates .com and Twitter are the other two, but Twitter only alerts a user if you proactively click **Follow.**) When logged into your own account and view the profile of another user, LinkedIn will report your name, title, employer, and geographic location (from your profile) to that user so they know exactly who has viewed his or her profile. Luckily for searchers who do not want to leave a trail, LinkedIn gives you the ability to turn this option off. To do so, click **Me** (under your profile picture in the upper right-hand corner of your profile) and from the drop-down menu, click on **Settings & Privacy.** On the later screens, click the **Privacy** tab at the top of the screen, and then **Profile viewing options.** You can then choose from two levels of anonymity. You can choose **Private profile characteristics** (e.g., **Business Owner in the Legal Services industry from Albuquerque, New Mexico Area**) or you can choose **Private mode,** leaving no trace of your identity when you visit the other user (e.g., **Anonymous LinkedIn Member**).

Note that when others view your LinkedIn profile, the highest level of information you get about their visit to your profile will be the level of information you have opted to leave about yourself (even if visitors have selected to leave a higher level of information about themselves).

**Ethics Alert!** Before selecting a jury or when a jury is empaneled, if you plan to research jurors' profiles, set your **LinkedIn** privacy settings to **Anonymous LinkedIn Member** so LinkedIn alerts no one you've searched their profile. Some ethics opinions find that LinkedIn's automatic alert constitutes *you* communicating with a member of the venire or jury and *you* violating MRPC Rule 3.5 Impartiality and Decorum of the Tribunal, which says except during official proceedings before and during trial, a lawyer shall not: communicate with a member of the venire or jury. The same admonition goes for when you are in anticipation of, or in, litigation. You don't want to have a social media site contact a represented party; this would violate MRPC Rule 4-2 (no communication with a represented party). These same warnings apply to **Twitter,** which also alerts a user you have researched their account, but only if you proactively click **Follow,** so don't click **Follow.**

You are only allowed to download your own LinkedIn profile, so if you want to download someone else's profile (e.g., an opposing party), you must move to compel that person to log in to their account and then visit this link: http://bit.ly/LinkedInDownloadProfile to begin the download process. (This link only works when logged in to the account to be downloaded.) Then, the account owner would click the radio button to the left of **Download larger data archive, including connections, contacts, and your account history** or click the radio button to the left of **Want something in particular? Select the data files you're most interested in.** After making one of two choices, the account owner would then click the **Request archive** button.

## PINTEREST

Pinterest (http://www.pinterest.com) is a different kind of social network that provides users with virtual "boards" where they can "pin" images they create or find on the Internet. The boards are usually categorized into topical collections that the user can then share with other users. Pinterest's value is more as a background research tool to learn about an individual's interests, hobbies, and so on. Our search at Google Scholar for case law in the first quarter of 2019, using the keywords *pinterest* and *evidence,* produced only 13 case results.

You do have to be logged into your own Pinterest account in order to search the site. Once logged in, use the search box at the top of the page to search for individuals by name. The default set of results (All Pins) utilizes the OR Boolean connector and displays pins that include either the first or last name (or both) of the individual for whom you searched. Click the Pinners named option at the bottom of the drop-down/suggestions list beneath the search box to see user name matches for your search terms. Some users are easy to identify in the search results because they have included a photo of themselves in their profile—but not all users have done this.

Like any social networking site, some people use their real name and some use a pseudonym. If you have identified a profile at another social networking site where your target has used a pseudonym, use that pseudonym as a keyword to search Pinterest (or at any other social network you are searching for that person) as people often reuse the same pseudonym at multiple sites.

While the primary purpose of Pinterest is to collect and share images, users do have the ability to create "secret boards" that can only be seen by the creator and anyone they invite to view the board. Since pictures pinned to secret boards don't show up anywhere else on Pinterest, so be sure to ask at deposition or in interrogatories if your subject has any secret Pinterest boards.

## SNAPCHAT

Snapchat is a different animal than the social media sites we've been discussing. First, Snapchat is a smart phone application and not a website, so users send "Snaps" (pictures and videos) and "Chats" (text messages) to each other via their smart phone.

Other differences are that "Snapchat profiles are very basic, containing little more than a person's username and profile picture. You can only view the profiles of friends, people who've added you, or people who sent you a chat. You have to use the Snapchat app to see others' profiles" (https://m.wikihow.com/View-Snapchat-Profile) and Snapchat is searched by username, not a person's real name.

The final difference is the ephemeral nature of Snapchat. Snaps are automatically deleted after all recipients view them. If unopened, they are deleted from Snapchat's servers after thirty days (or twenty-four hours if the Snap was sent to a group Chat). Chats have similar rules, but they can be saved. If you create "My Stories" or "Custom Stories," they are deleted after twenty-four hours, but if you save "Custom Stories" to your "Memories" they are kept on Snapchat's servers until you delete them. Go to Snapchat's **Privacy Policy** and then click **Support Site** to learn more about how long Snapchat stores other types of content, how accessible the content is to others, and how "Custom Stories" can be saved by anyone in the Story who takes a screenshot.

Our search at Google Scholar for case law in the first quarter of 2019, using the keywords *snapchat* and *evidence,* produced 48 case results, but in a brief review of many of these cases, it seems that oftentimes, the actual content from Snapchat wasn't admitted into evidence. Instead, a witness testified about seeing an image posted from a particular user's Snapchat account. For instance, in *State v. Heard,* 2019 Ohio 1227, ¶27 (Ct. App. 2019), "Colpetro also testified that, sometime after the shooting, she saw an image posted from Appellant's "Snapchat" account showing a gun. . .."

## SOCIAL MEDIA PROFILE COLLECTION VENDORS

There are a number of services that have been created for the sole purpose of crawling the publicly available portions of profiles and storing copies of them as they change over time. Be aware, you cannot use a website collection vendor to surreptitiously capture a private profile (different rules apply for law enforcement officials). You can use a website collection vendor to capture public social media profiles, however. And, if you obtain written permission from your own client, you could use a website collection vendor to collect your client's private profile instead of having the client use the social media sites' download tools described earlier.

The advantage to using one of these services is that the collection and archiving of the information is done automatically, the archives are searchable, and the vendors (generally) provide some sort of verification and authentication of the captured information. Another advantage these services offer is the ability to manipulate the content as if it was live (e.g., expand comment threads, play videos, and enlarge photos).

Although you can research and capture the information yourself, it takes time and if you are going to enter the information as evidence, you may become involved as a witness in your client's case, which is not a position you want to be in. Another drawback to collecting information yourself is the inability to collect metadata about the content (e.g., dates, times, GPS information, and computers from which content was posted) that can be equally important as the content itself. The third-party services generally capture this metadata.

The following are some the best-known web content collection vendors:

- **ArchiveSocial** (http://www.archivesocial.com) captures content in its "native format" (e.g., images, videos, etc.) and offers the ability to "replay" the content you've captured as if you were viewing it the day it was captured. You can read and expand comment threads, play videos, enlarge photos, and so forth. ArchiveSocial also lets you export the archived content in its native format(s), PDF, or HTML. While the service is marketed primarily to the financial services industry and government agencies as a compliance tool, it can also be used for capturing content from opposing parties, and so forth. Prices start at $199 per month to capture up to 1,000 posts and other content from up to 10 social networking accounts. Prices increase for higher volumes of captured information.

- **Nextpoint** (http://www.nextpoint.com) captures available posts from the social networking accounts of your target and stores them on Nextpoint's secure servers. Data are stored in their native format. This includes not only the posts, but also links to content on other sites (e.g., "videos, news or Facebook posts linked to from archived records") and files embedded in the posts (e.g., PDF, Word, Excel). Previously, posted prices began at $295 per month for unlimited captures and storage for a single case. The company now requires you to contact them for pricing. A free trial is available.
- **PageFreezer** (http://www.pagefreezer.com) offers two separate solutions for capturing Web pages and available content of social networking accounts. The first solution is the company's managed account, which is designed to capture multiple-page websites or social media profiles and store them on PageFreezer's secure servers. The second solution, Web Preserver, is a plug-in for the Chrome Web browser designed specifically to capture single pages locally, on your own computer. (Multi-page captures may be available in future releases.) Both solutions capture content in their native format with date and time stamps for authentication. Captured pages and posts not only look the same as they did when they were captured, but you can also click through the links and be taken to captured versions of the content the link pointed to on the day the content and link was captured. Comment threads can also be expanded and contracted. Content captured with either solution can be keyword-searched and exported as native files or PDFs. Pricing for capturing a single social media account is $475. Web Preserver's monthly fee includes a set number of captures. Additional captures and sharing features are available at additional cost.

For more information about collecting social media profiles as evidence, see *Six Best Practices for Capturing Social Media for Use as Evidence in a Court of Law*, an article by a website collection vendor, **Page Vault** (https://www.page-vault.com), who posted a useful guest post at lawtechnologytoday.org on February 20, 2018 (http://bit.ly/pagevaultcapture).

## USING SOCIAL MEDIA TO RESEARCH LAWYERS OR LEGAL TOPICS

See Chapter 17 to learn about lawyer-oriented blog and tweet sites.

# Chapter 17

# RESEARCHING LEGAL PROFESSIONALS

### FINDING BACKGROUND INFORMATION ABOUT ATTORNEYS, JUDGES, AND OTHER LEGAL PROFESSIONALS

## CONTACT AND LICENSING INFORMATION

Researching people is an entire book in itself, so this chapter will focus only on researching legal professionals (primarily attorneys and judges). (For a book on investigative research co-authored by one author of this book, see *The Cybersleuth's Guide to the Internet: Conducting Effective Free Investigative & Legal Research on the Web*, 14th edition, by Carole Levitt and Mark Rosch, available at http://bit.ly/cyberabalp.)

Whether it's an attorney you are opposing, hiring, referring a matter to, or with whom you are associating, it's always a good idea to first research the status of his or her license. For information about attorneys' license status, disciplinary action taken against them, and their contact data, check the appropriate state bar site if membership in the state bar is mandatory (commonly called unified or integrated) in that jurisdiction. But if the state bar is voluntary, check the state's attorney licensing site (often the state's supreme court).

In some states, an attorney may opt out of being listed on the association's directory (or even on the attorney licensing site), and some states don't even offer an online searchable database. To help with these issues, the **Internet For Lawyers** website provides a state-by-state directory of attorney licensing databases (http://bit.ly/ifllawyerlicense). Use the drop-down **Select a State** menu to link directly to the searchable databases of attorney licensing boards (or to the unified state bar association) in forty-five states, and the District of Columbia. There are also tips on getting information from bars that don't offer an online searchable database or from those that allow members to opt out of the online database.

The **ABA Division for Bar Services** provides a useful color-coded map of the United States to help determine whether a state's bar association is unified or voluntary at http://bit.ly/volbarorunified. (The map is on the right side of the page; you may need to scroll down to see it.) Voluntary bar associations are shown. You can also search for a particular bar's website by entering the state name into the search box at the ABA's State & Local Bar Associations Directory and then clicking the link (http://bit.ly/findabar).

## LAWYER DIRECTORIES WITH BIOGRAPHIES

To locate background information about attorneys, there are several free lawyer directories with biographical information. There are three major ones: **Martindale-Hubbell** (Martindale; https://www.martindale.com), the **FindLaw Lawyer Directory** (https://lawyers.findlaw.com), and the **Justia Lawyer Directory** (https://www.justia.com/lawyers), and a few others. Some directories also offer lawyer ratings.

### Martindale-Hubbell

From 1868 until the Internet became popular, **Martindale-Hubbell** had been a print national lawyer directory and was the only game in town. Martindale eventually became an online directory, **Martindale.com** (https://www.martindale.com). Many other online directories soon became available, making the lawyer directory business fairly competitive. Martindale.com is now part of the Martindale-Avvo network (which includes Avvo.com, Lawyers.com, and Nolo.com). And, Martindale is not just a directory of attorney and law firm names and addresses (which included its AV rating system), but is now a site that expanded to include ratings from clients and peers and provides lawyer and firm website design, among other marketing tools.

To search or browse Martindale's directory, use the **Find an Attorney** page (https://www.martindale.com/find-attorneys) and then **Search by name, law**

**firm, organization, school, articles, or location** by entering them into the top search box (see Figure 17.1). In the search box below that, you are instructed to **Search by name, area of practice, or location.** We are not sure why there are two different search boxes.

**Figure 17.1** Martindale.com Find an Attorney: Search or Browse. Screenshot from Martindale.com used with permission.

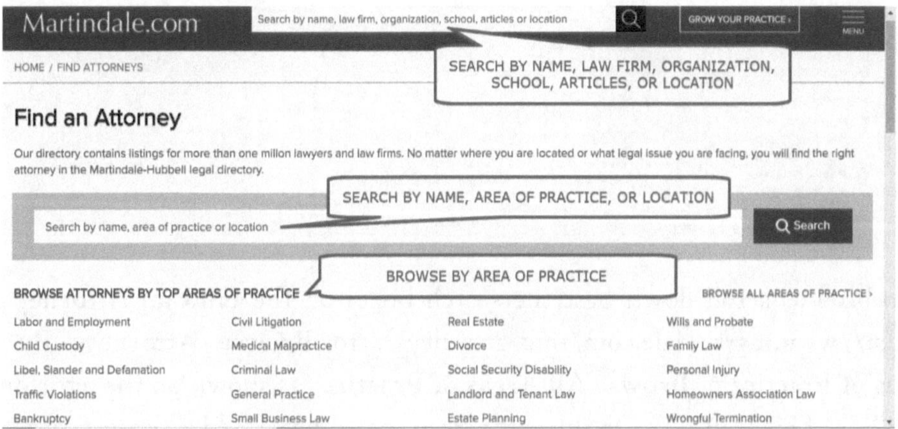


Although it appears that your searches can include a mix of criteria, not all lawyer profiles are as complete as others, so you might miss a result if a profile doesn't include all that criteria. Our search for *criminal law Chattanooga Levitt* retrieved two results, but one was a **Sponsored** result (Figure 17.2) for a firm that did not include *Levitt*. The other result matched our criteria. Results will show the firm name, city and state, and ratings (**Client Reviews** and **Peer Reviews**), if any. If a lawyer or firm has paid to be a **Sponsored** firm, the results page will include a **Contact** link (which allows a potential client to send a message to the firm from within Martindale.com), a **View Phone** link, and a **View Website** link on the right side of the page (Figure 17.2). When you click the firm name, you will see these links again and also the firm's address.

If you retrieve too many results, you can use the **Filters** (Figure 17.2) in the left-hand column to narrow by **Areas of Practice, Location, Peer Reviews, Client Reviews, Firm Size,** and **Bar Registry.**

**Figure 17.2** Martindale.com Find an Attorney search result. Screenshot from Martindale.com used with permission.

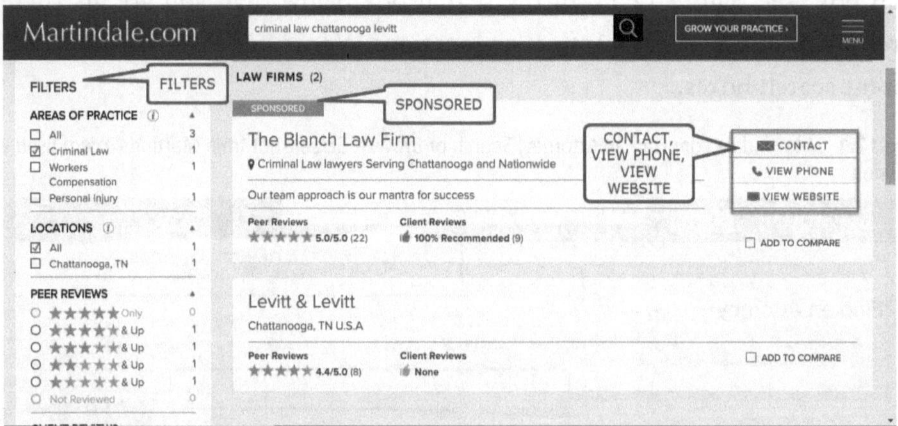


To browse, scroll down past the search boxes on the **Find an Attorney** page (https://www.martindale.com/find-attorneys), to **Browse Attorneys By Top Areas of Practice** or **Browse All Areas of Practice** (as shown on the left side and right side of Figure 17.3). On the next screen (not shown), add a location, otherwise you will see a very long list. As you continue to scroll down the initial **Find an Attorney** page, you can also browse attorneys by **Popular Cities**, the **United States**, **U.S. Territory**, **Canada**, **Other Countries**, or **States** (U.S.).

**Figure 17.3** Martindale.com Find an Attorney: Browse and Other Searches. Screenshot from Martindale.com used with permission.

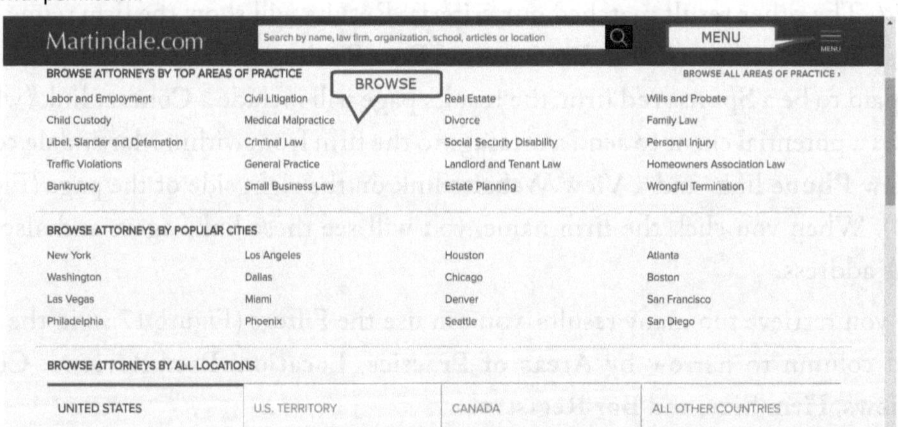

To conduct a variety of other searches, use the **Menu** icon on the top right-hand side of the page (Figure 17.3) and click one of these links: **Law School Alumni, Legal Library**, or **Bar Associations.**

The **Law School Alumni** search looks useful. You can search by a lawyer's name if you want background information about an individual. Or, you can click on a law school to display a list of their alumni. For instance, you could choose The John Marshall Law School, and view the list of over 10,000 alumni. To narrow your search even further, from there you can find one or more attorneys who match your needs by filtering by: areas of practice, locations, ratings (e.g, Peer Reviews by number of stars), Client Reviews (by percentage), Admissions (state and federal courts), languages, and so on.

The **Legal Library** section is not a search of libraries or librarians, but a content section divided into these categories: **Legal Alerts/Articles, White Papers, Court Documents,** and **Presentations.** Mostly, all these categories appear to be articles, although we did find some briefs in the **Court Documents** category. We did not see any forms in the **Forms** category; nor did we see any PowerPoints, videos, or audios in the **Presentations** category. The **Bar Associations** link allows you to obtain contact information for all U.S. State Bars and some foreign and international bars. The site no longer includes its **Experts and Services** database.

## FindLaw

The **FindLaw Lawyer Directory** (https://lawyers.findlaw.com; see Figure 17.4), owned by Thomson Reuters, provides two search boxes. The first is **What's your legal issue?** After you click into that box you can enter a legal issue or click **Legal Issues** from the **More Options** drop-down, where you can then click one of the listed **Legal Issues.** The second search box, to the right of **What's your legal issue?** is **Location** (Figure 17.4), which allows you to enter a city, ZIP Code, or state. The **More Options** (Figure 17.4) drop-down menu also offers other search and browse options (**Name Search, Browse Lawyers, Browse Law Firms, Browse Types of Cases** and **Help**).

If you don't click into the **What's your legal issue?** search box, you will see links to **Browse by: City, State,** or **Legal Issue** (the **More Options** drop-down menu is covering these links in Figure 17.4).

Figure 17.4 FindLaw's Find a Lawyer. Originally appeared on FindLaw.com. Used with permission.

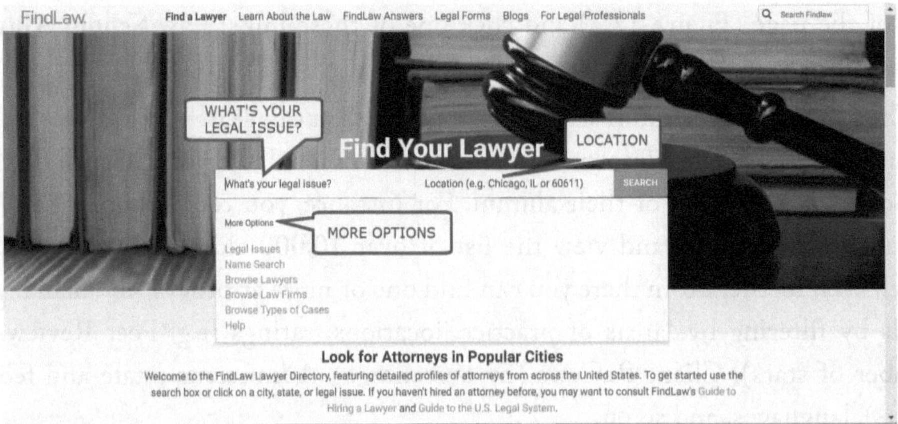


Once you retrieve a result you will see the name of the firm on the left side, and the following information (if available) will appear on the far right: the firm's phone number, a link to the firm's FindLaw Profile, a link to the firm's website, and a **Contact us** link.

## Justia

The **Justia Lawyer Directory** provides a basic search at https://www.justia.com/lawyers (see Figure 17.5). There are two search boxes at the top of the page. In the first search box, you can search by **Legal Issue** or **Lawyer Name**, and in the second search box you can enter a location. (Your city and state are automatically detected and filled in based on your Internet connection but can be easily changed.) Scroll down the page to browse by **Practice Area, State**, or **City**. All lawyers have a free listing with basic information and contact information. Justia allows lawyers who have a free Justia account and an active profile in the Justia Lawyer Directory to rate other lawyers on a scale of 1–10, based upon: Legal Knowledge, Legal Analysis, Communication Skills, and Ethics and Professionalism. Lawyers can "claim" their profiles by clicking **Update your profile now!** This is a free service that allows lawyers to create a more complete profile that can include their photo, biographical information, education and experience, websites and blogs, social media profiles, and more.

**Figure 17.5** Justia Lawyer Directory. Screenshot from Justia used with permission.

## Additional Directories

Here are a few other directories, some of which include a rating system for the lawyers listed:

- **Nolo** (https://www.nolo.com/lawyers) allows users to browse by **Location** or by **Practice Area.** Results include attorney and/or firm profiles and may also include licensing and disciplinary history information. You cannot search by attorney name. As mentioned in the Martindale entry earlier in this chapter, Nolo and Martindale are part of the same network.
- **Superlawyers.com** (https://www.superlawyers.com) includes "outstanding lawyers from more than 70 practice areas who have attained a high degree of peer recognition and professional achievement. This selection process includes independent research, peer nominations and peer evaluations." To search, first click **Search Lawyers** or **Search Firms** on the homepage. Then enter a lawyer or firm name into the search box. This same search box can also be used to search by legal issue instead. In the second search box, you can search by location. Click the **Browse All** link to browse by **Practice Area, Top Cities, State,** or **Region.** Once you click the **Browse All** link, another option appears, **Advanced Search.** Click that to enter criteria into a variety of search boxes, such as name, law school, international criteria, etc. **Superlawyers.com** is owned by Thomson Reuters.
- **Avvo.com** (https://www.avvo.com/find-a-lawyer) is a directory that also includes a rating system for lawyers. The Avvo Rating is based on information the lawyer has included on his or her profile besides the information

Avvo collects from public sources like state bar associations and lawyer websites. As explained by Avvo: "We create profiles and collect publicly available data for over 97% of US attorneys. Claiming your profile on Avvo allows you to add more information about you and your practice, allowing us to provide a more accurate Avvo Rating. We do not 'adjust' ratings by request, nor do we remove attorney profiles" (http://bit.ly/avvoremove). Clients can leave reviews for attorneys with whom they have worked, but only peer endorsements affect an Avvo Rating. You can search the directory by attorney or firm name or practice area, and location. (As with Justia, your city and state are automatically detected and filled in based on your Internet connection but can be easily changed.) You can also browse by city, state, or practice area. Avvo joined the Martindale Legal Marketing Network in 2018 and the network is now called Martindale-Avvo.

## JUDICIAL DIRECTORIES

Although a few of the resources discussed above provide limited information about judges, some specific sources are available for background information about judges.

All current and former Article III federal judges (i.e. judges appointed under Article III of the United States Constitution) can be searched at the Federal Judicial Center's **Biographical Directory of Article III Federal Judges, 1789–present** (https://www.fjc.gov/history/judges). Article III federal judges include judges from the:

- Supreme Court of the United States
- U.S. Courts of Appeal
- U.S. District Courts
- Court of International Trade
- U.S. Court of Claims
- U.S. Court of Customs and Patent Appeals
- U.S. Customs Court

To search the Biographical Directory of Article III Federal Judges by name, enter a last name only or a last name, first name (you must use the comma as shown) into the search box or browse names alphabetically by clicking a letter of the alphabet (see Figure 17.6).

**Figure 17.6** Biographical Directory of Federal Judges.

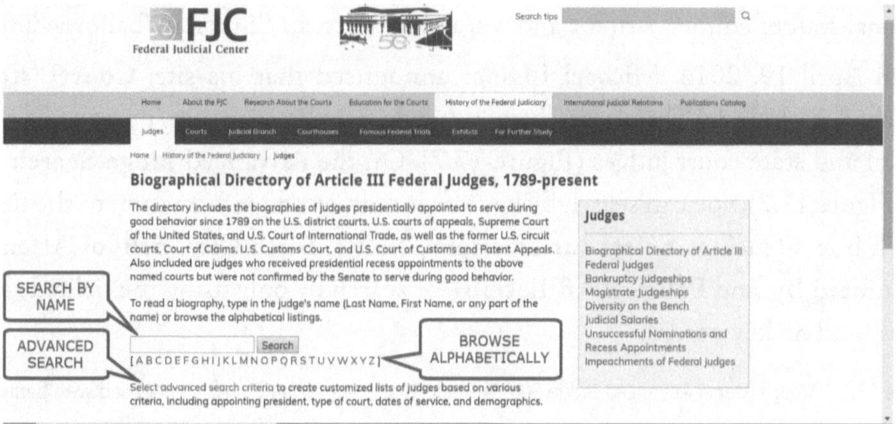


Besides viewing biographical information, you can create customized lists of judges based on various criteria, including the name of the president who appointed them, the type of court, dates of service, and demographics (Figure 17.6). To invoke this advanced search, click the **Select advanced search criteria** link on the home page (or visit http://bit.ly/FJCAdvanced). To create a customized list of female judges in the Court of Claims, click **Court** to choose Court of Claims and then click **Personal Characteristics and Background** to choose **Gender: Female.** (There are none.)

There is no official biographical directory for all Article I Judges. (Article I Judges include those from the: United States Court of Appeals for the Armed Forces, United States Court of Appeals for Veterans Claims, United States Tax Court, United States Bankruptcy Courts, and U.S. territorial courts in the Northern Mariana Islands, Guam, and the Virgin Islands.) There is also no official biographical directory for all state and local judges.

However, **Judgepedia,** now merged into **Ballotpedia,** filled this gap. **Ballotpedia** is an online encyclopedia of American politics and elections, but it also offers biographies (that vary in length and depth) of:

- U.S. Supreme Court justices (http://bit.ly/sctballot)
- state and local judges from the municipal and magistrate level up through state appeals courts judges and state supreme courts (http://bit.ly/stlocaljud)
- Article I Judges (http://bit.ly/art1judge)

The site also includes 269,707 encyclopedic articles written and curated by a professional staff of editors, writers, and researchers (https://linkon.in/ballotpedia).

On April 19, 2016, Michael Lissner announced that his site, **CourtListener**, launched its **Judicial Database** (https://www.courtlistener.com/person) of 8,500 federal and state court judges (Figure 17.7). On the **Advanced Judge Search** page (see Figure 17.7), you can search by keywords only, or add information to the fielded search boxes (such as **Select Jurisdictions, Name, Birth City, School Attended, Appointed By**, and **Political Affiliation**), or search by only using the fielded search boxes (and no keywords).

**Figure 17.7** CourtListener Advanced Judge Search Menu. Screenshot from CourtListener used with permission.

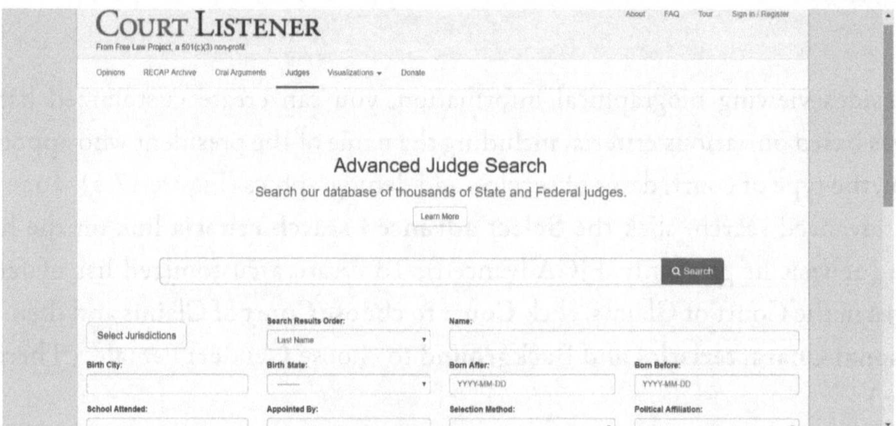


Results may include a judge's "biographical and educational background, judicial and non-judicial positions held, political affiliations, American Bar Association ratings, campaign finance data, and opinions authored [by a particular judge]" as shown in Figure 17.8 (https://www.courtlistener.com/person). Some judicial profiles are more complete than others. For instance, our search of *william guild democrat* yielded no results, but our search for *william guild* yielded one result. As it turns out, his profile was not as complete as others because his lacked his political affiliation.

As to the judicial and non-judicial positions held, Lissner added the following details (https://linkon.in/ctlistabout):

- The judicial positions they have held: The core of this data is a list of courts and dates for each judge, but it also includes details about their specific position, how they were nominated or elected, what the voting outcome was, who appointed them, the clerks they supervised, and nearly a dozen dates about the timing of their nomination process.

- The non-judicial positions they have held: The database aims to include comprehensive timelines of a judge's full career both before and after being a judge. This includes work in other branches of government, in private practice, and in academia.

In 2016, CourtListener also launched a project to gather and curate judicial portraits. Although the site does not yet have a portrait of every judge in its database, many profiles include a portrait of the judge. Many profiles also include links to the opinions that the judge has authored (see Figure 17.8). Some information may be incorrect. For instance, in our result for Judge Guild, we noticed he was born in 1993 but served as a judge from 1969–1980. A **Google** search with a link to **Wikipedia** showed he died in 1993. Fortunately, **CourtListener** allows you to report errors; scroll down to the end of the profile to **Something isn't right?** If you click **Get in touch with a correction,** a **Contact Us** form is offered where you can provide a correction.

**Figure 17.8** CourtListener Judge Search results: biographical information and links to opinions. Screenshot from CourtListener used with permission.

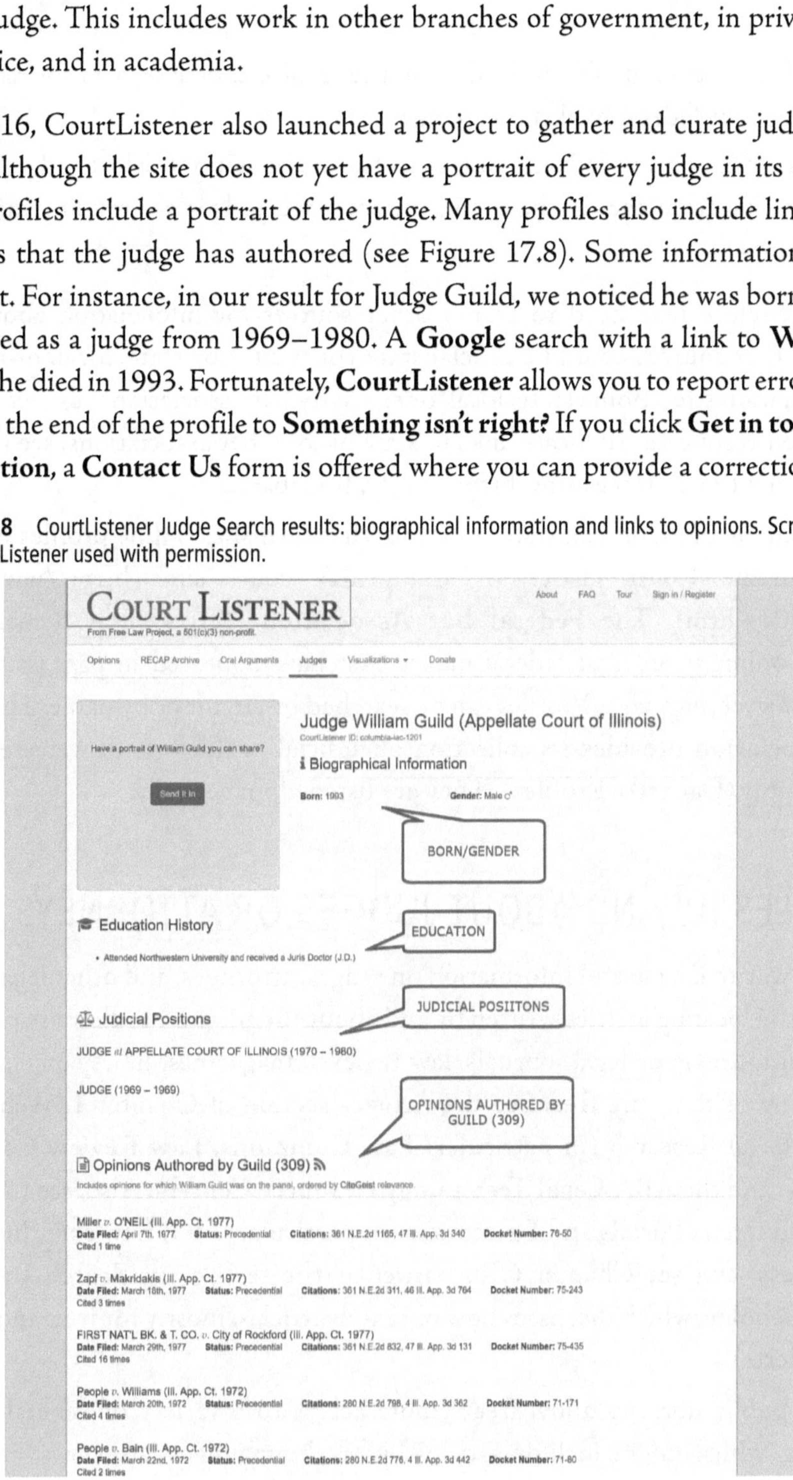

Although Lissner's original announcement about CourtListener's Judicial Database proclaimed the database was comprehensive, he added that (https://linkon.in/ctlistabout):

- We have been unable to find a comprehensive source of data for magistrate judges or federal bankruptcy judges.
- The data on lower court judges in the states is poor. Most judges are still missing from the database and the included judges are missing many data points.

You therefore may need to search other sources for information about some judges. Other sources could be official state court sites or state, local, or specialty bar association sites. Some state, local, or specialty bar associations restrict who can access their resources. To locate links to state or local bar associations, see the **ABA Division for Bar Services** site (http://bit.ly/findabar).

An example of an official state court site that furnishes online profiles of its sitting Supreme Court justices is California's court site (http://www.courts.ca.gov/3014.htm). The **Federal Bar Association** (http://bit.ly/fedbarproind) provides online profiles of federal judges that have appeared in past issues of its *Federal Lawyer* magazine. Profiles can be searched by circuit or by name. The **Dallas Bar Association** provides its collection of judicial profiles to all website visitors (http://bit.ly/DallasBarProfiles). They are listed alphabetically.

## ARTICLES BY AND ABOUT JUDGES OR ATTORNEYS

Another way to find useful information on judges, attorneys, and other legal professionals is by locating articles written by and about them, whether they are published in general journals or legal journals/law reviews, magazines, newspapers, or websites. Many of these are free. See the Articles section of Chapter 1, Websites for General Legal Research (in particular: **Law Commons, Law Review Commons, Lexology**, and the **ABA Legal Technology Resource Center**). Also, see Chapter 4, Free Commercial Portals and Directories (in particular: **HG, Law.com, Justia,** and **Nolo Press,** and see Chapter 6, in particular the section on **Search Results in Google Scholar,** which discusses how to search articles, mostly for free, and also set up free alerts).

Some public libraries allow free remote access to a variety of general or legal databases, which might include articles by or about judges, attorneys, and other legal professionals. You can use a search engine to find your library's URL and then visit the library's site to learn which databases your local public library subscribes to that you access remotely for free. One of the databases some libraries offer remote access to is **LegalTrac**, which indexes articles from legal periodicals and legal newspapers. While **LegalTrac** primarily offers abstracts, some articles are available in full text.

# USING LEGAL PROFESSIONAL-ORIENTED SOCIAL MEDIA TO RESEARCH LEGAL TOPICS, LAWYERS, OR JUDGES

## Justia's LegalBirds

As we mentioned in Chapter 16, you can use Twitter to figure out the best people who write about your practice area and then follow them on Twitter, but to narrow your search down to just legal professionals, see **Justia's LegalBirds** (http://legalbirds.justia.com). It's a directory of legal "tweeters" arranged by **Categories** and **Practice Areas** (see Figure 17.9).

**Figure 17.9** Justia's LegalBirds. Screenshot from Justia used with permission.

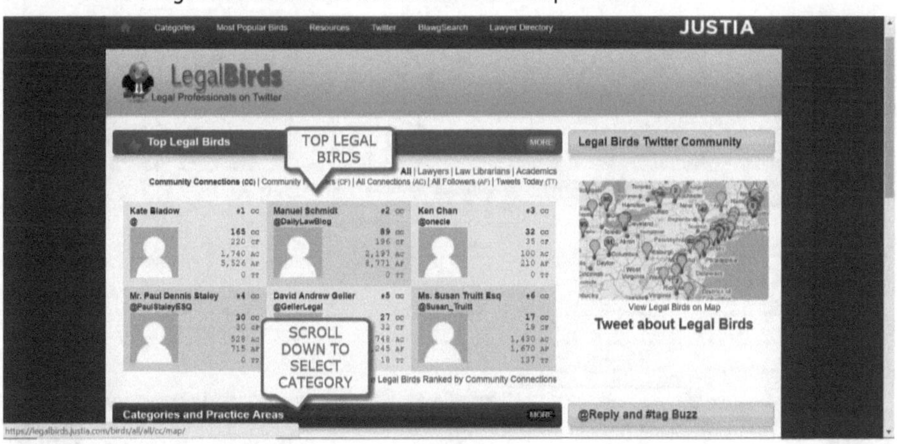


If you choose a category, the results list will show the lawyer's name (e.g., Carole Levitt) and her Twitter name (e.g., @carolelevitt). Clicking on the lawyer's name will take you to her Justia profile and clicking on her Twitter name will take you to her Twitter profile. At the top of the LegalBirds home page, you will also see a list of Top Legal Birds, but you will no longer see keyword search box, unfortunately, now making this site less useful.

## Justia's BlawgSearch

Another type of social media are law-related blogs (sometimes called "blawgs") that can be useful for researching lawyers or legal topics. Blawgs are basically web sites, with a social media aspect when the blawg owner also allows subscribers to comment. Some blawgers allow you to subscribe to an RSS feed or receive an e-newsletter. To search for a blawg that could be useful to your research, visit Justia's BlawgSearch at https://blawgsearch.justia.com/ (see Figure 17.10). It is an annotated, topically arranged list of blawgs, which is also keyword searchable. To keyword search, simply enter keywords (e.g., child kidnapping) into the search box at the top of the page. Beneath the Most Popular heading, you can hover over a blawg title to read a description of that blawg or just click the blawg title to visit it. You can also click any category from the list of Categories to view all blawgs in just that category. Once the list is displayed, you can hover over a blawg title after to read a description of that blawg or just click the blawg title to visit it. On the right-hand column, notice:

- Recent Search Terms: click a term to see a list of blawgs that include that term
- Featured Blawger

**Figure 17.10** Justia's BlawgSearch. Screenshot from Justia used with permission.

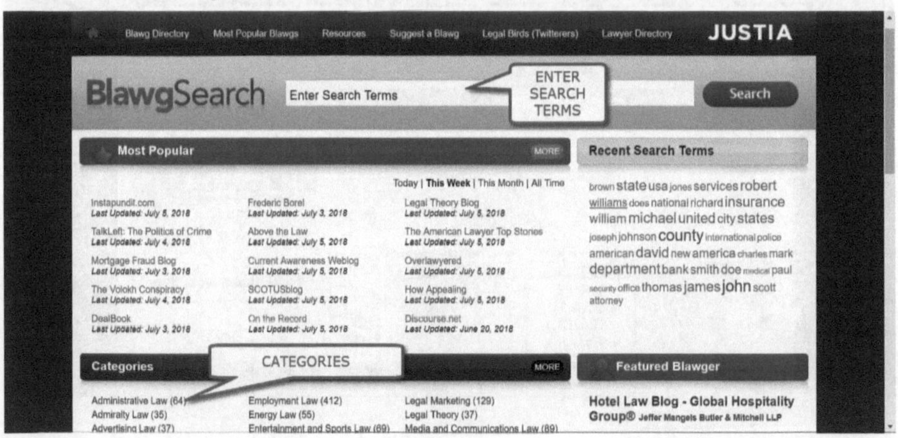


Another source for locating useful blawgs is The ABA Journal's Blawg Directory (http://www.abajournal.com/blawgs), arranged by: Topic, Author Type (e.g., consultant, judge, etc.), Region (by court, state, or country), Law School, and Courts. Although there is a keyword search box powered by Justia, it does not work as well as the one at Justia.

Every year since 2007, ABA Journal staffers have assembled a list of their 100 favorite legal blogs (Blawg 100) for the December issue of the Journal. In 2017, Blawg 100 was renamed Web 100 so it includes more than blogs; it now includes 50 blogs, 25 law podcasts, and 25 tweeters (http://bit.ly/bestweb100). Scroll down to find the left-hand column which links to Best law blogs, Best law podcasts, or Best law Twitter to view each of the most current lists. You will also see Blawg Hall of Fame in this column, which links to a list compiled since 2012 of "consistently outstanding law blogs." The list has grown to 55.

LexBlog (https://www.lexblog.com) is a blog site where you can keyword search for relevant blog posts, and if you are a Fastcase user, when you perform a search through Fastcase's entire database, LexBlog blog posts show up in your Fastcase search results. You can also limit your search to only LexBlog posts at Fastcase.

# Part V

## CITE CHECKING YOUR RESEARCH

The final step in a legal research project is to conduct cite checking to verify that your cases are still "good law." It can also be a first step if you want to expand your research by finding more cases and other materials that cite to your cases. One of the questions that people conducting legal research on the Internet most often ask us is *Can I Shepardize (or KeyCite) cases anywhere for free on the Internet?* The answer, in the strictest sense, is no because the free cite-checking services rarely offer any editorial treatment (or at least not full editorial treatment). Instead, the free services usually bring back a list of cases that cite to your case, and it's up to you to determine how the citing cases treated your case. You must read those cases to decide if a later case overruled, reversed, or affirmed your case. This should be your approach to using any citator, however, since you are ultimately responsible for how you use the cases you find.

# Chapter 18

## CITE CHECKING CASES

### FREE ALTERNATIVES TO FEE-BASED CITE-CHECKING PRODUCTS

In this chapter we will not be discussing the fee-based cite-checking products (Shepard's, Keycite, and Bcite), but will only discuss the free alternative cite-checking products (**Google Scholar's How cited** service for all federal and state cases; **CourtListener's** citator; the **World Legal Information Institute's LawCite** service for U.S. and foreign law; and **Casetext's** limited free citator features). Besides the alternative cite-checking services discussed in this chapter, there is also another citator "option" which we call the "party name as keyword" citation search. It can be used in any jurisdiction, and we will discuss it at the end of this chapter.

See Chapters 8 and 9 for details about Casemaker's Citing References and Fastcase's Authority features, which provide a list of every case that has cited the case you are reading but do not provide editorial signals (e.g., reversed, affirmed, etc.) to indicate subsequent history. (Instead, you must review each of these subsequent cases to learn how they treated your case.) Also, see Chapters 8 and 9 for details about Casemaker's Casecheck+ and Fastcase's Bad Law Bot, which provide editorial signals to show negative subsequent treatment of the case you are reading, but do not provide editorial signals for affirmative subsequent treatment. Although Casemaker and Fastcase both include unpublished cases (cases not reported in an official reporter) in their databases, neither tracks the subsequent history of these unpublished cases. The "party name as keyword" citation search, which we mentioned above (and will describe later), can be used to track the subsequent history of unpublished cases if you are using Fastcase and Casemaker.

We will not be discussing the online cite-checking services that most attorneys are familiar with (Bloomberg Law's BCITE, LexisNexis's Shepard's, and Westlaw's KeyCite). These commercial citation services offer superior and quicker cite checking compared to the free citators discussed in this chapter and to Casemaker and Fastcase discussed in Chapters 8 and 9. The pay citator products are the only ones that (1) offer full editorial treatment (indicating both affirmative and negative treatment, etc.), and (2) include citation history for unpublished cases, which is especially important if an unpublished case is later affirmed or reversed by a published case.

Finally, we focus on cite checking cases in this chapter because the resources we discuss are also devoted primarily to cases. You should also cite check any statutes you use, however, and always make sure they have not been repealed or amended.

## GOOGLE SCHOLAR

In Chapter 6 we discussed the Google Scholar free case law database (https://scholar.google.com) and mentioned that it includes a rudimentary citation service to update any case found at Google Scholar. To use this rudimentary citation service, begin by clicking the **How cited** link next to the **Read** link in the upper left corner of the case view page (see Figure 18.1; note that as in Chapter 6, Google screenshots do not contain callout boxes or other superimposed graphics for copyright permission reasons).

**Figure 18.1** Google Scholar's How cited link for cases. Google and the Google logo are registered trademarks of Google LLC, used with permission.

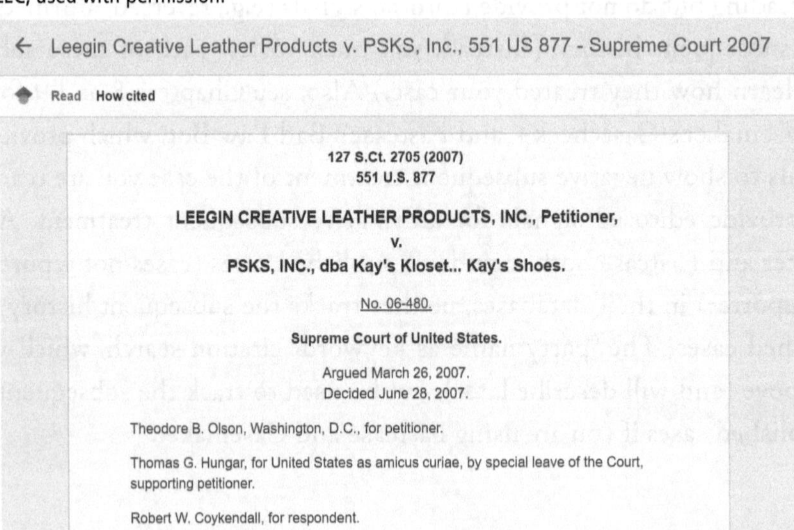

> **CAVEAT**: Unpublished cases are not included in Google's citator (or in Fastcase or Casemaker), so you must run a keyword search using the party names to update these cases. Details on how to run a keyword search using the party names are provided later in this chapter.

Figure 18.2 shows the citator (How cited) page. It contains sections labeled **How this document has been cited** (left column), **Cited by** (upper right column), and **Related documents** (lower right column). Google does not document the differences among the three sections, but we will explain them here.

**Figure 18.2** Google Scholar's How cited page. Google and the Google logo are registered trademarks of Google LLC, used with permission.

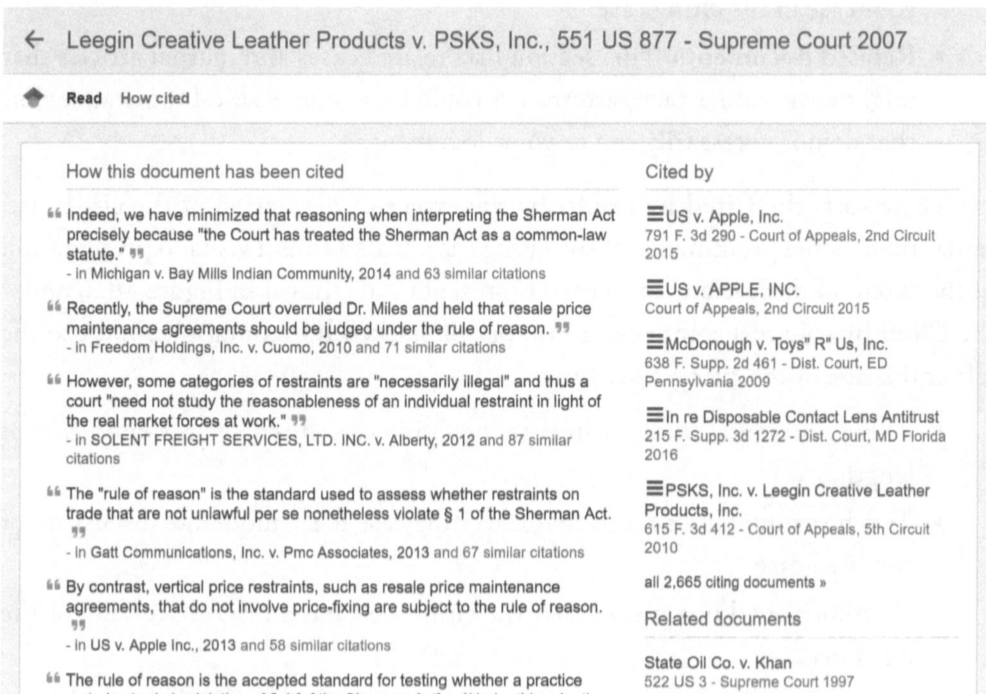


- **How this document has been cited.** A snippet of text is displayed that attempts to show how your case was treated in select citing cases or journal articles. Clicking a snippet takes you directly to the location of the snippet in the citing case—which should also be the location where your case is cited—if the citing case is in Google's collection of free cases. Journal citations are also included in this list. Some journals coming from non-Google sources are in PDF format. In those instances, you're taken to the beginning of the article or to a log-in/payment page of the database vendor.

- **Cited by.** While **How this document has been cited** lists only select documents, the **Cited by** section appears to be comprehensive, at least as to cases. For example, in Figure 18.2, if you click the **all 2,665 citing documents** link (at the bottom of the **Cited by** section), it would link to all the cases that cite to the case you're reading, in addition to many books and journal articles. **Cited by** also differs from **How this document is cited** in that clicking a case citation link takes you to the first page of the case, not to the exact, pinpoint page where your case is cited, so use the Find function (explained earlier in this chapter) and enter a party name from your case to find the reference to your case in the citing case.
- **Related documents.** This section lists related cases and journal articles that might have similar fact patterns (or could be a countersuit, for instance) but that do not necessarily cite to your document.

Google sorts the **Cited by** results by the extent of discussion of the cited case, rather than by the prominence of the citing case. It also adds a visual representation of the extent of discussion. The visual representation (shown in Figure 18.2, under the **Cited by** column) comprises a number of stacked horizontal blue lines to the left of the title of the citing case.

- Three horizontal lines mean that the citing case discusses the cited case at length.
- Two horizontal lines mean that the citing case has a moderate discussion of the cited case.
- One horizontal line means that the citing case has a brief discussion of the cited case.
- No horizontal lines means that the citing case only cites but does not discuss the cited case.

To go directly from the search results list to the visual representation of discussion depth, click the **Cited by** link listed below the case annotation (see Figure 18.3).

**Figure 18.3** Google Scholar search results and Cited by link. Google and the Google logo are registered trademarks of Google LLC, used with permission.

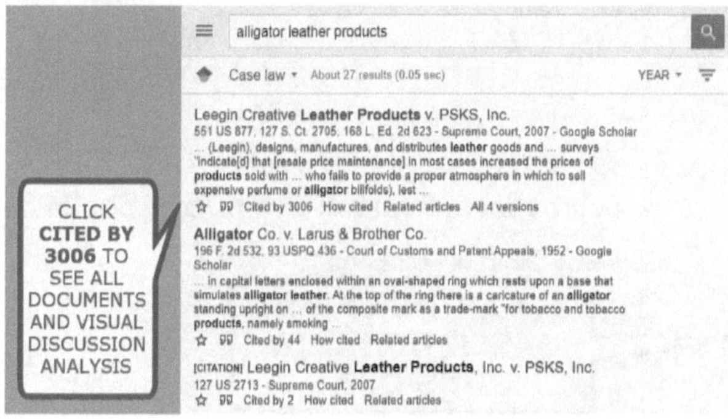


Use your web browser's **Find** function to jump to the place where the citing case cites to your case (described earlier in this chapter). You can then read that part of the case to see how (or if) the new case affects your case.

## COURTLISTENER

CourtListener, discussed earlier in Chapter 6, also provides a free citator tool. Once you have found a case (see Chapter 6 for instructions), a **Cited By** column on the left side of the page provides cases that have cited the case you are reading (see Figure 18.4). The "top five cases" (according to CourtListener) that cite your case will be visible, and you can see all cases that cite your case by clicking the **View All Citing Opinions** link below the five visible cases (see Figure 18.4). CourtListener also parses the case you are reading and provides a linked list of cases that it cites (in other words, the cases that the judge(s) relied upon when writing the case you are reading). This list, called **Authorities**, appears below the abbreviated Cited By list on the left side of the page (see Figure 18.4).

**Figure 18.4** CourtListener's citator feature. Screenshot from CourtListener used with permission.

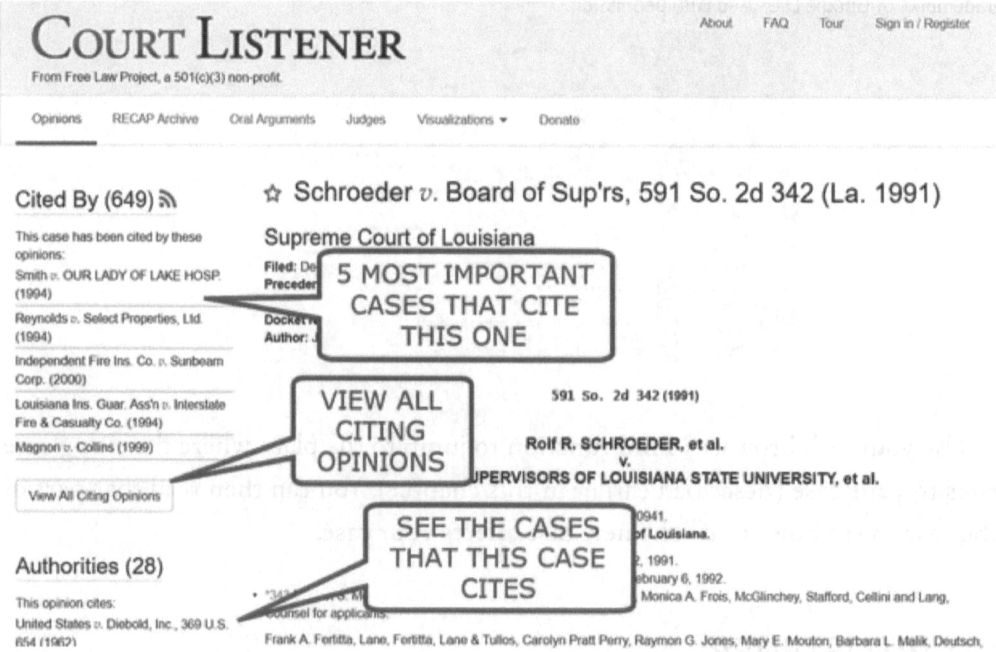


If you click **View All Citing Opinions**, you will be taken to the complete list of cases that cite your case. Although CourtListener does not provide positive and negative or depth-of-discussion information about citing cases, it allows you to sort and filter the results (see Figure 18.5). You can filter results by jurisdiction and precedential status. In addition, you can sort by relevance, newest/oldest, or most/least cited. It will be up to you to interpret how the cases treat your case, however. You can also subscribe to a results feed in order to be alerted if a new case cites to your case (see Figure 18.5).

**Figure 18.5** CourtListener's citator results page. Screenshot from CourtListener used with permission.

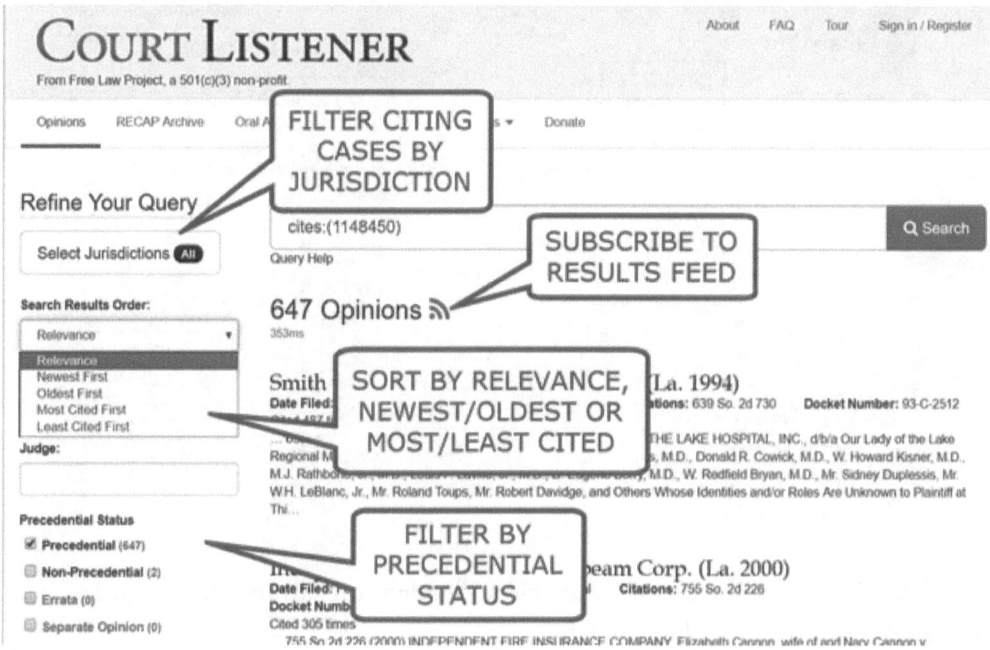


## WORLDLII'S LAWCITE

WorldLII (discussed in Chapter 14 Foreign, International, and Comparative Law Resources) has a citator feature called **LawCite** (http://www.worldlii.org/LawCite). LawCite will work not only for foreign and international case law and articles, but it will also work for U.S. cases and articles, as long as they are in WorldLII's databases. (NOTE: WorldLII's databases come from many sources around the world, and their coverage is not well documented. Therefore, as with any resource, we recommend that you do not rely on this citator to be 100% complete or accurate.)

To use LawCite, enter the information for a case or law journal article into the search form (see Figure 18.6). Then click **Search** for a list of results, or click **I'm Feeling Lucky** to see the one most relevant result. The search form provides fields such as Citation, Parties, Author, Year, and more. If you receive more than one search result, choose the case or article you want by clicking its title in the list of results. You will then be taken to the LawCite record for that case or article, where you can view a list of documents that cite to it (see Figure 18.7).

**Figure 18.6** WorldLII's LawCite citator. Screenshot from WorldLII used with permission.

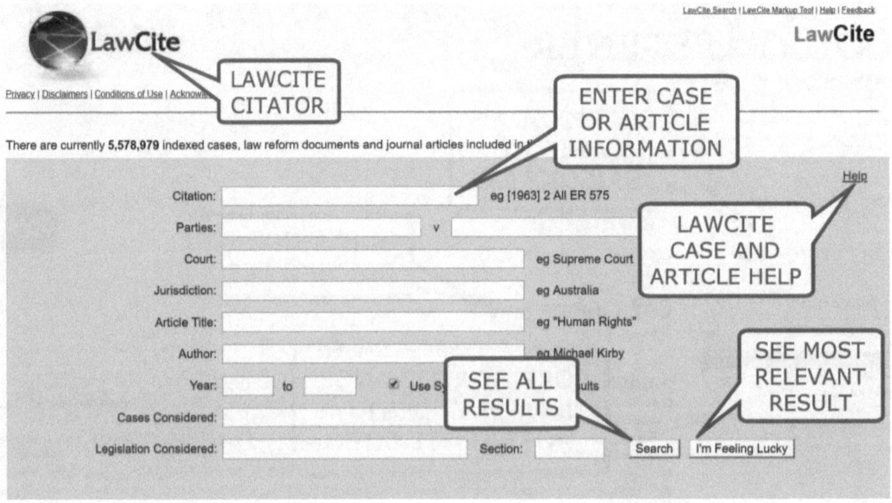


A LawCite record for a case or article is divided into up to five categories, with links to the citing material, if available:

- Legislation Cited (by this case or article)
- Cases and Articles Cited (by this case or article)
- Cases Referring to this Case or Article
- Law Reform Reports Referring to this Case or Article
- Law Journal Articles Referring to this Case or Article

Each category provides information about the citing document, such as the citation, author or court, jurisdiction, and a Citation Index that indicates approximately how many documents in WorldLII's database cite to your case or article. You can click the title of the citing document to go to its LawCite record, or click the citation to go to the document itself. For more information on using LawCite and interpreting results, click the **Help** link near the upper right corner of the search form or on the Case record (see Figures 18.6 and 18.7). No editorial enhancements are provided. You must read the cases and other documents to see how they treat your case.

**Figure 18.7** LawCite Case record. Screenshot from WorldLII used with permission.

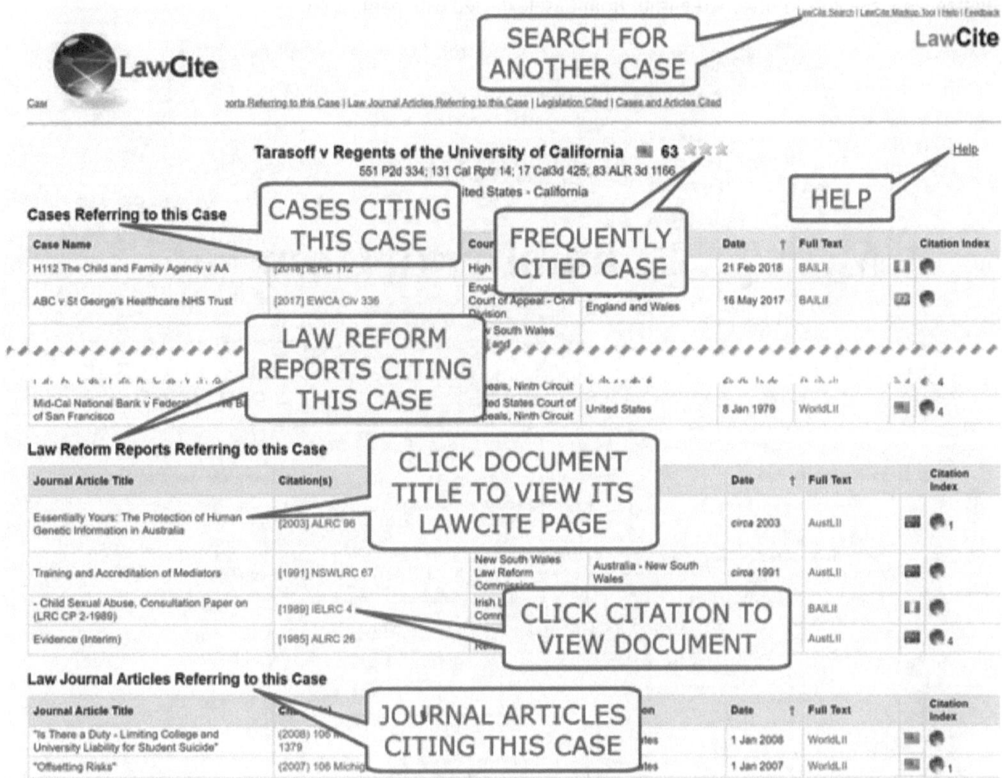


## CASETEXT

Casetext, discussed in Chapter 6, has some citation capabilities, but the most useful ones are no longer free. Casetext's citator information page is at http://bit.ly/CasetextCitatorInfo. It provides additional information about the citator, such as its coverage, how often it is updated, and how it was built. Much of the information on this page is for the paid citator features, but some of the free ones are explained, too.

**Figure 18.8** Casetext shows the number of citing cases and briefs, up to two citing cases, and all attorney-written legal analyses for free. Screenshot from Casetext used with permission.

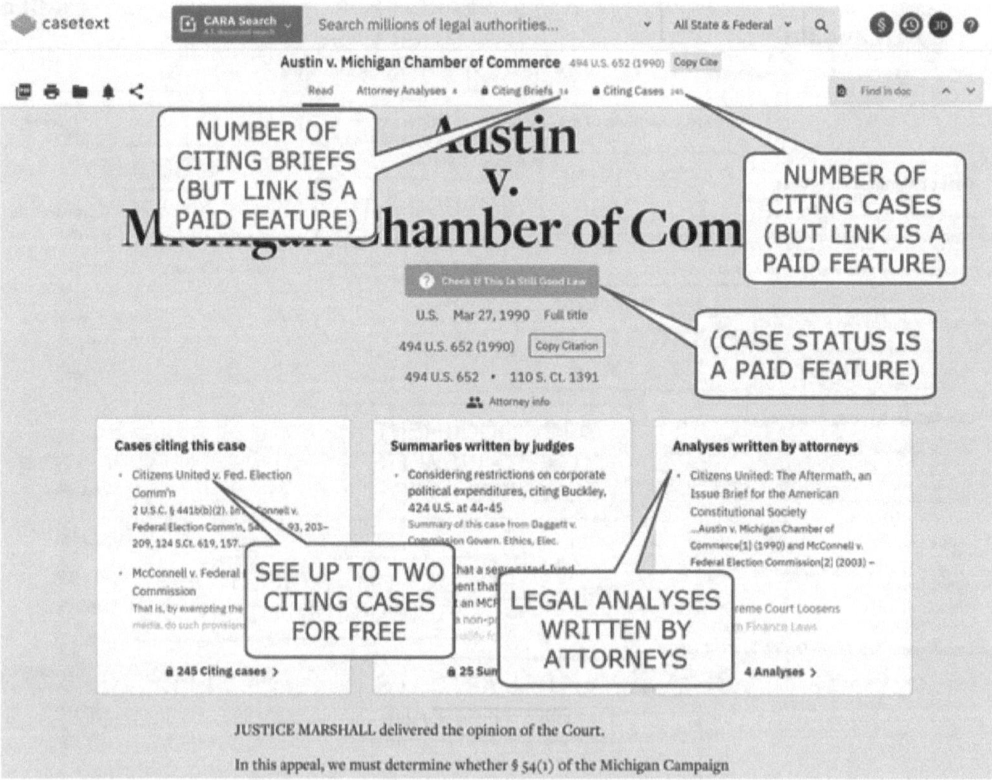


Casetext provides the following free citator features that may be useful:

- At the top center of each case page are four links: Read, Attorney Analyses, Citing Briefs, and Citing Cases. **Citing Briefs** and **Citing Cases** have a number (see Figure 18.8). If the case has not been cited, the number will be 0. Although the option to click the link and see all the citing cases is a paid feature, you can at least get an idea of whether the case you are viewing might be seminal, based on its number of citations.
- Also on the case page, below the case name and citation information are three columns: Cases citing this case, Summaries written by judges, and Analyses written by attorneys. In the left column, **Cases citing this case** shows up to two case names with snippets of text displayed below them (see Figure 18.8). You can click the titles of these two cases to read them for free, although you will need to use **Ctrl F** or **Command F** (described earlier in this book) to find the part where they cite your case. (A link for **# Citing cases** below the two case names is also a paid feature.)

- You can also view citation counts and the number of **Legal Analyses** for each case listed in your search results. For example, to the right of the *Celotex Corp v. Catrett* case citation in Figure 18.9, **Cited 172,597 times** indicates that many cases have cited *Celotex*. And to the right of **Cited 172,597 times**, the notation **17 Legal Analyses** indicates Casetext has 17 articles that relate to the *Celotex* case. If you are looking for seminal cases such as *Celotex*, you can use a drop-down menu near the upper right corner of the search results page (see Figure 18.9) to sort results by **Cite Count** (as well as by Relevance, Newest to Oldest, or Oldest to Newest).

**Figure 18.9** Citator feature in Casetext search results. Screenshot from Casetext used with permission.

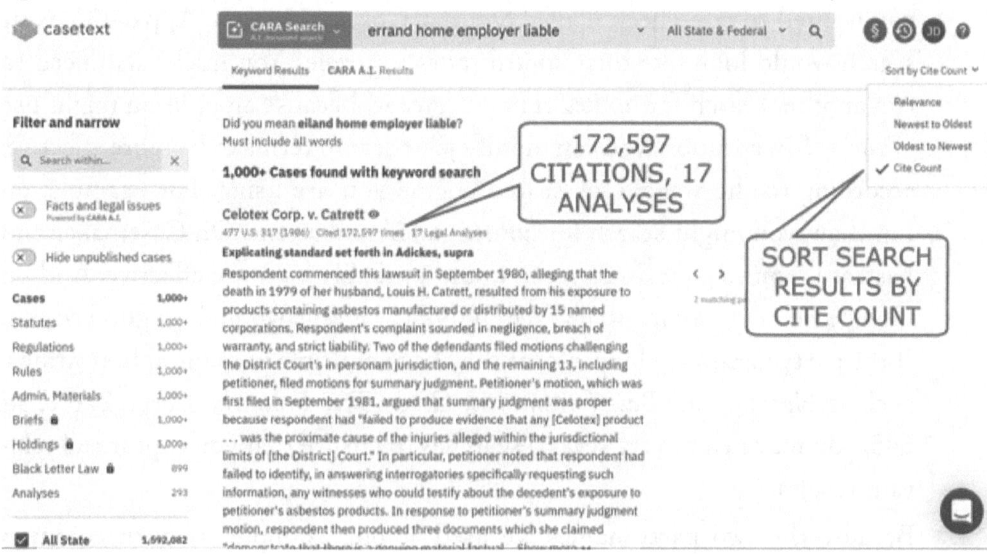


## "PARTY NAME AS KEYWORD" CITE CHECKING

The final method for cite checking we will discuss is the "party name as keyword" citation search process. As noted earlier, this is the method you must use to cite check unpublished cases in Google Scholar, Fastcase, and Casemaker because none of their citator products include unpublished cases. It would also be important to know if the unpublished case you want to rely upon has been reversed or affirmed by a higher court or overruled and possibly become a published case. You will also want to learn which other opinions have cited your unpublished opinion and why. Since FindLaw doesn't even have a citator, you must use this method to update cases from FindLaw.

This process is rudimentary and the results do not include the editorial treatment for which the pay services are known. We only recommend using the "party name as keyword" citation search for fairly recent cases because cite checking older cases with this method might bring back too many citing cases—thousands in some instances—all of which you would have to read to determine if they were relevant.

To conduct a "party name as keyword" citation search, follow these steps:

- Enter the plaintiff's and defendant's names from the case you want to cite check into the database's keyword search box in quotation marks. Also, if the database has a date range field, add the date of your case's decision as the beginning date and the current day's date as the ending date. For instance, if you wanted to cite-check *United States v. Greene*, 239 Fed. Appx. 431, your search would look like this: *"united states v. greene."* You might also need to run another search for *"united states vs. greene"* because an opinion might use "v." or "vs." In addition, you can modify your search terms to be more effective, according to the website or search engine you are using. For example, on FindLaw, you might search for *"united states" and greene*. On Casemaker and Fastcase, *"united states" /2 greene* would probably be more effective. And on Google Scholar, *"united states" AROUND(2) greene* would be a good search. If the party names are longer, or if they have multiple possible abbreviations, such as *Florida State Bd. of Admin. v. Green Tree Financial Corp.*, 270 F. 3d 645, you may need to try several searches to ensure that you capture all relevant results.
- Because the two party names we used as our example are such common words, you will probably retrieve too many irrelevant cases. If that happens, you can refine your search technique. First, add some descriptive keywords or phrases from the case being cite checked. For instance, if the issue in *United States v. Greene* was tax evasion, you could add the keywords *tax evasion* and run the following search: *united states greene tax evasion* (or *"united states" /2 greene AND "tax evasion"* on Casemaker or Fastcase, or *"united states" AROUND(2) greene "tax evasion"* on Google Scholar).
- If your search still retrieves a large number of irrelevant cases, try searching for the citation of your original case—in this instance 239 Fed. Appx. 431—in quotation marks: *"239 Fed. Appx. 431."* Once you have successfully used your citation as a keyword search, you should receive a list of cases that cite your case, including your case.

This last step can be tricky for two reasons: (1) some case law databases may attempt to convert it to a citation search and retrieve only your original case, and (2) court opinions may not always refer to the full citation of your case (e.g., they might sometimes refer to a pinpoint cite). For these two reasons, we have more success using the "party name as keyword" cite-checking alternative over the citation method.

# Index

## A


ABA. *See* American Bar Association (ABA)
ABA Center for Professional Responsibility (CPR), 27–28
ABA Law Journal, 349
  Blawg Directory, 348
Academic portals and directories, 64
Accurint, 285
AdLaw By Request, 17
Administrative codes. *See* Code of Federal Regulations (CFR)
Administrative law, 227–244. *See also* Federal executive and administrative law
  federal, 227–244
  state and local, 245–262
Administrative Office of the United States Courts (AOUSC), 110
Administrators in Medicine DocFinder, 27
Advertising law, 17
Alerts. *See* E-alerts
American Association for Justice (AAJ)
  Exchange and Litigation Packets service, 14
American Bar Association (ABA), 69
  Center for Professional Responsibility (CPR). *See* ABA Center for Professional Responsibility (CPR)
  Division for Bar Services, 336
  Legal Technology Resource Center, 5–6, 346
  preview of U.S. Supreme Court cases, 131, 133
  research resources, 69
  State and Local Bar Association Resources, 69
American Immigration Council, 22
American Intellectual Property Law Association (AIPLA), 26
American Legal Publishing, 258–259
American Medical Association (AMA), 26–27
American Society of International Law (ASIL), 266–269
Amicus briefs, 316
Appellate materials, 69. *See also* Case law databases
  on Casemaker4, 151
  on Fastcase, 168
  on FindLaw, 86–91
  on Google Scholar, 76
  in Justia court opinions e-newsletters, 47
  PACER Case Locator, 290
  on PACER docket site, 286
  on Public Library of Law site, 106
Apps
  case law, 34
  Casemaker, 34
  Constitution, 38
  criminal law, 36
  ethics, 37

Apps, *continued*
- Fastcase, 34, 179–183
- federal regulations, 35
- legal dictionary, 36–37
- professionalism, 37
- state statutes, 37
- taxation, 37
- United States Code, 38

ArchiveSocial, 331–332
Articles. *See* Legal articles; Law journal articles
Association of Federal Defense Attorneys (AFDA), 36
Asa V. Call Law Library, 68–69
Attorneys. *See* Lawyers
Audio recordings, 299
Avvo.com, 341–342

## B

Bad Law Bot, 169–170
Ballotpedia, 343
Bankruptcy courts, 10, 14, 74, 76, 110, 283, 286, 294, 295, 299, 300–301
- cases, 286, 300–301
- dockets, 284, 285, 301

Bankruptcy law, 18, 35, 36, 50, 133
Bar associations. *See also* American Bar Association (ABA)
- judicial profiles, 346
- member-benefit databases, 123–124, 157–158. *See also* Casemaker4; Fastcase
- state and local bar associations, 69, 346
- voluntary associations vs. unified/integrated, 336

BCite. *See under* Bloomberg Law
Best Interests of the Child State-by-State, 21
Bills, 205
- federal, 57, 214, 215, 220, 222–223, 224
- state, 253, 254–255, 256

Bing search engine, 54–56
Biographical Directory of Federal Judges, 342–343
Bissett, Jan, 12
Black's Law Dictionary, 36
Blawgs, 17–32
- advertising law, 17
- bankruptcy law, 18
- Blawg Directory, 348
- business law. *See* Corporate law
- class action lawsuits, 18
- corporate/business law, 20
- directory of, 348
- family law, 21–22
- immigration law, 23
- index of, 348–349
- intellectual property, 26
- Justia's BlawgSearch, 348–349
- LexBlog, 349

BlawgSearch (Justia), 348–349
Blogs (law-related). *See* Blawgs
Bloomberg Law, 12, 140, 283, 354
- BCite, 85, 140, 354
- Law Dockets, 283

Boolean connectors, 56, 57, 78, 79, 88, 93, 94, 103, 106, 107, 113, 115, 117, 118, 126, 127, 161, 162, 190, 196, 207
Briefs, 14, 15, 26, 30, 34, 48, 116, 311–312, 316
- AIPLA, 26
- federal courts, 14
  - PACER, 286
  - RECAP, 300–301
- Los Angeles Superior Court, 14–15
- sample, 14
- securities fraud, 30
- U.S. Supreme Court, 15, 34, 48, 116, 311–312, 316

Budget of the United States Government, 57
Business law. *See* Corporate law

## C

California case law databases, 116–121
California Official Reports Public Access, 116–121
CaseCheck+ (Casemaker4), 140–141
Case documents, 14–16
- fees for searching, 284–285
- Los Angeles Superior Court, 284–285
- New York State and local courts, 285
- PACER, 286–300
- RECAP, 300–308
- use of, 284
- of U.S. Supreme Court, 311–316

Case law apps, 34
Case law databases, 71–280
  apps for, 33
  bankruptcy cases. *See under* Bankruptcy courts
  California Official Reports Public Access website (LexisNexis), 116
  Casemaker4, 123–156
  Casetext, 101–105
  Fastcase, 157–186
  federal case law, 74, 76, 86–87, 94, 101, 106, 108, 109–116, 133–136, 163
  FindLaw, 48–50, 85
  free commercial online, 73–108
  free governmental online, 109–121
  Google Scholar, 73–85
  governmental databases, 109–122, 201, 218, 229
  Justia, 48, 107–108
  PACER, 286–300
  Public Library of Law, 106
  state, 256
  Supreme Court of the United States official website, 112
Case Locator (PACER), 289–290, 295–298
Casemaker apps, 34
Casemaker4, 123–155
  advanced searching, 137–139
  alerts in, 149–151
  citator products, 140–141
  content, 124
  documents in, 145–149
  help with, 153–154
  outside vendor products with, 154
  personalization with, 151–153
  printing, 146–148
  searching, 124–140
  searching cases, 124–133
  searching statutes in, 142–145
  time keeping with, 154
Case Management/Electronic Case Files (CM/ECF), 286, 298. *See also* PACER (Public Access to Court Electronic Records)
Case name search. *See* Party names, searching by
Cases. *See* Case law databases
Casetext, 101–105, 361–363
Catalogs of Copyright Entries (CCEs), 24
Center for Professional Responsibility (CPR), 27–28
CiteCheck (Casemaker4), 141
Cite checking
  Authority Check (Fastcase), 166–167
  Bad Law Bot (Fastcase), 169–170
  BCite (Bloomberg), 85, 140
  CaseCheck+ (Casemaker4), 140–141
  Casemaker, 140–141
  cases, 353–365
  CiteCheck (Casemaker4), 141
  Fastcase (Authority Check), 166–167
  FindLaw, 363
  Google Scholar (How cited), 354–357
  How cited (Google Scholar), 354–357
  Interactive Timeline (Fastcase), 167–169
  KeyCite (Westlaw), 85, 353–354
  party name as keyword, 363–365
  party name and keyword process, 363–365
  red flags (Fastcase), 169–170
  research, 351
  Shepard's (Lexis), 85, 353–354
City and county websites, 257–258
  codes, 258–262
  ordinances, 260–262
Class action law, 18
Classified: The Class Action Blog, 18
Classmates (websites), 320
Code of Federal Regulations (CFR), 229–232, 233–236
  apps for, 35
  on Casemaker4, 172–173
  CFR Parts Affected, searching, 235–236
  on Cornell Law School Legal Information Institute (LII), 200–201
  e-CFR, 231
  on govinfo, 62
  List of CFR Sections Affected, 233–235
Codes. *See* Local law; Statutes; United States Code (U.S.C.)
Committees of the U.S. Congress, 217–219
Commonwealth Legal Information Institute (CommonLII), 278–279
Company law. *See* Corporate law
Comparative law resources, 266, 270–271

Compilation of Presidential Documents, 237–238
Complaints, 316–317. *See also* Dockets
  civil, 316–317
  federal, 316–317
Congress.gov, 206–220
  committee reports, 206, 218–219
  Committees of U.S. Congress page, 206, 217–218
  congressional bills, 208, 214–215
  Congressional Record, 206, 216–217
  Glossary, 216
  legislation pages, 206, 214–216, 220
  members of Congress, finding, 206, 219–220
  searching, 207–213
Congressional Record (CR), 35, 216–217
Congressional reports database (govinfo), 220–224
Congressional Research Service (CRS), 224–225
Constitute Project, 280
Constitution, 35–36, 38, 187–191
Contact information, 335–336
Copyright law, 24–26
Cornell's Divorce Law Overview, 21
Cornell Law School Legal Information Institute (LII), 64–68, 199–201, 247–249, 279
  Code of Federal Regulations (CFR), 65, 200–201
  searching, 65–67, 200
  state law materials, 247–249
  U.C.C., 65
  U.S. Code database, 199–201
  U.S. Constitution database, 65, 187, 190
  Wex legal dictionary, 66
  world legal materials, 279
Cornell University Library, 21
Cornerstone Research, 306
Corporate law, 19–20
County websites, 257–258
Courthouse News Service, 316–317
CourtLink, 283
CourtListener, 15, 94–101, 301–302, 344–346, 357–359
Court of Chancery, 19
Court rules
  apps, 35–36
  websites, 6–9
Courts
  judge profiles, 344–346
  searching cases by, 61, 74–76, 79, 82, 86–87, 89, 91, 103, 106, 110–112, 130
  websites, 6–9, 10, 112–116
Criminal law
  apps, 36
  websites, 20
CyberCemetery, 243–244
*Cybersleuth's Guide to the Internet, The* (Levitt and Rosch), xviii, 321, 335


# D


Dallas Bar Association, 346
Davis, Judy, xi, xiii
Declaration of Independence, 187–191
Delaware State Court, 19–20
Dictionaries. *See* Legal dictionaries
Directories
  academic, 64
  assessment of, 40–41
  free commercial, 43–52
  government, 53–63
  judicial, 342–346
  lawyer, 336–342
DivorceNet, 21
DocFinder, 27
Dockets, 9, 283
  federal, 308–310
  fees for searching, 284–285
  local, 256, 284–285, 316–317
  Los Angeles Superior Court, 284–285
  New York State and local courts, 285
  PACER, 286–300
  RECAP archive, 300–308
  state, 256, 284–285, 316–317
  Supreme Court, 116, 311–316
  use of, 284
  websites, 285

## E


E-alerts, 298–299. *See also* E-newsletters
  docket-related information, 298, 308
  federal regulations, 228
  new cases, 76–77, 358
Eble, Timothy E., 18
e-CFR, 231–232. *See also* Code of Federal Regulations (CFR)
eCode360 Library, 261
e-Code of Federal Regulations (e-CFR), 231–232
EDGAR, 29
EISIL. *See* Electronic Information System for International Law (EISIL)
Electronic Information System for International Law (EISIL), 266–269
Electronic Resources Guide (ERG), 266
Employment law, 20–21
Employment Law Information Network (ELIN), 20–21
E-newsletters. *See also* E-alerts
  immigration law, 52
  legal news, 47, 107–108
  new cases, 48, 52
Ethics
  apps, 37
  Formal Ethics Opinions, 28
  websites, 27–28
ETHICSearch, 28
European Union, 275–276
Executive and administrative law. *See* Federal executive and administrative law
Expert witnesses, 13–14


## F


Facebook, 321–323
Family law, 21–22
Fastcase, 34
  HeinOnline partnership, 175, 176
  red flags, 169–170
  syncing, 34, 179–180
Fastcase 7
  apps, 179–183
  authority check in, 166–167
  Bad Law Bot in, 169–170
  case law in, 163–166
  documents in, 176–179
  finding resources on, 158–163
  interactive timeline in, 167–169
  law reviews in, 175–176
  regulations in, 172–173
  searching on, 161–163
  secondary resources in, 173
  statutes in, 170–172
  treatises in, 174–175
Federal agencies, 240
  defunct agencies, finding, 243–244
  forms from, 240
  websites of, 240
Federal agency forms, 9–10
Federal case law databases, 74, 76, 86–87, 94, 101, 106, 108, 109–116, 133–136, 163
*Federal Class Action Practice Manual Internet Edition* (Eble), 18
Federal court opinions, 299
Federal dockets. *See* Dockets
Federal executive and administrative law, 199–217. *See also* Code of Federal Regulations (CFR)
  CyberCemetery, 243–244
  e-CFR, 231
  federal agencies websites, 240
  Federal Register. *See* Federal Register (FR)
  List of CFR Sections Affected, 233–236
  presidential materials, 237–239
  United States Government Manual, 241–242
  USA.gov, 242
  U.S. Regulation Tracker (Justia), 236–237
  White House website, 240
Federal Judicial Center Biographical Directory of Federal Judges, 342
Federal Register (FR), 57, 227–229, 231, 232, 235–237, 241, 257
Federal regulations, 35
Federation of Tax Administrators, 32
Fees
  for docket search, 284–285
  for local codes, searching multiple, 259
Financial Industry Regulatory Authority (FINRA), 31

FindLaw, 48–50, 85–94, 253, 262, 316, 339–340
briefs (Supreme Court), 316
case law databases, 86–87
federal case law databases, 86–87
Lawyer Directory, 339–340
Opinion Summaries Archive, 90–94
searching, 88–90
state case law databases, 86–87
state statutory materials directory, 253
Foreign constitutions, 280
Foreign law, 41, 50–51, 252, 263–280
GlobaLex, 270–271, 279
HG.org, 50–51, 273–276
Latin American law resources, 41, 276–277
Law Library of Congress, 264–266
WashLaw Legal Resources on the Web, 252, 279
Formal Ethics Opinions, 28
Forms. *See* Legal forms

## G

General Code, 261
GlobaLex, 270–271
Global Legal Information Network (GLIN), 264–265
Global Patent Search Network (GPSN), 25
Google Patents, 26
Google Scholar, 73–85, 346, 354–357
Advanced Search, 74–81
case law database, 354
cite-checking services, 354–357
courts covered, list of, 73–74
date range searches, 82
How cited link, 354
keyword searches, 78, 83–85
patents and patent articles, 26
searching, 74–81
search results, filtering, 84–85
Government agency resources, 54, 240–244
Governmental case law databases, 109–122
Google Translate, 263–264
Government portals and directories, 53–63
Government Publishing Office (GPO), 56–57, 109–119, 231, 241, 243. *See also* govinfo.gov
Governors' websites. *See* State governors' websites
govinfo.gov, 56–63, 109–112, 201–203, 220–224, 237–239
Advanced Search page, 60–63
CFR database, 229–231
CFR Parts Affected, 233–236
court opinions, 109–112
searching, 56–63, 201–203
United States Government Manual, 241–242
GovRegs, 35
Guide to Law Online, 264–265

## H

Heinen, Margi, 12
HG.org. *See* Hieros Gamos (HG.org)
Hieros Gamos (HG.org), 21, 50–51, 273–276, 346
House of Representatives Office of the Law Revision Counsel (OLRC) United States Code Online. *See* Office of the Law Revision Counsel (OLRC) United States Code Online
How cited (Google Scholar), 84, 353, 354–357

## I

Illinoisdivorce.com, 22
Immigration Bulletin, 52
Immigration law, 22–23
ImmigrationProf Blog, 23
IngentaConnect, 3–4
Instagram, 326
Insurance law, 23
Insure.com, 23
Intellectual property, 24–26
Intelligize, 30
International law-related resources, 41, 50–51, 252, 263–280
American Society of International Law (ASIL), 266–269
Electronic Information System for International Law (EISIL), 266–269
Electronic Resources Guide (ERG), 266, 279
GlobaLex, 270–271, 279
HG.org, 50–51, 273–276

Latin American law resources, 41, 276–277
Law Library of Congress, 264–266
WashLaw Legal Resources on the Web, 252, 279
Internet For Lawyers, 335–336
Internet Legal Research Group (ILRG), 12
Investigative research, 284, 286–287, 321, 324
docket materials, 284
investigative databases, 285
IRS forms, 10–11

## J

Journals, 3–4, 6, 24, 27, 81, 136, 175, 276, 279, 346, 355–356. *See also* Law journal articles; Legal articles
Judgepedia.com, 343
Judges, 80–81, 95–96, 131, 137–139, 161, 309, 316, 342–346, 346–347, 356
articles written by and about, 346–347
judicial directories, 342–346
searching cases by, 80–81, 95–96, 131, 137–139, 161, 309, 316
Judicial directories, 342–346
Jurisdiction
browsing by, 44, 49, 89, 252
searching by, 34, 74, 89, 96, 103, 106, 133–136, 152, 174, 180, 316
Jurispro.com, 13–14
Jury instructions, 12–13
Jury verdicts, 13–14
Justia, 43–48, 107–108, 308–310
blog directory (BlawgSearch), 348–349
case law, 107–108
court opinion e-newsletters, 47–48
Federal Dockets database, 10, 41, 308–310
Latin American law resources, 276–277
Lawyer Directory, 336, 340
LegalBirds, 347
Legal Practice Areas directory, 43
Legal Research & Law Practice directory, 43
Legal Web search engine, 46–47
state court links, 256
Twitter directory (LegalBirds), 347
U.S. Regulation Tracker, 228, 236–237
Justia's BlawgSearch, 17

## K

KeyCite, 48, 79, 85, 140, 169, 354
Keyword searching
Bing-powered search engines, 54, 247
Casemaker4, 125–127, 142
Cornell Law School Legal Information Institute (LII), 64–65, 200
Delaware Court of Chancery opinions, 19
Fastcase, 161–164
Google-powered search engines, 5, 43, 44–46, 51, 274
Google Scholar. *See* Google Scholar
USA.gov, 54, 242, 247

## L

Labor law, 20–21
Latin America, 41, 276–278
Law blogs. *See* Blawgs
Law.com, 346
Law Commons, 4, 346
Law dictionaries. *See* Legal dictionaries
Law Dictionary & Guide, 36
Law journal articles, 5–6, 81, 279, 359–360. *See also* Journals; Legal articles
Law Library of Congress, 264–266
Law review articles. *See* Law journal articles
Law Review Commons, 4–5, 346
Laws. *See* Legislative research
Law school websites, 64
LawStack, 35
Lawyer directories, 336–342
Lawyers
articles written by and about, 346–347
background information on, 304–305, 336–342
directories of, 336–342
licensing databases, 335–336
research on, 335–349
searching cases by, 114, 131, 137–139, 285, 293, 304
Twitter and, 324–325
social media research on, 347–349

Legal articles, 3–6, 21, 51–52, 73, 76–77, 274–275. *See also* Journals; Law journal articles
  attorneys, written by and about, 346–347
  Google Scholar database, 73
  HG.org, 21, 50–51
  judges, written by and about, 346–347
  LegalTrac, 347
  Nolo Press, 51–52
Legal association portals, 69
LegalBirds, 347
Legal briefs. *See* Briefs
Legal dictionaries
  apps for, 36–37
  Black's Law Dictionary, 36
  Law Dictionary & Guide, 36
  Nolo's English Law Dictionary, 36, 51
  Wex, 66–67, 199, 249
  Wolfram Lawyer's Professional Assistant, 36–37
Legal Dictionary by Farlex, 36
Legal Dictionary—Law Definitions and Thesaurus, 36
Legal directories, 39–41
Legaldockets.com, 285
Legal ethics. *See* Ethics
Legal forms, 12, 154
  agency forms, 9–10
  business forms, 12
  court forms, 9–11
  employment and labor law forms, 20–21
  immigration law forms, 22–23
  intellectual property forms, 24
  personal forms, 12
  tax forms, 10–12, 31–32
Legal Information Institute (LII), 64–68. *See also* Commonwealth Legal Information Institute (CommonLII); Cornell's Legal Information Institute
Legal portals. *See under* Portals
Legal research
  defined, xvii–xviii
  general legal research resources, 3–15, 33–38
LegalTrac, 347
LegalZoom, 12
LegiScan, 255–256
Legislation, federal, on Congress.gov, 206–220
Legislative research
  bills. *See* Bills
  comparative, 266, 270, 280
  Congress.gov, 206–220
  federal, 205–225, 245–247
  foreign, 264–266, 270–279
  govinfo.gov, 220–224
  international, 264–276, 279
  local, 250–251, 257–262
  state, 247–256
  tribal, 256–257
Levitt, Carole, xi–xii, xiii, xiv, xvi, xviii, 325, 327, 335, 347
LexBlog, 349
LexisNexis
  California Official Reports Public Access, 116–121
  CourtLink, 283
  Martindale-Hubbell, 336–339
  Shepard's, 79, 85, 119, 140, 169, 353, 354
  Terms and Connectors searching, 118
Lex Mundi, 50, 273
Lexology, 6, 346
Library of Congress, 24, 35, 38, 187, 191, 206, 251, 264–266
Licensing information, 335–336
LII. *See* Cornell Law School Legal Information Institute (LII)
LinkedIn, 320, 326–329
List of CFR Sections Affected (LSA), 233–236
Local government law, 259–261
Local law, 245–262
Los Angeles Superior Court, case documents and dockets, 15, 284–285


# M


Magazines, 3–4
M&A Profs, 20
Martindale-Hubbell, 336–339
Medicine, 26–27
Mergers and acquisitions, 20
Merit briefs, 316
Mexican law resources, 277

Milberg, 18
Model Rules of Professional Conduct, 27, 320
app, 37
MoreLaw.com, 13
Municode, 259–261

## N

NAFTA resources, 270
National Association of Counties (NACo), 257–258
National Association of Criminal Defense Lawyers (NACDL), 20
National Association of Insurance Commissioners (NAIC), 23
National Association of Securities Dealers (NASD), 31
National Center for State Courts, 6, 12
National District Attorneys Association (NDAA), 20
National Indian Law Library (NILL), 256–257
National Library of Medicine (NLM), 27
National Student Clearinghouse, 14
Nations of the World, 265
Native Americans, 246
Nature of Suit (NOS) codes, 284
*Newberg on Class Actions* (Eble), 18
Newspapers, searching, 3, 24, 346–347
New York University School of Law, 270–273
Nextpoint, 332
Nolo, 51–52, 341, 346
articles by or about attorneys and judges, 51–52, 341, 346
attorney directories, 51, 341
blog, 51
dictionaries, 36, 51
DivorceNet, 21
legal research, 51
Nolo's English Law Dictionary, 36

## O

Office of the Law Revision Counsel (OLRC) United States Code Online, 191–199. *See also* United States Code (U.S.C.)
advanced searches, 194–197
help features, 195–196
search tips, 196
OLRC. *See* Office of the Law Revision Counsel (OLRC) United States Code Online
Open States, 254–255
Oral arguments, 14–16, 314–316
Ordinances, 260–262
Oyez, 15, 34, 108, 315

## P

PACER (Public Access to Court Electronic Records), 14, 284, 286–300
Advanced Search menus, 290–292, 293–295
automatic case notification, 298–299
case documents, 286–287, 289–290, 295–298
dockets, 286–287
help, 300
NOS (Nature of Suit) searches, 284
pleadings, 286–287
registering, 287–288
PageFreezer, 332
Party names, searching by
Casemaker, 138–141, 363–365
Fastcase, 363–365
FindLaw, 89, 91–92
Google Scholar, 79, 363–365
Justia, 107, 309
PACER, 295–296
Public Library of Law (PLoL), 106
RECAP, 304–306
Supreme Court of the United States, 89
Patents, 24–26
PeopleMap, 285
People, researching, 335–349
Personal injury law, 27
Pinterest, 329–330
Pleadings, sample, 14, 284. *See also* Dockets
Portals
academic, 64
assessment of, 40–41
free commercial, 43–52
government, 53–63
legal, 39–41
legal association, 69
Presidential materials, 237–239

Princeton University Center for Information Technology, 301
Printing, 34, 35, 118–120, 146–148, 152–153, 176–177
Private laws database, 224
Professionalism
apps, 37
websites, 27–28
Property law, 21, 28–29
Public laws
classification tables and, 194, 196–199
Congress.gov, 224
Cornell Law School Legal Information Institute (LII) U.S. Code database, 191–192, 199–201
govinfo.gov, 203, 224
researching, 199
Publiclegalforms.com, 12
Public Library of Law (PLoL), 106
Public Papers of the Presidents of the United States, 237
Public Record Retriever Network (PRRN), 283
PubMed Central, 27
PushLegal's Statutes and Case Law Library, 34

## R

Rank and Filed, 30
Real estate law, 28–29
RECAP, 14, 300–308
Recordings, 299
Red flags (Fastcase), 169–170
Reed Smith, 17
Regulation Tracker, 236–237
Regulations
Code of Federal Regulations. *See* Code of Federal Regulations (CFR)
copyright, 24
federal, 172–173, 191
state, 172–173, 247, 253
Treasury, 37
Researching people, 335–349
Robbins Geller Rudman & Dowd LLP, 18
Rosch, Mark, xii, 322, 335
RSS feeds, 298–299, 307–308, 348
Rulebook, 35

## S

Sample briefs and pleadings. *See* Briefs; Pleadings
Scholar. *See* Google Scholar
Search engines
Bing, 54–56
Boolean connectors, 45, 55–57, 78–79, 93–94, 125–127, 162, 196, 327
Google Scholar, 73–85
field searching, 95, 304–305
SEC Info, 30
Securities and Exchange Commission (SEC) site, 29
Securities Class Action Clearinghouse. *See* Stanford Law School Securities Class Action Clearinghouse (SCAC)
Securities law, 29–31
Session laws, 124, 136–137, 142, 170
Settlements, 13, 18, 31, 37
Securities Class Action Clearinghouse, 31
Shepard's, 79, 85, 119, 140, 169, 353, 354
Snapchat, 330–331
Social media, 319–333
Social Science Research Network (SSRN), 4
Social Security number redaction in PACER, 286–287
Stanford Law School Securities Class Action Clearinghouse (SCAC), 30
Stanley, Tim, 41, 48
State and Local Government on the Net, 250–251, 258
State bar associations. *See* Bar associations
State case law databases, 256
California, 10, 94, 101, 116–121
Cornell Law School Legal Information Institute (LII), 247–249
Fastcase, 34, 157–160, 163–166
FindLaw, 85–90, 253, 262
Google Scholar, 34, 73–75, 79
Justia, 10, 108, 256
Public Library of Law, 106
State constitutions, 247
State court rules, 35
app for, 35
State governors' websites, 246

State of the Union addresses, 237, 239
State statutes, 34, 37, 67, 68, 247, 249, 253, 262
State Tax Agencies, 32
State tax forms, 12
Statutes. *See also* City and county websites; Local law; State statutes; Statutes at Large; United States Code (U.S.C.)
  Casemaker4, 138, 142–145
  Casetext, 101
  on Cornell Law School Legal Information Institute (LII), 191, 199–201
  Fastcase 7, 170–172, 180, 184, 185
  federal. *See* United States Code (U.S.C.)
  govinfo, 224
  on PushLegal, 34
  state, 34, 37, 67, 68, 247, 249, 253, 262
Statutes at Large, 61, 224
Stern, Stacy, 48
Stored Communications Act (SCA), 322
Superlawyers.com, 341
Supreme Court of the United States, 112–116, 311–316
  apps, 34, 35, 38
  audio files, 15, 34, 315
  briefs, 15, 48, 116, 316
  court rules, 6
  dockets, 89, 116, 311–314
  forms, 10
  justices, biographical information, 342–343
  opinions, 76, 90–91, 101, 112–113, 114–115, 316
  oral arguments, 15, 34
    audio, 15, 34, 315–316
    written transcripts of, 15, 314–315
  Rules and Guidance, 116
  searching cases, 86, 88–90, 106, 107–108
  slip opinions, 114
  transcripts, 15, 314–315
  website, 15, 112–116
Susser, Siskind, 23, 52

# T

Tax Court. *See* U.S. Tax Court
Tax forms
  federal, 10, 11
  state, 12
Tax law
  apps, 37
  websites, 31–32
Territories, resources for
  foreign territories, 154, 264–267
  U.S. territories, 53, 254, 247–250, 253
THOMAS.gov, 206
Thomson Reuters's PeopleMap, 285
TLOxp, 285
TouchTax Code and Regs, 37
Trademark Electronic Search System (TESS), 26
Trademarks, 24–26
Tribal law, 256–257
Tribal Law Gateway, 256–257
Twitter, 320, 324–325

# U

United Nations, 263, 265, 271, 275
United States. *See* U.S.
United States Code (U.S.C.), 170–172, 191–203
  apps for, 38
  on Casemaker4, 142–145
  Cornell Law School Legal Information Institute (LII) U.S. Code database, 199–201
    CFR parallel authorities links, 201
    citation searching, 199
    keyword/phrase searching, 200
    Parallel Table of Authorities, 199
    results, navigating, 200
    Table of Popular Names feature, 192
  on Fastcase, 170–171
  govinfo.gov United States Code database, 191
  metadata, displaying, 203
  Office of the Law Revision Counsel (OLRC) United States Code Online. *See* Office of the Law Revision Counsel (OLRC) United States Code Online
  popular names of acts, 192, 199
  researching, 35, 38, 61, 142, 170, 191–203
  on United States official government websites, 191
  updating of, 197–199

United States Government Manual, 241–242
University of North Texas Libraries, 243
  CyberCemetery, 243–244
University of Southern California (USC) Gould School of Law, 68–69
Upcounsel, 12
U.S.
  U.S. administrative codes. *See* Casemaker4; Code of Federal Regulations (CFR)
  U.S. bankruptcy courts. *See* Federal case law databases
  U.S. bankruptcy courts dockets. *See* PACER (Public Access to Court Electronic Records)
  U.S.C. *See* United States Code (U.S.C.)
  U.S. Congress
    members, finding, 206, 219–220
    researching, 206–220
  US Constitution & Federal Laws, 35–36
  U.S. Constitution Annotated, 38
  U.S. Copyright Office, 24
  U.S. courts. *See also* Federal case law databases; PACER (Public Access to Court Electronic Records)
    of appeals, 10, 88–90, 110, 301, 308, 342–343
    district court dockets. *See* PACER (Public Access to Court Electronic Records)
    district courts. *See* Federal case law databases
  U.S. Government Manual, 241–242
  U.S. Government Publishing Office. *See* Government Publishing Office (GPO)
  U.S. House of Representatives
    members, finding, 206, 219–220
    website, 225
  U.S. Patent and Trademark Office, 25
  U.S. Regulations. *See* Casemaker4; Code of Federal Regulations (CFR); Fastcase; Federal Register (FR)
  U.S. Regulation Tracker (Justia), 48, 228, 236–237
  U.S. Securities and Exchange Commission, 29–30
  U.S. Senate
    members, finding, 206, 219–220
    website, 225
  U.S. Supreme Court. *See* Supreme Court of the United States
  U.S. Tax Court, 31, 343
    Google Scholar case coverage, 73–74
USA.gov, 53–56, 242, 245–247
  Advanced Search page, 54–56
  federal agencies links, 9–10, 53, 242
  local government materials, 9–10, 53, 245–247
  territorial materials, 53, 245–247
  tribal law and government resources, 9–10, 53, 245–246

## V

Visalaw.com, 52

## W

Washburn University School of Law, 252, 279
WashLaw Legal Research on the Web, 252
  foreign and international law resources, 279
WebCivil Local, 285
WebCivil Supreme, 285
Westlaw, xv, xvi
  FindLaw, 48
  jury instructions, 12
  KeyCite, 48, 79, 85, 140, 169, 354
  PeopleMap, 285
Wex, 66–67, 199, 249
White House, 240
Williams Institute, 22
Wisconsin State Law Library, 256
  tribal law materials, 256–257
Wolfram Lawyer's Professional Assistant, 36–37
Workplace Fairness, 21
World Law Guide, 279
World Legal Information Institute (WorldLII), 271–273, 359–361

## Y

YouTube, 324

## Z

Zillow, 28